The Green Economy

ENVIRONMENT, SUSTAINABLE DEVELOPMENT
AND THE POLITICS OF THE FUTURE

Michael Jacobs

Pluto Press

London • Concord, Mass

First published 1991 by Pluto Press
345 Archway Road, London N6 5AA
and 141 Old Bedford Road
Concord, MA 01742, USA

British Library Cataloguing in Publication Data
Jacobs, Michael
    The Green economy : environment, sustainable development and the
    politics of the future.
    1. Environment. Economic aspects
    I. Title
    304.2

ISBN 0-7453-0412-5 pb

Library of Congress Cataloging in Publication Data
    Jacobs, Michael, 1960-
        The green economy : environment, sustainable development and the
    politics of the future / Michael Jacobs.
            p. cm.
        Includes bibliographical references and index.
        ISBN 0-7453-0312-9
        1. Economic development–Environmental aspects. 2. Environmental
    protection. 3. Green movement. I. Title.
    HD75.6.J33 1991
    363.7'058–dc20   91-2824
                                                                  CIP

Typeset by Stanford Desktop Publishing Services, Milton Keynes
Printed in the United Kingdom by
Billing and Sons Ltd, Worcester

The Green Economy

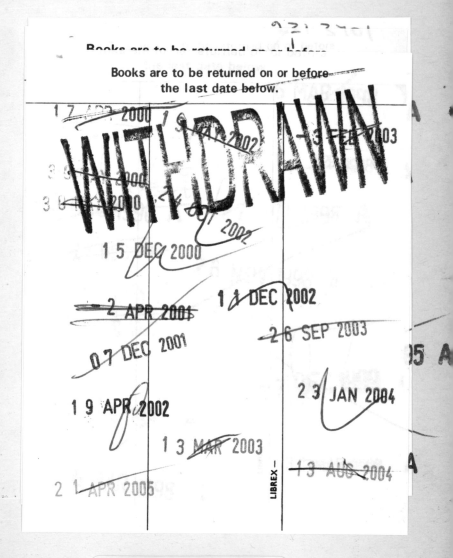

Contents

List of Figures

List of Tables

For my parents
Betty Upton Hughes and Arthur Jacobs

If it took England the exploitation of half the globe
to be what it is today, how many globes will it take India?

Gandhi

Preface

Apart from students of the subject, not very many people read books with the word 'economics', or one of its variants, in the title. On the other hand in recent years a large number have been buying books labelled 'Green'. This one is intended to appeal both to those with a scholarly or professional interest in economics and to those, in whatever capacity, concerned about the environment.

For this reason the book is written in a rigorous but not an academic style. There are very few ideas which cannot be expressed in a manner understandable to the layperson: despite the best efforts of some economists I have certainly not come across many in economics. This book therefore assumes no prior knowledge either of economics or of environmental science, and I have tried to avoid unnecessary complexity of expression. I have not shied away from using technical terms, since it is important that the lay reader can participate when others use them. But all such terms are explained, I hope simply, when they first appear; and the index should aid recollection in their subsequent use.

For the same reason I have largely omitted academic references in the main body of the text. I do not wish to conceal or deny the source of the ideas in this book – I happily acknowledge that almost all of them were first thought of by someone else – but I know that for the lay reader it is irritating to find constant references to writers and works one has not read and may not even have heard of. The academic debates in environmental economics, politics and philosophy from which this book is drawn are interesting and important; but my primary concern here is with the ideas themselves, not their sources. Readers who wish to know whose arguments are being adopted or challenged and where else these debates have been aired will find detailed references in the footnotes.

I also use the footnotes to expand on points made in the main text and to address possible counter arguments. In a work of this sort there is always far more to say than will be interesting to the average reader. Moreover a detailed discussion of one point will often obscure the wider argument being made. So the intention has been to make the main text carry the principal line of thought as clearly as possible, with the rest relegated to the notes.

The term 'environment' in this book refers to the natural environment, not to the wider concept of our 'surroundings', which includes human-made structures. It is in one sense true, as Einstein noted, that 'the environment is everything which is not me'; and there are good reasons why the built environment should be incorporated into debates about environmental policy. For many people in urban areas, particularly the poor, the quality of housing and the appearance of the streets are often more important factors in living standards than the number of trees and butterflies. But conceptually the natural and built environments are different, and the process of policy making in many cases raises different issues. So this book is limited in its coverage.

Some notes on language. I use the term 'South' to mean the countries of Africa, Asia and Latin America, often collectively called the Third World. Despite the evident problems with the meaning and implications of the word 'development', I follow common practice and use 'developing countries' where necessary as an alternative. On account of these problems, however, I don't contrast developing countries with 'developed' ones; I generally prefer 'the North' or the 'industrialised' or 'rich' nations.

I have tried to avoid the use of 'green' to mean 'environmental', but where this is unavoidable (as in 'green consumer') it takes a lower case 'g'. 'Green' with a capital letter denotes the political ideology, or a person holding it. As far as possible I have tried to distinguish between 'Greens' and 'environmentalists'. Environmentalists I take to be people (usually, in the current discussion, writers and activists) concerned about the environment, whatever their wider political allegiance. Greens are those whose commitment to the environment is part of a broader ideology (sometimes called here the 'Green view', or similar) which places emphasis on humankind's relationship with the rest of the natural world, and seeks a society based on non-materialist, decentralist and cooperative values. Not all Greens, it should be noted, belong to or support Green political parties, and my use of the capital letter should not be taken to denote the party view. I explore these questions of ideology and political allegiance a little further in the Introduction.

This book owes its existence to two people more than any others. Several years ago it started out in life as a joint project with Victor Anderson. For a variety of reasons its character changed during the writing and Victor's direct involvement became less. But the many hours of stimulating intellectual argument (and laughter) we shared remain a source of much of my thinking, and Victor's indirect contribution to the final text is therefore considerable.

Anne Beech, my editor at Pluto Press, has stood by this book for far longer than it deserved. As deadlines and promised completion dates passed Anne's perfect understanding of the psychology of writing always provided me with just the right combination of encouragement and reassurance. I am immensely grateful to have had such support.

My ideas have been tested and developed in enjoyable discussions with many people, including Martin Carter, Tim Crabtree, Paul Ekins, David Fleming, Mike Flood, Nick Hanley, David Kemball-Cook, Duncan McLaren, Anne Miller, Henry Neuberger, Susan Owens, John Pezzey, Stephen Smith, Anders Wadeskog and Perry Walker. Tim Jackson helped me sort out my ideas on energy policy; Peter Hopkinson and Chris Nash reviewed the chapters on monetary valuation and cost benefit analysis; Ian Spellerberg checked my ecology. Rachel Stringfellow, Robert Atkinson, Ann Giletti and Beverly Cox provided expert research assistance.

Very helpful comments on early drafts of the book were made by Frankie Ashton, James Cornford, David Kemball-Cook, Anne Miller, Robin Murray, James Robertson, Amanda Root and Martin Stott. The final text has benefited from detailed and perceptive criticism by Monica Ali, Victor Anderson, Julian Jacobs, Henry Neuberger and Susan Owens. I am extremely grateful to all these people; I know I have taken far too little notice of their comments; none of them are therefore implicated in the final outcome.

I should like to thank John Arnold and the Department of Adult Education at the University of Southampton for providing me with accommodation and facilities during one part of the writing of this book; and my colleagues at C.A.G. Management Consultants for their assistance during another. I have not only been given extensive time off to complete the work but consistent personal support in doing so. I could not have had more concrete proof of the value of cooperative working.

Finally I'd like to acknowledge the help of the many friends (including my family) who have supported me, morally and emotionally, during the long period that this book has been in progress. They will know who they are; many of them must have despaired of ever seeing the final product appear. It wouldn't have done without them.

Michael Jacobs
London, March 1991

Introduction

The integration of environmental and economic policy

We have in the past been concerned about the impacts of economic growth upon the environment. We are now forced to concern ourselves with the impacts of ecological stress – degradation of soils, water regimes, atmosphere and forests – upon our economic prospects. We have in the more recent past been forced to face up to a sharp increase in economic interdependence among nations. We are now forced to accustom ourselves to an accelerating ecological interdependence among nations. Ecology and economy are becoming ever more interwoven – locally, regionally, nationally, and globally – into a seamless net of causes and effects.

World Commission on Environment and Development, *Our Common Future* (the 'Brundtland Report')[1]

In the last few years mounting evidence of global environmental degradation has apparently convinced most of the world's political leaders that the planet faces a serious crisis. Speeches have been made, conferences attended, declarations published. But economic policy has so far remained largely unaffected.

At first sight this might seem surprising, since it is evident that the causes of environmental damage lie in economic activities – in agricultural and industrial production, in the consumption of energy and the discharge of wastes. Few will deny that it is the scale and pattern of these activities which are responsible for the pollution and exhaustion of natural resources now causing so much alarm. To the naive observer it might then appear obvious that, if the crisis is to be tackled, economic policy must be changed.

But of course from another perspective the unwillingness of governments to address the economic causes of the crisis is not surprising at all. It is equally evident that repairing the damage done so far and preventing its spread will not simply cost money (perhaps very large sums), but may represent a challenge to the very structures of the economic system itself. Environmental degradation is not an incidental consequence of economic activity. As we shall show in this book, in many ways it is a central feature of the ways in which

xiii

production and consumption are currently organised. If this is so, it is only to be expected that governments will hesitate before confronting the problem. The interests ranged in defence of the economic status quo are wide and powerful: most people in the industrialised world, indeed, have some stake in them. And the consequences of taking action are often uncertain.

Yet it remains true that environmental protection cannot be achieved unless an environmental perspective is integrated into economic policy. This book is therefore an attempt to show what such an integration would mean, both in theory and practice. Its intention is threefold: to clarify just how current economic processes cause environmental degradation; to explore the concept of 'environmental protection' and in particular the objective described as 'sustainability'; and to show how economic policy and policy making can be designed to achieve environmental objectives.

In doing this the book tries to bring together two strands of thought which have historically been kept apart, despite their common concerns: the academic discipline of environmental economics and the political ideology of the Green movement.

The distance between them has been maintained from both sides. Many Greens have rejected the whole subject of economics. They have pointed out the almost complete failure of mainstream economic theory to acknowledge the environmental basis or consequences of economic activity, and they have noted how few economists have shown much interest in the problem. More recently, the work of the rather small band of environmental economists has achieved greater prominence. But far from welcoming the potential convergence, many Greens have viewed it with alarm. By placing monetary values on living things and by proposing (for example) that firms should be sold 'licences to pollute', the new economists in their view undermine the very basis of environmental concern. For Greens the environment is to be understood as humankind's spiritual home, not simply as its source of wealth; our proper relationship with it one of stewardship and harmony, not simply more efficient exploitation. Such an understanding, in the view of many Greens, simply cannot be accommodated within the narrow assumptions of 'rational' self-interest and cost-benefit calculation upon which economics rests.[2]

For many environmental economists, this emphasis on the spiritual basis of humankind's relationship with the environment is precisely the problem. The Green worldview is all very well, but it doesn't provide much of a guide to policy making in the real world. The economist argues that it is only by understanding how firms and households make economic decisions – which, whatever we would like, *are* generally based on some kind of self-interest – that the impact of their behaviour on the environment can be changed. Knowing how much people value the environment gives policy makers stronger arguments for protecting it; using instruments such as marketable pollution licences can then reduce the cost of doing so. To many environmental economists, the Green position simply doesn't *help* very much in moving towards a common goal.[3]

This book is an attempt to bridge the gap. It springs from the Green movement's deep concern about the degradation of the environment and the relationship of industrialised societies to the natural world; it shares the Greens' belief that this must undergo a fundamental change if the threat of environmental catastrophe is to be averted. But it acknowledges that such change requires the application of sober and considered policies in the world as it is, and that the perspectives and techniques of environmental economics have an important role to play in designing these.

Environmental economics

As such the approach taken in this book should probably be described as 'unorthodox' both from a Green and from an environmental economics point of view.

Most of the academic work done in environmental economics may be described as an attempt to incorporate the environment into the conventional or 'neoclassical' framework of economic analysis. The environment is perceived as a set of commodities (goods and services), valued, like other goods and services, by individuals in society. But because environmental commodities are usually available free (that is, at zero price), this value generally goes unrecognised. The result is that they get overused, leading to environmental degradation. To bring the environment into the economic calculus, prices or monetary values therefore need to be assigned to the various goods and services it provides.

Once this is done, it is argued, the models of economic behaviour used to analyse the rest of the economy can also be applied to the environment. Demand for commodities is expressed by households and firms in markets; their preferences are self-interested and 'rational' (profit-maximising and consistent). The tastes and desires on which they are based are assumed to be determined outside the economic process (in culture or biology, for example) and are therefore taken as given rather than analysed. When the environment is unpriced, markets do not on their own fully express preferences for the environment. But they can be made to do so by applying taxes or subsidies to products or processes with particular environmental impacts. By increasing the environment's price, these measures will change consumers' behaviour. The objective of policy is then to produce a socially 'optimal' use of resources. This is defined as the point at which the benefits of those participating in the market exceed their costs by the maximum possible amount. The neoclassical approach is particularly concerned that this should be achieved 'efficiently', that is, most cheaply for society as a whole.[4]

Not all work done in environmental economics would answer to this description, but it is fair to say that it represents the dominant or 'orthodox' tradition. It is, moreover, this broad approach which has received considerable public attention in the last few years through the publication and media coverage of popular environmental economics texts such as (in the UK) the so-called 'Pearce Report', *Blueprint for a Green Economy*.[5]

The approach taken by this book is not a simple rejection of the neoclassical framework. On the contrary, the considerable analytical power of this framework is widely employed – it underpins the explanation of the causes of environmental degradation in Chapter 3, for example.[6] In many fields it provides useful techniques and tools for policy making: the proposal for 'environmental taxes', for instance, is sympathetically discussed in Part III. But in more fundamental respects the neoclassical framework is not an adequate basis for thinking about the environment.

In the first place, the apparent (or claimed) ethical 'objectivity' of the orthodox approach is misleading. Environmental decisions do not only affect people who can make their preferences count in the market. People (and other creatures) in distant places are also affected. So are those who are not yet born – 'future generations'. Even those who can participate in markets do not do so on a basis of equality: some have more purchasing power than others. To accept the outcome of market preferences as 'optimal' is therefore an ethical choice, which is rarely recognised by neoclassical writings. The present work starts from the assumption that the ethical basis of environmental economic policy needs to be made explicit; and an attempt is made in Part II to explore the implications of doing this. The conclusions reached inform the rest of the book.

The narrow behavioural assumptions of the neoclassical framework are also questioned. People do not only have private preferences of the sort expressible in markets; they also have public preferences (particularly for public goods such as the environment) which may be more appropriately expressed through the political process. Much behaviour is indeed self-interested and 'rational' in the economic sense; but some is not, and a recognition of the concern felt for the environment and other people which is not simply reducible to self-interest inevitably affects the nature of economic analysis. Moreover we see no reason to ignore the sources of people's tastes and preferences; it seems evident that the economy itself can affect these, and that this process is therefore also worthy of analysis. In general this book takes as its premise that economic behaviour must be understood within the wider institutional and cultural context in which it operates, a context rarely reflected in the abstract market models of orthodox theory.[7]

These disagreements with the neoclassical framework are not simply assumed here; they are argued out. To be criticised the framework needs to be understood. So the book is intended to be an explanation of orthodox environmental economics as well as a critique of it. Unfortunately, however, it should not be thought that this has led to the formulation of a theoretical 'synthesis', let alone to the development (as sought by many Greens) of a 'new economic paradigm'.[8] Acknowledgement of the environmental dimension of economic activity clearly does have a profound effect upon economics, and it may well be that a completely new framework for the subject will subsequently be developed; there is certainly some interesting work being done which may herald such an advance.[9] But this book does not claim to be it. In its stead the eclectic and perhaps rather ad hoc approach taken here will have to suffice.

Utopianism and feasibility

If such an approach places us outside of the economic mainstream, it is also likely to attract criticism from the Green side. There will be many Greens for whom this book is insufficiently radical; some will question whether it should really be described as 'Green' at all.[10] There is no arbiter of ideological purity, but the charge would be understandable. Much Green writing has been devoted to the goal of far-reaching social change. A Green society is envisaged as 'post-industrial'. In it people live in politically decentralised communities. Voluntary changes in values and lifestyles lead to a drastic reduction in material consumption, allowing a harmonious relationship to be developed between humankind and the natural world. Paid industrial employment correspondingly declines, as people find greater satisfaction in other forms of work, at home or in the community. A principal goal of economic policy is to increase self-reliance, particularly for local economies and 'bioregions'. The state is noticeable mainly by its absence.[11]

That such a society is not foreseeable in the near future does not mean that radical social goals should not be advocated. Any movement for change, however pragmatic its policies, needs a vision of where it is going. As Oscar Wilde said, 'a Map of the World that does not include Utopia is not worth even glancing at.'[12] But equally, knowing where Utopia is is not much use unless the roads leading there (or at least the cycle paths) are also marked. Of course, when asked the way, a Green would be perfectly entitled to answer, 'Well I wouldn't start from here.' But we *are* starting from here, and there will be many intermediate destinations to reach before the journey ends.

This book is therefore about the path and perhaps some of the rest stops on the way rather than about the ultimate goal. The Green economy it describes is a *feasible* rather than a Utopian one. (It is certainly 'a' Green economy, not the only type which could be so described.) By feasible is meant two things.[13] First, one can imagine the measures described here being introduced in industrialised countries over the next ten to twenty years. Though perhaps not likely, they are not beyond the bounds of reasonable possibility given sufficient political will. Second, these measures do not rely on wholesale transformations in people's values to bring them about.

Some Green writing seems implicitly to assume that in a Green society environmental sustainability will be achieved because people's attitudes and motivations will have changed: they will be non-competitive and non-materialistic and 'in harmony with nature'. Some writers have indeed gone so far as to say that sustainability cannot be achieved *until* such a transformation has occurred.[14] But this is surely a counsel of despair. Whether or not such a change may one day happen, it does not look imminent, and we certainly cannot wait around for it before acting, or there will be little nature left for our descendants to be in harmony with. Sustainability is an item on the current agenda, not on some contingent future one. This book therefore presumes that the people for whom, and about whom, environmental policies are designed will be much like the people we see around us today.

Of course, any philosophy which seeks to change society must assume that people's values will change to some degree – both to win consent in the first place and because new institutions will require new social attitudes. Sustainability certainly requires people to become less materialistic and to respect the natural world more deeply. But it is a mistake to believe that, because (as may readily be accepted) the present economic system cannot be changed fully without a transformation of culture and values, it cannot be changed at all until the transformation is completed. As we suggest in this book, shifts in values and lifestyles can be encouraged at the same time as, and indeed through the process of, institutional and policy reform. In the meantime environmental policies must be designed for the world we live in. We cannot, as Bertolt Brecht observed, dissolve the people and elect a new one.

Green politics

Describing the economic policies proposed here as feasible nevertheless raises the question of what sort of politics can bring them about. The subtitle of this book is deliberately ambiguous. As we shall show, environmentalism may well be described as a politics of a *concern* for the future; whether it will also become the character of politics *in* the future is a matter for conjecture.

There are a number of different ways of looking at this question. From one perspective the most important issue is 'how?'. Anxiety about environmental problems is clearly now a significant factor in the politics of most industrialised countries. This is registered by opinion polls and by the rising membership of environmental pressure groups and Green parties. It is reflected in the higher profile of environmental issues within mainstream politics. There is consequently an important question about how this concern gets translated into political results. What are the respective roles of the pressure groups and the parties; of the available arenas such as central government, local government and industrial bargaining; of more individualised actions such as 'green consumerism' and lifestyle change? What are the processes and forces required?

In the main these issues are not addressed in this book. Indeed it starts from a rather different premise. What if environmental concerns *already were* a major priority of government? What economic policies could then be implemented in order to achieve the desired environmental goals? Although this premise assumes away the political 'how?' question, the resulting discussion nevertheless makes a contribution to the answer. For a clarification of what protecting the environment will involve is likely to be an important part of the process by which environmental concerns actually do get turned into action. If people can be convinced that Green policies are practical and need not be too expensive, they may be more likely to vote for them, and politicians subsequently more likely to implement them.

Of course this begs many questions about the relationship between voters and politicians, and between politicians and the economy. The focus of this book is on economic policies for national governments. For reasons we explain, most of the critical changes that need to be made are the responsibility of the state. But the implicit view of the state and the process of economic policy making that runs through this book is certainly open to criticism. The assumption may seem to be that when a majority of voters want something, governments will decide to do it, and when governments decide to do something, it happens. This is not the case. On the contrary, we recognise that in the real world there are many forces at work influencing the course of the economy, and the power of governments, let alone electorates, to determine the final outcome is often severely constrained.

If a government wishes to impose an environmental law curbing some kind of pollution, for example, a simple analysis might say that companies would react simply by reducing their pollution, since it would become illegal. But in practice a much more likely (or at least more immediate) response would be a lobbying campaign by the companies against the law. Given the power that very large, often transnational companies can wield, in many cases this might defeat the proposal. In other cases, environmental measures might never achieve the status of proposals, however 'popular' among voters, because of the existence of other forces within the political arena. Governments are not simply vehicles for the expression of democratic choice.[15]

All this is acknowledged. The liberal view of the benign state and the democratic process is not an adequate picture of the real world. But it is nevertheless useful in a book of this sort. The purpose here is to show what types of policy are available, and how they would work if they could be introduced and did operate as intended. That this may not happen is not a reason for refusing to propose them, or to know how they are designed to work. Perhaps more to the point, the democratic process, however flawed, is still the best (and probably the only) means by which environmental economic policies can be introduced, and through which the majority of people can participate. To take part in this process a degree of what might be called 'knowing naivete' is almost certainly essential, and policies for change must be proposed on this basis. This is the stance taken here.

A second element of the question about the nature of environmental politics concerns its ideology. Environmentalists have long argued about whether they belong essentially on the Left or the Right of the political spectrum, or are divorced from the old conflicts altogether ('neither Left nor Right,' as the German Green Party put it, 'but forward'). This debate is partly about the values underlying the environmental worldview. Some have argued, for example, that a concern for the welfare of future generations is at root an extension of a commitment to present equality, and therefore left-wing; others have related conservation to conservatism; while a third group have claimed that the 'ecocentric' basis of the Green philosophy sets it fundamentally apart from other ideologies. To some extent the debate is about the nature of the economic analysis. Is environmentalism compatible with capitalism, or does it require a major change? If so, is this the same change that socialists seek, or does environmental protection require a different type of economic system altogether?[16]

This book is not an exercise in political philosophy, nor a discourse on the nature of capitalism. Nevertheless it is impossible to write about environmental economics without addressing these issues in some form. Chapters 2, 7 and 8 explore a few of the questions about values, though the directly political connections are left implicit. On the relationship of environmentalism to the economic system we are inevitably more concrete, Chapters 3, 4 and 10 setting out some fairly explicit views. But none of these arguments are developed into a full-blown political theory, and the wider implications are not explored. Some of these implications – for the character of politics beyond environmental issues – are extremely interesting and deserve a full discussion. Unfortunately, space and the confines of the present task require that this take place elsewhere.

The structure of the book

The book is divided into four parts. Part I is an attempt to explain the nature and causes of the environmental crisis. Chapter 1 is a description of the crisis from an economic perspective, introducing some of the basic concepts upon which the rest of the book is built. It is not intended to provide a complete account of the world's environmental problems: this can be found in many other places. Rather, particular problems are used to illustrate the economic framework proposed. Chapter 2 then examines the crisis from a social perspective, looking at who principally suffers from its effects. Chapter 3 is intended to explain how environmental degradation occurs, viewed as an economic process. This analysis of how the economic system works (or doesn't) informs the subsequent policy proposals for its reform. Chapter 4 addresses criticisms of the analysis, looking at a number of alternative explanations that have been proposed, particularly by Greens.

Part II describes the objectives of the Green economy. Chapter 5 is a discussion of two possible goals widely discussed, though not always with much clarity: 'zero growth' and 'sustainable development'. It is hoped that some light may be thrown on them. Chapter 6 begins the exploration of what is meant by the aim of 'environmental protection'. It examines the approach taken by orthodox environmental economics, based on the concept of the 'value' of the environment. Chapter 7 proposes an alternative approach, that of 'sustainability'. This concept is defined and defended against various criticisms, and in Chapter 8 an attempt is made to show how sustainability can be converted into concrete policy objectives. Chapter 9 then broadens the discussion to relate sustainability to other economic objectives, and explores the environmental limits to economic activity.

Part III moves from analysis to practice. How would a sustainable economy actually work? Chapter 10 sets out the broad framework of environmental economic policy making, picking up on the analysis of Chapter 3. It looks at the principles, the processes and the scale of government required. Chapters 11–15 then examine the various methods available to the policy maker. Chapter 11 is essentially a description of the possible instruments of policy, including environmental taxes, regulations and government expenditure. Chapter 12 looks in more detail at the debate, familiar in environmental economics, between the comparative merits of financial incentives (such as taxes) and the regulatory approach. Chapter 13 explores the particular role of government expenditure.

Chapters 14 and 15 then examine the wider implications of these policies, picking up the issues raised in Chapter 2. Chapter 14 looks at how the costs of environmental policies are distributed amongst different groups in society, and investigates their impact on employment. Then chapter 15 extends the analysis to the international sphere. It explores the way in which environmental assistance can be given to the developing countries of the South, and the possibilities for global environmental agreements.

It should be stressed that Part III does not set out a blueprint for environmental policy. It does not propose answers to every environmental problem. Rather the purpose is to provide a framework for understanding the options open. These are illustrated with many examples of possible policies, but comprehensiveness is not claimed, and the structure is not intended to provide 'solutions'. For instance, energy policy is discussed here in four different places. Chapter 12 discusses the idea of an energy or 'carbon' tax in the context of an argument over whether (as is often claimed) taxes are more 'efficient' than regulations in meeting environmental targets. The tax proposal then reappears in Chapter 13 as an example of how tax revenues can be used to subsidise environmentally benign products. In Chapter 14 the case of energy is used to illustrate the distributional implications of environmental taxes, and in Chapter 15 the difficulties of international environmental agreements are explored with respect to the same (because it is the most important) policy area. This structure may sound confusing, but it is quite deliberate. Readers who wish to know what should be done about energy policy can look elsewhere; the intention here is to explain the principles of environmental policy making in general, so that they can then be applied to specific issues.

A further comment needs to be made. This book is primarily about environmental economic policy in industrialised countries. It is the North which is mainly responsible for the environmental crisis. The discussion of environmental policy in the South is therefore limited to its relationship with the industrialised world. Even then it is hardly adequate. The issues of international trade, debt, aid and power are extremely complex and merit at least a book on their own (there are indeed many available).[17] It is hoped that the analysis in Chapter 15 is at least an acknowledgement, if not a satisfactory resolution, of the problems.

Part IV looks at how the environment is measured for the purposes of economic policy. Chapters 16 and 17 examine how the costs and benefits of environmental protection can be weighed in the process of decision making. Chapter 16 is a discussion of the method known as 'cost-benefit analysis' or CBA, which is often used (or at least advocated) by orthodox environmental economists. Chapter 17 is a more detailed analysis of the techniques by which – in order to incorporate the environment into CBA – economists have put monetary values on the environment. This chapter is in places quite difficult, but the importance of this debate within environmental economics, and for policy making, merits a full discussion.

Chapter 18 explores the long-running argument about the indicators which should be used to measure economic performance, looking at environmentalists' criticisms of Gross National Product (GNP) and the alternatives they have proposed. Finally Chapter 19 asks the question which for many readers, conscious of the nature of politics in industrialised countries, the previous chapters will surely have raised: will environmental policies reduce people's standard of living? This involves an examination of how the 'standard of living' is defined; the consequence is perhaps more hopeful – judged by the criterion of political feasibility – than might be anticipated.

Part I
Analysis

1

The Economy and the Environmental Crisis

The economic functions of the environment

For those of us who live in towns and cities, where much of the world around us is human-made, it is easy to forget how dependent we are on the natural environment. Imagine that we could put a large glass bell-jar over a town, reaching down through the soil to the bedrock. The town would get sunlight through the glass, but no air or rain. It wouldn't take long before the inhabitants of the town were dead. Even before they starved through lack of food and raw materials they would have choked to death from the smoke of burning fuels, been drowned in their own sewage or crushed beneath solid wastes.[1] It is the abundance of the natural environment that prevents this happening to us. It is from the earth and the atmosphere that we get the resources with which we produce food and other goods, and it is to the soil, the rivers and oceans, the air and winds that we discard our waste. Without them we couldn't survive.

The 'environmental crisis', put simply, is the result of a reduction in the abundance of the natural environment. We don't live under a bell-jar. But the glass is closing in on us.

We can understand this more systematically. The natural environment or 'biosphere' consists of water, soils, atmosphere, flora and fauna, with energy being provided by the sun. Some of the biosphere is living (plants and animals) and some is not (minerals, air and water). The whole achieves balance through the continuous flow of energy and recycling of matter. Living and non-living parts interact in self-regulating communities or 'ecosystems'.

The biosphere performs three principal functions for the economic activities of humankind.

It provides us with *resources*. Some resources, such as air, water, and many plants and animals used for food, are consumed fairly directly. Others are raw materials or energy sources which are used in production to make goods and services. There are three main types:

'Non-renewable' resources are those which (in a human time-scale) cannot be regenerated by natural processes: fossil fuels (coal, oil, gas), minerals and other materials. Fossil fuels can of course be 'regenerated',

3

but only over a period of several billion years, which is longer even than the 'long run' of which economists speak. Non-renewables are therefore ultimately in fixed supply: all use depletes the total stock.

In practice, however, the relevant supply is not the total stock of a resource (some of which may not yet have been discovered) but only that proportion which is 'economically accessible': that is, profitable to mine. This proportion may increase if the price of the resource rises or if a new technology is developed which makes mining cheaper. In this way use of non-renewables does not necessarily imply depletion in economic terms. In addition, some metals can be 'regenerated' by recycling – using them more than once.

'Renewable' resources are those which, through natural regeneration processes, can continue in supply despite being 'used' by humankind. Plants and animals, of course, reproduce and regrow. But clean air and fresh water are also renewable: the elements oxygen, hydrogen, carbon and nitrogen (among others) are constantly recycled by living organisms in processes such as photosynthesis, respiration, nitrogen-fixing and decay.

The stock of a renewable resource can to all intents and purposes remain indefinitely, though it may be affected by evolutionary or other natural changes in ecosystems. But it *can* be depleted and ultimately exhausted by human activity. If a resource is harvested faster than it regenerates, the stock will decline: this is known as 'over-exploitation'. Renewables can also be depleted 'indirectly' by altering the ecosystems of which the resource is a part. Water, for example, may be lost when trees – which hold it in the soil – are cut down. Renewable resources are therefore 'exhaustible', though exhaustion is not inevitable.

'Continuing' resources, by contrast, are inexhaustible. They are those sources of energy the supply of which is unaffected by human activity. (They are often called 'renewable', but this is not strictly accurate.) The two principal original sources of continuing energy are the sun, which generates solar radiation and wind energy, and gravity, which generates tidal and wave energy and hydropower (though this, dependent on water, is also partly renewable). Some geothermal energy (heat from the earth's crust) is also a type of continuing resource.

The biosphere's second function is to assimilate our *waste products*. Whether natural or human-engineered, all uses of energy generate waste. Energy itself ends up as waste heat. Plants and animals (including human beings) generate organic waste, most importantly physical excreta, dead matter and carbon dioxide. Human economic activity – production – generates both more complex organic wastes such as plastics and inorganic residuals such as metals.

It should not be thought that only the unwanted by-products of economic activity, such as the smoke from a factory chimney, or left-over materials, are wastes. Ultimately the intended products themselves end up as waste too. Since matter cannot be destroyed, everything ultimately becomes waste, and returns in some form to the environment.

The biosphere assimilates waste in a number of ways. It disperses concentrations of gaseous and liquid chemicals in the atmosphere, rivers and seas, and reconstitutes matter into smaller and/or more stable compounds. Organic wastes (and small quantities of minerals) are then absorbed into natural cycles – where through processes of regeneration they are effectively transformed into resources. Finally, those wastes which cannot be absorbed are stored in the environment. Stored wastes may be 'inert' (non-interactive), in which case they may have no adverse effect on the environment, or they may interact in harmful ways. This is commonly called pollution.

Finally, the biosphere provides us with various *environmental services*. This function is less economically obvious than the first two (and is often ignored by economists), but is no less important.

There are two types of environmental service. The first are amenities which the environment provides for direct and conscious consumption. For example, it provides space for recreation and scenery and wildlife for aesthetic enjoyment. Both living and non-living matter enable human beings to expand knowledge through scientific study. While it is difficult to put a value on these services, it is clear that overall human well-being is considerably enhanced by them.

The second type of environmental service can be called, broadly, 'life-support'. Human beings are dependent on the natural processes which maintain the working of the biosphere. These include such functions as the maintenance of genetic diversity (the variety of different species) and the stabilisation of ecosystems; the maintenance of the composition of the atmosphere; and the regulation of climate. These services are often intangible and they are 'consumed' only indirectly – indeed, mostly unconsciously – but they are no less crucial. Life depends on them.

It is essential to recognise that human economic activity relies completely on these functions of the environment. There could be no economic activity without them. The environmental crisis is a crisis of all three.

The depletion of resources

It used to be thought, and one may hear it still said, that the principal environmental problem facing humankind is the depletion of non-renewable resources, particularly fossil fuels and metals. But this is not the case. In the first place, as we show below, the depletion of *renewable* resources, and problems of pollution, are considerably more critical issues, with an earlier and larger effect on human life. Pollution caused by the production of non-renewables is likely to require constraints on their use long before they are in danger of running out.

But in any case many of the dire predictions which were made about non-renewables being exhausted have been proved false. Due to the discovery of new reserves, and through recycling and substitution by other materials, scarcity of key resources is less imminent than was once feared. For example, the famous Club of Rome report *The Limits to Growth*, published in 1972, projected that the supply of tin would run out in 1987. In reality in that year there was a worldwide glut and tin mines had to be closed for lack of demand. This was mainly because in most of its industrial uses, such as the manufacture of cans, tin had largely been replaced by other materials, notably steel and aluminium. At current consumption rates, reserves of iron ore are estimated to last 160 years, and aluminium 220.[2]

Nevertheless the depletion of non-renewables is still a cause for some concern. The estimated years of supply of some minerals, given known reserves and current consumption rates, is quite short: under 25 years for lead, zinc and mercury.[3] It is important that these resources (as well as others in longer supply) are conserved through efficient use and recycling. While some metals are easy to substitute, others, such as platinum and chromium, are at present irreplaceable. The continuing development of substitution technology is therefore vital.[4]

The depletion of fossil fuels is more acute. Coal remains in plentiful global supply: at present consumption rates known reserves should last over 200 years. But the equivalent figure for natural gas is just 58 years, and for oil a mere 41.[5] These statistics do not take into account the possible discovery of new reserves, nor the extraction of oil from other sources such as oil shale and tar sands; they also ignore the likely effects of rising prices on rates of consumption. Nevertheless, it is fairly obvious that our current dependence on oil (it accounts for about 40% of global commercial energy) must decline fairly soon, requiring the development of alternative sources.

The major raw materials crisis, however, is that of the renewable resources. Unlike non-renewables, depletion is not inevitable; but it is occurring, in some cases very rapidly. Throughout the world marine stocks, topsoil, forests and water are being exploited at much faster rates than they are being renewed. Indeed, we are frequently so destroying the environment that they cannot be renewed at all.

This process is evident, for example, in the world's seas. Since 1950 the total global fish catch has almost quintupled. But this growth conceals major falls in regional catches of particular species. Herring numbers in the North Sea are down by 75%, North West Atlantic haddock have declined by over 90%, Californian sardine stocks are only now recovering after a complete collapse in the 1950s. The reason in each case is that overfishing has exhausted stocks. The Food and Agriculture Organisation of the United Nations estimates that catches in nine of the world's sixteen major marine fisheries have now exceeded their 'maximum sustainable yield', with a decline in stocks likely to follow. The near extinction of at least four species of whale serves as a grim warning that overfishing can be terminal. Such depletion has obvious implications for food supplies.[6]

On land, the basis of food production is topsoil. Here too exploitation is far outstripping natural regeneration rates. It takes between 100 and 2,500 years, depending on the type, for 2.5 cm of topsoil to form. In some places soil erosion is destroying this quantity in as little as ten years. The phenomenon of 'desertification' in Africa, with the resulting threat of famine, is now well known: worldwide nearly 51% of productive drylands are now 'moderately' or 'severely' desertified, and 80 million people live in areas at great risk.[7]

But soil loss is also occurring in Europe, Australasia and North America. The US loses, net of natural replacement, well over one billion tonnes a year, equivalent to more than 300,000 hectares of land. Over-production is the principal cause, with part also due to chemical toxification. The result is that approximately a third of all US croplands are experiencing a marked decline in productivity. The same effect is occurring on about half of all arable lands in the world. Combined with other causes (such as conversion to non-agricultural uses) at current rates 275 million hectares, or 18% of the global total, will be lost by the year 2000. With another billion people being added to world population in the same period, the prospect for food production is extremely serious.[8]

Tree loss is both a major cause of soil erosion and desertification and important in itself. While the coverage of temperate forests in the Northern hemisphere has remained fairly constant due to reforestation, tropical forests are being rapidly destroyed. Recent studies estimate that over 20 million hectares (an area larger than Britain) are lost each year. Total coverage will have fallen by half between 1950 and 2000; by 2025, unless current trends are checked, only isolated pockets may remain at all. Because much of this land has been completely bulldozed or burnt, there is little chance of the forest regrowing. Effectively the forests are being 'mined': they have been turned into a non-renewable resource.[9]

The significance of such depletion is not just the loss of timber, though with two billion people dependent on wood for fuel, in addition to pulp, construction and industrial demand, this is serious enough. The forests also supply a wide variety of foods, gums, resins, oils and medicines. These products, which can be collected without damaging the forest, are actually more valuable in financial terms per acre than commercial timber or cattle, which ultimately destroy it.[10] Tree loss also causes water supplies to dry up, both in the ground and from rain, with severe effects on agriculture throughout the watershed area.

Perhaps most importantly, rainforests are the 'genetic reservoir' of the earth. It is thought that they contain at least two million species; of these, fewer than one in six have been identified. Amongst those that have are a large number of plants with potential economic uses. (A recent small US survey of the Amazonian rainforest identified more than a thousand.[11]) The forests have already proved an invaluable source of drugs, including those used to treat leukaemia, Hodgkin's disease and other types of cancer: the potential for future discoveries is immense. New foods and sources of industrial materials are almost certainly also available. The importance of the latter is emphasised by the depletion of non-renewable resources, which will force the development of renewable substitutes. Yet all this is being lost. As the forests are destroyed, the genetic reservoir is drained, irreversibly. We are therefore not just losing existing resources; we are eliminating the possibility of finding new ones. Effectively, we are depleting the resources of the future, even before they have been developed.[12]

And all this is quite apart from the immediate human cost of rainforest destruction. The forests are home to hundreds of thousands of people, many of whom have been forcibly removed, killed by imported diseases and brutally massacred as their lands and livelihoods have been taken away. Future generations may well regard this process as comparable to any of this century's worst examples of genocide; they will also have cause to regret the huge loss of knowledge about the rainforests which indigenous cultures have accumulated. At a time when genetic, medical and materials research will be most needed, it will take scientists decades to rediscover what these people have known – if the resources are still there for them to try.[13]

Pollution

Some wastes, particularly organic compounds produced by plants and animals, need not be a cause of pollution. So long as they are returned to the environment at rates and in concentrations which permit their absorption into natural cycles, their production is itself unproblematic. Unfortunately, in industrialised societies, such wastes are rarely separated out and disposed of in this way. Moreover, many of the other kinds of waste generated by economic activities are very difficult for the environment to degrade. Incapable of being absorbed, these substances must simply be stored in the environment. Pollution then occurs when concentrations of stored wastes reach such levels that they begin to cause harmful effects to living organisms.[14]

Most obviously, human health is endangered. Familiar problems include lead, sulphur and ozone in the atmosphere, nitrates and aluminium in water supplies, radioactive nuclear wastes and pesticide residues left on fruit and vegetables. Pollution does not merely cause discomfort; it kills. A study by the US Environmental Protection Agency of just one-third of toxic emissions to the atmosphere suggested that they alone cause 2,000 cancer deaths each year. In developing countries between 10,000 and 40,000 deaths may result annually from pesticide poisoning.[15]

Pollution can also cause stocks of resources to be reduced. Acid rain (caused by sulphur and nitrogen oxide emissions) has caused extensive damage to forests in parts of the US, Canada, Scandinavia and Central Europe, and is now noticeable in many other parts of the world. The West German timber industry is estimated to lose US$800 million each year from the effects of acid rain, with agriculture suffering further costs of $600 million due to the resulting loss of soil fertility.[16] Meanwhile marine pollution severely reduces fish stocks. Shellfishing has been stopped in a third of all US estuarine waters due to industrial and sewage dumping; the overall loss to offshore fisheries is estimated at $80 million per annum.[17]

The damage to environmental services

The effect of pollution on resource stocks is an example of how the various economic functions of the environment interact. Another lies in the impact of both pollution and resource depletion on the third function, the performance of environmental amenity and life support services.

The loss of amenity from natural habitat degradation – both through pollution and through simple destruction – is evident to anyone who enjoys the beauties of the countryside or coast. In the last 40 years Britain has lost 224,000 kilometres of hedgerows as farms have been enlarged, while half of the country's old deciduous woodlands have been eliminated. In the US, 20,000 square kilometres of coastal wetlands have gone: dredged, filled in, polluted and developed. All these habitats are notably rich in wildlife.[18]

For many people, such damage would be regrettable even if no particular losses were experienced by human beings. But in fact it is evident that people do derive well-being from the existence of areas of natural beauty and the wildlife they contain. The widespread pleasure obtained from household pets, flowers and plants, gardens, parks and beaches suggests that human beings have a genuine need to be in contact with the natural world. Its loss is therefore their impoverishment. Moreover, the loss is not just experienced by people directly affected. Surveys show that even those who never actually visit the countryside want there to *be* one. The natural world has *existence value*. We want it to be there, in all its beauty and diversity, and its loss affects our well-being.[19]

For many people in industrialised countries it is the loss of amenity which is the most direct manifestation of the environmental crisis. But the loss of habitats has ramifications also for the basic life support services which the environment provides.

The biosphere is maintained through the complex interaction of living organisms. As habitats are destroyed, ecosystems are upset, with sometimes unpredictable and wide-ranging effects. Pollution in particular is frequently self-reinforcing, since it reduces biological diversity and therefore makes it harder for the ecosystem to withstand further pollution. The reduction or elimination of one species may affect many others dependent on it. Food chains may be disrupted, the balance of species altered so that pests become dominant, and ultimately evolutionary processes themselves may be threatened. The complete collapse of ecosystems is possible: this occurred, for example, in Lake Erie in the 1970s, when pollution killed off almost all life. More critically, the famines which have claimed the lives of hundreds of thousands of people in Africa are the result – in part – of almost complete environmental bankruptcy.[20]

Since we do not know how many species inhabit the Earth (estimates range from four million to over 30 million) it is almost impossible to give accurate figures for the rate of their extinction. But careful estimates suggest that we are now losing over 35,000 species every year.[21]

The risks are considerable. Not only are ecosystems made more unstable, but the possibilities of righting them are reduced. In agriculture, for example, monocultural breeding (farming a single strain of crop) has left huge areas of cropland highly susceptible to diseases and pests. It is possible through genetic manipulation to strengthen and diversify crop strains to improve disease resistance and increase productivity. But this can only occur if the genetic material exists to work from, and it is precisely this which is rapidly being lost. Many potential new materials, chemicals and drugs which could be engineered from genetic resources may never be developed.

In part it is our ignorance about the workings of the biosphere which makes the reduction in genetic diversity so troubling. We simply do not know the ecological effects of many of our actions. The environment has been well likened to a tapestry, the threads of which are gradually being unwoven: at some point the whole picture may fall apart. We do not know when.

The impact of human economic activities on other major life-support functions of the environment is now well known. The release of chlorofluorocarbons (CFCs) from aerosols, solvents, fridges and packaging foam is causing the depletion of the atmospheric ozone layer, which protects the earth from the sun's harmful ultra-violet rays. The result will almost certainly be an increase in skin cancers and cataracts; there is the likelihood also of crop damage, and possibly the disruption of major foodchains if, as suspected, the photosynthesising processes of phytoplankton in Antarctica are affected.[22]

Finally, and perhaps most dramatically, the 'greenhouse effect' is seriously affecting the regulation of the earth's climate. Here again the exhaustion of the environment's waste absorption capacity is the principal cause. Human activities have been releasing carbon dioxide and other greenhouse gases (nitrous oxide, CFCs, methane and water vapour) into the atmosphere for centuries. Until recently these were absorbed without noticeable effects. But now the limits of absorption have been reached: not simply because emissions have increased but because so much of the key carbon dioxide 'absorbers' – forests – have been destroyed. Heat consequently trapped in the atmosphere is causing temperatures to rise. This may already have started: the five hottest summers on record were all in the 1980s, with the 1989–90 US grainbelt drought a possible early result.[23]

The imprecise nature of climatic models makes prediction hazardous. But the projections of the Intergovernmental Panel on Climate Change, which reported in 1990, are widely accepted. These suggest that on current trends the global mean temperature is likely to rise by 1°C by 2025, and a further 2°C before the end of the twenty-first century. Temperature increases will be higher the further the distance from the equator. Such rises are likely to cause significant changes in crop production patterns, with resulting stresses on food distribution. In addition there is a severe risk of coastal flooding if, as predicted, sea levels rise.[24] Catastrophic disruption of human settlements (two-fifths of the world's population live in coastal regions) may then occur, with some experts forecasting the likely creation of between 60 and 300 million 'environmental refugees'.[25] The economic, social and political impact of such events can only be guessed at.

The laws of thermodynamics

Understood in this way it is clear that the environmental crisis is also an economic crisis. It is caused by economic activities and it undermines the very functions on which the economy depends.

But even this is not the full story. So far the three economic functions of the environment have been considered separately. It is already obvious however that they are inter-related. The depletion of forests affects the regulation of climate and genetic diversity as well as raw material supplies. Pollution reduces available resources and disrupts ecosystems as well as damaging health. Climatic change can reduce the productivity of the soil. These interconnections are not just a general demonstration of the 'wholeness' of the biosphere – though this lesson is very important. They are a crucial feature of the relationship between the environment and the economy. The economic functions of the environment are related in quite specific ways, by the first two laws of thermodynamics.

The laws of thermodynamics are the physical rules which govern the behaviour of matter and energy. The first law is very simple. It states that matter and energy cannot be either destroyed or created. There is a fixed total, which is always conserved in some form or another.

This law has a rather profound bearing on economics, because it calls into question what exactly economic activity does. Clearly, for all the effort that goes into production, nothing 'new' is actually created. All that happens is the *transformation* of materials and energy from one state into another. In terms of environmental functions, what economic activity does is turn resources into wastes. Every quantity of resources which enters the economic process must emerge at the end as the same quantity of waste. Of course, much of the resource input will go to make a product, which is used; this is the point of the exercise. Initially, therefore, only a proportion (sometimes known as the 'residual') will emerge as waste. But when the product is used up, or wears out, it too re-enters the environment. The energy employed in production must similarly end up eventually as waste heat. There is simply no escaping this: what goes in to the economic process must come out of it. It can't just disappear.

The quantitative relationship between the first two environmental functions is therefore straightforward. The more resources are used, the more wastes need to be assimilated. Resource depletion and pollution are essentially the *same* problem, two sides of one coin.

But the relationship has a qualitative dimension to it as well. The transformation of resources into wastes follows a specific path dictated by the second law of thermodynamics, or 'entropy law'. Entropy can be understood as a measure of the 'disorderedness' or 'unavailability' of matter or energy. Thus a lump of coal has low entropy: it is concentrated in form and the energy it contains is available for use. But once the coal is burnt it has high entropy, becoming dissipated as heat and carbon dioxide, neither of which are available for use. The example illustrates the workings of the second law, which states that (so long as there are no external sources of energy) entropy always increases. The universe is constantly becoming more disordered, its energy and matter less available for use. In economic terms, it means that wastes are always more dispersed and useless than resources. (Any visit to a landfill site will confirm this.)

Entropy is thus indeed a way of defining resources and wastes: the former have low entropy, the latter high entropy. In turn economic activity may be thought of as a process by which low entropy materials are converted into high entropy ones, while useful services are derived from them en route. In doing this the economy conforms to the general (and irreversible) direction of the universe: from low entropy to high entropy.

It is here, however, that the third function of the environment (the performance of environmental services) enters the picture. For it is not quite true that entropy always increases. Note that the second law only insists on this if there are no external sources of energy. This is of course the case with respect to the universe as a whole. But it isn't so for the earth. On the contrary, the biosphere is powered by a continuous flow of energy from the sun. And this enables the flow of entropy within the biosphere to be reversed. Carbon dioxide is recovered from the atmosphere in photosynthesis and reused. After excretion, waste products are broken down and reconstituted as foods in the soil. Water, minerals and other chemicals pass out of living organisms into the environment, and are then taken up again as new inputs. We may say that this is what the living world is about: not just converting resources into wastes, but using the energy of the sun to reverse the path of entropy and convert the wastes back into resources.

This 'circular' activity is made possible and carried out by the performance of environmental life support services. Climatic regulation and the biogeochemical cycling of elements such as nitrogen and oxygen are directly involved in reversing entropic flow; habitat maintenance and genetic diversity ensure that there are sufficient animals and plants to enable it to occur.

The three economic functions of the environment are therefore clearly linked. Resources and wastes are ultimately the same quantities. They differ only in entropic value; but high entropy is constantly being converted back into low entropy through the life support services which the environment performs.

It will be apparent that these connections increase the complexity of the environmental crisis. It might be thought possible, for example, to reduce the problem of resource depletion if wastes could be recycled faster or more efficiently. But the damage being done to life support services actually reduces the ability of the environment to assimilate wastes and recycle them; an increasing quantity simply gets stored as pollution. More recycling could be done by the economy. But the entropy law tells us that this can only be done if additional energy is applied, which if it comes from fossil fuels only adds to the pollution problem.

A new picture of the economy

The laws of thermodynamics thus have important implications for environmental policy, and we shall return to them in Chapter 9. Here it is perhaps sufficient to note that they enable us to see the economy in a new light. Traditionally economics has pictured the economy as a circular flow of money, a continuous (and frequently expanding) loop connecting firms and households. Firms pay workers, who buy goods and services from firms. Households also save money, which firms then borrow to pay for investment, paying interest in return. This investment goes to produce more goods and services, which households buy with their increased incomes, and so on. (The flow can be complicated by adding in government, imports and exports, but the basic pattern remains the same.)

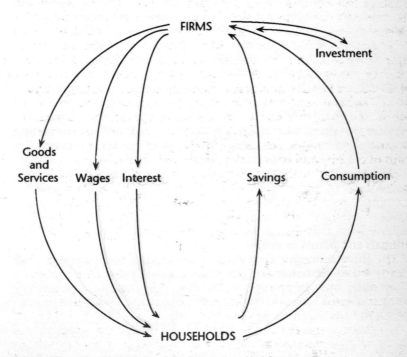

Figure 1.1 The orthodox model of the economy

This picture, which can be found in any introductory economics textbook, ignores the physical aspects of economic activity altogether. In thermodynamic terms it represents a perpetual motion machine, the flow of money apparently unpowered by any external source of energy. In fact, as we have seen, the economy is fuelled by both the sun and commercial energy sources. A physical description of the economy is portrayed in Figure 1.2. Here there is a circular flow, but it is one of matter: taken from the environment, used in production and consumption and then returned to the environment as waste.

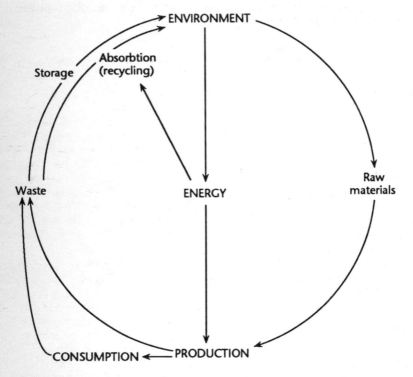

Figure 1.2 A simple thermodynamic model of the economy

Note that this picture of the economy also describes the workings of the biosphere itself. Animals and plants take food (raw materials) from their environment and use energy (from the sun or from other living things) to grow and develop. They excrete wastes, which are then recycled by other organisms – using the energy of the sun – to become food. In this sense we may draw a new connection between the economy and the environment. In the first part of this chapter we attempted to show how the environment could be seen as part of the economy, providing it with critical functions. It should now be clear that the economy is equally part of the environment. It is constrained by the same physical laws and its processes mirror those of the biosphere.

There are two major differences between the two systems. The first is that far more of the wastes produced by living things in the biosphere are absorbed back into the productive cycle. In the economy, although all wastes return to the environment, they generally do so dispersed as high entropy materials of low usefulness. They are therefore simply stored, leading in many cases to pollution. This has led to the second difference. So far the human economy has taken fewer measures to ensure its own survival. As we shall see, addressing the second problem will require us to do something about the first.

2

Whose Environment?

Is the environment a middle-class issue?

Two contradictory observations are often made about environmental problems. One is that the environment is a 'middle-class issue'. This is said to be so because it is only when people have high incomes that they can afford the luxury of worrying about 'the quality of life', and because the membership of environmental pressure groups is almost wholly middle class. The other observation is that, on the contrary, since everyone shares the environment, income and status differences are irrelevant. The environmental crisis, it is claimed, signals the end of 'old-fashioned' politics based on class.[1]

Both these arguments are false. First, the fact that poor people cannot afford to buy a good 'quality of life' does not mean that they do not want it. The argument is a good example of the fallacy that demands registered in the market are a full expression of consumers' desires. They aren't. Market demand is based on consumers' income; but consumers' desires clearly don't always match the resources they have for meeting them. The evidence of surveys (rather than consumption patterns) indeed shows that working-class people would like a clean environment just as much as middle-class people. The fact that for poorer people other needs may take precedence when it comes to spending limited income does not diminish this finding.[2]

Meanwhile pressure group membership is of course no indication of the social spread of environmental concern, being a culturally middle class phenomenon (in industrialised countries) in all fields. On a global scale it is actually inaccurate to say that pressure groups are middle class. This is mostly so in rich countries, but in the South the environmental movement is mainly a movement of the poor, whose environments are the worst degraded.[3]

This reveals the mistake in the second argument. It is simply not true to say that the shared nature of environmental problems makes income differences irrelevant. It is certainly the case that everyone, irrespective of class, will experience effects such as global warming. Pollution is no respecter of residential boundaries. But the *impact* of the ecological crisis is not felt in the same way by everyone. Like most other good things, the benefits and costs of the environment are unequally distributed. The poorer you are, the worse the crisis you will experience.

The environmental crisis and the poor

It is almost universally true that poor people live in the worst environments. Indeed one of the advantages of greater income is precisely that it allows those who have it to buy pleasanter surroundings. Affluent people live in leafy suburbs or the country. Poor people get greenless inner cities and housing estates. The most polluted places in the world are the urban slums of Mexico and Brazil, in the shadow of huge industrial complexes. When the Union Carbide factory at Bhopal in India leaked poisonous gas in 1984 it was the poor, living on its doorstep, who were killed; the better-off, in the suburbs, escaped with less serious injuries.[4]

In many parts of the world degraded environments practically define poverty. Most people in the South make their livelihoods from agricultural activities: farming, grazing animals, fishing, collecting wood, fruits and other products from forests. They live in what are sometimes called 'biomass societies', places where practically all human activities use organic materials. Food is unprocessed, fuel comes from a combination of firewood, dung and crop wastes, buildings are made of wood, mud, brick and thatch, clothing from cotton and wool. Water supplies depend on soil maintenance and tree cover. For biomass societies the environment is not a 'luxury'; it is the very means of existence.

In these circumstances environmental degradation can have devastating consequences for the poorest communities. Over recent years television pictures of famines in Africa have brought home to Northern viewers the terrible effects of soil erosion and desertification. But hunger, malnutrition and forced migration also follow from other examples of degradation, such as the depletion of fishing grounds and forests. In many countries deforestation compels women to walk for many hours every day just to collect water, fodder and firewood for cooking. (This is perhaps the real 'global energy crisis'.) Whole peoples are uprooted, and frequently killed, when the rainforests are destroyed. For the poorest people in the world, those directly dependent on biomass resources for their very survival, the environmental crisis can literally be a matter of life and death.[5]

Further, as global environmental problems worsen, rich nations and rich people will almost everywhere suffer less than the poor. It is true that no one will be able to escape increased ultra-violet radiation from the depletion of the ozone layer. But those who can afford it will cover themselves in protective creams, while those who cannot will get cancer. Rising sea levels will cause coastal flooding in many parts of the world. But the citizens of Florida will be resettled inland; those of

Bangladesh will become displaced or drown. If energy becomes scarce and prices rise, the rich will cut down on luxuries; the poor will freeze.

This is not to say that rich people and poor people do not have a common interest in addressing the environmental crisis. Clearly it hurts both groups. It simply hurts the poor more. Two factors are involved. One is the nature of the environmental problem concerned; the other is its extent. Where scarcity is the problem, wealth will always be a source of advantage. As resources are depleted their prices are likely to rise. Similarly, as unspoilt areas become threatened by development, the cost of land (and of visiting it) will increase. In both cases, unless rationing of some sort is introduced, richer people will be able to afford higher prices where poor people will not.

In the case of pollution, the question of inequality turns on its extent. Thus at the moment, when not all parts of the atmosphere and not all rivers and beaches have been polluted, it is possible to use one's money to secure a better environment. One can pay extra to live in a less polluted area and travel further to enjoy a more pleasant holiday. But as pollution spreads wider, the possibility of escape diminishes. If high lead levels in the air are confined to cities the rich can live elsewhere. But if all air is poisoned, they cannot breathe something else.

Within industrialised countries inequalities in the experience of environmental problems are probably diminishing. This is both because resource scarcity has *not* yet become a serious issue, and because pollution is increasingly widespread, making escape an option only for the very rich.

In addition, many environmental services are provided collectively. Since everyone receives the same piped water, everyone is equally harmed by its pollution (and benefits from its cleaning-up). We all travel on the same roads, so cannot buy our way out of congestion. If the greenhouse effect were to cause coastal flooding, evacuation and resettlement would (presumably) be organised by the state, and would not discriminate between rich and poor people. Progressive taxation moreover means the rich pay proportionately more for such environmental protection than the poor.

Such equality is not of course irreversible. The privatisation of water supplies makes 'two-tier' provision possible, enabling the rich to pay more for purer water. Proposals for private toll roads and motorway lanes are precisely designed to allow the rich to escape congestion. It would be entirely possible for the state to insist that resettlement programmes were financed by private insurance.

Whether or not this occurs, between rich and poor *nations* major inequalities in the experience of the environmental crisis will remain – unless deliberate action is taken to ameliorate them. First, scarcity of resources is much more directly an issue in Third World countries. In the North, physical depletion of a local resource need not induce scarcity. New stocks are simply imported from elsewhere. In the South poverty often precludes this option. Scarcity is physical: when a local forest disappears, there are no alternative supplies.

Second, as stricter pollution control measures are enforced in the North, many dangerous industries may be (and in some cases already are being) transferred to poorer nations where regulations are more lax. A desperate need for foreign exchange, along with lower public sensitivity due to poverty and lack of information (and often lack of power) make it hard for many Southern countries to resist such imports. Such a literal 'trade in pollution' will make the difference in cleanliness between Northern and Southern environments more marked.[6]

Third, environmental services in the South are not provided 'collectively' with the rich countries. Whereas the costs of coastal defences in East Anglia, Holland and Florida are paid for by both seaboard and inland residents of Europe and the United States, the equivalent costs in Bangladesh and Indonesia are not being met by the citizens of the world as a whole. Clean water is piped to practically everyone in Europe, irrespective of income; but not to everyone in the world. As the costs of protection against environmental problems rise, they will therefore be proportionately much higher for poor countries than for richer ones.

Future people

On an international scale, the environmental crisis is therefore not equally distributed. But there is another scale of inequality too. This is *intergenerational*. There can be little doubt that the environmental crisis is already with us. But its worst effects are being stored up for the future.

By definition, the continuing depletion of resources causes more problems to future generations than to present ones, since each generation has less available than the last. Certainly, for consumers in the North, the current rapid destruction of resources such as rainforests is not yet causing shortages or even significant price rises. But when, some time (on current trends) in the next century, they have been lost altogether, then the effects will be noticed. In particular, as we have already seen, the elimination of their genetic resources, along with those in other habitats, will be deeply regretted. In every case, as a resource is run down, current economic activity effectively benefits present generations by impoverishing future ones.

It could be argued – and indeed it often is, by industrialists accused of impoverishing future generations – that using resources today creates wealth which enriches future people. Indeed this wealth enables scientific and technological knowledge to be enlarged; by producing new materials and industrial processes, this will reduce the future need for the resources which are depleted.[7] But this is a very thin argument to justify generalised resource depletion. It assumes both that the only way to devote more money to scientific and technological research is to increase income through depleting resources; and that wealth is always a substitute for the resources foregone. But neither of these things is assured. It is quite possible for useful research to be funded by redistributing expenditure from other areas (for example, from defence, which currently consumes half of the world's entire scientific research spending). It is also not the case that increasing financial wealth inevitably requires the depletion of resources. Finally it is by no means clear that human-made wealth and technology can always substitute for natural resources – in regulating climate, for example, or maintaining genetic diversity. We shall deal with these questions more fully in Chapter 7. What we can say here is that *at least* in terms of the availability of the resources themselves, and quite possibly in a wider sense, resource depletion causes future generations to bear a loss.

Many other environmental problems exhibit a similar time-separation of benefit and cost. The greenhouse effect may already be causing temperatures to rise, but its most dramatic effects are not likely to occur for 50 years. Nuclear power provides electricity for people living now; but people not yet born will have to cope with the radioactive waste it leaves behind. In this way the environmental crisis is not just a question of the world we live in today, but of the world we bequeath to our descendants.

This question of intergenerational distribution gives the economics of the environment an added twist. The argument that resource depletion makes future people better not worse off may not be convincing but it does express an assumption fundamental to orthodox economic theory. This is that so long as present society continues to invest some of its resources (that is, spend them on capital which will subsequently create more wealth), people living in the future will always be richer than people living now.

The environmental crisis throws this assumption into doubt. Future people may be richer financially, but at the same time they may inherit an environment which is severely degraded, which in turn will force them to undergo major and possibly disastrous changes in their style and patterns of life. If in this sense it seems likely that future generations will be poorer than us, this should have an important bearing on how we value different economic decisions. For example, in weighing the effects of an action, economists tend to 'discount' future costs and benefits, giving them less weight than present ones. One justification for this is that future people will be better off than current people, so a pound or dollar will be less valuable to them. But if future people will in fact be poorer, this justification no longer holds. Economic decisions may be forced to take the interests of future generations into account in a more direct way.

We shall investigate these issues further in the second part of the book. For the present a different conclusion can be reached. This is that, although it is important to understand the physical biosphere as a whole, so that the links between different environmental problems are clear, this cannot be said of the environment as an economic phenomenon. There is not one environmental crisis, affecting everybody in the same way. There are many different crises, and the one each of us experiences depends on a number of facts about us – where we live, how much money we have, what generation we belong to.

This has obvious consequences for the design of environmental policy. Environmental problems cannot be regarded simply as scientific issues, with purely scientific solutions. Just as each environmental problem has a distributional element, so will any solution to it. Whose environment will be protected? Who is to get the benefit of any improvements? Who will pay for them? As we shall see, such distributional questions must inevitably have political answers.

3

The Invisible Elbow:
Market Forces and
Environmental Degradation

A technological fix?

The environmental crisis raises many questions, but one seems to stand out above all others. Why is it that industrialised societies have arrived at a position where the natural environment, on which they depend, is being so rapidly and apparently dangerously degraded?

At first sight this is indeed a puzzle. It has after all hardly been the stated aim of governments (or anybody else) to cause environmental collapse. On the contrary, ever since the severity of the damage began to emerge in the 1960s governments throughout the world have claimed to be committed to environmental protection and improvement. Yet in so many aspects the situation has grown steadily worse.

This divergence between intention and result provides one possible answer to the question. The environmental crisis, it might be argued, is an accident. It is an unintended and unforeseeable consequence of industrial development, occurring because society has been ignorant of the effects of its actions, and because technological progress has not kept pace with environmental impact. This view sees the environment as primarily a *technical* issue. The crisis will correspondingly be solved by the development and application of improved and new technologies, both to repair existing environmental damage and to prevent such damage occurring in future.[1]

There is some validity in this position. Ignorance has clearly contributed to the problem. It is only recently, for example, that many metals and chemical compounds have been identified as toxic. When CFCs were first developed they were specifically welcomed as inert and therefore safe. It is also true that environmental problems are largely – though not completely – unintended: very few industrialists or governments will confess to deliberate degradation of the environment. It occurs rather, they will claim, as a regrettable by-product of other, economically beneficial activities.

But here the argument begins to weaken. Seen in relation to each individual economic activity, environmental degradation may perhaps be described as a 'by-product'. But considered in relation to the economy as a whole, this seems quite the wrong term. Degradation is too pervasive, occurring in too many different ways, from too many different sectors of industry, for such an incidental description. Viewed on a global scale, environmental degradation on the contrary looks like one of the *main* products of industrialised economic activity. It is only *because* we have chosen largely to look the other way that the damage can be perceived as merely a side-effect.

Moreover, while it may not be intended, degradation is certainly foreseeable. Depletion of fisheries and forests, for example, is an obvious consequence of unfettered exploitation. The harm caused by agricultural chemicals has been clear for 30 years. We have had sufficient knowledge of ecology to understand the consequences of habitat loss for at least 60.[2]

It may of course be argued that, even if adverse environmental effects could be foreseen, the technologies have not been developed to deal with them. But in some cases this is not relevant – control of forest or fishery depletion requires primarily political or economic, not technological, change. In other cases it isn't true. Environmentally safe methods of pest control, for example, have been available since at least the early 1960s.

But even if this were the case, the question arises of why technological solutions have not been found. In other fields, after all, technological progress over the last 30 years has been spectacular: we have put people on the moon, engineered new forms of life and invented extremely complex ways to kill one another. One might think that greater scientific and technological advance in solving the environmental crisis – if that is all solving it involves – might have been made too.

Unfortunately, although technological development will be crucial to the process, it cannot be sufficient. New technologies are not invented, still less applied, merely because they might be said to be needed. Technology does not develop of its own accord, and its progress is not random. It must be chosen and financed, and these decisions, made primarily by private businesses, are inevitably based mainly on *economic* calculation.[3] The problem is that it has not been in the interests of businesses to develop technologies which might better protect the environment. The question, then, is why it hasn't. To answer this we must go deeper than the issue of technology, to the economic context in which it is developed.

Market forces

In most parts of the world, the economic context is one governed by market forces. This term needs to be defined strictly. Market forces come into being, at the level of the whole economy, when the majority of decisions made at the level of individual firms and consumers take place in markets, and there is no one determining the collective consequences. Market forces are thus the overall sum of many millions of separate individual parts.

In much of the public debate about the operation of the economic system there is considerable confusion as to the nature of markets and market forces. One may often hear these two phenomena being spoken of as if they were the same thing, subsumed under the single label of 'the market'. Moreover, questions concerning markets and market forces are often mixed up with questions about the *ownership* of businesses, which are not the same at all.

Part of the problem is that these issues carry around with them a great deal of ideological baggage, sporting labels such as 'capitalism' and 'free enterprise'. While the ideological debate is important it can often get in the way of a better understanding of how the economic system – whatever it is called, and however it is judged – actually works.

In the current context, for example, the ownership of firms is not very important. As experience has amply shown, a nationalised or cooperatively owned firm is as capable of causing environmental damage as one in private hands. This is because what matters with respect to the environment is the mechanism by which resources are allocated, and this has no necessary bearing on ownership. Different types of companies can coexist with a variety of mechanisms, from relatively 'free' markets to centrally administered (planned) systems. Certainly socially owned firms can (and frequently do) operate in markets, just as privately owned ones can be monopolies.

It is important also to distinguish between markets and market forces. Market forces are a macroeconomic phenomenon, operating at the level of the economy as a whole. Markets by contrast are a microeconomic mechanism, operating at the level of individual products, businesses and households. They are defined by the existence of a number of suppliers and purchasers free to choose with whom they trade, where changes in price mediate between supply and demand. Markets can be and are regulated by government intervention, for example through taxes and laws: there are no completely 'free' markets. But even where markets are regulated, market forces can still operate. They do so whenever the overall result of individual decisions made in markets is unplanned. Regulation of markets *may* be designed to plan the overall outcome, but it usually isn't. In the case of most market-regulating laws its purpose is simply to prevent certain micro level occurrences, such as exploitation of workers or consumers. In the case of taxes it is generally to raise revenue for the government. So long as the collective outcome of behaviour in individual markets is not determined, market forces may be said to operate.

This is what happens in most sectors of the economy, on both national and international scales. The overall allocation of resources and commodities (energy, raw materials, money, labour, goods and services, wastes) is not planned by a single agency. It is left, rather, to the undetermined, combined result of many different agents' decisions. These decisions are made privately; that is, without reference to others' similar decisions, on the basis of each agent's own interests. In general it is impossible for individual economic agents to take into account the wider effects of their actions, since these are dependent on millions of other individual agents' actions, which cannot be known. Added together, market forces thus generate an overall result which no one has determined.

This is the 'invisible hand' which Adam Smith argued brought general prosperity. But it can equally be an 'invisible elbow' which brings general ruin. The anatomical choice is not arbitrary. Elbows are sometimes used to push people aside in the desire to get ahead. But more often elbows are not used deliberately at all; they knock things over inadvertently. Market forces cause environmental degradation by both methods. Sometimes there is deliberate and intended destruction, the foreseen cost of ruthless consumption. But more usually degradation occurs by mistake, the unwitting result of other, smaller decisions. People do not deliberately cause the greenhouse effect or the depletion of the ozone layer. Individual consumers do not intend to destroy the rainforests or plunder the fisheries. And indeed individually they do not do so. These outcomes occur overall, because small individual decisions add up inexorably to large collective ones, and no one is counting. Market forces are at work.

Of course, particular types of environmental impact, notably certain forms of pollution in industrialised countries, are regulated. But mostly these regulations govern the emissions and discharges of individual firms (and sometimes consumers); they do not control the total level of pollution caused as a result of all the discharges together. It is the total level, however, which matters to the environment. Some of the most damaging forms of waste (such as toxins) are indeed only subject to minor local controls; in relation to the environment as a whole they effectively escape restraint. Meanwhile resource exploitation – of minerals, fossil fuels, timber, fish, soil – is in most cases completely uncontrolled; it is frequently positively encouraged. Moreover, even when strong regulations apply in industrialised countries, they are frequently far weaker in the South. Since both the economic system and many environmental problems are global in nature, the result is that the overall impact is mostly unplanned.

The result is an economy which may fairly (if not very elegantly) be described as *environmentally unconstrained*. What happens to the environment is determined by the arbitrary interplay of market forces, not by planned decision-making.

Another feature of the operation of market forces which has a direct bearing on the environment is the pressure they generate for economic growth. Where market forces operate – that is, in the absence of coordination between firms – competition tends to stimulate increased production. Clearly, where decision-makers are motivated by the prospect of increased earnings, growth is attractive. But even where the owners or managers of a firm have no particular wish to grow, it may be necessary, simply to ensure survival. If one firm reinvests its profits to buy more productive machinery, or to increase production, its competitors are often required to do so also, for fear of losing markets and eventually going bankrupt. Even where large firms have only a few competitors, the pressure for growth arises from the institution of tradeable shares. A firm that does not expand, particularly in terms of profit, will see its shares fall in value, thereby risking takeover. (The structure of private ownership *is* therefore relevant here.)

In general market forces thus encourage the constant expansion of production. Such expansion can have obvious environmental implications, if resources come to be over-exploited and waste emissions exceed absorption capacities. And clearly, where the overall environmental impact of economic activities is unconstrained, this is what tends to happen.

It is the *combination* of these two features of market forces which defines the economic system in relation to the environment. Neither, by itself, is sufficient. If economic growth had not 'taken off' in the Industrial Revolution, for instance, if production had remained at pre-industrial levels, the absence of environmental constraints would be of little account, since resource use and waste emissions would be at such low rates. Similarly, the pressures for economic growth do not *of themselves* result in environmental degradation. The pressure on firms is to increase earnings, not to increase the use of resources or emission of wastes.

This is an important point. Many Greens have argued that the environmental crisis is caused by economic growth. But growth *per se* is not responsible; it must be environmentally unconstrained growth. The qualification may seem pedantic, but, as we shall see later in the book, it has critical implications for policy.

A simple example may illustrate. Growth can take different forms. In some cases an increase in resource use and waste emissions may be necessary, but in others it may not. A firm which expands production of financial services, or recycled paper, or solar panels, may succeed just as well as one which builds nuclear power stations (probably better!) or imports tropical hardwood. Yet its impact on the environment may be much less. It may even improve it. It is *material* or physical growth which matters for the environment. But what the economic system requires is *financial* growth. Firms must expand their profits; they do not have to use up more resources. In theory at least, financial growth could still occur even if physical expansion were environmentally constrained.

We shall return to this argument in more detail in Chapter 5, where we consider whether 'zero growth' is necessary to prevent environmental degradation. For the moment however it need not detain us, because environmental constraints are *not* applied, and growth is therefore not purely financial. It can hardly be denied that 200 years of industrial expansion has indeed caused major environmental degradation. We can now begin to see why.

Externalities: the problem of third parties

To understand environmental degradation we need to add to our description of the economy a crucial fact about environmental problems. This is that they are rarely experienced – or at least their full extent is not experienced – by the people who cause them.

After all, by themselves, the pressures for growth and the absence of environmental constraints do not explain why degradation actually occurs. If, as we have argued, degradation is harmful to people, it might be reasonable to presume that it wouldn't happen. If (to take a somewhat allegorical example) I believe that adding an extension to my house risks the entire building collapsing, perhaps killing me, I am unlikely to do it, however much I might want the extra space. There might be nothing stopping me building it, and indeed I might experience pressures to do so from my bank manager (who wants to lend me money), but if I am going to put myself in danger, I will resist.

Unfortunately, this direct connection between the decision-maker and the effects of the decision is absent in respect of most environmental problems. They constitute what economists call *externalities*: effects which are 'external' to the decision-makers.

Externalities may be both positive and negative. Keeping bees in one's garden, for example, can both benefit the neighbours (their flowers will be more abundantly pollinated) and harm them (they may be stung occasionally). Both effects are external, being the result of one's own decision, not theirs. Most environmental problems come into the category of 'negative externalities'. They represent the costs of production and consumption decisions which are not borne by the agents involved in the transaction.

Take a simple case of pollution. If a chemicals factory releases effluent into a river, the fish catch in the estuary further downstream may fall. Two things may then happen. Either the income of the fishing industry will be reduced, or the authorities may be forced to spend money cleaning the water. Meanwhile, the chemicals firm will price its products on the basis of the costs it bears in making them: rent, material inputs, labour and so on. These 'private' costs will not include the cost of releasing the effluent, since this is not paid by the firm. The result is that the consumers of the chemicals will effectively pay less than the full ('social') cost of making them, while the fisheries workers or taxpayers are forced to bear the difference. The pollution is thus an externality of the agents involved in its generation (the chemicals firm and its consumers); it is a cost falling on third parties.

Since it does not pay the cost itself, the chemicals firm actually has an economic incentive to pollute. It is cheaper to pollute the river than it is to clean up the effluent before it leaves the factory. So long as this is the case, and the firm is not legally prevented from doing so, rational economic behaviour suggests that, for the firm, polluting is the right action. In this sense, pollution is not an accident, but a deliberately chosen occurrence.

External costs can be both monetary and non-monetary. In some cases, as in the example of the authorities cleaning up the estuary, expenditure is actually incurred by another agent. In others, such as in the fishing industry's reduced income, money may be lost rather than spent. Sometimes harm may be done which cannot be valued in financial terms.

For example, one of the external costs of motor transport is the dirtying of buildings from exhaust emissions. These costs are borne by the owners of the buildings, who have to spend more on cleaning than they otherwise would. Such costs can be estimated in money terms whether or not the cleaning is actually done. But another type of cost is borne by children whose brains are damaged by atmospheric lead. This cost cannot be given a monetary figure, because people's lives are not amenable to financial calculation. Though it might be possible to add up the costs of hospital treatment, the employment of remedial teachers, and so on, this will not reflect the real cost to the child. It is non-monetary.

Many environmental costs have both monetary and non-monetary components. When a new motorway bulldozes a stretch of countryside, the loss in value of nearby houses can be calculated, but the loss in pleasure, and the worth of all the animals and plants destroyed, cannot.[4] The importance of non-monetary externalities lies in the fact that, unlike monetary costs, they cannot generally be 'paid for' by the participants in the original causal transaction. Vehicle owners can be taxed to give a rebate to landlords; homeowners near the new motorway can be compensated. But no financial transfer will compensate the brain-damaged child.

An important feature of external costs is that they increase in the process of industrial modernisation. As population rises, particularly in cities, more people are affected by pollution. There are fewer places where wastes can be deposited without harm. Moreover, as pollution and resource use rise, their impact is likely to be cumulatively greater. Each emission or unit of resource extracted adds to previous ones. In this sense external costs can form a vicious spiral, each one worsening the effects of the next.

Nearly all examples of pollution are externalities. This is most obvious where wastes emitted in one place cause damage elsewhere: sulphur and nitrogen oxides from US power stations fall as acid rain in Canada; British chemicals dumped in the North Sea foul German beaches. But it is also true in cases where those who cause the problem also experience it, if they are not the *only* people to experience it. Motorists, for example, do not avoid the air pollution they generate; but neither do non-motorists. If taxation rises to pay for the safe disposal of wastes, the company which produces them may pay more, but it shares the burden with non-polluting firms. The entire population of the world is at risk from ozone depletion, not just those fortunate enough to have fridges and spray-on deodorants.

Resource depletion is also a form of externality. Sometimes the harmed third party is a group of people who would otherwise have used the resources in the present day: Indians, for example, in the Amazonian rainforest, whose traditional harvests of rubber and fruit are destroyed; fishing communities near depleted waters, deprived of income and food. In general, resource depletion will affect people living in the future, whose opportunities may be lessened by the reduced availability of the resource.

It will be recalled from Chapter 1 that the biosphere not only provides resources and assimilates wastes, but performs various 'environmental services', both amenities (for example natural beauty, scientific information) and life support services (for example genetic diversity, climatic regulation). Where pollution and resource depletion impair these services the third parties affected may therefore be very widespread. Life support services in particular benefit all life on the earth, so the external cost involved in such problems as rainforest destruction and carbon dioxide emissions is very great.

Three types of externality

Environmental externalities occur in all economic systems. It is impossible to insulate third parties entirely from the effects of economic decisions. But they pose especially difficult problems in a system governed by market forces. This may be understood more clearly by looking in more detail at three particular types of externality.

Common Resources

The first arises from the existence of *common resources*. Many of the world's renewable resources are not formally owned. They are publicly available for use by private actors, without restriction. For example, ocean fisheries are (in the main) common resources. Anyone can fish in them, and there is no limit to the size of catch. This means that it is always in the interest of each fishing boat to catch a few more. But of course when each fishing boat does this, the total fish stock may begin to decline. The more boats join in, the more likely the catch is to fall, eventually perhaps to zero.

The problem here is that, in the short term, the full cost of overfishing is not borne by the people who do it. Each boat gains the entire income earned by the extra fish caught, but pays only a part of the penalty in reduced catch. The depletion is therefore an externality to each boat. In the long term, of course, the decline of stocks will seriously hurt each boat's income, but by then it will be too late.

The problem is made worse by the fact that for any boat to *refrain* from catching the extra fish will not actually help. Unless each boat can be sure that all the other boats will also refrain, the likelihood is that the others will simply catch the extra fish themselves. The 'refraining' boat will then have lost the extra income while still being forced to pay the cost of depletion. So long as market forces govern the total catch, therefore, each boat has a powerful economic incentive to overfish.

This situation is sometimes called the 'tragedy of the commons': it is an application of the famous 'prisoner's dilemma' problem of cooperative behaviour.[5] No individual actor wants depletion to occur, but rational economic behaviour for each combines to give that collective result. This process is exhibited throughout the world where resources are held in common, and not restricted in use: pasture lands eroded by overgrazing, forests degraded by overfelling, whales made almost extinct by uncontrolled hunting.

One solution to the problem that is frequently suggested is to turn common resources into private ones. It is argued that if the oceans were made private property, then overfishing would not occur, because the owners would suffer the cost of depletion themselves. What is now an external cost would become an 'internal' one. This suggests that it is not really market forces which are the problem, but the absence of private ownership.[6]

But this argument is incorrect. It is true that a formal owner, if he or she could control all use of the resource, would want to prevent over-exploitation, in order to maintain future income.[7] But this would not be done by allowing 'market forces' to work. The 'market forces method' would mean allowing the fish catch to be determined according to the demand for fish and the financial cost of catching them. But since these are not necessarily related to the number of fish in the sea, there is no guarantee that overfishing would not occur. Indeed, market forces would actually *encourage* depletion. As fish became scarce their price would rise, encouraging the fishing industry to catch even more.

To prevent overfishing the owner of the oceans would precisely *not* allow market forces to determine the total fish catch. He or she would set specific limits to the number of fish which could be caught. This limit would be the maximum number possible compatible with the prevention of depletion. The right to catch this number would then presumably be auctioned off to the highest bidder. In this way the fish stock could be kept constant, while the price of fish would rise. A higher price would cut demand to such a level that it met the reduced supply.

An owner controlling fish stocks and catches in this way would have to be a monopolist, that is, the *only* owner of the ocean. If there were several owners in different 'zones', competing with each other to attract fishing boats to fish in their waters, the 'auction' pricing mechanism could not be used. This is because an owner who allows unlimited fishing will make much more money than one who imposes limits. In the long term the latter might do better, but by then he or she may have gone bankrupt through lack of custom.

Of course, if ownership needs to be monopolistic, it would be better if it were public ownership, since private monopoly leads easily to abuse. (In particular a private monopolist, motivated by profit, is likely to charge higher prices, since consumers cannot buy from anyone else.) So the solution to the problem of common resources turns out not to be private ownership and market forces at all. Rather, it is social ownership and the direct limitation of the total harvest. This is an important conclusion to which we shall return later in the book.

It is important to note here that 'social ownership' need not mean 'nationalisation'. Many so-called 'primitive' societies have kept common resources such as grazing lands and fisheries ecologically stable through the operation of cultural and moral controls. This is a perfectly valid way of limiting harvests, though it is not one (unfortunately) which large-scale industrialised societies can often use.[8]

Public goods

The second type of externality which causes problems for market forces occurs in the case of *public goods*. These are a type of common resource with a special feature, namely the impossibility of dividing the resource up into separate parts. The obvious example is the air. Not only is the air not formally owned, but it cannot be partitioned. The air you breathe is the same air I breathe, and anything I do to my air is also done to your air – whether or not you want it.

Being a common resource, the use of air is unrestricted. Moreover it is free. Unless specific controls are introduced it costs nothing to discharge wastes into the atmosphere: all the costs of doing so are offloaded onto third parties. Yet it is fairly clear that many of those third parties – people suffering from lung diseases, foresters with declining harvests – would be prepared to pay to get clean air. (In the case of the forester, its worth could be measured, being the difference between the cost of the clean air and the greater loss of timber from pollution.)

But a system of market forces cannot give people clean air, however much they are prepared to pay for it. This is because no one can sell a public good in a market. If a company comes along and offers to clean up the air, in return for an annual charge, it can't keep the clean air restricted only to those who pay for it. Everyone else will also benefit. But of course if it is possible to benefit from something without paying for it, why should anyone pay for it? We can all 'free ride'. The net result is that no one pays, and the air remains dirty.

This problem occurs whenever a good is 'public'; that is, when it cannot be restricted only to paying customers. Lighthouses, national defence and crime prevention measures all fall into this category. In these cases it is generally recognised that the state must provide these services, charging *everyone* for them through taxation. The same is true of environmental public goods, notably clean air, and (if access to them cannot be restricted) clean rivers and seas and beautiful countryside. It is of course possible in some cases to charge those who *cause* pollution, if their emissions can be monitored, but 'ownership of the air' must still be public, since it is a common resource. Clean air then is just like a fishery, and the same arguments apply to it as already discussed.

The important point to recognise here is that market forces cannot provide clean air *even if there is demand for it.* In some cases of pollution, the people suffering could not afford a better environment even if one were on offer. The slum dwellers of Brazil, for example, would not have enough money to pay the neighbouring factories to clean up their waste emissions even if the companies were prepared to do so. But for supporters of market forces the more damning observation is that even if those suffering from pollution *can* pay, the system will not allow them to do so. This is because they do not take part in the transaction which causes the pollution: they are, precisely, third parties.

It is possible, in theory, to add up how much clean air is 'worth' to people. They can be asked how much they would be prepared to pay for it. Imagine that, in a particular town affected by pollution from a chemicals factory, the total sum which the residents, asked individually, said they were prepared to pay for clean air exceeded the cost of cleaning up the harmful emissions. We could then say that, overall, the cost of the pollution exceeded its 'benefit' to the factory causing it. (It would pay the firm to clean up the emissions in return for this sum.) The 'optimum' or rational solution would therefore be for the emissions to be stopped.

But how could this occur? It isn't the people who suffer the pollution who decide whether it is generated or not: they are third parties to the transaction between the factory and its customers. Even if they were prepared to pay the factory to stop its emissions, this would only work if they all paid. But how could you get everyone to pay? Clean air is a public good: it is indivisible. So everyone benefits from it whether or not they pay for it. We come back to the same problem: if each person would benefit whether or not they paid, why should anyone pay?

The conclusion, therefore, is that wherever externalities involve public goods, market forces cannot generate the optimum or best solution.[9] The only way to get clean air would be to *make* everyone pay through taxation. But even this raises a problem. Why should people have to pay for clean air? Surely the correct solution is for the firm which causes the pollution to pay? But this will not occur unless you charge them for using the air as a waste disposal site. And as we saw with the case of the fisheries, this can't happen in a market forces system either.

Future generations

The third type of externality is where those affected by the environmental damage are not yet born; that is, where the harmful impact of current activities is felt by *future generations*. The difficulty here is evident. We have seen that, in cases of public goods, the problem is that third parties cannot express their desires in the market. But this is even more obviously problematic where the third parties do not actually *exist* at the time of the causal transaction.

As we have seen, this is to a large extent the case for many of the key environmental issues: depletion of resources, the greenhouse effect, damage to the ozone layer, the destruction of habitats and extinction of species, and so on. In many cases the impact on future generations will be extremely serious. It is a fair bet that, if such generations were able to influence current decision-making, they would try to prevent the damaging activities. But they are not able to.

Of course, future people cannot take part in any economic system. But the crucial point here is that, so long as decisions are made by market forces, their interests cannot even be taken into account. Market forces are governed by the demands of individual actors in the market, and unborn people are not in the market. They have no purchasing power to wield.

Now it has been argued that the interests of future generations *are* taken into account, because current actors want to preserve their resources for the future. An agricultural landlord does not want the soil to be eroded, the argument runs, because his future income will fall. Even if his *own* income won't fall, because the soil erosion won't take effect until after he's died or sold up, the value of his land will fall, since its value is dependent on its future productivity. Therefore in a market system private owners *do* effectively take the interests of the future into account.

Unfortunately, this argument is flawed, for two reasons. First, people don't make decisions about future income in the same way that they make decisions about present income. The future is 'discounted'; that is, less value is placed on it than is placed on the present. If I am weighing up, for example, whether to plant trees which will yield a future return, but cost money now, or save the money now and forgo the earnings in the future, I shan't count one actual pound or dollar now as equal to one prospective pound or dollar in fifty years' time. A bird in the hand is worth two in the bush! After all, anything might happen in the next fifty years. I might go bankrupt, or disease might kill off the trees, or the price of timber might fall.

This process of giving the future less value than the present, or 'discounting' it, is very important in the economics of the environment, as we shall see later. Here we can see that it creates a problem for a market system. The landlord deciding whether to spend money on soil conservation measures will not be so concerned about loss of productivity in, say, the year 2050. But the people who *will* be living in 2050 will be concerned; they would have wanted the farmer to have taken every measure for conservation, to keep the soil at least as productive. Discounting thus means that a market system does not provide fully for the future.[10]

This is especially true for resources which regenerate very slowly, such as tropical forests and whales. Then the period over which conservation measures will prove worthwhile is very long, much longer than the period in which investors expect their investments to show a return. So it pays a timber company or whaler to deplete the resource as fast as possible, making maximum profits while spending the minimum in interest payments on their capital equipment.

Second, resources do not only have value to their owners. As we saw earlier, renewable resources in particular provide environmental services which are of benefit to many other people. They may be valued for their beauty, or their scientific interest. Even more importantly, they may contribute to essential life support services, such as the maintenance of genetic diversity and regulation of climate. These benefits are 'external' to the resource owner, and therefore they do not come into his or her 'private' cost-benefit calculations on whether to preserve the resource for the future.

For both these reasons, an economic system based on market forces cannot cope with externalities which affect future generations. This is true not only in the case of common resources, but of privately owned ones too.

Unequal demands

Nearly all of the major problems which make up the environmental crisis can be classified under the heading of at least one of these three types of externality. The consequence is clear. An economic system based on market forces not only cannot prevent environmental degradation occurring; it can actually encourage it. In many cases economic actors are given positive incentives to deplete resources, to generate pollution and to impair environmental services.

The problem of externalities is made worse by a final important feature of the current economic system. This is the gross inequality of income and wealth between nations, and between different groups within nations.[11]

In a system governed by market forces, resources are allocated where demand for them is greatest. Economic agents with greater income and wealth will always be able to outbid those with less. This means that many more of the world's resources, regardless of their geographical origin, go to richer nations and groups than to poorer ones. The 26% of the world's population who live in the industrialised countries consume, for example, 80% of the world's commercial energy, 79% of its steel, 86% of its other metals and 85% of its paper. And they generate 92% of all industrial carbon dioxide emissions.[12]

In some cases of pollution, inequalities of income and wealth make little difference to the pattern of environmental degradation. Sweden and Norway are richer countries than the UK, but this does not help them in trying to prevent acid rain coming over the North Sea from

British power stations. But in many cases it is precisely inequality which generates the environmental problem. The export of toxic wastes from industrialised to developing countries, for example, is only possible because the former are able to outbid local people for use of the dumping grounds. By contrast, affluent countries are refusing to take such waste. The spectacle of ships such as the 'Karin B' (in 1988) carrying toxic cargoes from port to port around Europe being refused entry contrasts starkly with the regular trade carried on between North and South, demonstrating the difference economic power can make.[13]

In the case of resources, inequality is a direct cause of degradation. This is because rich economic agents are not dependent simply on one source for their raw materials; they can look anywhere for cheap supplies. They can therefore offload the cost of depletion or pollution onto those poorer, local agents who cannot afford to buy elsewhere.

The example of the Latin American rainforests is instructive. There is considerable local demand for the renewable harvests of the forest, such as, rubber, fruits and oils. However this cannot compete with the demand for timber and ranching land which comes from the United States and Europe, since consumers in the industrialised countries are so much richer. The result is that the forests are felled and cleared to provide mahogany tables and beef for export, while the harvests of the local people are destroyed.[14] It is the inequality of income and wealth which enables rich consumers in the industrialised countries to impose such costs; if the local people were as rich, they would not allow it. This is why forests in the US and Europe are not being comparably depleted.

Wealth enables rich consumers to escape the external costs of depletion because, so long as resources are relatively abundant, they can always buy elsewhere. The fact that clearing rainforests for cattle causes rapid soil erosion and loss of productivity barely matters when there is so much other forest land which can be converted. Virtually all the ranches established in Amazonia prior to 1978 have now been abandoned; their owners have simply moved on to pastures new. Therefore the industrialised countries don't actually experience depletion at all: it is notable that, despite the rapid destruction of rainforests, the prices of tropical hardwoods and beef have not risen. The depletion is experienced entirely by the local people, who cannot afford to buy from wherever the resource is cheapest. They have their own local resource or nothing. The external costs are therefore offloaded directly from rich onto poor.

The same process can be seen wherever demand for a resource is exercised by consumers in the industrialised nations. In many of the world's coastal fisheries, for example, the local catch has been decimated by industrial fishing for export to the industrialised countries. When a fishery is exhausted, the export fishing boats move elsewhere, leaving the local people to pay the cost – often in terms of malnutrition from reduced protein consumption. In many parts of the South soils are eroded under the same pressures to export crops. Much greater demand is wielded by consumers in the North than by local people, so intensive farming techniques are used to produce exportable cash crops. Local people may actually go hungry while this occurs; they are certainly forced to pay the long-term costs of erosion.[15]

When unequal demand transfers resources from poor to rich, environmental degradation is frequently given added impetus by the actions of the poor. Unable to harvest their traditional resources, which they used to do sustainably, they are forced into 'marginal' or less productive areas which frequently cannot support them. This leads to further depletion, as soils are overgrazed or overcultivated, fisheries exhausted, trees cut down for firewood. (When the export industries have moved on, what were formerly fertile areas will have themselves become marginal.) This process is occurring throughout the world, as the very poorest people attempt to survive on already degraded lands and seas, causing further degradation as they do so.

As a result, it is often said that many of the world's environmental problems are caused by the actions of the poor. But this is a *consequence* of the crisis, not its cause. Poor people only degrade their own environment – thereby imposing long-term costs on themselves – when their short-term survival depends on it and they have, literally, no option. Responsibility for the environmental crisis should therefore not be laid at their door; it rests with the earlier and greater environmental demands of the industrialised nations which bring them to this position.

Third World debt

In the last decade the transfer of resources from poor to rich nations under the pressure of unequal demand has been exacerbated by the expansion of international debt. The trillion (thousand billion) dollars owed by nations in the South to Northern banks and governments is now responsible for a great deal of the most damaging examples of environmental degradation. The debt was created in the first place because of the huge inequality between nations: in the 1970s and early 80s Northern banks needed somewhere to lend the huge sums of money deposited by the newly rich oil exporting nations, and poor developing countries keen to industrialise were the obvious target. It is now itself a source of further inequality, as interest repayments – at rates more than double those at which the loans were originally taken out – impoverish Southern nations and enrich Northern ones. In many cases the flow of repayments from poor to rich countries actually exceeds aid given in the other direction.[16]

There are two primary mechanisms by which the debt crisis causes environmental degradation. First, many of the so-called 'development' projects which the loans have been used to finance are themselves ecologically damaging. This is most notably true in the case of the huge dams built in Brazil, India and other countries to provide irrigation and hydro-electric power. Such dams flood very large areas, causing immense destruction of ecosystems, loss of forest and arable resources, increased salinisation and reduced fertility of downstream agricultural land, higher incidence of water-borne diseases and the forced resettlement of hundreds of thousands of people. These costs are almost always excluded from the cost-benefit calculations which determine a project's 'viability'; they are rarely compensated for by the benefits the dams provide. Smaller-scale hydro-schemes have been shown to be more efficient in the production of energy, as well as less environmentally destructive.[17]

Second, the means by which debts are repaid are often environmentally damaging. Deforestation is the most obvious example. In Latin America the need to earn foreign exchange causes much of the rainforests to be cleared. This is not only because the timber and beef harvested from the (ex-)forest lands are themselves lucrative, but because the forest is used to resettle peasant farmers displaced from agricultural land elsewhere. This agricultural land has been turned over from subsistence farming to huge plantations (both private and government-owned) growing soya beans and other cash crops. The crops are required not to feed local people but for export, to earn money to pay debts. Since such massive production of soya beans actually depresses its price, more and more must be grown just to maintain revenue.

Dispossessed from their land, the peasant farmers have been encouraged to resettle in forest areas. But the fertility of forests lies in the vegetation, not the soil, and degraded forest land cannot long support agriculture. Water is lost, soil is eroded and harvests rapidly decline. The farmers move on, clearing more trees to survive a few more years. A great deal of tropical deforestation is carried out in this way by poor peasant farmers; but again the first link in the chain lies in the demands of industrialised nations.[18]

This process, by which international debt leads to environmental degradation, is repeated throughout the South. It is no coincidence that many of the key countries where tropical rainforests are being destroyed – Brazil, Indonesia, Zaire, Peru, Colombia – are among the top debtors. Meanwhile other methods of financing debt are also found. Peru's anchovy stocks have been fished almost to extinction, Bolivia exports its endangered animals, Mexico is permanently draining groundwater to produce vegetables for export to the US; and so on.

Population and causation

One obvious conclusion from this brief account is that, in many parts of the South, a prerequisite for solving the environmental crisis is ending the debt crisis – in essence, by eliminating or greatly reducing debt repayments. But the impact of 'unequal demands' in general suggests a wider conclusion, which refers to the issues raised in the last chapter.

There we stressed that the environmental crisis had important distributional features: the effects of environmental problems were not experienced equally by different groups. Now we must add that the *causes* of the crisis are not distributed equally either. In understanding how environmental degradation occurs it becomes clear that inequalities of wealth and income are a crucial component in the process. Put bluntly, it is caused largely by rich nations – and rich groups within nations.

This has an important bearing on one of the factors most commonly cited when causes of the crisis are discussed, namely population growth. There is no question that the continued rapid expansion of global numbers is making the crisis worse. World population is currently at around 5 billion. It is expected to exceed 6 billion by the year 2000, and is unlikely to level off until it hits 10 billion, or double today's number of people, near the end of the next century.[19] Most of the extra people will live in the South, where population growth is fastest, and many will live where there is already great pressure on food supplies, often because of soil erosion and other forms of environmental degradation.

But population growth in the South must be put in the perspective of resource consumption by the North. For if the object of our concern is the potential divergence between the number of people in the world and the biosphere's capacity to support them, then the way in which the biosphere's resources are divided up is of crucial importance. As we have seen, the slices of the cake are not of the same size. The average person in a rich industrialised country eats three times as much food as his or her counterpart in the Third World. Overall, it is estimated, citizens of the US get through environmental resources 500 times faster than those of India.[20] In these circumstances, extra people in the South are of much less concern than extra people, or even a constant number, in the North. Reductions in the population of rich countries would do far more to ease the problem than equivalent reductions in poor ones.

This is not to argue that slowing the pace of population growth in the South is not important: by and large, the fewer people wherever they are the less likely the environment is to be degraded, and the easier it will be to feed everyone and to improve living standards. But the primary issue is who has access to the resources; whose consumption is actually causing the problem. The world currently has adequate resources with which to feed its population. It is in fact likely that given improvements in agricultural productivity and environmental stability there will be sufficient capacity to feed 10 billion people.[21] But the food has actually to be available to the poor, and that means increasing the resources they have to produce or to buy it. Indeed, as experience has widely shown, the richer communities become the more slowly their populations grow. It is therefore possible to address both sides of the problem – Northern consumption and Southern population growth – together, by slicing the global income cake more equally. This, of course, is a political question as much as an economic one.

4

Capitalism, Industrialism and Green Politics

Business values and the environment

In the last chapter it was argued that the environmental crisis is a result of a global economic system governed by market forces. We attempted to show that market forces not only cannot prevent environmental degradation; they may actually encourage it.

There are two sorts of argument which might be used to counter these claims. One is that it is not inevitable that the economic system should cause degradation. It may do so now, but in the future it could be 'greened'. The other is that an *economic* analysis misplaces the root cause of the environmental crisis. This lies, rather, in the *social values* which inform industrial economies. This argument points to the degraded environments of Eastern Europe under communism to show that it is not market forces which are the primary problem, but the values common to both communism (as was) and capitalism.

We shall deal with this second argument later. We may notice, however, that the two arguments are linked by their emphasis on social values. Those who claim that capitalism can be 'greened' base this view on the assumption that growing environmental concern will affect the decisions of companies and consumers in the market system. They argue that this is already happening, pointing to the growth of 'green' sectors of the economy and the phenomenon of 'green consumerism' as evidence that market forces need not always cause environmental degradation.

For example, a leading British environmentalist, John Elkington, argues in his book *The Green Capitalists* that it is not the market system *per se* but only the *particular form* of it we have experienced that gives rise to environmental problems. Describing the activities of a number of 'sunrise' companies engaged in environmentally beneficial activities, he suggests that

> what we are seeing is the emergence of a new age capitalism, appropriate to a new millenium, in which the boundary between corporate and human values is beginning to dissolve ... The argument

now is about what sort of capitalism we want ... One dimension [is] the green dimension.[1]

There can be no doubt that over the last twenty years environmental concerns have grown in importance for many private sector firms. Huge corporations such as IBM, BP and ICI have adopted environmental policy statements. Along with many others they devote considerable resources to the research and development of new products and processes which will reduce resource use and pollution. Meanwhile whole new industrial sectors have grown up whose very purpose is environmental protection: energy conservation, renewable (continuing) energy generation, various forms of biotechnology, 'low and no waste' technologies, materials recycling, waste disposal, pollution control and many more. Other industries, such as information technology, fibre optics and financial services, have expanded rapidly with minimal environmental impact.

But unfortunately these examples do not prove that an economic system based on market forces can secure protection of the environment. That some firms can make profits while benefiting (or not harming) the environment does not mean that all firms are likely to. As we have seen, firms do not have to be malicious to act in a damaging way. They merely have to respond rationally to economic signals. In many industries, these signals still encourage environmentally harmful activities. The fact that they do not in others may reduce the problem but does not eliminate it. Since controlling pollution is almost always more expensive than ignoring it, voluntary corporate 'greening' is unlikely to be widely practised.[2] The advocates of 'green capitalism' have to show that the entire economic system could be environmentally benign; evidence of a few green companies does not do this.

The issue in general is not the behaviour of individual firms, but the collective result of all their actions. Individual firms contribute to pollution, but none of them need be responsible on its own. Since no firm can know the collective result when it decides its own action, even environmentally-conscious companies can unwittingly cause damage. A 'good' factory may reduce its own toxic emissions by half, for example, but if other 'bad' ones are increasing them by the same amount the overall environmental impact is unchanged. The existence of good firms on their own will not solve the problem. (Moreover, of course, even the 50% of emissions still produced may be dangerous to health.)

Evidence that firms have become environmentally conscious either 'voluntarily' (as a result of changes in corporate values), or because market forces have encouraged them, is in fact rather thin. The vast majority of new environmental activities have been explicitly developed as a result of the statutory regulation of markets or of political pressure from environmentalists. Elkington, for example, cites the development of alternative aerosol propellants to replace CFCs. But it was governmental regulation which first forced companies to search for alternatives in the 1970s, not market forces. Indeed, when American regulations were relaxed in 1980 the huge American transnational Du Pont, a leading producer of CFCs, actually shelved its research programme into alternatives, regarding it as uneconomic.[3]

This story is common to nearly all examples of 'environmental sensitivity' among large companies. If they are forced by regulation – or sometimes, by political pressure – to change their practices, they will do so. They will often then invest large sums of money in the development of new products and processes. But they will not do this until regulation is imposed or threatened. The reason is evident. Environmental protection is expensive. In a competitive market, voluntary action will put a firm at a cost disadvantage. But if all firms are forced to act, none will be worse off in comparison with the others.

Companies do not merely wait for regulation. Though a situation where all firms in the industry face the same costs may be preferred to one where costs are unequal, the best situation is usually where no costs are imposed at all. Any cost, depending on how far it can be passed on to consumers, threatens profits. So firms will often resist regulation fiercely.

The history of unleaded petrol is instructive in this regard. Throughout the 1970s and 1980s the oil companies and the motor industry did their utmost to prevent and then delay legislation enforcing unleaded petrol.[4] Now that it has been introduced, of course, they are cheerfully proclaiming how green they are. The moral is not so much to beware corporate hypocrisy as that market forces are not responsible for environmental improvement. Firms have to be specifically constrained.

Green consumerism

It might be argued that what the 'green capitalists' are doing is responding not so much to political pressure as to consumer demand. As consumers increasingly desire environmentally non-damaging products, so profit-making companies will be forced to make them. According to this argument, the very market forces that we have claimed cause the degradation of the environment will in fact compel its protection.

Thus, it might be pointed out, as consumers have worried more about the links between diet and ill-health, so food manufacturers have been forced to produce foods without artificial additives, and supermarkets have taken to stocking 'whole' and organic foods. No regulations were necessary to effect this change; just the operation of 'consumer sovereignty' in the market.

The 'healthy food revolution' is indeed impressive testimony to the power of the market to change production and retailing behaviour by private firms. If markets could always register consumer preferences for environmental protection in this way, the case against market forces might indeed collapse. No doubt more people would need to be educated about the environmental crisis more urgently. But if they were, and they could be encouraged to express their concern in their buying habits, the system would respond. 'Ecologically-sound' products would become profitable, and market forces would produce them. No change in the system, just in the preferences of its consumers, would be necessary.

Unfortunately, this is too simple. To begin with, consumers must have sufficient information to be able to make informed decisions. Only when statutory regulation forced food companies to label the additives in their products did additive-free foods become widely available. It is still impossible to find out what pesticide residues are left on fruit and vegetables. Information is often not provided by firms unless they are forced by regulation. So a consumer may wish to exercise an environmentally-informed choice but be unable to do so.

But more importantly, foods are not a very typical product in this context. They are characterised by the fact that their 'polluting' qualities are experienced by their own consumers. They are one of the few cases where the environmental hazard is not actually an 'externality', because it is not a third party who is harmed. It is the consumer him or herself. This makes it very easy for the consumer's environmental preferences to be registered in the market. The person at risk can simply not buy the product.

This is not the case with most instances of environmental degradation. As we have seen, the large majority are examples of external costs, where the person or group harmed is *not* the purchaser of the hazardous product, and therefore cannot avoid the risk simply by not buying. In these cases, consumer preferences will not necessarily prevent the damage, because it isn't the consumer who is damaged. Production and consumption of hamburgers, for example, have extremely serious environmental effects, in the destruction of rainforests for cattle ranching. But those who suffer these effects are not customers of burger joints. And there is unfortunately no sign that the people who are customers are changing their eating habits because of concern about tropical deforestation.

'Green consumerism' should not be written off. Clearly there are many people in industrialised countries who are now expressing their environmental concerns in their shopping, and market forces are meeting their demands. The remarkable worldwide success of the Body Shop is evidence enough that individual 'green capitalist' firms are possible, while the growth of 'ethical' investment and pension funds demonstrates that even financial markets can respond to non-monetary motivations. These developments should certainly be encouraged (and later on in this book we encourage them). But this is not a mechanism which can solve the environmental crisis, for a number of reasons.

First, environmentally-sensitive products are usually more expensive than those which are not, since they involve extra costs in production. (Cosmetics appear to be an exception, which may explain the Body

Shop's success.) So long as environmentally 'unsound' products remain on the market, the appeal of their 'ethical' competitors is therefore likely to be limited to more affluent consumers. It cannot be expected that poorer people will buy more expensive products, if they have a choice, simply in order to prevent a distant or future external cost. Only if the price differential is eroded will consumer behaviour change on a sufficient scale, and in general this will not occur through market forces. It will have to be regulated.

The marketing of unleaded petrol demonstrates this. Even when it was held at the same price as leaded petrol it failed to sell. Only when government tax policy brought its price considerably below leaded petrol did motorists buy it in significant quantities.

Second, consumers have to be offered a choice to express their environmental concerns. If all the available products are equally damaging, consumer preference cannot be exercised. Although orthodox economists may pretend that consumers have 'sovereignty' in a market, one can actually only buy what is offered by producers. There is no guarantee that firms, especially those which are near-monopolies, will invest unbidden in the development of new products and processes in order to satisfy consumers' putative environmental concerns. Many people, for example, may want to buy goods with less wasteful packaging; but they cannot do so, because no one is offering them. Similarly, many people may want to reduce atmospheric pollution by using their car less. But if the public transport system can't take them where they want to go with reasonable efficiency, they may have effectively no choice at all.

Third, and related to this, many environmental problems are very remote from the final consumers of products. They are caused by the activities of firms far down the 'production chain'. Toxic waste may be generated by a company which makes the metals for the machines which makes the plastics which are used to make the TV bought by the consumer. In such cases it is very difficult for consumers to make informed choices, even if a choice is theoretically available.

Lastly, of course, it has to be doubted whether enough consumers actually *do* want to make such choices. As we have seen, many environmental problems are experienced by people far distant from the consumers of industrialised societies, either in developing countries or in the future. It isn't obvious that, even if green consumption behaviour could solve these problems, the interests of such people are sufficiently important to Northern shoppers. They may become so, but the environmental crisis cannot, unfortunately, wait until they do, for by then it may be too late.[5]

A 'green capitalism', then, whether it is based on the development of new, environmentally-motivated firms or on environmentally-sensitive consumer behaviour, cannot be the solution to the crisis. Market forces have to be controlled, not promoted, if the overall environmental impact of economic activity is to be reduced.

There is, of course, another type of argument in support of 'green capitalism'. This accepts all the foregoing but claims that capitalism can quite happily coexist with the overall regulation of environmental impact. Environmental controls are after all quite widespread already: a few more won't mean the end of the system. But then we are into a semantic debate about the name the system is given, not an argument about the changes necessary to solve environmental problems. We shall explore the extent of regulation necessary in Chapter 10. Whether it is felt that these charges would so alter the nature of the economic system as to make 'capitalism' an inappropriate label is a matter of definition, not of substance. The issue is what must be done, not what to call it.

The argument from communism[6]

We said that there were two arguments which might be put forward to counter the claim that market forces are responsible for the environmental crisis. The first was that capitalism might be 'greened'. The second is that focusing on the mechanics of the economic system makes for too shallow an analysis.

Proponents of this view point out that environmental degradation is not confined to countries with capitalist economies. Until recently the countries of Eastern Europe had economic systems based on centralised state planning. To a large (though declining) extent the Soviet Union and China, along with some Third World nations such as Cuba and Vietnam, still have such systems. In these countries market forces have been to a considerable extent absent. Yet this has not prevented immense environmental damage. Resources were and are depleted and pollution generated just as in the West and the capitalist South; often, indeed, much more severely. Therefore market forces, the argument runs, cannot be held responsible for the environmental crisis. Its causes must be located elsewhere, in the characteristics that these systems share, not in those by which they differ.

Many Greens have argued that both capitalism and communism are indeed part of a single, larger system, which they call 'industrialism'. In his book *Seeing Green*, for example, Jonathon Porritt, former director of UK Friends of the Earth, observes that both systems are

> dedicated to industrial growth, to the expansion of the means of production, to a materialist ethic as the best means of meeting people's needs, and to unimpeded technological development. Both rely on increasing centralization and large-scale bureaucratic control and co-ordination. From a viewpoint of narrow scientific rationalism, both insist that the planet is there to be conquered, that big is self-evidently beautiful, and that what cannot be measured is of no importance ... the similarities between these two dominant ideologies are of greater significance than their differences ... they are united in one, all-embracing 'super-ideology' ... industrialism.[7]

In this view it is insufficient to analyse the environmental crisis in terms of economic processes, for its real roots lie deeper, in the fundamental ideology and culture of industrialised society – both capitalist and communist. It is here, in Northern materialist values, that the real problem, industrialism, is to be found. We degrade the environment, this view claims, because our culture has become alienated from it; unlike so-called 'primitive' societies – which have lived for centuries without degrading their own environments – we no longer feel a part of the natural world, but superior to it, and so acquiesce in its destruction.[8]

This argument leads to an important conclusion, namely that the principal focus for change must be ideological. Since industrialism is the root of the problem, the environmental crisis will not be solved until it is overcome. As the communist experience has demonstrated, merely reforming economic structures and mechanisms cannot be enough. If the ideology and culture don't change too, environmental degradation will continue to occur. From this follows a political standpoint which emphasises individual lifestyles and values: changing what people consume and how they live and think, rather than the structures of the global (or even national) economic system. Indeed, attempting the latter kind of reform is regarded by many 'deep Greens' as merely tinkering with the problem – and may actually be dangerous if it reinforces the idea that economic change is sufficient – since it is not economic processes and mechanisms which are its fundamental cause.[9]

This argument must be taken seriously. It is unquestionably true that the environmental record of the communist system has been no better, and has often been worse, than that of the capitalist world.[10] And there can also be little doubt that the ideology of both capitalist and communist societies has indeed in many ways legitimised and encouraged the exploitation of nature.[11] There are clearly powerful cultural mechanisms underpinning the expansionist consumerism which characterises Western society (though one might question how far this has been a communist value: it was not exactly a surfeit of consumerism which caused the revolutions in Eastern Europe.) But none of this is incompatible with an economic analysis of the environmental crisis.

There are two mistakes here. The first is the assumption that, because communism also produces environmental degradation, therefore it must do so for exactly the same reasons and in the same way as capitalism. This doesn't follow, and indeed isn't the case, as we shall show below. Second, there is no reason to suppose that ideological change must be an alternative to economic reform, or take place prior to it, rather than be a complementary and simultaneous activity.

Communism and capitalism cause environmental degradation in quite different ways. Under communism, ideology *is* a crucial part of the economic process. This is because production and consumption in most sectors of the economy are determined according to centrally-decided plans rather than markets. Companies do not compete with each other, but are given production targets by the state. Environmental degradation therefore doesn't occur through the operation of market forces: there is a central agency planning the overall outcome of individual economic activities. Externalities can in theory be taken into account in decision-making, since the state is involved in all decisions. Even non-monetary costs can be recognised, since economic accounting need not be governed by financial profit. We can therefore say that it is precisely because the state has *not* been concerned about environmental degradation that it has been allowed to occur. Had communist ideology included a concern for the environment it would actually have been relatively easy (at least in theory) for environmental criteria to be incorporated into production plans, since these plans are centrally coordinated. (This is indeed precisely what happens with respect to employment, where the ideological emphasis on full employment ensures that everyone has a job irrespective of its efficiency.)[12]

The demise of communism in Eastern Europe may make these arguments seem academic, but they are important in the debate about the nature of capitalist societies. The 'deep Green' view is that the mechanics of the economic system are much less important than the underlying ideology. But the mechanics are not the same in the two systems. Therefore ideology cannot be a sufficient explanation of why environmental degradation occurs: the ideology generates its environmental impact through different processes. Only by understanding these processes will it be possible to understand how the ideology is put to work in practice in degrading the environment. And only if the processes are understood will it be possible to change them.

This is particularly true in relation to capitalism, because here the industrial ideology is not nearly so direct a factor in generating environmental degradation. Indeed the 'deep Green' argument, that (in environmental terms) nothing would be achieved by reform of the economic system unless the ruling ideology were also changed, can be turned on its head. A change in ideology without a change in the economic system would be similarly ineffective. This is because, as we have seen, market forces tend to generate degradation whatever the desires of producers and consumers. Firms which voluntarily refrain from environmental damage are liable to be bankrupted by competitors, while individual market demand for environmental protection frequently goes unmet because of external effects. Even if the majority of people rejected consumerism and firms abandoned their expansionist impulses, society would still have to find some mechanism for controlling the overall result of their individual decisions. The whole point of the 'invisible elbow' is that consumers and firms do not have to *want* to degrade the environment for degradation to occur. It is the overall effect that counts, and however environmentally conscious individual agents are, they are not able to know how their own actions will combine with others to produce a collective result. So long as market forces remain the determinants of environmental impact, therefore, ideological change on its own cannot guarantee that the environment will be protected.

This is not to reject the Green concern with ideology. It seems indisputable that the economic system is buttressed by important features of Western culture and its set of dominant values. There is clearly a strong link between consumer demand and environmental damage, and that demand must to a considerable extent derive from cultural sources rather than from within the economic system itself. (However, the way in which the system generates demand through marketing and advertising should not be disregarded.)[13] Perhaps most importantly, it is difficult to see how the economic system can be changed unless culture and values change also. In democracies fundamental reform can only occur by popular consent (whether such consent is *sufficient* is another question), and this will not be forthcoming unless attitudes and values have shifted.

Our argument is therefore not that ideological change is not important, merely that it is not enough on its own. Reform of the economic system – essentially, the control of market forces – must also occur if further environmental degradation is to be avoided. The two types of change must go together.

'Neither Left nor Right but forward'?

This conclusion has an important bearing on the nature of Green politics. Some Greens and others have argued that environmental issues can be divorced from 'old-fashioned' Left–Right conflicts. For them Green lies not along but outside the traditional spectrum running from red to blue. This view derives from two sources. One is the perception, discussed in Chapter 2, that environmental issues affect everyone irrespective of class or income. The other is the analysis of capitalism and communism as a single system united by the ideology of 'industrialism', with its accompanying emphasis on ideological rather than structural economic change.

It should now be clear that neither of these sources lends strength to the 'neither Left nor Right' position. Without doubt (as we shall see in the rest of this book) the environmental crisis changes many of the assumptions which have underpinned political life in the twentieth century – about growth, markets and national sovereignty, for example. The new glare of environmental awareness will certainly expose some old Left-wing positions as barely distinguishable from Right-wing ones. But this does not mean that the differences between alternative types of economic system (capitalist, communist or other forms of socialist) can simply be ignored; nor that traditional divergences between Left and Right over distributional questions are suddenly obsolete.

Since the different mechanisms by which different economic systems generate environmental degradation *are* important, conflating them into a single ideological construct such as 'industrialism' does not help in understanding how degradation occurs and how to prevent it.

In particular it doesn't help our understanding of capitalism. Ideology is indeed important, but in this context it is the dominant belief in the efficiency and liberty of market forces which is perhaps the most crucial element of the Western value system, rather than those aspects which are shared with communism. So long as industrialised societies persist in seeing the beneficent invisible hand rather than the destructive invisible elbow, they will find it hard to protect the environment. But of course *this* ideological debate, concerning market forces and their control, is a familiar one. It has long been the battleground of Left–Right conflict.

An analysis of the processes causing environmental degradation within capitalism further reveals the role played by unequal distributions of income and wealth. As we saw in Chapter 3, it is primarily the rich countries of the world, and the rich groups within them, whose actions (even if unwittingly) are responsible for the major environmental problems, due to their much higher consumption of resources and generation of wastes. Even where the immediate causes appeared to be the actions of poor people, such as in the tropical forests, a chain of causes and effects can usually be traced back to the unequal demands of Northern countries. In both cases it is clear that a redistribution of resources and income from rich to poor, particularly on a global scale (from North to South), would be likely to ease the environmental problem. But this, again, is not a conclusion which stands outside traditional political disagreements between Left and Right, but squarely within them.

As environmental problems are tackled, a related set of questions will emerge concerning their distribution. We saw in Chapter 2 that the benefits and costs of the environment are not equally shared. The questions of who gets the resources, and who suffers from pollution, do not generally yield the same answer. At present richer people and countries, and current generations, are benefiting more than poorer and future ones; indeed, frequently at their expense. Questions further arise about who is to bear the cost of environmental improvement. Is it each person and nation to their own? Are costs actually to be transferred from rich to poor, as in the example of toxic waste? Or are those who cause the problems going to pay for them?

These are intensely political questions. In this sense the environment is quite comparable to more traditional political subjects such as education, welfare policy or taxation. So long as Left and Right are distinguished according to their views on distributional issues – on equality and inequality – the environment will therefore prove, not a relief from 'old-fashioned' conflicts, but a fertile new ground for them. Those who have hoped that environmental problems could somehow be kept apart from the unpleasant world of politics, or that the Green movement could somehow supplant old arguments altogether, are doomed to be disappointed.

That environmental concern cannot create a new political value-system on its own, but has to be attached to older positions, does not however mean that Green politics must simply be submerged beneath traditional ideologies. There are without question elements of the Green worldview which are different from both Left and Right – the emphasis on humankind's relationship with nature, for example, the rejection of materialism as the most appropriate means of meeting human needs, the revalued work ethic. These constitute a crucial new contribution which the Green movement has brought to the political debate, and they are not (as some have supposed) reducible to other traditions. Rather, what these arguments suggest is a synthesis: a new framework, drawing on both Green values and older ideology, within which the environmental crisis can be addressed. The rest of this book may be taken as an attempt to explore, in part, what such a synthesis would imply.

Part II
Objectives

5

Sustainable Development: Beyond 'Zero Growth'

Economic growth and the environment

Perhaps the most famous idea to emerge from the Green movement concerning the relationship between the environment and the economy has been that of 'zero growth'. Over the past twenty years many Greens have argued that it is economic growth which is the primary cause of environmental degradation; therefore the objective of policy should be 'no growth'.

An important inspiration for this argument was the Club of Rome report, *The Limits to Growth*, first published in 1972.[1] The report focused attention in particular on the problem of 'compounding'. Its authors pointed out that global industrial activity was increasing not steadily, in linear fashion, but at an accelerating or 'exponential' rate. A growth rate of, say, 3% per annum represents a larger increase in output every year, as the base on which it is calculated rises. In fact, constant 3% growth involves a doubling of production every 24 years. The report calculated that exponential increases in resource use, waste production and world population would lead to scarcity, pollution and famine on a catastrophic scale 'within the next hundred years' unless something were done to arrest the trends.

The Limits to Growth was widely criticised. It was shown, for example, that much more optimistic predictions resulted if different assumptions were made about the economy's 'feedback mechanisms' – the ways in which, by raising prices, resource scarcity automatically reduces consumption and encourages the development of reserve stocks, more efficient technologies and new materials.[2] But far from quenching the debate about the desirability of economic growth, these criticisms only served to fuel it. However the computer models were manipulated, it seemed indisputable to many environmentalists that industrial production could not carry on increasing indefinitely. 'Zero growth' became the Green movement's most pressing, and most notorious, economic objective.

Unfortunately the 'growth debate' has generated much more heat than light. Indeed in many ways it has distracted attention from the real issues of the environmental crisis. By linking environmental concern to 'zero growth' it has allowed those dismissive of this position consequently (but irrationally) to dismiss the environmental problems it seeks to address. Two simple mistakes have been responsible. The first is a failure to distinguish between alternative meanings of 'economic growth'. The second is a fault in logic. Because current patterns of economic growth are environmentally damaging, it does not follow that the solution to environmental problems is no growth.

To economists, and in most political discussion, economic growth refers to annual increases in Gross National Product (GNP).[3] To environmentalists and Greens, it often means an increasing consumption of natural resources. These are not the same.

GNP and its growth are measures of income flows around the economy. They are *not* measures either of natural resource consumption or of pollution. Any activity which involves the exchange of money in return for a good or a service contributes to Gross National Product. But the environmental impact of different activities is clearly different.

Some products (for example, tropical hardwood furniture, cars, pesticides) result in a great deal of damage to the environment, either from production or consumption, or both. But others, such as most direct services, natural fibre clothes, temperate softwoods, need have relatively little adverse environmental impact. They rely primarily on human energy, or use resources which are not scarce, or they generate little pollution. Some industries, such as organic farming, recycling and pollution treatment, positively improve the environment. Even an industry whose product doesn't change can reduce its environmental impact by altering its production methods, for example by using less energy or generating less waste.

The extent to which any given rise in GNP is damaging to the environment therefore depends on what it is that is growing. As a mere monetary aggregate, GNP does not distinguish between different types of economic activity: it simply records the overall total. It is quite possible for GNP to go up with fewer resources being used, and less pollution being generated, if the *content* of growth tends away from environmentally-degrading activities.

The crucial concept here is what might be called the 'environmental impact coefficient' (EIC) of GNP. We can define this as the degree of impact (or amount of 'environmental consumption') caused by an increase of one unit of national income. If the content of economic activity is changing, so that an extra unit of GNP tends to consume fewer resources than last year, EIC can be said to be falling. If an equivalent rise in GNP results in a higher level of environmental consumption, EIC is constant or rising. Then the overall impact of the economy on the environment can be measured by the difference between the rate of change of EIC and the rate of growth of GNP. If EIC is falling faster than GNP is growing, then overall environmental impact falls. If on the other hand GNP is rising faster than the reduction in EIC, net environmental impact increases. (Of course, if the environmental consumption caused by a unit of GNP is *rising*, GNP would have to fall to hold out the hope of an overall improvement.)

The concept of the environmental impact coefficient is not meant (at this stage) to be precise: for one thing it demands a way of measuring environmental consumption or impact, which we have not yet developed. It also runs the risk of assuming that if consumption of resources does not rise from one year to the next, environmental quality remains unchanged, when in fact some environmental impacts, such as fossil fuel depletion and certain kinds of pollution, are clearly cumulative over time. (This problem can in fact be eliminated in the definition of EIC.[4]) But it is useful as a way of understanding the relationship between the rate of economic growth and environmental degradation. It shows that rising GNP does not have to mean that the environment is getting worse.

For some resources the environmental impact coefficient of GNP has indeed been falling. Since the Second World War, technological progress (which raises the productivity of material and energy inputs) and the trend away from manufacturing towards services have combined to reduce the 'materials intensity' of national income. That is, there has been a reduction in the quantity of resources needed to produce each unit of GNP. For some minerals such reductions have exceeded the growth rate of GNP; thus economic growth has been accompanied by a *reduction* in resource depletion rates, not the reverse. On the other hand, similar reductions in EIC with respect to energy have failed to reduce overall energy consumption. Between 1970 and 1987 energy intensity in industrialised countries fell by 23%, but output rose faster, by 62.5%.[5]

The relationship between economic growth and environmental degradation is not a simple one, as the Green movement has tended to assume. It is certainly true that *current patterns* of economic growth are causing major ecological problems. This is happening both because in many cases the environmental impact coefficient of GNP is still increasing (every year a unit of GNP causes more damage) and because, where EICs are falling, they are not falling fast enough to counteract rising GNP. But it is certainly conceivable that both these trends could be reversed. If major shifts in the content of GNP occurred, through technological change in production processes, or changes in the products consumed, it is possible to imagine the fall in EIC outweighing any increase in national income. In that case economic growth could coincide with a reduced environmental impact.

Indeed, this is a likely result of many proposed policies for environmental protection. Recent studies have shown, for example, that a major reduction in carbon dioxide emissions could be achieved with negligible impact on growth. By changing the mix of fuels away from coal and towards gas, and by raising the efficiency of energy use, it is estimated that Britain could reduce CO_2 emissions to the so-called 'Toronto target' (a 20% cut in the 1988 level of emissions by 2005) while output continued to to grow at about 2.3% per annum.[6] Similar projections have been made for the US, Australia and Norway.[7] The example of Japan, which has the highest growth rate in the industrialised world and the lowest energy intensity, confirms that such a 'decoupling' of growth and energy consumption is possible.[8] Meanwhile other models suggest that (so long as the economy is not at full employment) a significant investment in pollution control would positively increase the rate of growth.[9] These results are not really surprising. Environmental protection tends to require investment in new equipment and materials, and this investment stimulates growth.

It might be argued that even if zero growth is not sufficient for environmental improvement, it would at least help, since the lower the growth rate the more effective is any reduction in EIC. But even this is not the case. It depends on what is not growing. If zero growth means no increase in energy efficiency and pollution control, overall environmental impact will be worse than with positive growth of these industries. In these circumstances growth would be environmentally better than no growth.

Perhaps even more to the point, it is quite possible for environmental degradation to get worse even when growth is zero or negative. If EIC is increasing, even negative growth may lead to overall damage. This is what happened, notably to many African countries during the 1980s. GNP contracted at the same time as environmental degradation increased. (Negative growth is indeed widely accepted as one of the causes of natural resource depletion in Africa.)[10]

The moral is clear. GNP does not measure environmental degradation, nor is it necessarily correlated directly with it. It therefore cannot be used as an environmental indicator. Since no rate of economic growth, whether positive, zero or negative, can on its own tell us what is happening to the environment, none is a useful target for environmental policy. Whatever the Greens' economic objective should be, 'zero growth' is not it.

Growth of environmental consumption

This does not necessarily mean, however, that environmentalists are wrong when they argue that 'growth' should be reduced, if they are using the term to mean, not increases in national income, but growth of environmental consumption, measured in physical not monetary terms. ('Environmental consumption' here refers to the usage of any or all of the environment's functions.) It should be noted that *The Limits to Growth* itself never referred to GNP: its definition of economic growth was always in terms of physical outputs.

The consumption of physical resources is indeed important. In a finite world with growing population, there clearly are limits to the quantities of resources which each person can consume, both because of scarcity and – probably more importantly – because of the inability of the biosphere to absorb the consequent wastes. But even on this definition of growth, 'zero' isn't what's required.

First, it is not simply *growth* which is the problem: that is, the *rate of increase* of consumption of environmental resources. For non-renewables, since any use increases scarcity, it may be reasonable to measure the extent of 'degradation' by the increase in the rate at which they become scarce: that is, by the growth rate of depletion. But with respect to renewable resources, growth is not necessarily the problem at all. Often, it is simply the *rate of consumption*, whether or not this is growing.

Take the case of tropical rainforests. The principal problem is not that this year's destruction is larger than last year's (that is, that there has been growth), because last year's was also too great. Even if there were no growth in destruction – even if, in fact, there were a fall – the output might still be too high. The problem is that the rainforests cannot regrow at the same rate as the trees are being felled and burned, not that this year's excessive destruction is greater than last year's.

As we shall show in Chapter 8, much environmental degradation is not caused by growth, but by a rate of consumption (whether growing, static or declining) which is above the natural regeneration (or 'sustainable') rate. If too many fish are being caught, so that the total stock is falling, it is not sufficient to keep the catch at the same level as last year, that is, to have 'zero growth'. To prevent the stock from dwindling further, the catch must actually be reduced. By the same token, if the catch is below the sustainable level, it may be perfectly possible to increase it up to that point (to have 'growth') without doing ecological damage. By focusing on growth, Greens may actually obscure the real extent of degradation, which can occur without it.

The same argument can indeed be applied to non-renewable resources. The greenhouse effect makes it almost certain that consumption of fossil fuels should be reduced. But there seems little point in having zero growth of, say, silicon consumption, or even consumption of iron ore. These materials remain in plentiful supply, are relatively inert when disposed of and can also frequently be recycled. (It is indeed likely that silicon-based products will do much to reduce the environmental impact of economic activity.[11])

It might be argued that 'zero growth' is not meant to be applied to individual resources, but to overall environmental consumption. Growth in some is possible, but will have to be accompanied by reductions in others. But it is by no means clear what 'overall' means in this context. In what unit are different resources measured, such that an increase in the consumption of one can be weighed against a fall in another? Consumption clearly cannot be limited to a certain total weight or volume: this would be no guarantee of environmental impact. Nor can resources be valued in money terms for this purpose, since prices do not reflect environmental damage either. But without a way of measuring the consumption of different resources, the concept of 'overall zero growth' is not meaningful.

There can be no doubt that the consumption of some resources will have to be limited. But these resources are specific and nameable. It does not mean that somehow there is a figure for 'total resource consumption' which must be kept static.[12]

'Zero growth', therefore, is not a sensible environmental objective whichever meaning of economic growth is used. Either way, we have to *disaggregate* economic activity, to isolate exactly what is causing the environmental degradation about which we are concerned. Aggregate targets and indicators, whether financial or physical, are little use in this.

This is an important conclusion, but given the misunderstandings this subject is apt to generate, it is crucial to be clear just what has been concluded. We have *not* shown that, because the goal of 'zero growth' should be rejected, therefore economic growth is environmentally acceptable. No rate of growth *per se* is a helpful objective. Nor have we denied that current patterns of growth are causing immense environmental degradation throughout the world and will have to be changed, radically, if the degradation is to be reversed. It is incontrovertible that environmental impact coefficients are not currently falling anywhere near fast enough.

We have not even claimed that a reduction in all forms of environmental degradation will or even can in practice be achieved (and continue to be achieved) while growth continues. Reducing EIC by a sufficient amount to counteract rising GNP will require a continuing improvement in technology and a shift in consumption patterns which are by no means guaranteed. Given the extent to which global GNP can be expected to rise as poorer countries develop, they may not in fact be achievable at all. At this stage we simply do not know. What we have said is that it is conceivable that they might be achieved, and that only by examining the relationship between particular types of output and particular forms of degradation can we discover what the possibilities are. In doing this we shall find that the overall rate of growth is secondary, and at any given time it will tell us little about our prospects of environmental success.

The concept of sustainable development

There is a further reason why 'zero growth' is not a helpful objective. This is that, however measured, growth rates do not take into account the distributional effects of economic activity. As we showed in Part I, the questions of who pays for and who benefits from the environment (and who doesn't) are very important. Aggregate growth rates – including zero – have nothing to say on these questions: any rate of growth can coincide with any type of distribution.

In the past few years, in order to overcome these problems of 'zero growth', a new objective has been proposed. Since its first major public appearance in the World Conservation Strategy of 1980,[13] the term 'sustainable development' has come to represent a more considered approach to the interaction of economic activities with the environment. The 1987 'Brundtland Report' of the World Commission on Environment and Development indeed proclaimed it the central goal of economic policy. Sustainable development, the report declared, is 'development that meets the needs of the present without compromising the ability of future generations to meet their own needs.'[14] In promoting improvements in living standards, economic policy has to ensure that the environment is sustained for the sake of future people's welfare.

Thus defined, the goal of sustainable development has received apparently widespread acceptance. It was endorsed by the leaders (including Mrs Thatcher and President Reagan) of the G7 group of industrialised nations at the Toronto summit of 1988. It has been claimed as an approach to policy equally applicable to First and Third Worlds. Industrialists as well as environmentalists have adopted it. It has consequently entered not just the language of the media but that of academic debate. Many articles, books and conference papers have discussed and defined it more closely.[15]

For some, this apparently near universal embrace induces suspicion. Can a term which commands such support actually mean anything? In the environmental movement the suspicion is founded in a genuine anxiety. By linking environmental protection to economic development, 'sustainable development' appears to smother the conflicts between these aims. For many years Greens have struggled to show how industrial expansion causes environmental damage. This was the whole point of the 'zero growth' argument, however misplaced the actual policy. Now, just when the extent of damage threatens to give them a conclusive case, the term sustainable development appears like a magic wand to wave away such conflicts in a single unifying goal. We can have our cake and eat it, it seems to say: no longer need industrial advance cause environmental degradation. We can have sustainable development instead; everyone can be both rich and green.

Yet, environmentalists rightly point out, the conflicts remain. Environmental protection *does* mean constraints on economic activity. Although economic growth and conservation are not incompatible, they remain uneasy companions. There is surely a grave danger in glossing over their differences: the risk that, whatever the motives of its originators, sustainable development will effectively provide a green cover for 'business as usual'. By failing to specify exactly what degree of environmental protection is required, Greens warn, the term offers governments and industry a means of embracing environmentalism without commitment. The British government's official published response to the Brundtland Report serves as a salutary illustration: a document wholly in favour of sustainable development which argues that British economic policy already conforms to it.[16]

But these anxieties are not grounds for rejecting the notion of sustainable development. They demonstrate only that it is a 'contestable concept': one that affords a variety of competing interpretations or conceptions. Many political objectives are of this kind: liberty, social justice and democracy, for example. These concepts have basic meanings and almost everyone is in favour of them, but deep conflicts remain about how they should be understood and what they imply for policy. So it will be with sustainable development. In the 1990s it will be hard to find anyone to oppose the ideal; but this will still leave much room for disagreement over what it entails.

The key to sustainable development, as with other contestable concepts, lies in its core meaning, that part which remains however it is interpreted. There are three elements to this. The first is the entrenchment of environmental considerations in economic policy-making. In the past, as we have already noted, environmental and economic policy have been kept apart, their connections barely acknowledged. Sustainable development insists on their integration, in both theory and practice. The conflicts between environmental and expansionist economic objectives are not hidden; they are merely placed within a common framework in which a variety of parallel objectives can be recognised. In this sense sustainable development goes beyond both the traditional economic orthodoxy which ignores environmental considerations altogether, and the simplistic integrative stance of 'zero growth'.

Second, sustainable development incorporates an inescapable commitment to equity. The use of the term 'development', along with the explicit reference to 'needs' in the Brundtland definition, are drawn from the vocabulary of the Third World, where improvements in living standards are meaningless unless they include those of the poor. Sustainable development thus implies not simply the creation of wealth and the conservation of resources, but their fair distribution. A commitment to global equity requires at least some measure of redistribution between North and South.

By qualifying development with the adjective 'sustainable', another dimension of equity is also incorporated. If something is sustainable it is able to last or continue. Sustainability expresses a concern that the environment is conserved in some way for the use and enjoyment of future generations as well as the present one. It is not necessary at this stage to elaborate on what precisely this means (we shall do so in the next chapter); we may simply note that sustainability is thus a commitment to some form of *intergenerational* equity, or the fair distribution of environmental benefits and costs between generations.

The third element of the core meaning of sustainable development also arises from the word 'development'. It is notable that the Brundtland report did not use the phrase 'sustainable growth' (though others have tried to reduce it to this).[17] Although the terms are sometimes used interchangeably, 'development' does not simply mean 'growth'. Economic growth is represented by increases in national income, but development implies something wider than this, a notion of economic welfare which acknowledges non-financial components.

These might include the quality of the environment itself: it is evident that national income does not record pollution levels or the beauty of natural scenery, both of which affect our welfare. They might also include factors such as the state of people's health and their level of education, the quality of work, the existence of cohesive communities, the vibrancy of cultural life. None of these things is measured by growth rates (or other purely monetary measures): all might be counted towards sustainable development.

How such counting could be accomplished we shall return to in Chapter 18, although in the wider sense this book is not concerned with the non-environmental elements of 'development'. It is important to note their existence nevertheless; the concept of sustainable development suggests a new perspective on economic policy from a variety of angles.[18]

Although still open to contestable interpretation, the core meaning of sustainable development is thus neither empty nor insignificant. It can indeed be distinguished quite clearly from more conventional economic objectives, being based not simply on the narrowly financial interests of the current generation of rich world consumers. In both its two-dimensional commitment to equity, and its embrace of non-monetary components of welfare, sustainable development suggests a radical departure for global economic policy. As the Brundtland report noted, sustainable development is *not* the objective of policy which has been followed by the industrialised world in the post-war period. On the contrary the report's stark conclusion is that current rates of environmental degradation are neither meeting the needs of the present nor permitting future generations to meet theirs. Under almost any interpretation (if not quite that of the British government) sustainable development therefore implies that economic policy must change.

The issue, then, is exactly what changes are required, and how they are to be put into effect. It is in this debate that the real conflicts will be revealed. Greens and other environmentalists are right to warn that sustainable development may be used as a means to legitimise environmentally damaging and inequitable policies. But this implies not that the concept be rejected, only that alternative interpretations are formulated and argued for. Acceptance of the objective of sustainable development is the beginning of the debate, not its end.

6

Valuing the Environment: The 'Orthodox Economist's' Approach to Environmental Protection

The problem of 'nature'

Central to the concept of sustainable development, however interpreted – indeed, central to any considered response to the environmental crisis – is the idea that the environment must be 'protected' or 'conserved'. But this is not as simple an idea as it sounds. How is 'the environment' defined? What, precisely, should be protected? Should no tree ever be cut down? How many members does a species need to have to be adequately conserved? If environmental protection is costly, are there limits to what we should pay to achieve it?

As soon as these questions are asked problems emerge. It is easy to say, for example, that environmental protection requires that the characteristic beauty of the English countryside is preserved, with urban development curtailed. But the way most of the English countryside looks today is quite different from how it looked a couple of hundred years ago, let alone a thousand. Countless forests have been removed, crop and grazing patterns have changed, human settlements have developed. These features could change again in the future, as a result both of 'unintentional' changes such as the greenhouse effect and of social developments such as a desire to plant more hedgerows. In these circumstances it is not evident what 'protecting the environment' means. Which environment? What faces us here is evidently not a static concept of 'nature', separate from human society, which can somehow be frozen in time and 'conserved'. Rather there are various alternative forms of nature, each at least partly created by human activity.

The same applies to other aspects of the environment, such as air quality. What is to be protected here? What levels of atmospheric pollution (or its absence) constitute 'nature', such that all else represents the excessive impact of human beings which should be eliminated? Methane, for example, one of the principal greenhouse gases, is emitted quite naturally by animals; emissions are increasing as global livestocks rise. What level of emissions is the 'natural' rate? Carcinogenic and ozone-forming hydrocarbons are emitted from vegetation and microbial decomposition as well as human-made sources. As global vegetation cover has been cut these emissions have fallen. It is not then obvious what constitutes the 'natural' level. Even if we could identify such a level, for example for a non-organic pollutant such as atmospheric lead, does this mean that we should reduce lead levels that far? What if this is extremely expensive, and shows no more benefit to human health and ecosystems than slightly higher levels? How do we weigh the environment against the costs of conserving it?

These are not mischievous questions. They do not show that because different levels of pollution might be considered 'natural' any of them is therefore acceptable. Neither do they show that environmental protection is simply a matter of trading off costs and benefits. Rather they demonstrate that the environment cannot provide its own answers. It might be thought that a concept of 'ecological equilibrium' could be used, defined as the state of the environment when it is stable, or not in the process of degradation. But natural ecosystems can equilibrate (or stabilise) at many different levels of diversity and quantity, including states which we would describe as polluted or degraded. Nature evolves not simply of its own accord but in conjunction with human development: just as human society is not independent of nature, it is not independent of us. What we see around us in the natural environment (apart from in a few wilderness areas, and even these are rarely unaffected by any human society) is in this sense as much 'produced' as the more obviously human-made structures of our towns and cities.[1]

The concept of environmental protection is therefore not to be found in nature itself, and cannot be a simple matter of conserving what currently exists. Outside wilderness areas which we choose to leave altogether alone, the options open to us all involve different ways of interacting with nature, and all will change it in some way. Environmental protection means making choices about the sort of nature we want, not leaving it somehow 'as it is'.

Valuing the environment

One way of approaching the question of what 'protecting the environment' means is to ask how much we value it. It is after all because people value the environment – albeit for a variety of different reasons and in many different ways – that we wish to preserve it. So a logical approach might be to say that we should protect the environment insofar as its value to us exceeds the cost of preserving it. When that point is reached, any further protection will cause us to forgo other things that we value more. This then gives us a clear criterion for making choices about what aspects of the environment should be conserved, which enhanced, which changed and so on.

This way of thinking about environmental protection dominates the academic discipline of environmental economics: it is what we might call the 'orthodox environmental economist's approach'.[2] It is based on a simple premise, namely that the rational way to make economic choices is to compare the costs and benefits of alternative actions. Protecting the environment almost always involves costs. Some of these are direct expenditures, for example on extra pollution control equipment, or on game wardens to guard wild animals against poachers. Others are the costs of *not* doing things we might otherwise have done, such as using a forest for timber, or a stretch of land for development. In both cases we can speak of the 'opportunity cost' of environmental protection: the things we have forgone by choosing conservation.

It is then reasonable to ask whether these costs are worth paying. But this can only be decided by weighing them up in some way with the benefits we are getting in return – in this case, the benefits from protecting the environment. And these are dependent on how much we value the environment. In general it seems likely that a great deal of environmental protection will be regarded as worth the cost; but that there will come some point where an extra 'unit' of protection – reducing air pollution by another part per billion, for example, or maintaining another acre of countryside – will not. It is at this point – where, in the economist's terms, the marginal cost equals the marginal benefit – that the amount of environmental protection is just right or 'optimal'.

It is likely that if some such cost-benefit approach were followed, the environment would be more protected than it is now. At present, where the environment has what we might call 'competitive functions', only some of its benefits are measured. When there is a choice, for example, between using the air of a particular urban area as a sink for polluting factory discharges, or as a source of health and quality of life for local residents, the value of the first function is precisely calculated, but the value of the second not at all. The factory company is able to say exactly how much it would cost it not to pollute the atmosphere (either the cost of installing pollution control equipment or of not producing the product involved at all); but no one asks the residents what clean air is worth to them. So in the balance sheet from which decisions are made, the bottom line is clearly on the side of pollution. If on the other hand some attempt *were* made to value clean air to local people, the result might well turn out in their favour. For instance, it might be found that to get clean air they would collectively be prepared to pay the factory more than it cost the latter to install pollution control equipment. At the very least there would be more chance of this happening than if no valuation were done and no cost-benefit trade-off applied.

It is not in fact true that clean air is completely unpriced. Pollution regulations, which prevent factories discharging whatever levels they want, are effectively ways of valuing the environment. They reflect the fact that people do desire clean air (and water, etc.), and the extra costs which factories bear to meet the regulations can be thought of as the environment's price. Regulations prevent decisions being made on purely financial criteria.

But an environmental economist might argue that such regulations do not reflect the 'real' value of the environment – as measured by the benefits people get from it. Pollution standards are not set by asking people how much clean air is worth to them – whether, for example, they *would* be collectively prepared to pay the factory enough to stop it polluting. Little or no effort is made to gauge the benefits provided by a given stretch of countryside, either in terms of, for example, the use people make of it for recreation, or the contribution to carbon dioxide absorption made by its forest cover. If these benefits were measured, it could be argued, we would find much higher environmental values than are currently reflected in pollution control and land use regulations, because the environment provides us with far more benefit than has hitherto been acknowledged. Using the orthodox economist's approach would thus generate a much greater degree of environmental protection than is currently afforded.

This conclusion is almost certainly correct. When alternative options for use of the environment are being considered, the case for recognising the many different benefits it provides in its undegraded state is surely incontrovertible. When arbitrating between competing demands, asking people how much they value the environment is usually preferable to not asking them. But this does not mean that the orthodox approach is sufficient to address the deeper issue of what 'environmental protection' means.

The problem of measurement

One objection to the 'valuation' approach is that it cannot actually be carried out. Of the two sides of the cost-benefit equation, the first side is fairly straightforward. In most cases we can reasonably calculate how much any particular measure of environmental protection will cost (though the more extensive the measures required, the more unreliable the estimates will be). But the benefit side is much more problematic.

In the first place, we may not know what the benefits are. Our knowledge of the environmental impacts of economic activities is often tentative at best. We may be unsure, for example, of the effects of discharging particular chemical wastes into the sea or of storing them in landfills: neither the immediate effects on ecosystems and water supplies nor the subsequent effects on human health and welfare may be certain. But if we do not know these costs, we cannot estimate the benefits of preventing them. There are particular problems when environmental impacts are far-reaching. Global warming, for example, is likely to affect (among other things) agriculture, coastal resources, forests, water resources, human-made infrastructure and human health.

But we do not know exactly how, nor what the costs of these changes will be to the economy or to society at large. There is the possibility, to take one aspect, that global warming will cause major migrations of population in some parts of the world. But estimating the costs of such migrations (and therefore the benefits of preventing them) is almost impossible.

Indeed, it is not clear that it is meaningful. In order to compare the costs and benefits of environmental protection in the way that the orthodox approach requires we must place them in the same units. But it is not obvious that it makes sense to put a monetary value on 'the benefits of preventing the migration of peoples'. What exactly is being valued here? Or to take another example, it is widely acknowledged that the tropical rainforests play a critical role in maintaining genetic diversity and absorbing carbon dioxide, as well as preserving water stocks and soil quality. But exactly how are these benefits – benefits whose exact nature is uncertain but which may well be extremely extensive – given monetary values? Since to estimate the 'optimal' level of rainforest protection we should need to know the benefits obtained from protecting different amounts of forest (that is, from spending different amounts of money on protection) it is not enough simply to get an overall figure for the benefits of the forest; we should need figures for different areas or parts of it.

Environmental economists have in fact devised a number of ways of giving the environment monetary values. We shall review these methods in Chapter 17. But for now the ability of the methods to overcome the problems of measurement is not the primary issue. For in one sense these objections do not dent the orthodox argument. The environmental economist could acknowledge that it is very difficult to put a value on the environment, and that in practice this approach will prove highly imperfect. But he or she could argue nevertheless that its *conceptual basis* is correct. That is, whether or not it can actually be undertaken as the theory suggests, the rational way of *understanding* environmental protection is still as a trading-off of costs and benefits. The 'marginal cost equals marginal benefit' rule, with the environment given a value, remains the goal towards which we should aim. Any other way, the economist could claim, will lead to a 'suboptimal' solution, involving either too much or too little environmental protection in comparison with its benefits. In this sense the problems of measurement are important, but they do not overturn the basic principle.

Whose value?

This defence, however, does not secure the claims of the orthodox approach. There are more basic objections. One of these is that the orthodox approach is entirely 'anthropocentric': that is, it measures the environment's worth only in terms of what it provides to human beings. Many Greens have rejected this view. They have argued that the environment has 'intrinsic' value, independent of any benefit that human society derives from it. According to this 'ecocentric' position, animals and plants and the ecosystems to which they belong possess moral rights which may override human interests in determining the appropriate level of environmental protection.[3]

We shall explore this argument further in the next chapter. For the moment, however, we shall concentrate on a second objection to the 'valuation' approach. This accepts the assumption that it is the welfare of human beings which ultimately matters, but points out that not all the people for whom the environment has value are included in the orthodox calculus. When the environment is valued, it is asked, who does the valuing?

This is a practical problem for any attempt to apply the approach in the real world – it is obviously impossible to ask everyone affected by a decision to value the environmental feature concerned. But this can be overcome by statistical methods to get a 'representative sample' of respondents. The much more serious problem is the prior, conceptual one of who the sample should be representative of. So far we have talked as if it is obvious whose valuation should be taken into account, and as if, once decided, this value can at least in principle be measured. But it is by no means obvious; nor are all people's valuations always measurable, even in theory.

Take an example of a new road, which it is being proposed should be built through what is now a forest. The orthodox environmental economist would want to find out how much the forest is valued by the people who live near it, and by those who go walking there. He or she might want to add an element of value felt by people living elsewhere who, even if they don't visit that area now, might want to at some time in the future (or might want their children to), or who are simply glad that the forest exists, irrespective of any direct use they or anyone else might make of it.[4]

But (leaving aside the practical problems of measurement) this is not a sufficient measure of the value of the forest. For forests do not only provide benefits to people in the area, or even in the country, where they are located. As absorbers of carbon dioxide they play a role in the global absorption of carbon dioxide, which is important for climatic regulation. As natural habitats they contribute to the maintenance of genetic diversity and ecological stability. Moreover the environmental effects of the construction of the new road cannot be confined to the loss of forest. New roads tend to increase traffic (this is usually their purpose): they thus add both to global carbon dioxide emissions and to acid rain.

Some of these wider effects fall on local people, and therefore (if they are aware of them) may be included in their valuations. But they also fall on those who might be called 'distant people', whose valuations are not included in the orthodox economist's calculus. These distant people belong in two categories. First there are those living in other countries, affected in this example by acid rain or global warming. It is difficult enough ensuring that the local sample is representative of all those living locally who are affected by the new road. Asking that the valuations of people living in other countries should also be included presents a conceptual as well as practical problem. Which countries? Which people? How can the very small impact on total global carbon dioxide emissions caused by this single new road be divided up between all the world's people who might possibly be affected? Yet if every small increase in emissions is ignored, the total will also be ignored, since it is precisely made up of many small emissions.

This problem of whose valuations to include is particularly acute if the valuations are measured by money, since many of the world's people are very poor, and their monetary valuations are therefore likely to be very low. It is conceivable, for example, that we could get some sort of valuation of acid rain damage from countries such as Canada and Norway, which are likely to have similar scales of valuation to the countries causing it (such as the US and Britain). But if beef consumption in the North causes rainforest destruction in the South, the valuations of the forest dwellers are likely to go unnoticed, since they do not have the income to compete with the valuations of richer consumers.[5]

But if it is difficult for people geographically distant to express their environmental valuations, it is impossible for members of future generations. Such 'temporally distant' people do not exist at all, so their valuations cannot be measured by any techniques. Yet they may well be affected even more than people living presently. On current projections unchecked global warming is likely to cause severe social and economic dislocation in thirty to fifty years' time and beyond, while long-term destruction of habitats may cause various kinds of ecological collapse. These effects imply that the forest has a value to people living in the future as well as to those alive now. Yet these values cannot be taken into account by the orthodox approach, since there is no one here to express them.

This suggests that the orthodox economist's method for determining the optimal level of environmental protection is flawed. The method rests on the notion that the environment can be valued. But a significant proportion of the environment's value cannot be known, since it comes from people excluded from the valuation process.

The environmental economist has an answer to this objection. He or she will point out that this account assumes that present people in the North do not care about people in the South, nor about future generations. Yet there is considerable evidence that they do. Campaigns in Western countries to protect tropical rainforests and wild animals such as elephants and whales, along with large donations made to famine relief, demonstrate that people *are* concerned about people and the environment in distant places.

Perhaps even more importantly, there is strong evidence that people do care about the future. In surveys it is clear that as well as valuing the environment for the immediate use they get out of it, most people also place some value on the possibility of using it (or their children and grandchildren using it) in the future: what economists call 'option' and 'bequest' values. Moreover the environment has 'existence value': people make clear that they want it to exist whether or not anyone will ever see or use it or get any other direct benefit from it.[6] All these types of value are effectively valuations of the future.

Unfortunately, however, such valuations cannot do what the environmental economist wants them to. In order to preserve the orthodox approach to environmental protection, the value given to the distant or future environment by people living in the 'here and now' should equal the value which would be given by those directly experiencing its degradation. But there is a fundamental difference between the concern I have for your welfare and the concern you have for it. However much one cares about other people, their interests very rarely carry the same weight as one's own when these are in conflict. And the further distant a person is, the less weight they will have. People may give money to famine relief, but they don't give nearly as much as they spend on themselves or their families. They don't give enough to prevent famine. However great the concern felt by people in the North about the destruction of the Amazonian rainforests, it surely isn't as much as the concern felt by the Indians who actually live there.

Economists call this phenomenon of reducing the value of distant people's interests 'discounting'. It is most commonly applied to the future. As we saw in Chapter 3, most of us discount the future quite normally in our everyday behaviour. Offered £100 now or in ten years' time, even inflation-proofed, most of us would take it now. We are impatient, we cannot guarantee that we will be alive to enjoy the money in ten years' time, and if by chance we were much richer then it wouldn't actually be worth so much to us as it is now. Moreover if we invested it now we would have *more* than a hundred in ten years' time. This is an example of discounting our own future: but the same practice occurs however long the period under consideration.[7] Indeed, the value of future returns becomes smaller and smaller the further into the future they are estimated. For example, if an investor has a 'discount rate' of 10% (meaning that each year a given sum of money is held to be worth 10% less), a projected income of £1 million in a hundred years' time is worth just £73 today. Yet of course to the person living in a hundred years' time (leaving inflation aside), £1 million is worth £1 million.

This divergence between the 'present value' of the future and its 'own' value (so to speak) is particularly important in relation to the environment. Many decisions taken now will affect the environment in the future. But, because of discounting, the value placed on the future environment by current people is likely to be much less – for the further future, very much less – than the value felt by the people who will actually have to live in it. The orthodox approach of trying to accommodate the problem of future environmental value through the mechanism of current people's valuation is therefore doomed to fail.

Indeed, it may fail catastrophically. The examples of 'option', 'bequest' and 'existence' values which are usually cited by orthodox environmental economists are ones where the costs of preserving the environment are not very great – where degrading the environment does not bring much current benefit. Thus it is not surprising that the value placed on the Grand Canyon and the grizzly bear by current people is sufficient to preserve them for the future: the benefits to be had by developing the Canyon or making the bear extinct are negligible.[8] But not all distant environmental effects are like this. Some of the most serious cases of degradation both in the South today and in the likely future are much more closely linked to current benefits. Preventing tropical rainforest destruction almost certainly requires a major transfer of wealth from North to South, quite apart from a reduction in beef and hardwood timber consumption. It is by no means clear that the value placed on the rainforests by current citizens of Northern countries is sufficient to outweigh the costs they would be required to pay for their protection.

Future degradation is even less certainly valued. Food prices remain low in the North to a large extent because of agro-chemical practices whose effects on soil erosion and groundwater pollution may prove extremely serious in the longer term. Future global warming will occur because of the direct benefits current people gain from burning fossil fuels and running cars. In both these cases, as in others, future generations face potentially catastrophic environmental impacts. Yet it is not at all certain that the value placed on these impacts by the current generation is sufficient to prevent them, given the costs such prevention will involve. It should be noted that – unlike the development of the Grand Canyon or the extinction of the grizzly bear – some of the most serious future environmental effects do not involve visible degradation today. So the benefits of protection to future generations are not matched by similar benefits to current people – benefits which might raise their valuations to protective levels.[9]

The orthodox 'valuation' approach to environmental protection therefore not only fails to generate the full value of the environment to distant people. It also cannot guarantee that environmental catastrophe will be avoided. Something more than this approach is clearly required.

7

Sustainability: Protecting the Future

Beyond valuation

In the last chapter we noted that there were two fundamental objections which could be made to the 'orthodox' approach to environmental protection. One was that, in 'valuing the environment', the values of distant people, particularly future generations, were excluded. The other was that, in addition, the orthodox approach ignored the 'intrinsic' value of the environment existing independently of any benefit gained by humankind.

Clearly any alternative approach must take these objections into account. But this immediately poses a problem. Whatever other difficulties it has, the orthodox method can at least say how it derives its concept of environmental 'value'. It asks people how much they would be willing to pay to protect the environment, or observes their behaviour to reveal their implicit preferences. But such a method is not available to obtain the values of people who are not yet born, or the 'intrinsic' value of the environment in itself. How do we find out what these values are? Can they be incorporated into a decision-making framework? Is it even correct to speak of them as 'values' in the same sense as that used by orthodox economists, speaking of people living now? We shall take each in turn.

The interests of future generations

It is true that we cannot know what value future generations will place on the environment, and in particular what view they will take of those aspects of our current environmental behaviour which will affect them. But it is not unreasonable to try and guess. After all, some members of 'future generations' actually are alive today – a child born in 1990 will reach retirement age in the middle of the twenty-first century. Many others will be known to us in our lifetimes. The grandchild of a person currently aged 20 is likely to see in the twenty-second century. We have a fair idea of what will happen to the environment over this period, if current trends are not changed. It may be impossible to predict future people's 'values'. But their interests are surely not beyond speculation. A thought experiment may help.

Imagine we were living in a hundred years' time. What would we want previous generations to have done with respect to the environment? Two intuitive answers spring to mind. One is that, at the very minimum, we would want them not to have left us facing environmental catastrophe. If in a hundred years' time global temperatures have risen as far as currently predicted, it seems reasonable to suppose that the generation living then will not thank us for the legacy. Indigenous people in the rainforest today, or farmers facing starvation on desertified lands in Africa, would surely make the same judgement of generations before the present one, wishing that something had been done to reverse the trends towards degradation.

But a sufficient degree of environmental protection to avoid catastrophe is not all we might want if we were living in the future. We might say that we wanted to experience at least as high a level of 'environmental consumption' as previous generations. After all, if one generation degrades the environment it is effectively robbing the next of the opportunities it has enjoyed, whether these are in terms of resources for wealth creation or aesthetic benefits. Where the environment is degraded irreversibly, such as in the extinction of species or loss of unique habitats, there may be a particularly acute feeling of injustice. In this view, though one generation may not have an obligation to *increase* the potential level of environmental consumption of future generations, it is only fair that it leaves at least an *equal* oppportunity behind.

Such an idea of 'intergenerational equity' is the basis of the concept of *sustainability*. This term is often used today simply as a general indication of environmental goodness; it risks becoming bland if not meaningless. But sustainability does have a useful intuitive meaning – the capacity to last or continue. Our thought experiment now suggests that this can be made precise. Two interpretations of sustainability follow from it.

A 'weak' or 'minimal' version of sustainability would require that the environment is sustained only in the sense that future generations are guaranteed the avoidance of environmental catastrophe. It asks that we should refrain from acting 'as if there were no tomorrow', but – apart from an avoidance of catastrophe – there is no requirement on what tomorrow should bring. By contrast the 'strong' or 'maximal' version of sustainability would demand rather more: that future generations are left the opportunity to experience a level of environmental consumption at least equal to that of the present generation. The maximal version might thus be seen as a reflection of the favourite Green adage: 'we do not inherit the world from our parents, we borrow it from our children.' If we are borrowers not owners it is incumbent upon us to leave the world as beautiful, productive and stable as it was lent to us.

Exactly what this means, of course, needs to be elaborated. Can we define 'environmental consumption' in such a way that it becomes reasonable, in practice, to speak of leaving future generations the opportunity to enjoy an 'equal' level? How far into the future are the generations to go?

The concept of environmental consumption may be understood in terms of the economic functions provided by the environment which we identified in Chapter 1. The biosphere provides human beings with resources; it assimilates wastes, and it performs a variety of amenity and life support services. Environmental consumption can be regarded as the enjoyment of all these functions. We can then say that future generations are left an equal opportunity of such consumption if the capacity of the environment to provide these functions at current performance levels is preserved. Sustainability will then be meaningful in so far as we can identify the different capacities and define 'current performance levels'. As we shall see in the next chapter, this is indeed generally possible.

As to how far into the future sustainability requires the present generation to look, this is not so difficult. So long as each generation looks after the next (say, over a period of 50 years) each succeeding generation will be taken care of. Of course, if an effect in the further future is foreseen, then it too can be taken into account. No generation can be expected to guarantee results it cannot foresee; but equally none should be allowed to ignore those it can.

The two versions of sustainability, minimal and maximal, could in theory dictate quite different courses of action. If environmental resources are abundant, ensuring that the next generation does not suffer catastrophe will be a much less demanding requirement than bequeathing them the *same* degree of environmental capacity. The capacity at which catastrophe is threatened (say, a minimum number of trees or volume of topsoil) might be much lower than currently obtains. Whereas maximal sustainability would require that the number of trees and volume of topsoil were held constant, the minimal version might allow quite significant degradation.

This difference is of some historical interest – do we think previous generations should have left us the same capacities they inherited? – but it is of little relevance today. This is because over the last 50 years the gap between the minimal and maximal versions of sustainability has significantly narrowed. Whereas in the first half of the century the size of tropical rainforests or the fertility of arable land did not appear to threaten environmental crisis, this cannot be said now. Then, preventing future catastrophe did not require maintaining the acreage of forest or volume of topsoil: the two versions of sustainability diverged. But now it appears that such objectives are precisely what is required. Indeed, it is probable that more trees will have to be planted and soil grown. If this is so then the minimal version of sustainability has actually become *more* demanding than the maximal. The distinction between the two has effectively collapsed.

As the extent of the environmental crisis has been revealed, it is evident that such a collapse has occurred with respect to a large number of environmental functions. In fewer and fewer fields can it be plausibly argued that continued environmental degradation is consistent with avoiding future catastrophe. In nearly all of the most important examples, preventative action requires at least the maintenance of environmental capacities; in many, improvements are now required. Whatever the theoretical differences, therefore, between the 'maximal' and 'minimal' versions, in present circumstances sustainability generates a single demand.

Intrinsic value

The concept of sustainability thus gives us a means of taking into account the interests of future generations. But this is still an 'anthropocentric' approach to the environment: it identifies the environment's value in terms of human interests. It therefore doesn't satisfy the second objection to the orthodox approach, which insists that the environment also has 'intrinsic' value. This 'ecocentric' objection can now be applied to the concept of sustainability too.

Or so it would seem. In fact, before making this claim, we need to examine the concept of 'intrinsic value' more closely. We are looking for a rule which will guide environmental policy, defining how much and what kind of environmental protection is justified. In practice, what does 'intrinsic value' mean?

There are broadly two versions of the ecocentric view. One of these ascribes intrinsic value to *individual members* of non-human species. It is argued that the differences between human beings and members of other species are not material to moral concern. Those who highlight such differences are accused of being 'speciesists' or 'human chauvinists'.[1] We may readily agree that seeing only human beings as ends in themselves, and all other species as merely instruments to serve human interests, constitutes a failure of moral imagination. But how far does the 'moral community' extend? What exactly is the characteristic feature which gives an object intrinsic value?

For some philosophers it is consciousness or sentience: the ability to have experiences, in particular the experience of pain.[2] This is intuitively justifiable. But it cannot be sufficient to act as a guide to environmental policy, since it does not apply to animals and plants lower down the evolutionary scale. Other ecocentrists have therefore argued that the possession of life itself is sufficient to give intrinsic value.[3] But this leads to the problem of how to rank different life forms in the moral scale. Some 'deep ecologists' have argued for 'biotic egalitarianism in principle'.[4] But few people will acknowledge moral equivalence between a plankton and a human being, even if this could in any way act as a basis for action. In the absence of a guide to moral ranking, ecocentrism does not provide much help in the formulation of environmental protection policy.

More importantly, locating intrinsic value in individual members of non-human species doesn't actually achieve the result desired by ecocentrists: it doesn't provide an argument for preserving species as a whole. There are many circumstances in which the interest of one, perhaps endangered, species requires the control of another species which is its predator or competitor for space. But if all individuals have equal moral rights, culling or other methods of control are not available, leading to the possible extinction of the endangered species.[5] It is in addition not clear what an individualistic ethic has to say about how many members of a species there should be. It is doubtful that individual animals and plants can be said to have an interest in the number or diversity of the species as a whole; yet it is this which is often the key question at issue in environmental policy.

Finally, an ethic concerned only with protecting individuals offers no guarantee of protection to the ecosystems of which they are a part; indeed, to what is characteristically thought of as 'nature' itself. Imagine that a development corporation wanted to build a theme park on a wetland noted for its many and rare species. The park would be so profitable that the corporation could offer to remove (humanely) all the animals and the plants on the wetland and place them in a zoo, where they could be protected even from one another. Few ecocentrists would regard this as desirable, yet an ethic concerned solely for the welfare of individuals would have difficulty arguing against it.

It is for these reasons that the second approach to ecocentrism has been developed. This locates intrinsic value not in individual members of non-human species (or at least, not just in individuals) but in ecosystems *as a whole*. The most famous expression of this view is the 'Land Ethic' proposed by the ecologist Aldo Leopold. Leopold argued that 'a thing is right when it tends to preserve the integrity, stability and beauty of the biotic community. It is wrong when it tends otherwise.'[6] Such an approach overcomes the problem of discriminating between individuals in order to protect species, since such discrimination will enhance the diversity of ecosystems. And it offers an answer to the question of numbers: in general, the more the better. But it raises other problems.

One is that the concepts of 'integrity, stability and beauty' are not evidently clear-cut. (Beauty in particular seems unavoidably anthropocentric.) Given that nature both changes over time and stabilises in different states, it is not always clear what will be required of environmental policy. What for example would the Land Ethic regard as an acceptable rate of carbon dioxide emissions? Would it have a view on depletion of mineral resources?

The more important problem however is that the Land Ethic seems to lead to unacceptable conclusions with regard to human life. If human beings, like other living things, have value only insofar as they contribute to the integrity, stability and beauty of ecosystems, we would seem to have a justification for culling people, or at least allowing them to die. It is incontrovertible that human society is destroying the diversity of ecosystems, particularly in places such as the Sahel region of Africa, where without aid many people may indeed die. The idea that people in the Sahel should be allowed to starve in order to protect the environment will surely fill most people with horror.[7]

It would be possible to rescue the Land Ethic from this conclusion if it were acknowledged that both ecosystems *and* individuals have intrinsic value. But such a 'pluralistic' position does not yet appear to have been worked out in any detail, and it is indeed difficult to see how it could be used in practice. How would ecosystems and individual human beings (or indeed members of other species) compare with each other when they came into conflict? This would not be merely a problem of comparing the worth of different individuals, but of different kinds of things, namely individuals and ecosystems. Could the intrinsic value of a particularly rare ecosystem outweigh the intrinsic value of the life of a person, or a human community?[8]

These arguments are not intended to show that ecocentrism has no moral basis. On the contrary, there are strong intuitive grounds for wanting to extend the class of morally valuable things beyond just human beings. The attitude of 'reverence for nature' which is the foundation of the ecocentric view is almost certainly an essential psychological and cultural element of any policy towards its protection. What has been shown is simply that, as yet, the ecocentric view does not offer a coherent approach to what is meant by environmental protection, and therefore to the formulation of policy.

But this is not the end of the argument. The more important conclusion to be reached is that the concept of sustainability can perform most if not all of the tasks desired in practice by most ecocentrists. That is, sustainability (in its strong or maximal version) offers at least as much environmental protection as a coherent ecocentric position would be likely to. In declaring that future generations should be left the opportunity to experience a level of environmental consumption equal to that of the present generation, sustainability imposes a substantial constraint upon economic activity. There is no question that species and ecosystems would be preserved, if not always (in the latter case) exactly as now. It is true that precisely how these protective policies would be formulated (which we discuss in the next chapter) rests on a concept of 'environmental consumption' which is essentially anthropocentric. But this is simply a means of overcoming the problem raised at the beginning of the last chapter, that there is no immutable thing called 'nature' which can be preserved. In practice, as we shall demonstrate, sustainability will prove a *sufficient* moral basis for a conserving environmental policy, even if supporters of the ecocentric view are unhappy with its philosophical foundation.

We can in fact see why this is so. There is no doubt that sustainability is anthropocentric: it wishes to preserve the environment for the benefit of future generations of people. But unlike the orthodox approach it does not see 'benefit' in terms of economic demands. It makes no attempt to calculate how much future generations will value the environment in terms of their willingness to pay for it. It simply recognises that future people *probably will* want the environment to be preserved, and that the current generation therefore has an obligation to give them an opportunity to enjoy it. This enjoyment is understood in the widest terms: not just the use of resources but the appreciation of all nature's diversity and beauty. This emphasis on equality between generations leads to a view of environmental protection which has more in common with the ecocentric standpoint than with that of the orthodox, 'valuation' approach.

Sustainability and morality

It will already have been noticed that these arguments are ethical in character. This makes them quite different from the sort of arguments which were used to justify the orthodox approach. Indeed, they appear to make sustainability a different sort of concept from environmental valuation.

Advocates of the valuation approach to environmental protection have one apparently strong argument on their side. They can claim that theirs is what economists would call a 'positive' approach, one which rests on (in theory) objectively measurable desires and interests – the desires and interests of living, accessible people who can be asked what they are, or who reveal this information in their behaviour. This approach generates an 'optimal' level of environmental protection which is not based simply on what the economist him or herself prefers – what 'ought' to be – but which reflects the world as it is. By contrast, the economist would say, sustainability is a 'normative' concept. It cannot be proved by an appeal to facts (such as empirically measured valuations), since it involves imputing interests to future generations rather than discovering them. It does so by use of an arbitrarily chosen method (the thought experiment) which inevitably reflects the values of the chooser. It thus goes beyond what is to what should be. In short, sustainability is an *ethical* concept.

To the orthodox economist this is a criticism; indeed, it places sustainability outside the realm of economics. Economics is a positive discipline whose hypotheses are empirically testable, not based on value judgements. Agreed, any policy decision on the environment will involve an ethical choice, since different options will affect different groups of people (and other living things) in different ways. Whether society should *adopt* the optimal level of environmental protection is an ethical question. But the optimal level itself is not an ethical concept. It is not derived from value judgements about what the economist thinks should be done, but from the interests and desires of the affected people, objectively (in so far as is possible) measured. Sustainability, on the other hand, has value judgements built into it. It is impossible to impute interests to future generations without specifying what those interests are, and the choice cannot but express the chooser's view of what level of environmental protection is morally right. In conducting our thought experiment – indeed, in choosing to conduct it – ethical concepts such as 'fairness' and 'justice' acted as guides.

This analysis of the ethical nature of sustainability can be readily accepted. But it is not, as the orthodox economist supposes, a criticism. This is because *no* concept of environmental protection is able to avoid value judgements. The very fact which made the thought experiment necessary – the impossibility of measuring future people's environmental valuations – ensures this. This impossibility leaves two options. Either future generations' interests are ignored (as in the valuation approach); or they are imputed (as in sustainability). A choice must be made; and even if it is unconscious such a choice will be ethical in character. The question must be answered: how important are the lives of future people?

The recognition that the very concept of environmental protection is a moral one therefore does not damage the idea of sustainability. (On the contrary, its chief victim is the notion of a 'positive' economics.) Rather what it does is to reveal the essential issue at the heart of the environmental crisis, namely the relationship between current and future generations.

The particular relationship expressed by sustainability itself, that of intergenerational equity, has a number of alternative ethical sources. At its simplest, as our thought experiment suggested, it expresses the Kantian injunction that each generation should do as it would be done by. A more complex interpretation can be derived from the method of John Rawls, who attempted to derive the principles of justice by asking what distribution of resources it would be rational to choose if one were ignorant of the group (or generation) one would oneself belong to.[9] In both cases there is a refusal to treat other generations as if they are morally less important than the present one, to 'discount' their lives. This again stands in contrast to the valuation approach, which incorporates the practice of discounting into its concept of 'optimal' environmental protection. Sustainability makes a simple moral claim: that while discounting one's *own* future may be acceptable, discounting the lives of *other people* (those not yet born) is not.[10]

Sustainability and intragenerational equity

It will be noted that our original objections to the valuation approach rested on the exclusion not only of future people (those distant in time) but of people distant in spatial terms, particularly (when decisions were being made in the North) those living in the South. Yet sustainability has been here defined solely in terms of intergenerational, not intragenerational, equity. This is partly because advocates of the valuation approach could claim that (even if only in theory) they can accommodate the interests of distant living people; it is only future people who are *necessarily* excluded. But more importantly it is because the point of sustainability is to establish a standard for environmental protection, and this inevitably means protection over time. Words such as 'degradation' and 'conservation' refer to changes occurring (or not occurring) over a period; sustainability expresses a principle by which such changes can be understood and evaluated. Hence its definition in terms of relationships between people living at different times.

This does not imply, however, that sustainability has no concern for equity within the present generation. If it is to have any meaning, it must be global in scope. In our thought experiment we need to ask not only what we would want if we were living in the future, but if we were living in the future in another place. Sustainability refers to the maintenance of environmental capacities throughout the world, not just in particular regions. It cannot allow one environment, say in the North, to be preserved over time by the simple expedient of exploiting resources in or exporting pollution to another area, such as the South. A national economy can only be described as 'sustainable' if its activities not only do not reduce environmental capacities within its own borders, but do not cause their reduction elsewhere. In practice this means that sustainability requires that the current geographical distribution of environmental consumption is made more equal, since this distribution is (as we have seen) one of the prime causes of degradation over time.

Yet sustainability should not simply be merged with ideals about equity between North and South. Although strongly linked, these are conceptually different. It is possible to imagine a 'sustainable' world economy, with environmental capacities maintained over time, which nevertheless exhibited significant disparities between income and wealth (and environmental consumption) between different groups and regions. Even after sustainability has been achieved – and therefore even while sustainability is being fought for – the question of intragenerational equity remains both distinct and important. If we are concerned about the interests of future generations, we must also surely be concerned about people living in poverty today.

The behaviour of the present generation

The concept of sustainability arose out of the need to define what is meant by 'environmental protection'. It is now possible to propose a working principle. *Sustainability means that the environment should be protected in such a condition and to such a degree that environmental capacities (the ability of the environment to perform its various functions)*

are maintained over time: at least at levels sufficient to avoid future
catastrophe, and at most at levels which give future generations the opportunity
to enjoy an equal measure of environmental consumption.

How this principle can be put into practice still requires elaboration:
this is the task of the next chapter. But before we do this a number of
objections to it need to be addressed. Is sustainability, so defined,
really a coherent concept?

The first objection points to an apparent flaw in the logic of the
argument. Sustainability rests on an implicit rejection of 'discounting'.
It is because the current generation is likely to discount the interests
of future generations that the 'valuation' approach was rejected. Yet
is there not a self-contradiction here? The crucial fact about intergenerational relationships is that they are entirely in the hands of the
present generation: all decisions about the environment are made by
people living now. So what do the interests of future generations
mean in practice? If the current generation discounts the future (as we
have said that it will), sustainability won't be achieved. On the other
hand if the current generation *doesn't* discount the future, then the
valuation approach will produce the same result as the sustainability
approach. Either way 'sustainability' appears to get squeezed out. In
the one case it won't be achieved; in the other it will, but it's not needed.

This argument, however, mistakes the concept of sustainability
with its realisation. It is quite true that, if the current generation
behaves as it normally does with respect to the future, sustainability
may not be achieved. But this does not mean that there is no value in
defining *what* is not being achieved, and examining the ethical basis
of such behaviour. The point of such exploration is to demonstrate the
environmental implications of conventional discounting, and through
this to encourage change. The concept of sustainability may in this sense
act as a campaigning tool itself, one whose definition and clarification
are in themselves attempts to encourage its political adoption.

In many cases, no doubt, sustainability will not be adopted. In
some cases, protecting the interests of future generations to the extent
demanded will cost more than the present generation is prepared to
pay. In others (particularly in the South) the immediate survival of the
present generation may actually be in conflict with that of future
ones. But even in these cases it will still be important to know the cost
of such decisions, and to be clear about what such costs will mean to
future people. This is what sustainability does. Unlike the valuation
approach, which simply ignores such costs, sustainability brings them
into the decision-making frame. The interests of future generations may
be traded off against those of the present, but at least the trade-off is
explicit, not swept under the carpet of discounting.

Sustainability does not in fact have to rely on a change in people's
'normal' attitude towards the future. Discounting is commonly practised
when individual consumers or firms are making private, self-interested
decisions concerning their own welfare. But this is not how sustainability will be chosen. Environmental protection is primarily a matter

of public policy, decided (at least in broad terms) in the political arena. But here people's behaviour is not private or simply self-interested. When they vote in elections or respond to opinion polls, individuals express public as well as private preferences, taking into account the good of society as a whole. This may certainly extend to the interests of future generations. In this way, in the political arena, sustainability may be chosen by the present generation despite the practice of discounting in consumption behaviour. As we shall show in Chapter 17, this contrast between 'citizen' and 'consumer' behaviour is a major difference between sustainability and the valuation approach.[11]

Discounting

This objection, however, is not the only one which the fact of discounting might raise. An orthodox economist will point out that discounting *doesn't* necessarily mean that future generations are made worse off. There are two rationales for discounting behaviour which, on the contrary, presuppose that future generations will be richer. Given economic growth, the first argument goes, people living in the future will have higher incomes than those living today. This means that they will get less value out of each pound or dollar they earn. (Most of us will agree that the same sum of money is worth less to a rich person than a poor person.) In these circumstances it is quite reasonable to discount, since money *is* worth more now than in the future. Moreover, it will be argued, discounting is justified because of the 'productivity of capital'. If we invested a given sum of money today it would earn interest, so that in fifty years' time it would be much larger. Discounting then simply reduces this increased future wealth back to its present value. If these two arguments are accepted, discounting cannot be held to discriminate against future generations, and therefore doesn't have the 'immoral' status which sustainability assumes.[12]

Neither argument, however, is convincing. Each rests on the same mistaken premise, namely that the environment behaves like, and can therefore be compared to, a sum of money. This view has no doubt arisen because in their attempts to incorporate environmental criteria into cost-benefit analysis – the arena where discounting is actually practised – environmental economists have tried to express the value of the environment in monetary terms. Having done this, they have then assumed that '£1 million worth' of environment is just like £1 million of cash.

But it isn't. As we saw in Chapter 5, economic growth expressed in financial terms does not mean that, in environmental terms, people are better off. The environment can be degraded even while growth occurs. So it cannot be said that because there is growth, future people will be 'better off', environmentally, than people living today, and therefore will place less value on a given environmental feature. On the contrary, current patterns of economic growth suggest that future people will be a great deal worse off: if anything, it is likely that the value they will place on what little environment is left to them will be greater than that felt today.

Similarly, the argument that the 'productivity of capital' provides a justification for discounting assumes that, because £100 invested today will grow at, for example, a compound rate of 10%, therefore '£100 pounds' worth' of environment will do likewise. But this is quite absurd. So far, certainly, biologists have yet to discover a relationship between interest rates and the expansion of the earth's surface.

We must conclude that, whatever its justification when applied to money, discounting the environment is indeed a form of discrimination against future generations. The need for the concept of sustainability remains.

Environmental and human-made wealth

Another sort of objection to our definition of sustainability protests that it is too limited. If the objective is to protect the interests of future generations, why should we only consider the environment? It could surely be argued that what future generations will want is not simply the same level of 'environmental wealth' as us, but the same level of *total* wealth, including human-made capital (buildings, machines, etc.), technological expertise, other kinds of knowledge and so on. Often, these latter forms of wealth are produced by the very economic activities which degrade the environment. Future generations might not thank us for slowing down the production of 'human-made' wealth simply in order to conserve 'environmental' wealth: they might value the former more. Indeed, it is human-made wealth – through scientific and technological progress – which will enable us to tackle the problems of resource scarcity and pollution. We would not be serving the interests of future generations, an industrialist or developer might say, by denying them the human-made resources to overcome environmental degradation.[13]

There is something slightly disingenuous, if not tautologous, about this argument: a Green could easily retort that new technologies to overcome environmental degradation would not be needed if the environment weren't degraded in the first place. In any case, only a tiny proportion of human-made wealth is actually devoted to developing such technologies: wholesale degradation is hardly justified by them. But beyond these simple ripostes there is a serious case to answer here. Much of human development has involved replacing natural resources by more productive human-made ones: steel substituted for wood, engines for animals. Where such substitutions can occur, would it not be more sensible to define sustainability as the maintenance of a constant stock of *total* wealth, including human-made capital, technology and knowledge, rather than simply environmental wealth? This would allow some environmental degradation if it generated a greater amount of human-made wealth.

The answer is no, for a number of reasons. First, many functions of the environment are unique: they simply cannot be substituted by human products. This is most importantly true of the life support services: climatic regulation, geochemical cycling, ecosystem maintenance and so on. If these are impaired there are no alternatives available. But it is also true of the environment simply as an amenity: most people do not regard leisure centres, for example, as adequate substitutes for the countryside, or animals in zoos as replacements for animals existing in the wild. Substitution between resources, meanwhile, cannot simply be calculated on the basis of the size of stocks: in producing human-made resources other environmental effects will occur (such as pollution) which must also be taken into account.

Second, environmental wealth is subject to *irreversibility*. Whereas it is possible to recreate most human-made capital if destroyed, this is not true of the natural environment. A species made extinct cannot be brought back to life. It is true that irreversibility is not necessarily absolute. In theory tropical rainforests could be replanted and in several hundred years might flourish again (though lacking many extinct species). It is possible that climatic trends could be reversed or atmospheric ozone replaced. But the timescale of such changes – in the context of intergenerational equity – justifies the claim of irreversibility. It should act as a warning against substitution of environmental wealth: if a mistake is made, there may be no going back.

Third, for all the scientific progress we have made, humankind is still to a considerable extent ignorant about the workings of the biosphere and the effects of current economic activity on it. We simply don't know what will follow from further degradation. This uncertainty suggests strongly that we should be cautious about depleting environmental resources even if they may yield apparently more productive human-made substitutes. Past environmental resilience, unfortunately, may be no guide to future behaviour. Ecosystems may be subject to 'catastrophic' change, in which a small external shock stimulates a very large reaction.[14]

Lastly, even if substitution were acceptable, it is not at all clear what 'total wealth' actually means. In order to aggregate environmental and human-made capital some common unit of measurement would be required. The only possible one would be money. But quite apart from the difficulty of putting a monetary figure on functions of the environment such as climatic regulation, such valuation would undermine the principle of sustainability, since it would be the value as defined by the current generation. We cannot know how future generations will value different aspects of the environment: the only fair way of expressing constant environmental capacity is in physical units (number of trees, volume of soil, etc.). But this would make substitution – and therefore 'total' wealth – impossible to measure.

For these reasons, sustainability cannot be expressed in terms of total wealth, both human-made and environmental. They are not substitutes; they have to be considered separately. It is the degradation of environmental wealth which is the crucial issue. It is therefore this which must be maintained – as measured in physical, not monetary units.

Population growth

The final objection which might be made to our definition of sustainability is that it ignores population growth. If population is constantly rising, what future generations will want is not a constant level of environmental capacity but an increasing one. Otherwise, far from experiencing intergenerational equity they will be progressively worse off than the current generation, with each person having less to consume. Leaving capacity at current levels might even lead to catastrophes such as famine, if the number of people exceeds the capacity of the earth to grow food for them.[15]

On these grounds it could be argued that what sustainability demands is not simply a constant level of environmental capacity but a constant *per capita* or per person level. Since the size of the next generation is the responsibility of the present one, insisting that sustainability took account of population growth would give an added incentive for the current generation to reduce it.

This is a strong argument, and there will often be cases where sustainability is best expressed per capita. But for reasons of simplicity we shall in general define sustainability in absolute terms. It will be hard enough to establish measures of environmental capacity without also having to divide them by figures for forecast population. Sometimes there may be no number which can be divided in such an arithmetically neat way. It is in any case preferable for the concept of sustainability, in so far as is possible, to be amenable to purely ecological interpretation; added complications concerning human numbers are more helpfully considered afterwards, once the basic concept has been clarified.

This does not mean, however, that population growth need simply be ignored. One of the principal consequences (and purposes) of technological development is that the rate of environmental 'productivity' increases. That is, the amount of consumption which is yielded by a given unit of a resource rises over time. New crop strains produce larger or more frequent harvests; mineral extraction becomes more efficient. If such increases in productivity keep pace with population growth, future generations need not be made worse off by the maintenance of environmental capacities. This is clearly the target at which we must aim.

In conclusion it seems that sustainability, defined as the maintenance of environmental capacities, can indeed be regarded as a coherent concept, one offering a standard for environmental protection which safeguards the interests of future generations as well as as those of the present one. One last question remains, however. Sustainability may be coherent. But can it be put into practice in the real world of economic policy? Can it, to use an ugly but descriptive phrase, be 'made operational'? It is to this question that we now turn.

8

Making Sustainability Operational: The Meaning of 'Environmental Capacity'

How useful is the concept of sustainability?

We have defined sustainability as the maintenance of environmental capacities, at levels which at least prevent future catastrophe, and which at most give future generations the opportunity to enjoy a measure of environmental consumption equal to that of the present generation. In defending this principle against various criticisms, we have shown that it performs the basic task required of it, namely to provide a way of understanding what we mean by 'environmental protection'. But there is still considerable work to do to demonstrate that sustainability, thus defined, is actually a *useful* concept. Does it help us put environmental policies into practice?

Two key questions need answering. First, we have to define 'environmental capacity' and 'environmental consumption'. Are these things measurable, in such a way that in any particular situation we can establish whether or not they are being 'maintained'? Secondly there is the problem of uncertainty. Given that scientific knowledge about the environment is incomplete, particularly in predictions of future ecological and climatic effects, can we actually identify the sustainable levels of our various (but inter-related) economic activities? How do we address the possibility that we might be significantly wrong?

We can begin to get a grip on these sorts of questions if – at least for the moment – we break the environment down into its three principal economic functions. It will be recalled from Chapter 1 that these are the provision of resources (raw materials and energy), the assimilation of waste materials, and the performance of environmental services. Such services include life support services such as climatic regulation, geochemical cycling, and the maintenance of biodiversity; and amenities of various kinds, including aesthetic, health-giving, recreational and scientific. The idea of 'maintaining environmental capacity' can be applied to each of these.

Renewable resources

A few years ago an environmental group produced a poster with a photograph on it of the Earth as seen from space. 'Here is the Earth', it said. 'Don't spend it all at once.' This is a useful metaphor to apply to the sustainability of renewable resources. These are resources, it will be recalled, which can regenerate of their own accord: soils, crops, animal and fish stocks and water supplies. Renewable resources are like savings accounts. A savings account grows every year: it accrues interest. And one can spend from it by withdrawing money. The size of the capital sum then depends on the difference between annual spending and interest. So long as they remain equal, the capital is maintained – and the same level of spending can be achieved next year.

Thus it is with a renewable resource. So long as the rate of harvest (spending) does not exceed the regeneration rate (interest), the resource stock is kept constant. The 'environmental capacity' of the resource is maintained – and sustainability achieved. This is a very simple rule, and one that has been well understood by agriculturalists throughout history. It is the reason why farmers keep fields fallow (allowing the soil and soil organisms to regenerate) and why traditional fishing and hunter-gathering communities have maintained strict social controls over the volume and seasonality of their consumption. It is, conversely, because commercial forestry and fishing practices have often *not* maintained the simple 'harvest equals regeneration' rule that fish and tree stocks in many parts of the world are declining.

It will be apparent that sustainability on this criterion does not rule out growth. Just as a higher interest rate will enable a higher annual level of spending, so if the regeneration rate of a resource can be increased, a larger harvest is permitted. Again, farmers have long applied fertilisers to the land and attempted to breed more fertile (or simply larger) animals in pursuit of this goal. More recently, scientists have developed higher-yielding and more frequently-harvested crops. Some of these attempts to raise regeneration rates are quite sustainable, having no adverse effects on soil fertility. Others, such as the application of artificial fertilisers and pesticides, may in many cases be unsustainable, causing a decline in the underlying fertility of the soil and long-term toxification of both soil and water.[1]

The fact that regeneration rates can sometimes be increased without long-term or external damage shows that 'environmental capacity' should not simply be equated with the size of the resource stock. For in these cases the resource has the capacity to produce the same output from a smaller stock. This is indeed an important aspect of sustainability. It is the capacity to yield a constant output over time which defines sustainability; this is what provides an 'equal level of consumption'. If this can be achieved by higher harvest and regeneration rates (for example through use of higher-yielding crop strains), then maintenance of the size of the stock is no longer demanded. In the case of the higher-yielding crop, for instance, it would allow land to be diverted to other uses. Of course, if sustainability is defined per capita, then the relevant figure is constant output per head. This might not permit reduction in the stock – in conditions of population growth, it could require an increase in the area under cultivation.

In general, increases in regeneration rates are one-off leaps to a different resource description rather than continuous trends. Once the new, more fertile type of resource has been established, therefore, the basic rule for sustainability reapplies: that the size of the stock should be maintained by making the harvest rate equal to the regeneration rate.

This rule, it will be noted, expresses the principle of intergenerational equity solely in terms of *flows*, of inputs and outputs. Holding harvest (output) rates equal to regeneration (input) rates ensures that the size of the resource remains constant. But this begs the question of what size the resource should be in the first place. This is the issue of *stock*. Why should the current size of the resource be the 'right' one, the size which should be maintained constant? This assumption might be challenged on the basis either that the current size is too large or that it is too small.

Those who suggest that it is too large could argue, after all, that the current stock level is arbitrary, the result of historical circumstances not principled decision. Why should the resource not be run down a bit further before applying the 'harvest equals regeneration' rule? Previous generations did not keep their inheritance intact for our benefit; why should we for our descendants?

One response to this question is that, although the current level of the stock is indeed arbitrary, it is not arbitrary to choose to maintain it. Sustainability expresses a relationship between the current generation and its successors. How the current size of the stock has been determined is not relevant to the principle of intergenerational equity applied from now on: one intergenerational unfairness does not merit another.

Another answer is that the 'minimal' version of sustainability is precisely designed to meet this complaint. By defining sustainability as merely the avoidance of future catastrophe rather than strict inter-generational equality, it does (in some cases) allow the depletion of current stocks – though only up to a certain point.

This is the point at which the current size of a resource should be regarded as too *small*. Reproduction of a species may become impossible below a particular critical population size. Failure of a species to survive certainly violates sustainability. A minimum stock may also be required where, as well as providing raw materials, the resource performs an important environmental service. Minimum areas of forests and other photosynthesising plants, for example, are needed to counter the greenhouse effect (by absorbing carbon dioxide). Forests also help to maintain regular water run-off. Particular populations and species may be essential to preserve the stability of the wider ecosystems of which they are a part.

In these cases the current stock size may not be the sustainable one. Maintaining it by sustainable harvesting will consequently not be sufficient. The size of the resource will have to be increased, which may require no harvesting at all.

We shall often wish to refer to the sustainability of individual resources. A 'sustainably managed' forest, farm or fishing ground is one which can maintain its output over time. Strictly speaking, however, the relevant capacity for terrestrial resources is only that of the soil, and for aquatic resources that of the aquatic ecosystem. It would after all be absurd if sustainability forbade farmers from changing their crops or the numbers in their herds. If it is found that a forest is less useful than cultivated cropland, then it should be possible (subject to the requirement that sufficient trees are preserved to retain water and to absorb carbon dioxide, and valuable habitats are not destroyed) to switch from one to the other.

The fertility of the soil would have to be maintained in this process, however. If (as in much of the Latin American rainforest) crops are planted for which the soil is unsuited, leading to erosion, this would not be a sustainable switch. But so long as soil fertility is maintained a future generation will have the opportunity to revert to the original cultivation pattern if it so wishes; no irreversible change is brought about. It is thus the maintenance of soil volume and fertility which is the key to sustainable agriculture. The actual balance of crops, trees, other vegetation and livestock should not be unduly constrained. Similarly, the actual balance of different species of fish may vary within a stable aquatic ecosystem.

For water supplies, sustainability means that the quantity and quality (purity) of both underground aquifers and surface stocks is maintained. This involves attention to vegetation cover and soil quality as well as pollution.

The important point about defining sustainability in this way is that each of these components of 'environmental capacity' – soil volume and productivity, the size of aquatic stocks and the quantity and quality of water supplies – is *measurable*. Moreover it is quite feasible, through proper management, to maintain them over time. This means that the principle of sustainability can be made operational. Rates of resource harvest and habitat quality can be identified which will maintain output (and therefore consumption) into the foreseeable future. If this is done, sustainability is turned from being a mere ideal into a practical guide to policy.

By the same token, it becomes possible to identify just how many current agricultural, forestry and fishing practices are *unsustainable*. As we saw in Chapter 1, in many parts of the world soil erosion is increasing faster than soil formation, fish stocks are declining as catches exceed regeneration rates, and forests are retreating as trees are felled faster than new ones grow.

Non-renewable and continuing resources

Applying the principle of sustainability to non-renewable resources would seem to be more difficult. Since they do not regenerate (at least, not within human timescales) all output reduces their stock. If sustainability means constant stock levels, it would appear to require us to stop using fossil fuels and minerals altogether. But of course this would be no help to future generations, since, if they were also bound by the sustainability principle, they couldn't use them either.

The depletion of non-renewables is therefore inevitable. The question is how quickly depletion occurs. Seeking maximum benefit over cost, orthodox environmental economists have identified the 'optimal rate of depletion', which is related to such factors as the interest rate, the capital gain from leaving a resource in the ground and the cost of extracting it.[2] But this is not what we are looking for. The 'optimal rate' is optimal for the current decision-maker; it is not necessarily the solution which best satisfies the interests of future generations, whose welfare is explicitly 'discounted'. (The equivalent 'optimal harvest rate' for renewable resources may sometimes lead to their extinction!)[3]

The issue for sustainability, rather, is what rate of depletion might be felt to accord with the principle of intergenerational equity. And here it is important to note that increasing *absolute* scarcity will not necessarily be of concern to future generations. Few people regard fossil fuels or minerals as having intrinsic value or as providing amenity in themselves, such that their existence *per se* is desired. Unlike soil, water and other aspects of the biotic environment, which are essential to the maintenance of life itself and which many people do regard as having intrinsic and amenity value, non-renewable resources such as coal and iron ore are valuable only insofar as they are required for the manufacture of products.

How valuable they are in turn depends on how great is the demand for them. And this is not fixed. As products and manufacturing processes change, demand for different resources changes. As we saw in Chapter 1, the demand for tin has declined dramatically in recent years as aluminium and steel have taken over many of its uses. Since aluminium and iron ore are still in plentiful supply, depletion of tin is therefore not a serious issue. Although the *absolute scarcity* of tin has increased, its scarcity *relative to demand* has not: on the contrary, the fall in tin prices almost certainly indicates a decline.

It is this concept of 'relative scarcity' (or its converse, 'relative stock size') which is important for the sustainability of non-renewables. The depletion of a given resource may be said to satisfy the principle of intergenerational equity if it occurs at the same rate as demand for the resource declines. Although the absolute stock level of the resource is reduced, the stock level *relative to demand* is then kept constant. In this sense, sustainability requires policy to be directed at demand as well as supply.

Relative stock maintenance is not an impossible requirement. On the supply side, the 'finitude' of fossil fuels and minerals is more complex than it may at first seem. There are in fact two forms of 'input' to the stock.

The first is an expansion of reserves. The recorded stocks of a resource do not equal the total amounts available in the earth's crust. They record only that which is *economically available* at current prices. As prices rise (or as extraction technology improves) exploration and mining become profitable and new stocks become available. This means that consumption does *not* necessarily increase even absolute scarcity – as mineral statistics demonstrate.[4] Clearly there is a limit to this process, especially if the energy or environmental costs of mining (for example, in Antarctica) violate other sustainability conditions. But for many resources it does appear that there is little danger of effective depletion.

Second, metals can be reused and recycled. (This is not possible with fossil fuels, whose energy cannot be used again.) By allowing further consumption of the metal without depletion, these activities effectively replenish the stock. As we shall see in the next chapter, recycling has its limits, but for most metals there is in principle considerable scope for expansion. Again, as prices rise, and as recycling technology improves, recycling becomes more profitable.

Meanwhile, demand for a scarce resource can be reduced through its more efficient use and through the substitution of other materials in less scarce supply. Design changes can reduce the quantity of a resource used in a product, often (for example in miniaturisation) quite dramatically. Making products more durable will similarly reduce overall materials demand. Substitution is already widely practised, not just for tin but for many other metals. Currently most substitutes are other, more abundant metals, but the use of silicon-based products such as ceramics is increasing. Substitutes are also being manufactured from renewable resources, such as non-fossil oils.[5] (In so far as this occurs, the sustainability of non-renewables obviously has implications for the required size of renewable resource stocks.)

Maintaining the relative stock of non-renewables is thus a function of three activities: the development of new 'economic' reserves; reuse and recycling; and a reduction in demand, including substitution by other materials. Relative stock size is a more difficult concept to measure than renewable resource output, requiring a calculation not only of the size of the aggregate stock but of projected demand, but it is not impossible: the long-term price trend of the resource will be some (though by no means a perfect) guide.[6] It is certainly possible to direct policy towards these three 'relative stock enlargement' activities. In this sense, though not an indisputable concept, the principle of sustainability does appear to be operational.

Since continuing energy sources (solar, wind, tidal, wave, etc.) do not run out, they pose no problems for sustainability. On the contrary, as we shall see below, their substitution for fossil fuels will be an essential component of any sustainability strategy.

The assimilation of wastes

Waste products from all kinds of human activity, including economic activity, are deposited in the soil, the air and water. They fall into two categories. Some are what can be called 'flow wastes': these can be assimilated by the natural environment through bio- and geochemical processes of dispersal, decomposition and recomposition. The wastes effectively 'disappear' or are rendered inert (non-interactive); some of them may then contribute to the growth of resources. Organic wastes generally belong in this category, along with chemicals such as carbon dioxide which are part of the biotic environment. 'Stock wastes', on the other hand, are not absorbed in this way. These wastes, such as heavy metals, remain in the environment in the condition they enter it. They are simply stored.

The capacity of the environment to assimilate flow wastes can be likened to a renewable resource. The quantity of wastes discharged into the environment constitutes the capacity's 'output': from the point of view of the economy, this is the desirable product. The 'regeneration rate' is then the rate at which the environment can absorb these discharges. The regeneration rate will depend on the biological and chemical composition of the recipient medium. For example, the more trees there are, the higher the rate at which carbon dioxide can be absorbed. The capacity of a stretch of river to assimilate organic waste depends on the number and type of microorganisms it contains, along with other characteristics such as volume of water, speed of flow, etc. Just as with a renewable resource, the purity of the recipient medium (its 'stock') will remain constant if the rate of discharge does not exceed the medium's rate of absorption. If this rate is exceeded, some of the discharged wastes will remain stored in the environment, decreasing its 'purity'. Where such wastes are at concentrations which are considered to cause damage to human health or to ecosystems, they constitute pollution. The concentration level at which damage becomes significant is known as the 'critical load'.

Note that if such storage of flow wastes occurs, not only the medium's purity but also its absorption rate falls. That is, the higher the level of pollution, the lower the environment's capacity to assimilate future wastes. This is again comparable to the behaviour of a renewable resource. If the output of a resource exceeds its regeneration rate, not only does the stock of the resource decline, but consequently its future output does too. If the purity of a river declines, its capacity to assimilate additional waste also falls.

Again, sustainability does not rule out growth. The rate of discharge of wastes can be increased if the regeneration rate of the recipient medium can be raised by the same amount. Thus if extra trees are planted, higher carbon dioxide emissions may become possible without an increase in pollution. Organic emissions into rivers can be increased without greater damage to health or ecosystems if the type and volume of microorganisms are changed, if water flow is speeded up, and so on. There are limits to the increases that are possible.

It is clear that the basic rule for sustainability is that the rate (and concentration) of flow waste discharges should not exceed the assimilative capacity of the recipient medium. This equality is indicated when the purity (pollution level) of the medium stays constant or falls.

As with renewable resources, however, this is not quite sufficient. For the rule only ensures that the level of purity of the recipient medium (the 'stock size') does not decline; it does not say what this level – the level of pollution – should be. Again, the *current* level of pollution is arbitrary, and holding it constant may therefore not be regarded as a desirable rule for policy.

The principle of intergenerational equity clearly rules out any (long-term) *increases* in pollution levels, where such increases will have damaging impacts on health and ecosystems.[7] The more interesting cases are those where the current level of pollution is considered too high, and it is felt desirable to reduce it. But these pose no problems for sustainability. There are two circumstances in which the current level of pollution may be considered too high. The first is where current pollution will have a long-term effect on health or ecosystems, such as in the case of CFCs or acid rain. But then sustainability *does* require a reduction in current pollution levels, since future generations will inherit a worse situation (a lower level of 'environmental consumption') than the present generation.

The second is where current pollution is causing *current* damage to health or ecosystems, with no additional long-term effects. Here sustainability of itself imposes no requirement to reduce pollution levels, since future generations will not experience lower environmental consumption than the present one. But equally it does not demand that current levels are maintained. There is nothing in the principle of sustainability to stop society reducing pollution if it wishes to.

In this sense sustainability is only a minimum condition for environmental protection. Its purpose is to protect future generations. It does this by ensuring that pollution does not increase over time. But if a society wishes pollution to decline, this is perfectly acceptable. Note that in that case it may be appropriate to apply some sort of 'valuation' exercise to determine the 'optimal' or 'acceptable' level of pollution for current society. By weighing the benefits of reducing pollution against its costs, society can decide whether reductions are an appropriate way of spending current resources. (This 'weighing' process does *not* have to use monetary measures: all that is meant is that some judgement is made between alternatives. We discuss this further in Chapters 16 and 17.) Where the conditions of sustainability have been met, therefore, the 'orthodox economists' approach' discussed in Chapter 7 may be regarded as reasonable.

Similar considerations apply in the case of stock wastes, such as nuclear residuals, heavy metals and other toxic materials. The environment's capacity to assimilate these may be likened to a non-renewable resource. Since they cannot be absorbed (that is, there is no regeneration), all discharges reduce the purity of the recipient medium. The 'stock' – the cleanliness of the environment – inevitably becomes depleted. Ideally, intergenerational equity would demand that such wastes are not emitted into the environment at all. As this is not at present practical, a rule similar to the 'relative scarcity' rule for non-renewable resources can be formulated. Insofar as safe sites can be found for such wastes, discharges may be permitted. As the space for safe deposits declines, discharges must decline too. When all safe sites have been eliminated, discharges must cease.

This formulation, of course, begs all the questions about what is considered 'safe'. This is a very complex issue, which involves not just technological questions about how toxic materials are stored, but economic and cultural questions concerning the perception and treatment of *risk*. Since the storage of toxic materials must be localised, extremely difficult issues of equity are also involved, as the 'not in my back yard' (NIMBY) phenomenon frequently demonstrates.[8] There is unfortunately no space to elaborate on these issues here. All discussions of 'acceptable' levels of pollution involve issues of risk; the principle of sustainability cannot avoid these issues, but nor does it throw any extra light on them. Suffice it to say that any considered approach to environmental protection requires much stricter control of toxic wastes than has generally been seen in the past; and that the eventual goal of environmental policy must be to phase out the production of such wastes altogether.[9]

What sustainability does do, for any given perception of risk, is offer rules to govern *changes* in pollution levels. Sustainability requires that neither pollution, nor its damaging effects, increase over time. Since both ambient pollution levels (the purity of air, water and soil) and the effects of such levels on health and ecosystems (diseases, tree loss, toxicity) are measurable, this is again an operational principle. Once 'acceptable' or 'optimal' pollution levels have been set, the waste emission rates which will maintain them can be identified, and policy then directed towards achieving such rates.[10]

Environmental services

For both resources and wastes, the concepts of 'environmental capacity' and 'environmental consumption' can be readily understood. In each case the environment provides a physical 'output' which is directly consumed. Sustainability can therefore be measured in terms of this output. But environmental services are not consumed in this way. There is no discrete time at which the capacity of the environment to regulate climate, for example, is 'consumed': this is a continuous process. There is no physical product which is 'depleted' by the ozone layer in providing protection against ultra-violet radiation.

Yet it is evident that in some sense we do 'consume' these life support functions. Their benefits are measured by indicators such as average global temperatures and the incidence of ultra-violet radiation. We can therefore use changes in these indicators to record changes in the environmental capacity and its consumption. If global temperatures are projected to increase, for example, we can say that the climatic regulation capacity has declined. If the ozone layer is depleted, its protective role is diminished. Similarly, if the number and variety of species is reduced (by extinction and habitat destruction), the capacity of the environment to maintain ecological integrity and genetic diversity can be said to have decreased.

The sustainability of environmental services can therefore be measured by the performance of these 'life support indicators'. Again it is clear that sustainability comes in two versions. The 'maximal' definition would demand that the indicators showed no change at all: future generations would then enjoy the same climate, level of ozone protection or degree of genetic diversity, etc., as the present one. 'Minimal' sustainability, on the other hand, would merely require the indicators not to change so much as to threaten catastrophe.

Exactly what constitutes 'catastrophe' is of course debatable. Would an average rise in global temperatures of 1°C be tolerable? At what point will the continued reduction in the numbers and varieties of species lead to unacceptable ecological consequences? These questions are both scientific and social. They make the minimal version of sustainability much less clear-cut than the maximal version. But they do not invalidate its conceptual basis. We have already acknowledged that sustainability is an ethical concept: it is explicitly an expression of the relationship between current and future generations. To be useful sustainability does not require any 'objective' definition of catastrophe. It requires only that some answer is given to the question: 'how much change is acceptable?' If a limit to change is set, this limit becomes the sustainability target, and policy can then be directed towards its achievement.

Again it is apparent that for the key life support services there is now little practical difference between the minimal and maximal versions of sustainability. It has become obvious that the changes in climate, agricultural production, land patterns and population movements already projected to result from global warming are sufficient to merit the description 'catastrophic'. Scientists cannot be certain what ecological effects will result from the current trends in habitat and species loss, but many are warning that the risks to food chains and wider ecosystem integrity are already serious enough to warrant cessation. Current damage to the ozone layer is generally considered above acceptable limits. In many cases sustainability may require not merely maintenance, but an *increase* in current levels of environmental capacity.

To make sustainability operational, limits expressed in terms of the environmental capacity itself (average temperatures, species numbers) must be turned into targets for the specific features of the environment which provide those capacities. Thus global temperatures are a function of a number of variables such as carbon dioxide emissions, the vegetation cover available to absorb CO_2, methane emissions, and others. Each of these will require a target such that, if all the targets (or some other specified permutation) are achieved, global temperatures will be held to the sustainability limit. Similarly, maintaining genetic diversity to a particular degree will require the conservation of minimum areas of particular types of habitat, development of new habitats, additional scientific breeding of some species to preserve critical minimum stocks, and so on.

In this way the sustainability of life support services can be measured and turned into policy targets. It is harder to say this of environmental amenities. Insofar as the environment provides the source of scientific discovery, future generations will be served by the general conservation of species. It is less easy to place the aesthetic and recreational amenity provided by beautiful views, landscapes and open spaces within the sustainability framework. It would be absurd for sustainability to require no change in any aspect of the environment on the grounds that this deprived future generations of a particular view or open space. The most that can be said, perhaps, is that especially beautiful or valuable areas should be designated inviolate. In this way, although the general use of land must be a matter for the present generation alone, certain areas can be given 'transgenerational' status. This is, of course, exactly what designated Wilderness Areas and other planning controls already do.

The scale of sustainability

Let us summarise the discussion so far. Our purpose in this chapter was to see how the principle of sustainability could be made operational: that is, how it could be expressed in terms of measurable policy targets. We have approached this question by looking separately at each economic-environmental function: resource provision, waste assimilation and the performance of environmental services. In each case we have identified measurable 'sustainability indicators' – of both stocks and flows – which can reveal changes in environmental consumption or capacity over time. In some cases, where the current stock level of an environmental feature is relatively high, a divergence has been observed between the 'maximal' definition of sustainability (intergenerational equality) and the 'minimal' definition (avoidance of catastrophe). In others the current level of stocks is so low that the two definitions coincide: sustainability may actually require an increase in capacity. Whichever definition is used, sustainability can be made into an operational policy by adopting limits or targets for the appropriate environmental indicators, and ensuring that economic activity does not cause these limits to be exceeded.

Of course, in practice such environmental targets cannot be determined independently of one another. The environment's functions are not isolated in this neat way. Depletion of resources may reduce waste absorption capacities; pollution can impair the performance of environmental services; impairment of life support services may cause resource depletion. Moreover depletion of one resource can affect another in the same or a related ecosystem. Air or water pollution may be caused by a number of different waste discharges acting in combination. These interconnections mean that sustainability targets for different environmental effects must be integrated with one another.

There is no question that such integration makes the task of setting them more difficult – our models will be more subject to error, our targets perhaps less precise. But it should not be an excuse for abandoning the attempt. We shall discuss the general problem of uncertainty about environmental behaviour below. Before we do this, however, one further question about the use of sustainability in practice needs to be answered.

This concerns the *scale* over which sustainability is intended to apply. When we speak of maintaining environmental capacities, is this an average global standard, or one applied to each local area? For example, are fish stocks to be kept constant in every fishing ground throughout the world, or can depletion in one area be compensated by increases in another? If the former, how can we define the local area (in this case, a 'fishing ground') whose individual sustainability must be preserved? If the latter, what effect does this have on the distribution of environmental costs and benefits between different areas?

These questions do not have fixed answers. In some cases it is clear that only a global standard makes sense. Since carbon dioxide or CFC emissions have global rather than local impact, they can only sensibly be measured on a global scale. The principle of balancing areas where emissions are rising against areas where emissions are falling then seems reasonable. (There is still a distributional issue over which nations should be allowed to increase their emissions and which must contract, but that is a question of current equity rather than sustainability.) On the other hand, carbon monoxide pollution in Bombay only affects people living there, so allowing emissions to rise because they are falling in London makes no sense. In this case sustainability has to be applied at a local level.

In between these examples, the scale on which sustainability is defined will vary according to circumstances. Take the case of forest cover. Let us assume that, in order to preserve environmental capacity, all trees felled need to be replaced. Now it could be held that every forest and copse should simply be preserved intact: this would guarantee both local and global sustainability. But it is reasonable to suppose that in many parts of the world trees do need to be felled for agricultural and urban development. Then the question is, where should the 'compensating' trees be planted?

If trees were merely required for timber and carbon dioxide absorption, sustainability might in theory allow them to be planted anywhere in the world: its only demand would be the preservation of the global 'capital stock'. But trees also have important localised water and soil retention functions. So the replacement trees must be planted in the same area. The size of this area would be determined according to geological and ecological considerations: so long as the pre-existing levels of water supply and soil volume were preserved, sustainability could be said to be secured.

The 'area of sustainability' could still be very large, however: water tables, for example, can cover thousands of hectares. Sustainability is therefore insufficient by itself as a decision-making principle: there remains the distributional question of which part of the area should be chosen for the replacement trees. This will no doubt depend partly on administrative boundaries: if sustainability projects are undertaken by governments (whether local, regional or national), compensating projects are likely to fall within the same borders. Considerations of equity, however, will also be crucial. Even if overall ecological equilibrium is maintained, people living in one area are unlikely to feel themselves compensated if their lost trees are replaced in another area, perhaps far distant. Allowing this could cause acute problems to communities in the South whose livelihoods depend on local forests and who have little money to import wood or other products from elsewhere. In general therefore it may be said that the smaller the 'area of sustainability', the more equitable the policy.[11] (We shall discuss this issue further in Chapter 10.)

Uncertainty, 'safe minimum standards' and the precautionary principle

While no doubt still open to argument, the approach to sustainability we have taken in this chapter seems reasonably workable. There is an important objection, however, which might yet be raised. This is that we have underestimated the difficulty of setting environmental targets. It is all very well, it might be said, blithely arguing that sustainability can be made operational by (for example) holding carbon dioxide emissions at the level which maintains global temperatures; but if we don't know what that level is, the whole notion becomes academic.

And indeed we don't know what it is. As the continuing debate within the scientific community confirms, extreme uncertainty surrounds predictions of climate change. Our understanding of the environment is in general highly underdeveloped. We have examined only a small proportion of species and still have much to learn about how ecosystems function. We do not know the long-term impacts of various kinds of pollution, or even how different toxins are dispersed by air or water. Where environmental effects are interrelated, trying to set simultaneous targets may lead to compound error. Uncertainty is not confined to the state of scientific knowledge. The environment may itself behave unpredictably. Subject to particular stresses, it may 'flip' from gradual adaptation into major or 'catastrophic' change.[12] Such behaviour might be impossible to forecast even if our knowledge of the underlying processes were much more advanced than it actually is.

In these circumstances, it may be asked, how can the notion of sustainability be made operational at all? As expressed so far sustainability appears to require perfect knowledge about the environment, both about the levels of particular indicators which will maintain environmental capacities, and about the means of achieving them. In the absence of such knowledge, is sustainability meaningful, let alone operational?

There is no question that uncertainty is endemic within environmental science. Inevitably, it makes sustainability in practice imprecise: environmental targets will often be ranges rather than points, and we will never be absolutely certain that they are correct. But uncertainty does not render sustainability meaningless. On the contrary, if anything it tends to reinforce the target-setting approach.

To start with, the fact that we do not understand the environment perfectly does not mean that we cannot use what understanding we do have as the basis for making decisions about it. No knowledge is ever perfect; society would be paralysed if we waited for certainty before acting. Scientific research must constantly strive for improvement: if our estimates of sustainable carbon dioxide emissions are found to be wrong, we must revise them. But acknowledgement that such revisions are bound to occur is not a reason for refusing to set the targets in the first place. If we did this, we would effectively be declaring that a risk of environmental damage is never worth the costs of preventing it – a proposition which in the light of the current crisis is surely insupportable.

What we have here, in fact, is a situation familiar from game theory. We are faced with two possible courses of action: controlling environmental effects and not controlling them. The financial cost of control is clear: beyond a certain point, reducing carbon dioxide emissions, for example, will involve higher electricity prices, a reduction in car use, and so on. But the cost of not controlling emissions is subject to uncertainty. It depends on whether our understanding of global warming is correct or not. If climatologists are right in predicting that current trends will cause catastrophic changes in living patterns, then the cost of not controlling CO_2 emissions is very great. Equally the benefit of controlling emissions is large. On the other hand if they are wrong, and no significant damage will in fact occur, the cost of non-intervention will be small or zero.

The situation is illustrated by Table 8.1. The question is then, what is the rational way to behave? The answer depends, of course, on the probability of each scenario occurring, and how 'risk-averse' we are. But one reasonable response to this situation might be to avoid very large costs. Most people are not tempted by gambles in which their losses could be very large, however great the possible gains. The crucial issue then is how large the two types of cost indeed are. It is difficult to compare the tangible financial burden of higher energy prices with perhaps barely imaginable changes in global population and agricultural patterns. But it seems reasonable to suppose that the predicted costs of global warming are considerably greater than the costs of controlling emissions. A policy of 'minimising the maximum cost' would then lead us to opt for control. If our predictions turned out wrong, we would pay the control costs without getting any benefit from them; but if we opted for *laissez-faire* and our predictions turned out to have been right, we would face catastrophe.[13]

Table 8.1: The payoffs of environmental policy under uncertainty

	Catastrophe	Non-catastrophe	Maximum cost
Environmental control	large benefit – control cost	control cost	control cost
Laissez-faire	catastrophe cost	0	catastrophe cost

This type of reasoning suggests that, far from the existence of uncertainty undermining the concept of sustainability, it lends support to it. Even where we do not know for certain the environmental effects of our actions, if we suspect that they could be catastrophic, we have good reason to control them. It is rational, in other words, to give the environment the benefit of the doubt. If the environmental effect in question involves an *irreversibility*, predictions of catastrophe are not necessary for conservation to be preferred. Since in such cases the losses are irreparable – that is, they are suffered by all future generations – even a small risk that they could occur suggests avoidance.

In practice this means, not just that environmental targets are set at what we believe to be the sustainable levels, but that we allow a considerable margin for error. With habitats and species, notably, there is a strong case for adopting 'safe minimum standards', in which rather more than the believed critical minimum stock is preserved, as a buffer against both unexpected environmental behaviour and the consequent risk of irreversible change. Given scientific ignorance, prudent pessimism should be favoured over hazardous optimism.[14]

We may put this another way. We have seen in this chapter that it is possible to make the concept of sustainability operational, by adopting limits or targets for key environmental indicators. Uncertainty means that in many cases it may not be possible to set these sustainability targets with great accuracy or confidence. But in most circumstances we shall find that setting some is preferable to setting none at all.

9

Environmental Efficiency, Entropy and Energy

Sustainability constraints

In the last two chapters we have argued that a sustainable economy is one in which environmental capacities are maintained; and we have attempted to show what this means in practice. For each element of environmental capacity – for each resource, for each waste discharged into the environment, for each service-providing environmental feature – a maximum stock or flow level can be identified beyond which environmental capacity begins to decline. For an economy aiming at sustainability, these maximums effectively become *constraints*: if economic activity trespasses beyond them, sustainability is no longer achieved. When added together, the individual sustainability constraints constitute an outer 'environmental boundary' for the economy as a whole. Within this boundary, economic activity is sustainable; outside it, it is not.

One way of picturing this is as in Figure 9.1. The inner circle is the economy, and it is placed inside a box representing the environment. The economy is ringed by a second circle, representing its environmental impacts. Somewhere inside the box is then a third circle, representing the sustainability boundary. This is the level of environmental impacts at which capacity begins to decline: the maximum sustainable yield of soils, water and marine life; the rate of depletion of non-renewable resources which maintains supply constant relative to demand; the maximum tolerable discharges of different pollutants; the minimum quantities of environmental features such as habitats, species and atmospheric ozone required to protect environmental services.

In this diagram a sustainable economy is one whose 'environmental impact' circle is inside the sustainability boundary. Here economic activity is within the limits of what the biosphere can tolerate without damaging the interests of future generations. An unsustainable economy, by the same token, is one whose environmental impact circle is outside the sustainability boundary.[1]

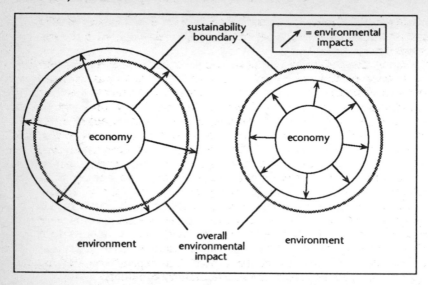

Unsustainable economy   *Sustainable economy*

Figure 9.1: Environmental impacts and the sustainability boundary

It is clear that the current global economy is represented by the left-hand diagram: many environmental impacts have strayed far outside the sustainability boundary. The primary objective of environmental-economic policy can thus be expressed as bringing the environmental impact circle back within the boundary: to ensure that economic activity does not violate the sustainability constraints. In Part III we shall describe the institutions and instruments – both economic and political – by which this can be done.

Environmental efficiency

But obeying constraints cannot be the only objective of economic policy. Even if society does accept the need for sustainability, this is unlikely to be its sole aim. A desire to protect the interests of future generations does not remove the desire to improve the well-being of the current one. A sustainable society will still wish to raise income and welfare and living standards, as economic policy has long attempted to do. There are important questions to be asked about how these things are measured: we should certainly not equate well-being with income levels, nor living standards with material consumption. (See Chapters 18 and 19.) But in general few people will deny the importance of income, particularly in developing countries, as one component of welfare; and and even fewer will question the broad proposal that welfare should, if possible, be increased – however it is measured. The question then is, how can these goals be made compatible with the sustainability constraint?

In some cases, of course, there will be no conflict between the two aims. Many policies to secure sustainability (like reducing waste emissions or saving an endangered habitat) are also likely to improve current welfare, while others (such as recycling and energy conservation) may raise GNP. But the other half of the equation does not so often hold. Most of the means by which modern industrial economies aim to raise living standards cause some degree of environmental degradation: particularly through the increasing use of energy, but in general through resource depletion and pollution. Indeed the conflict between current economic growth patterns and sustainability constraints hardly needs to be argued: it is the whole basis of the environmental crisis. If current patterns of economic growth were simply to continue, it can certainly be said that environmental degradation will get worse. In Figure 9.1, it is clear that as the 'economy' circle expands, so the 'environmental impact' circle expands too – taking it beyond, or further beyond, the sustainability boundary.

But this a priori incompatibility between the goals of economic growth and sustainability only holds if the patterns of economic growth remain unchanged. And this of course need not be the case. It will be recalled that in Chapter 5 we introduced the concept of the 'environmental impact coefficient' (EIC) of GNP: the degree of damaging impact caused by an increase in one unit of national income. We argued that if the composition of output was changed, EIC could be reduced, allowing GNP to rise without greater degradation. We can now explore this possibility a little further.

The relationship between GNP and environmental impact is in fact made up of a number of different links. Between any given impact and the intended increases in income (and welfare) which are its ultimate purpose, we can identify a chain of causes and effects.

Figure 9.2: The transformation process between GNP/welfare and environmental impact

Global warming provides an illustration. The build-up of carbon dioxide in the atmosphere is a damaging environmental impact. It is caused by the consumption of a variety of environmental outputs, notably fossil fuels. These in turn are wanted in order to manufacture various products – domestic energy for example. But the products are themselves only a means to two further sets of ends, namely warmth, light and power for households; and income for energy producers.

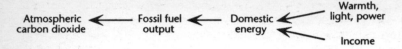

Figure 9.3: The transformation process: energy consumption

The 'environmental impact' link in the chain is the one which sustainability seeks to constrain. It is here that the 'limits to growth' lie: sustainability requires, for instance, that increases in atmospheric carbon dioxide are limited to the level at which global warming is considered tolerable. But a constraint here does not mean that there are limits to any of the other links in the chain. It is not the case that a quantitative increase in one link must necessarily result in corresponding increases in its subsequent effects.

Between each cause and its effect there is what we might call a *transformation process*, and this process has a ratio of *efficiency*: the quantity of the effect produced by a given quantity of the cause. Thus at present, we can observe, to get W hours of domestic warmth society needs to produce X therms of heat, while X therms of heat requires Y tons of fossil fuels, which in turn leads to the emission of Z tons of atmospheric carbon dioxide.

But none of these efficiency ratios are fixed. We know that by switching from one type of fuel to another, or by planting more trees, a smaller quantity of atmospheric carbon dioxide can be generated from the same use of fuel. Similarly, in the present energy production process there is considerable wastage of fuel. If this wastage were reduced, for example by 'co-generation' (combined heat and power production), the number of therms which could be generated from a given volume of fossil fuel would rise. And by insulating homes, an increasing amount of warmth can be obtained from the same amount of delivered heat.

For any particular economic activity, therefore, the environmental impact coefficient of GNP (or of welfare) actually consists of three different ratios. These are the amount of production required by a unit of GNP (or of welfare), the amount of environmental output required by a unit of production, and the degree of environmental impact caused by a unit of environmental output. If we can increase the efficiency of any of these ratios, we can reduce the EIC. And it is this possibility that is the key to solving the apparent incompatibility between growth and sustainability. Economic expansion need not cause further environmental degradation if the 'environmental efficiency' of production is increased by a commensurate amount. Indeed, if efficiency is increased by *more* than output, the environmental impact of an economic activity can actually be reduced. On a macroeconomic scale, this is precisely what is required, since for the economy as a whole the sustainability boundary is already being violated.

We can put this another way. At present the environmental impact of the global economy is unsustainable. In these circumstances there are two mechanisms available for achieving sustainability. One is simply to contract the scale of economic activity, without changing its content. The other is to change its content, to make it more efficient. In theory, if we can do this by a large enough amount, even further growth is not ruled out. (Though given the extent of current degradation, we should not count on it in the long term.) The raising of environmental efficiency may consequently be identified as the second objective of environmental-economic policy.

We may again imagine this pictorially. For simplicity we have shortened the chain of causes and effects, collapsing the links between income/welfare and environmental output. The length of the arrows indicates the efficiency of the transformation process between each stage: the shorter the arrow the higher the efficiency. By increasing efficiency, not only is the environmental impact circle brought back within the sustainability boundary, but this is achieved even while income and welfare are increased. This change may be described as the overall objective of economic policy: the progressive expansion of the inner circle while constraining all impacts within the fixed outer boundary.

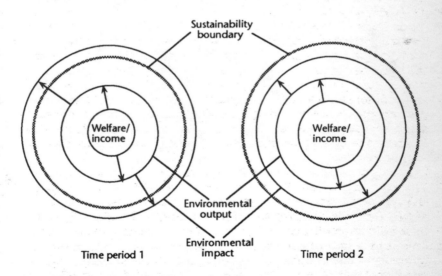

Figure 9.4: Raising environmental efficiency

Sustainability *does* place a constraint on economic growth. But the effect of this constraint can be progressively eased if the efficiency of economic activity is raised. In a sense sustainability offers conventional economic policy a quid pro quo: growth is possible, it says, but only if environmental efficiency is raised at the same time, so that overall environmental impacts remain within the sustainability boundary. Note that this lesson applies to the economy as a whole, not necessarily to each individual economic activity. For some activities merely increasing efficiency may not be sufficient to make good an unsustainable environmental impact. Some industries, for example, may have to be contracted, or closed down altogether, if sustainability is to be achieved. (Nuclear power production, rainforest farming, CFC production spring to mind.) But as we shall show below, there is still the possibility that they can be replaced by other, less damaging activities.

Raising environmental efficiency

It is not the task of this book to describe the specific technical advances which can increase environmental efficiency. Many such advances are already on the market; others are feasible but not yet available; still others (we may assume) have yet to be invented. From wind power to electric cars, from biodegradable detergents to recycling technologies, from home insulation to industrial ceramics, the technical means of raising efficiency are not generally in question, and they are described elsewhere.[2] What concerns us here are the *economic* means: the financial, regulatory and institutional policies by which we can ensure that the technical possibilities are actually introduced in practice. It is after all the fact that existing technical advances are not widely in use which is in many ways the key problem. We have the ability to tackle the environmental crisis, but the economic system is still not allowing these solutions to be implemented. Changing this state of affairs is the subject of Part III.

Nevertheless it may be helpful to classify in broad terms the ways in which environmental efficiency can be raised. This will allow us both to understand what the different types of technical advance are actually doing, and to ensure that all the possible means of raising efficiency are considered. It will also reveal an important limitation to the efficiency-increasing objective.

Using Figure 9.4, we may divide efficiency measures into two categories: those which seek to reduce the environmental impact of a unit of environmental output (that is, which allow the middle circle to grow without enlarging the outer circle), and those aimed at reducing the volume of environmental output required by a 'unit' of welfare or income (allowing the inner but not the middle circle to expand).

In each case we need to look at both ends of the production process. We pointed out in Chapter 1 that resources and wastes are ultimately the same quantities: this we know from the first law of thermodynamics. So for any given unit of environmental output there are two possibilities for raising efficiency: reducing depletion of the original resource, and reducing pollution caused by its consequent waste. We may identify a number of methods of doing each of these things.

1. Renewable resources

For renewable resources, an increase in environmental efficiency can be defined as an increase in sustainable output rates: that is, the ability to obtain a higher rate of harvest without causing either long-term depletion of the resource or other forms of associated environmental degradation (such as pollution of water stocks and loss of habitats). There are three principal methods of achieving this:

(a) Increases in the size of the resource stock, for example by cultivating previously unfarmed land or through fish farming. Clearly the wider ecological implications of this method (such as for habitat protection and genetic diversity) must be taken into account.
(b) Increases in the productivity of renewable resource species: for example by planting faster-growing or higher-yielding crops.
(c) Changes in agricultural production techniques. Modern irrigation methods and mechanisation, for example, or more careful tree felling, can increase the sustainable harvests of crops and forests.

Each of these methods, of course, is widely used. On a global scale there is clearly scope for further efficiency increases: it is estimated, for example, that the development of sustainable modern farming methods in the South (involving all of the above techniques) could increase the current average yield of global grain production by two and a half times, from 2 to 5 tons of grain equivalent per hectare. At current average consumption levels, it can be noted, this would be sufficient to support a global population of 11 billion, or slightly more than the number at which population growth is expected to stabilise at the end of the 21st century.[3]

There are limits to efficiency increases of this sort, however. The first is clearly dependent on available space. The second and third must ultimately be constrained by the thermodynamic limits to the efficiency of photosynthesis, which governs plant (and therefore animal) growth. Indeed it is already evident that, in areas practising modern intensive farming methods, grain harvests are levelling off, with a diminishing response to the added use of fertilisers. Maximum sustainable yields are being reached or exceeded. Morever in many cases the long-term environmental risks of raising efficiency by technological methods (such as genetic engineering) may well be felt to outweigh the potential benefits.[4]

2. Non-renewable resources

In the last chapter we defined the sustainable output rate for non-renewable resources as that which maintained the size of the stock relative to demand. As we showed then, growth of output is possible so long as the stock is increased. There are two principal measures available to achieve this:

(a) The discovery and exploitation of new reserves, thus increasing the size of the economically-available stock.
(b) The recycling of extracted resources, thus replenishing the stock.

Again, both these methods are widely used, though there is considerable scope for increasing the rate of recycling. Clearly, both are limited by the implications for other sustainability indicators: the ecological effects of mining new reserves, for example, may be considered too damaging. We shall return to recycling below.

3. Reducing pollution

To reduce the pollution caused by a given unit of environmental output, five principal methods are available:

(a) The production of more 'bio-degradable' products which can break down into harmless organic substances on disposal.
(b) An increase in the treatment of wastes before their discharge into the environment, to break up toxic and polluting substances into inert and harmless ones.
(c) An increase in the volume of waste recycling, to prevent wastes reaching the environment at all.
(d) An increase in the assimilative capacity of the recipient media for waste. A higher concentration of micro-organisms, for example, may enable a river to absorb greater quantities of sewage effluent. Similarly, more trees will allow higher carbon dioxide emissions without raising atmospheric CO_2. Again, there may be limits to these possibilities, as associated ecological changes occur.
(e) The discovery of new safe recipient media. It may be possible for some wastes to be assimilated, or safely stored, in new ways. The proposal that carbon dioxide could be deposited in the oceans falls into this category.[5]

Clearly, care must be taken with all these methods that other damaging environmental effects are not so caused; ignorance of how ecosystems work is a crucial factor here. Some proposals for safe waste storage, such as those for nuclear waste underground, are likely to be received with more scepticism than others.

In the transformation process between environmental outputs and income or welfare, we may identify three broad means of increasing efficiency – that is, of raising welfare and/or income without increasing either the volume of resources consumed or the amount of waste discharged. These are changes in production processes, changes in products, and changes in demand.

4. Production processes

Changes in production processes include:

(a) Reductions in the waste generated in production, through better use of materials, 'internal' (within-factory) recycling and use of 'low- and no-waste' and 'clean' technologies.[6]
(b) Increases in the volume of materials recycling: that is, use of the same volume of environmental output more than once. The possibilities for recycling post-consumer waste are particularly significant. Recycling both cuts down waste discharges and leads to a smaller demand for virgin resources.
(c) Reductions in the amount of energy used in production, through conservation and more efficient process and technology design.
(d) A switch to the use of continuing (renewable) energy sources. Solar, wind, wave, tidal, hydroelectric and geothermal sources are all less polluting than fossil and nuclear fuels, and the first four can't be depleted.
(e) A substitution of human labour for machine production. Human labour is 'powered' by solar energy derived from food. At present in industrialised economies fossil-fuel energy is cheaper than human labour for most industrial processes, but a change in energy prices in some cases could reverse this. Unlike machines, people consume approximately the same amount of energy when they are economically 'idle' as when they are 'productive'.
(f) Reductions in the resources used in distribution: in packaging, transport (the further the distance travelled by goods the higher their energy demand), and so on.

5. Products

Changes in products include:

(a) Reductions in the size of goods. Smaller goods, or simpler ones, require less material input than larger and more complex ones. The miniaturisation of microelectronic products is a case in point.
(b) Increases in the durability of goods. Longer-lasting products can provide the same benefits as a series of more rapidly obsolescent ones. Repair and reconditioning activity may generate as much income.
(c) Reductions in the energy required in using goods – from homes to washing machines. Both conservation measures (for example, building insulation) and more efficient design are possible.
(d) The production of more 'bio-degradable' products which can break down into harmless organic substances on disposal.
(e) Improvements in the quality of products. Higher quality products are likely to generate a higher value added per unit of material content, that is, their contribution to national income will be greater.

6. Demand

Changes in demand include:

(a) Shifts in the composition of demand to products with a lower material content. In the area of public expenditure, for example, preventative health care is likely to require less physical output for the same level of spending than, say, weapons production – and generate more welfare. Public transport may meet the same needs as private motor vehicles with lower energy and resource costs. In general, services often require a smaller physical output than goods per unit of income generated. We shall discuss these possibilities further in Chapter 19.

(b) Absolute reductions in per capita demand. Once the concepts of income and welfare have been distinguished, the possibility opens up that people could be happier with a lower level of material consumption; or at least, without the requirement for consumption constantly to rise. That 'money can't buy you happiness' is a commonplace; the contention that the costs of western consumer lifestyles might not actually be worth the benefits is probably not so widely held. But it has been argued by many radical writers in industrialised countries and we would be unwise to dismiss the possibility altogether.[7]

(c) A reduction in population. Clearly, if population can be reduced, total demand can fall even when per capita demand does not. The possibility that environmental degradation could be reduced by this means is generally accepted for the South, where population growth is often very rapid; it has been much less widely appreciated in the North. This is despite the much higher level of per capita environmental consumption, and therefore the much more significant effect population reductions could have.

The circular economy

Clearly, not all of these options for increasing efficiency will be available in every case; and which is most appropriate in any instance will depend on a number of factors, such as likely effectiveness and cost of introduction. Often it is indeed not the concern of economic policy exactly how an environmental target is achieved. Rather, it is sufficient to create the economic conditions for its achievement and then leave individual economic actors to choose the most appropriate technical method. We shall discuss this further in Part III.

One way of picturing the options is to use a more sophisticated version of the diagram of the economy which we introduced in Chapter 1. In Figure 10.5 we have identified where in the economic process each method of raising efficiency can be located. It will be noticed that many of the methods attempt to increase what we might call the *circularity* of the economy; that is, the various loops by which waste products are returned to the production process, either through natural regeneration or through recycling and reuse by producers and consumers.

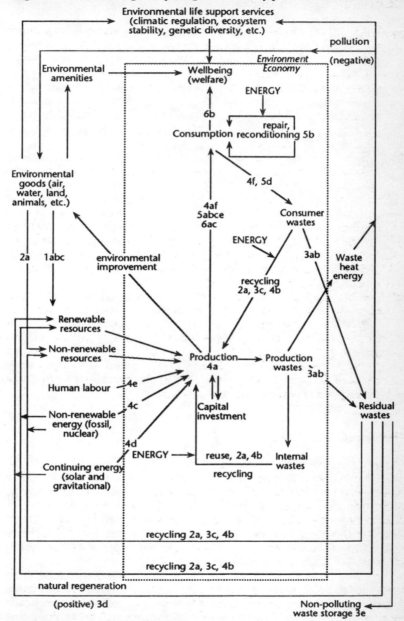

Figure 9.5: The thermodynamic economy

We might go so far as to say that increasing the circularity of the economy is one of the key goals of environmental-economic policy. After all, if all wastes could be returned to the economy in these various loops, both resource depletion and long-term pollution could be eliminated altogether.

One can imagine what a perfectly circular economy would look like. First, all wastes (other than heat) would be collected and separated out into different types. Then all those deriving from organic resources would be turned into biodegradable forms and returned to the land (or seas), while all those deriving from minerals would be recycled and used again. The net result would be no pollution, since no wastes would be stored in the environment: they would either be assimilated, or not be discharged at all. And so long as the rate of recycling kept pace with the demand for resources, the resource stock would not be depleted. Renewable resources would be harvested at their maximum sustainable yield, and mineral mining would not be required at all. Such an economy could even grow, if the efficiency by which resources were turned into products and income were raised.

Unfortunately, there are two snags to this rather cosy and reassuring scenario. The first is economic. It would be extremely expensive to collect, separate and treat all wastes in this way. Mining new resources is often cheaper than recycling old ones. Increasing circularity would therefore be 'uneconomic'. But this objection is not conclusive. After all, what is 'uneconomic' depends on a number of factors, and some of these can be changed. For example, governments could levy a 'resource tax' on mining, which would make recycling cheaper by comparison. Separation and treatment of wastes could be made compulsory in law, or subsidised. These are indeed precisely the sort of measures which we shall be proposing in Part III. Increasing circularity in these ways would without doubt have substantial economic ramifications, but it is certainly not impossible.

The second objection to the circular economy, however, offers fewer escape routes. It is based on an important technical observation about our description of the circular economy, namely that it is missing its most crucial feature. We noted that the first law of thermodynamics ensures that the quantity of resources which enters the economy equals the quantity of wastes which leaves it: this is the basis of circularity. But the second law is also significant here. The second law, it will be recalled, states that in any system without an external source of energy, 'entropy', or disorder, always increases. The very process by which resources get turned into wastes illustrates this: compare a lump of bauxite (aluminium ore) and a barrel of crude oil to the dispersal of milk bottle tops and carbon dioxide.

But it also means that wastes can't turn back into resources unless there is some external source of energy. 'Recycling' doesn't just happen on its own. Since its purpose is to reduce the entropy of the recycled material, it has to be powered by an energy source, and it is this which we have omitted to describe. Having criticised conventional economics in Chapter 1 for operating with a financial model of the economy which was essentially a perpetual motion machine, we are in danger ourselves of making exactly the same error. This is why our diagram includes not only the original sources of energy for the production process, but also the sources which power the recycling process. The moral is simple: if we want to recycle more wastes, we have to use more energy.

But *this* is extremely problematic, since if the energy comes from fossil fuels it will itself generate waste, notably in the form of carbon dioxide. Recycling more waste therefore reduces one pollution problem only at the cost of increasing another. Of course, carbon dioxide could be captured and converted back to solid carbon – but this would require more energy than was obtained from burning it in the first place. There is no escaping the entropy law.

It is true that in many cases obtaining a raw material by recycling requires less energy than making it from virgin resources.[8] But this is not a sufficient analysis. We must also take into account the energy required to collect, separate and transport the wastes to the recycling plant. And the more dispersed the wastes, the greater this will be. Currently recycling takes place only when these activities – collection, separation and transportation – are relatively easy. But if the objective is to increase the amount of recycling, the energy required will rise, as more dispersed and more intractable wastes are handled. (This is why recycling becomes more expensive the more of it is done.) At some point recycling will cease to save energy at all; on the contrary, so long as it is powered by fossil (or nuclear) fuels, it will start making a net contribution to pollution.[9]

And note that we cannot simply raise the efficiency of the recycling process, so that less and less energy is required per unit of output. Although advances are no doubt possible in current techniques, there is a thermodynamic minimum to the energy required for any chemical process, and beyond this it is not possible to go.

Recycling is not the only efficiency-raising measure we have listed which requires more energy. Treating wastes to render them biodegradable or otherwise non-polluting does too. Increasing the productivity of crops may involve the use of agrochemicals or farming machinery, both of which require additional energy inputs. Exploiting new reserves of mineral resources is extremely energy-intensive – indeed, as less-accessible reserves are mined, the energy cost per tonne of ore extracted rises. This is indeed true of energy itself. Acquiring energy requires energy! It is needed to manufacture the capital equipment, to power the extraction process and to transport the fuel to its point of use. Through a procedure known as 'net energy analysis' we can calculate how much energy is expended in these ways to bring a unit of energy to the market place. Unsurprisingly, we find that over time the 'energy requirement of energy' has risen, and is continuing to rise, as 'easy' reserves are exhausted and extraction becomes more difficult.[10]

Solving the 'entropic problem'

Two very important results follow from these observations. The first is that not all of the methods we identified earlier for increasing environmental efficiency are equivalent. Those which require greater energy inputs may relieve one type of environmental problem only at the expense of contributing to another. The most desirable methods, therefore, are those which do not require additional energy; those whose purpose, rather, is to *reduce the throughput* of the economy. Thus avoiding waste altogether is clearly preferable to recycling it. Reducing demand for materials should take priority over increasing waste assimilation capacities. Creating more durable goods is more important than making them recyclable. Ultimately we should be aiming to maximise the welfare obtained from economic activity while minimising the volume of matter and energy which flows through the economy. This is the most genuine measure of economic efficiency.[11]

Second, a new light is cast on the greenhouse effect. The seriousness of global warming is widely acknowledged, but the particular feature which makes it unique among environmental problems is rarely observed. This is its (almost) inescapable nature. Though difficult, we can do without CFCs and tropical hardwoods by substituting less damaging products. We can do the same for most toxins and heavy metals, even for pesticides and artificial fertilisers. But there is no substitute for energy. On the contrary, the very measures we might wish to take to mitigate other environmental problems – recycling, waste treatment, extraction of new resource stocks – themselves require additional energy. So long as this energy comes from fossil fuels, we shall risk making the greenhouse effect worse. Granted, there are many measures we can take to reduce the quantity of atmospheric carbon dioxide generated per unit of production, but if production continues to expand such measures will only ever postpone the problem; they cannot eliminate it. The second law tells us this.

There is, however, a solution. This is to do what we might describe as 'going back to nature'. After all, the biosphere is constantly recycling its waste products, including carbon dioxide, without apparently adding to pollution. It does this by using solar energy. Collected by plants in photosynthesis, and through the heating of the earth's water stocks, solar radiation is the external source of energy which enables the biosphere to convert high entropy wastes (such as carbon and nitrogen oxides) into low entropy resources, thus overcoming the constraints of the second law.

There are two ways in which humankind could harness solar power. One is by using plants and animals themselves to perform our economic recycling functions. This is what 'biodegradable' wastes do, for example: allowing the natural processes of organic decay to take effect. By planting more trees we could similarly cause a higher proportion of carbon dioxide to be absorbed, leading to a smaller greenhouse effect.

Substituting human labour for machines, where possible, would have a comparable result.

But there are limits to the availability of these methods. For one thing, they are not applicable to most non-organic substances, only tiny quantities of which can be safely absorbed in biochemical cycles. Separating out organic and inorganic substances is itself an energy-intensive process. Moreover, the chemical complexity of even many organic waste products makes biodegradability only effective over the long term, with pollution the immediate consequence of disposal. Breaking complex wastes down into faster-degrading substances, of course, requires more energy. Substituting human labour for machines, meanwhile, would in most cases cause a drastic fall in productivity; few people in industrialised societies would be prepared to accept the reduction in living standards that would result.

The other way in which solar energy can be utilised, therefore, is through its direct collection by human-made technology. Solar power and its variants (wind and wave energy; along with tidal energy, which is gravitational in origin) have long been recognised, of course, as potential 'alternative' sources of energy. But their real significance has rarely been grasped by politicians or economists.[12] Regarded merely as rather unfeasible alternatives to fossil and nuclear fuels, which might perhaps have some use in the distant future when coal and uranium are exhausted, the key property of these 'continuing' energy sources has been overlooked. This is not simply that they do not run out, but that they have no physical waste products. In contrast to both non-renewable and renewable (biomass) sources, they generate little or no pollution in use.[13] The only limits to their use, therefore, are the quantity of resources – including, in the short term at least, fossil fuels – required to build sufficient collectors for them, and the technology to turn collected continuing energy into all the forms and quantities of heat, electricity and motor power which modern industrial society needs.

Developing such technology therefore ranks among the greatest scientific challenges humankind now faces. If we can find ways of utilising solar and other forms of continuing energy directly, so as to replace fossil fuels in most (if not all) of their current uses, we will have gone a considerable way to solving our economic 'entropic problem'. Not only will the use of energy to extract and process resources cease to be a major cause of pollution, but recycling them will also become environmentally rational. The circular economy becomes a feasible goal.

It is this prospect which holds out some hope for the evolution of a global economy whose sustainability can be maintained even while economic growth occurs. We observed earlier that there were two ways in which the environmental impacts of the economy could be brought within the sustainability boundary. The first was simply for production to be contracted. But this is not a feasible option: given the gap between the living standards of North and South, the demand for economic growth in the South will not be assuaged even if Northern societies are persuaded to accept a lower level of material consumption.[14]

The second method, therefore, was for the environmental efficiency of production to be raised. We have now seen, however, that this possibility is itself constrained by the problem of entropy, as manifested in the greenhouse effect. In the short term we can mitigate global warming through a number of relatively easy measures of energy conservation. But in the longer term, as economic growth continues, the problem will remain. Meanwhile the very raising of efficiency, by recycling and so on, will itself require more energy. It is only through the development of continuing energy sources, therefore, that the vicious circle of economic entropy can be broken, and the virtuous one of sustainability put in its place.

Part III
Programme

10

Sustainability Planning

The two-stage process

In Part II we have described the principle of sustainability and how it can be interpreted in policy. In Part III we shall attempt to answer the question which obviously follows. How can an economy be constrained within environmental limits? What types of economic institutions, instruments and approach can achieve the sustainability objective?

Broadly, environmental-economic policy making can be thought of as a two-stage process. The first stage is to set targets for the key environmental indicators. These targets define the level at which environmental capacity is to be protected. The second stage is then to influence economic activity in such a way that it does not exceed these targets. Various instruments must be used (such as taxes, regulations and government expenditure) which constrain the behaviour of individual firms and households. We shall deal with each stage in turn.

It should be noted that this two-stage approach does not only apply if the targets chosen in the first stage are intended to maintain environmental capacity. It may well be that societies and their governments decide not to adopt the formal sustainability objective. As we have already observed, sustainability is a moral principle which has to be chosen, and may therefore not be. It is quite possible that the present generation will effectively trade off its concern for future generations (and geographically distant people) against the current costs of protecting them. This does not make the concept of sustainability redundant; on the contrary, if such a trade-off is made it is important to be clear what the costs are and who will pay them. It is simply an acknowledgement that the existence of a moral case for an action does not determine that the action will be taken.

But in these circumstances governments can still decide a level of environmental protection that they will maintain, and set targets on this basis. Though not 'sustainability targets', these will be of the same type, and will serve the same role in the first stage of the policy making process. The same instruments may then be used, in the second stage, to achieve them. In this sense, though we shall describe it as 'sustainability planning', the approach outlined in the following chapters does not depend on sustainability being the objective. It may be used even if less stringent policy targets are chosen.

Setting environmental targets

There are two types of environmental indicator for which targets need to be set. The *primary indicators* are those measuring quantities and qualities (stocks) of the key environmental features: soils; forests; land use; inland, underground and marine water resources (including levels of different kinds of pollution within them); non-renewable resource stocks; atmospheric composition (for example, carbon dioxide, lead, etc.); stratospheric ozone; numbers and diversity of species; coverage and stability of habitats; and others. These are the features which provide environmental capacity; they are therefore the key 'sustainability indicators' whose values we wish to maintain constant.

The *secondary indicators* are then those which measure the economic activities causing changes in the primary indicators. These are the flows into and out of the stocks represented by the primary indicators. They include for example emission and discharge rates for pollutants: these are what determine the primary indicators of water, air and land pollution. Others include economic activities such as agrochemical use, farming patterns, deforestation and reforestation, non-renewable resource exploitation and discovery, recycling rates and solid waste generation. It is only by setting targets for these secondary indicators that targets for the primary ones can be made operational.

Thus, for example, the key sustainability indicator for global warming is the quantity of atmospheric carbon dioxide. (There are a number of other relevant primary indicators as well, such as atmospheric methane, CFCs and nitrous oxide.) A target must be set for this in order to keep global warming within tolerable limits. But such a target can only be made operational if a target is then set for global carbon dioxide emissions, since these are the main determinant of atmospheric CO_2. (Other important secondary indicators are global afforestation and deforestation, since trees remove CO_2 from the atmosphere.) It is the primary indicator which measures sustainability; but it is the secondary indicator upon which the economic instruments of the second stage of policy making can act.

This target-setting process is increasingly being adopted as the basis for pollution control policy, particularly in the United States and by the European Community. It has not always been so. In the past – and in some countries and in some fields still – the predominant approach of environmental policy has been to focus on the instruments applied to individual economic actors rather than on the combined effect of these instruments on the primary indicators. In the UK, for example, air pollution control regulations have customarily given each factory permission to discharge a certain volume and concentration of pollutants. These amounts are obviously set with some concern for the level of pollution in the air into which the wastes are discharged (the 'ambient' level), but this is not their primary determinant. Instead, they are usually negotiated on the basis of a technical criterion, such as 'best available technology not entailing excessive cost'.[1]

More importantly, pollution controls of this kind are not limited by the ambient level. If the factory expands production, it can expect its permitted discharges to rise too. If another factory sets up in the same location, its additional emissions will not lead to the first factory's permitted discharges being reduced. In each case the result is that the ambient level of pollution in the air rises. The individual firms are controlled, but their combined effect is not.

This represents an important difference of principle. In the target-setting approach, the primary concern is the level of ambient pollution in the environment. The controls exercised over individual polluting factories are derived from this. If the combined effect of all the factories' activities causes the pollution level to rise above the target, their individual permits will be reduced. In the traditional approach, the primary concern is the individual discharge permits. The actual level of (collective) pollution is then secondary: it emerges from the combined impact of these permits. It is not predetermined, and can rise (or fall) according to the level of economic activity. As economic growth occurs, pollution and resource depletion may be expected, and are certainly allowed, to grow too.

The difference between the two approaches is clearly illustrated in the case of cars. Technically-based regulations to control exhaust emissions (notably the fitting of catalytic converters) have now been introduced in most industrialised countries. These are expected to reduce harmful emissions by up to a third. But air pollution will not decline, because the anticipated growth of car ownership and use will wipe out the gains within ten years.[2] The target-setting approach would recognise that to hold air pollution constant or to reduce it, either the regulations would have to become progressively more severe as car use rose, or car use itself would have to be controlled.

The traditional approach is clearly insufficient to meet the demands of sustainability. Sustainability is concerned with preserving, or reaching, particular ambient levels of pollution and of other environmental indicators, the levels which maintain capacity. It is not responsive to the rate of economic activity: when economic growth occurs, sustainability does not allow the level of pollution or resource depletion to grow correspondingly. It demands that the economy become more environmentally efficient, so that the *same* (or a lower) level of environmental impact is achieved. What matters is the condition of the environment; the permits given (or taxes set) for individual waste discharges or other environmental uses are entirely dependent on this.

This does not preclude the use of pollution controls based on technical criteria. The use of ambient standards clearly enables firms to operate at different levels of environmental care when the surrounding conditions are different. This can be anti-competitive: a firm located in an area of high air quality may be allowed to emit more pollution than a firm based in an area of low air quality, giving it lower costs. It also fails to enforce best environmental practices. There is a strong case therefore for firms being required to meet either target ambient standards or best-practice emissions standards, whichever are the tighter.[3]

Sustainability applies the target-setting approach, of course, not only to pollution but to all environmental impacts, including the depletion of resources and degradation of other environmental features that provide life support or amenity services. Traditional environmental policy has frequently ignored these altogether, placing almost no controls on the exhaustion of renewables such as soils and forests and often providing positive incentives to the depletion of minerals and fossil fuels.

Instruments

The second stage of policy making follows from the first. To hold the economy within the sustainability constraints set by the primary and secondary targets, economic activity must be restricted or changed in some fashion. (We may presume that, in the absence of any restrictions, the targets would be exceeded. This is, after all, the basis of the problem.) To do this various kinds of economic instrument must be employed to alter the behaviour of firms and households in such a way that their combined impact on the environment remains within the overall targets set.

In theory it might be possible for the government to administer environmental impacts directly, instructing firms what to produce and how and limiting the goods and services available to consumers. But as the Soviet system has shown, this would not only be authoritarian but also extremely inefficient. It isn't necessary either. Firms and consumers can be *influenced* in their behaviour without taking from them the freedom to make their own decisions, or requiring the state to have detailed information on what they are all doing. A number of instruments are available for this.

First, there are several *voluntary mechanisms*, simple forms of encouragement to people to engage in environmentally-benign activities. In some circumstances persuasion alone may be sufficient to make firms or consumers change their behaviour, perhaps through a moral appeal (for example, not to use aerosols with CFCs); in others, providing more information may help. Many people and firms for example may waste energy simply through ignorance of how they could conserve it. In other cases changing the legal context can have a stimulating effect: extending firms' liability for environmental damage, for example, or giving individual citizens and pressure groups the right to take firms and governments to court for violating environmental standards.

(Obviously, many environmentally beneficial activities by individuals and groups can take place without any government involvement at all.)

Second, damaging environmental activities can be *regulated*. Laws can be passed which prohibit certain types of behaviour or levels of harmful activity. Regulations can set standards, for example, for energy efficiency of electrical appliances or house insulation. They can prohibit particular quantities and concentrations of waste emissions from factories, or force a particular treatment method to be used. They can set upper limits on vehicle exhaust emissions or even make travelling on certain roads illegal in cars with only one occupant.[4]

The third instrument is direct *government expenditure*. Where governments control important elements of infrastructure such as waste management, energy production or transport, they can influence environmental indicators on a large scale. New methods of waste collection, treatment and recycling can be introduced; investments can be made in renewable energy production and public transport. Governments can also give subsidies and grants of various kinds to private firms and individuals, to support and encourage environmentally desirable activities such as recycling or habitat maintenance.

Subsidies are often classified as a form of *financial incentive*. This is a fourth type of instrument. Firms and households can be encouraged to behave in certain ways by giving them incentives to do so. Subsidies provide positive incentives. Placing a tax on damaging activities such as energy consumption or waste emissions alternatively creates a disincentive to undesirable behaviour. Another method is to set quotas for resource use or waste discharges and make these tradable between firms. In some cases people can be required to place returnable deposits on bottles and other containers. Incentives such as these change the effective price of the activity in question. Recycling becomes cheaper, energy consumption more expensive. The activity can be expected to change in consequence.

We shall discuss these instruments – their various forms, their effectiveness in different contexts and their wider impacts – in more detail in the next three chapters. For now it is sufficient to note that these are the principal tools of environmental economic policy. Each instrument, of course, can be applied in varying degrees. A pollution control regulation may specify quite high permitted levels of waste discharges or very low ones. A tax on an environmentally damaging product could be set at any percentage of its value from nought to a hundred or more (a 100% tax means a doubling of the price). The magnitude of the instrument required will obviously depend on the degree to which the economic activity in question is desired to change.

But this in turn demands that we know what effect a particular regulation or tax will have on the level of activity. For example, if we wished to use a tax on fossil fuels to cut energy consumption by 20% over a ten-year period, the level of tax needed would depend on how energy consumers reacted to a rise in price. Some profligate users might cut consumption by 20% if the price went up by only a little.

For others, requiring energy for essential purposes, it might take a very large tax before consumption fell by the required amount. (Since it takes time to introduce new energy saving equipment or practices, we would expect that the longer the period allowed the smaller the tax required.) If we wanted to cut water pollution by raising waste emissions standards we would similarly need to know how much it would cost firms to comply, what impact this would then have on their output and prices, whether the pollution would be 'displaced' from one medium to another (air or land), and other factors.

If we are to achieve our sustainability targets, we evidently have to understand how the indicators and the instruments are connected. In some cases this knowledge is available from existing data. For example, so-called 'input-output' tables can show the relationship between output in different industries and the energy and raw materials they consume. We also have the experience of how previous price changes have affected demand or production. In other cases we shall need to conduct new research into social and economic behaviour in different conditions. This might involve constructing new environmental input-output tables relating industrial production not just to resource inputs but to the emission of pollutants and other environmental impacts.

To enable the instruments to be used across the whole economy this information will then need to be built into new kinds of economic models incorporating environmental as well as more conventional economic indicators. Such models will help us to judge which instruments will achieve the targets most effectively, what adjustments are required when targets are initially 'missed' due to unexpected behaviour, the impact of these instruments on other economic activities, and so forth. Several models of these kinds are now being constructed in different research institutes; this is clearly an important task in the integration of economic and environmental policy.[5]

Planning, market forces and markets

This process of setting targets and then constraining economic activity to meet them through various kinds of intervention may be described as a form of planning. But this term must be used carefully. The phrase 'planned economy' has generally been associated with the old Communist bloc, referring to a system in which not only were almost all firms owned by the state, but a centralised bureaucracy made detailed decisions on what they were to produce and how. For every commodity the economy produced, the state chose the colour, style, size and material, as well as the volume and price. With none of these decisions being left to the choices of producers or consumers, there were virtually no markets at all. The entire system was effectively *administered* by the economic planning authorities.

But this is not what we mean here. By planning is meant simply the process of choosing the macroeconomic *outcomes* of economic activity, not the laying down of its microeconcmic *methods*. This distinction is quite crucial. In describing a sustainable economy as a planned economy, what we are saying is that the government must decide (in the first stage of policy-making) the level of the economy's overall environmental impact. It does not have to dictate (in the second stage) how this impact is achieved.

Planning in this sense stands in contrast to the operation of market forces, but it does not preclude the existence of markets. The difference between these two concepts will be recalled from Chapter 3. Markets are a microeconomic mechanism, operating at the level of individual products, businesses and households. They are characterised by the existence of a number of suppliers and purchasers free to choose with whom they trade, where changes in price mediate between supply and demand. Market forces by contrast are a macroeconomic phenomenon, occurring at the level of the whole economy. They come into being when the majority of decisions of individual firms and consumers take place in markets, and there is no one determining the collective consequence.

A planned economy is one in which market forces are controlled or superseded. That is, it is an economy in which there *is* some body which is determining the collective consequence of individual decisions – in the current context, determining the overall environmental impact of economic activity. This is what setting environmental targets does. However choosing macroeconomic outcomes in this way is not the same as deciding the methods by which, at a microeconomic level, the outcomes will be met. Markets can quite happily coexist with planning, so long as the conditions prevailing in the markets are adjusted to generate the targeted outcome.

The instruments previously discussed perform this function. None of them requires markets somehow to be 'abolished'; rather, what they do is to change the conditions in markets so that the choices facing suppliers and purchasers in them are different. Thus regulations prohibit or modify certain kinds of action, but they do not instruct companies or consumers to produce or buy any particular products or determine their prices. Taxes and subsidies change the prices in a market, but do not force any particular response. A government may invest in public transport, but this is no more coercive of firms and consumers than building roads.

Using these instruments to change the conditions in markets does not suddenly destroy the 'free market' system. Despite the rhetoric of some politicians, there aren't any 'free' markets in industrialised countries – and very few people who would wish there to be. Markets are already subject to all sorts of regulations and taxes, ranging from public health licences for restaurants and controls on the advertising of financial services to social insurance taxes on employers and VAT on consumer goods. All such measures restrict what suppliers and purchasers can do, and thereby influence their behaviour.

If the government did not intervene in the market in these ways, the outcomes would be different. Different goods and services would be produced, higher or lower prices charged, different social or environmental effects caused. Sometimes governments explicitly use market interventions to change social conditions: they tax alcohol and tobacco very highly, for example, or restrict the sale of pornographic material. At other times regulations and taxes may have unintended wider effects: by increasing the cost of employing people, for example, social insurance taxes tend to act as a disincentive to job creation. All that is now being proposed is that this influence on behaviour in markets should be more systematically directed to achieving certain predetermined ends, namely a particular level of environmental impact.

Note that it isn't usually the *individual* behaviour of firms or consumers which has to be influenced, but the collective behaviour of a whole set of actors. If a tax is put on energy, for example, in order to reduce its use, no individual factory or household is told to consume less. Rather, what happens is that the combined effect of all factories' and households' decisions in the new market situation results in the required decline in energy consumption. Although circumscribed in particular ways, the actions of producers and purchasers are still freely chosen, and prices still adjust to the differences between supply and demand. There is no need for governments to make decisions on behalf of individual economic actors (let alone to own them): they must plan the economy, but they do not have to administer it.

This two-stage approach is not new. Indeed, even governments which claim their adherence to market forces attempt to control them in some areas. A good example is provided by inflation policy. Governments do not let prices rise simply according to the 'invisible hand' of market forces. They actively seek to control them, often proclaiming a target inflation rate. How they go about achieving this varies, of course: some governments may rely mainly on high interest rates, others may use controls on credit; still others may directly dictate which prices can increase and which must be frozen. All these are interventions in the market (the latter of a particularly severe type) whose aim is to influence individual microeconomic behaviour so that the collective macroeconomic outcome meets the target set. The approach we have advocated for environmental policy parallels this process exactly.

It may be argued that, even if markets do still exist under such a system, planning in this way is still a curtailment of liberty. By choosing the outcomes of the whole economy and then 'influencing' people until they collectively act in the required way, the state is not allowing people to decide themselves how they will behave. Market forces leave choice in the hands of the people; planning expropriates it to the hands of the state.

This charge is justified in one sense – any kind of intervention in markets is a curtailment on the liberty of someone to do something – but it ignores the problem of externalities. As we saw in Chapter 3, most environmental problems are caused by one set of people but affect another: this is why they occur. In these circumstances it is quite reasonable to restrict the liberty of the offender in order to protect the liberty and welfare of the victim. This principle is common enough in other spheres: when, as in many environmental cases, the victim is geographically distant or even unborn, it seems particularly appropriate.[6]

Perhaps even more importantly, the offender and victim do not have to be different groups. The crucial characteristic of market forces is that they generate the 'invisible elbow': damaging collective effects which are not chosen, and may well not be desired, by any individual firm or household. Planning here, therefore, may restrict the liberty of the individual in order to produce an overall result that the *same* individual prefers, but cannot achieve on his or her own. Many environmental goods (such as clean air) are public goods which the individual choices of firms and consumers cannot obtain. In these circumstances individual actors may be happy to succumb to collective restrictions in order to achieve their desired ends. If the curtailment of liberty applies to everyone, it may actually be preferable to universal freedom.

In this sense – responding to the arguments put in Chapter 3 – we may describe planning as a way of coping with macroeconomic externalities. By choosing the overall outcomes of economic activity, sustainability planning overcomes the problem of the invisible elbow and allows unintended collective environmental effects to be taken into account.

The state and the citizen

The process of planning we have described gives the state the key role in environmental protection. Even though planning can be carried out through markets, rather than in opposition to them, there is no doubt that it requires a higher degree of state intervention than Western industrialised economies have been accustomed to. Targets must be set for each environmental indicator, and regulations, taxes or other instruments applied to constrain economic activity within them.

Moreover in practice this is almost certain to require a fairly 'hands-on' approach to industrial policy. To make sustainability constraints workable (particularly very general ones like carbon dioxide emissions), governments may need to break them down into targets for specific sectors of the economy. These targets will no doubt have to be negotiated with the industries concerned; this might actually involve signing agreements on how and over what time period particular environmental impacts will be reduced, with support for the development of new technologies offered in return. The impact of environmental policies on employment, local communities and other factors will also need to be considered. The form (though not the content) of industrial policy in Japan, France and elsewhere may provide some helpful lessons here. The pioneering National Environmental Policy Plan adopted by the Dutch government in 1989 offers an even more instructive model.[7]

Such an increase in state activity may alarm those people, particularly Greens, whose broad political goal is a reduction, rather than an increase, in the role of the state. But it is difficult to see how environmental protection can be achieved otherwise. The alternative is to allow the invisible elbow to operate uncontrolled. It would be a happy coincidence indeed if all the individual, separately decided actions of producers and consumers caused combined environmental impacts that stayed within the sustainability boundary, with no more than friendly exhortation on the part of the state. They have not done so in the past; there is no reason to believe that they will now.

A Green might argue in response that the changes in behaviour should be voluntary, not coerced. People should be encouraged and educated to want a less materialistic and high-energy lifestyle rather than being forced to adopt one through state intervention. But this is hardly a realistic strategy in the face of the urgent crisis which presents itself today. The more people who choose a voluntary change in lifestyle the easier the transition to a Green economy will be: both individual and group activities which protect the environment should of course be encouraged. But we can hardly wait until these are universal choices.

In any case such an argument misses the point of the invisible elbow. Because individual actions cannot be taken in the full knowledge of what everyone else is deciding, and therefore what the collective effect will be, a voluntary approach to environmental protection is almost certainly doomed to fail. Even individuals who wish to make a voluntary choice need to know how to do this, which can only come from a centralised authority setting targets and guiding behaviour to meet them. Indeed the 'free rider' problem means that many individuals will (quite reasonably) not be prepared to change their own lifestyle for the sake of the environment unless they know that everyone else is doing so as well. If sustainability is collectively agreed and enforced, it may actually win wider approval than if it is expected to rely on merely individual choice.

In this sense democracy is fundamental to sustainability. It is in their role as citizens, not consumers, that individual people will create a sustainable economy. Only governments can take the necessary measures, which means that only through active pressure on governments (for example, from voluntary environmental groups) and through the power of the electoral system will the objective of sustainability be adopted. It is only if people have voted for sustainability, moreover, that governments will gain the authority to impose the collective constraints on individual action which environmental protection requires. No one should decry the contribution that changes in individual lifestyles can make; but it is through collective political choices that sustainability will be achieved.[8]

The environmental constitution

The importance of the state in environmental protection, however, raises an obvious question: which state? We have already observed in Chapter 8 that sustainability targets need to relate to an appropriate geographical area; it is clear that the planning process by which the targets are adopted and implemented must do the same. But here there is often a mismatch between political constitutions and what we might call the 'environmental constitution'. Some environmental problems are quite localised: lead pollution in the air, for example, or the reduction of green spaces in towns. Others, such as the greenhouse effect and acid rain, affect areas which cross governmental boundaries. Clearly we shall need planning for sustainability to take place not simply at the level of the nation-state, but at a whole series of scales, from the local to the global, appropriate to the variety of environmental indicators which must be targeted.

In fact the appropriate scale of government is likely to be different for the two stages of policy making. Whereas it is evident that targets for environmental indicators have to be set at least at the geographical scale of the environmental indicator itself, applying the instruments which will be used to achieve the target need not. Thus, for example, targets for carbon dioxide emissions must be set at a global scale: it is not much good one country cutting emissions if others do not. But once targets have been agreed, it is possible for each country, and even provinces or states within countries, to decide what instruments they will use to achieve the targets. It is not necessary for the regulations, taxes or other measures actually to be decided and imposed by an international government or agency.

Nevertheless, in some circumstances this may be desirable. There are a number of different principles which might be used to govern the choice of scale at which sustainability planning occurs. Which scale is chosen will depend on which principle is considered paramount.

The first principle is that of *democracy*. In this context democracy might usefully be defined as the placing of decision-making power, over any particular issue, in the hands of the people affected by it (or their elected representatives).[9] We have already observed that environmental problems tend to be cases of externality, in which people not involved in the causal transaction are nevertheless affected by it. Democracy consequently implies that, for any given problem, decision-making power should rest at the scale of government which most closely coincides with the geographical area over which people are affected. At a smaller scale than this, some people affected are excluded from the process. At a larger scale, others who are not affected influence the decision, while government becomes unnecessarily remote from the influence and understanding of ordinary people. The principle of democracy thus suggests that environmental policy should be conducted at the smallest scale possible consonant with the environmental problem in question.

Applying this principle would mean that for localised pollution problems environmental targets should be chosen and enforced at a local level. Each city government, for example, would be allowed to set its own atmospheric pollution standards, which could be higher or lower than those prevailing elsewhere. Each region or state government could set its drinking water standards, while nations could set their own targets for beach cleanliness.

Unfortunately, such an approach runs directly into conflict with the second principle, that of *equality*. This demands that people living in different areas should have the right to an equal level of environmental protection; people in a poorer area should not be penalised for their poverty by lower standards than those applied in a richer area, and visitors to 'foreign' localities should be able to expect the same standards they are used to at home. In practice equality tends to be accepted when people identify with the larger area. Thus most people would expect air pollution and drinking water standards to be the same throughout their own country; and where there is some identification with an international community, may well expect them to be equalised more widely. The adoption of common pollution standards throughout the European Community, for example, is now widely accepted, even though this removes decision-making power from nations and regions.[10]

A third principle, that of *the single market*, reinforces the need to adopt common policies internationally. Where there are no barriers to free trade, businesses will tend to move to wherever environmental standards are lowest. Since this will threaten jobs and income in countries or regions with higher standards, it puts a downward pressure on environmental protection and makes it difficult for those standards to be maintained. In this context – again, the European Community or a free trade area such as North America provide good examples – equality is necessary not only for the sake of poorer areas but also for that of richer ones.

Indeed it may well be that not only are common targets required but also common instruments. At present, the European Community imposes some ambient pollution standards on its member countries, but by and large leaves it to them to decide how to achieve the targets. In practice different countries are adopting quite different approaches (and timescales) for doing this. But this creates the problem that firms operating in the Community face different regulations (particularly waste emissions standards) and taxes in different parts of it, giving rise to different costs and prices. These effectively violate the common trading standards which are the point of the single market. Increasingly, therefore, we can expect pressure to be brought to bear on the Community to 'harmonise' not just environmental targets but regulations and financial incentives as well.

Without such harmonisation it will almost certainly be impossible to control the activities of transnational corporations, which dominate world trade and which also frequently have the largest environmental impacts. Where companies can switch their activities from country to country, national economic and environmental policies will often be incapable of exercising the required influence over them; only supranational regulation may be able to do so.[11]

As harmonisation occurs, environmental policy in the Community is likely to become increasingly federal in nature. That is, it will involve different aspects of policy being decided and executed at different scales of government, from the local and regional through the national to the supranational. Which targets and which instruments are applied at which levels will be decided – at least in theory – according to the three principles we have outlined. Given the pressures of the single market, a likely trend is that power to decide targets and instruments will be transferred upwards to the Community as a whole, while the desire for democratic control will lead to the execution and enforcement of policy being transferred downwards to regional and local government. (It should be noted that so far the Community has found it much easier to impose common regulations than common taxes or charges. These are widely regarded as the responsibility of nation-states in a way that regulations are not, although harmonisation of VAT is a clear goal.) If this happens, the pressure for the institutions of the European Community to be democratised, with more decisions being made by the European Parliament (in public) rather than the Council of Ministers (in secret), will surely increase.[12]

One casualty of this process may well be the notion of 'national sovereignty' – the idea that all political power is derived from within the boundaries of the nation-state. We do not live in one environment, marked off by political borders. We live in many, radiating outwards in concentric circles from where each person stands. As environmental issues touch the lives and interests of people in different circles, we can expect them to want to participate in the decisions which affect them. Some issues will be local, some national, some international. If externalities are to be turned into democratic choices, policy will need to be made on a corresponding scale. This will have implications, it seems likely, for political ideologies, for definitions of citizenship and for electoral systems.

International environmental agreements

On a world scale, we are a long way from a political system which reflects the environmental constitution. It will be some years yet before national governments give way to a global authority. So outside communities such as the EC in which sovereignty is formally pooled international environmental policy must inevitably be made by agreement between nation-states. Such policy will almost certainly be limited to target setting: only genuinely supranational bodies (like the EC) can introduce and enforce environmental instruments.

International targets need to be set not only for global atmospheric pollutants like carbon dioxide and CFCs, but for marine pollution and fish stocks in international waters, for forests which play a global role in carbon dioxide absorption, for water supplies crossing national boundaries and for species and habitats of particular importance for global biodiversity. Ideally it would be valuable also to set targets for resources which belong to individual nations but whose products are consumed on a global scale. These might include fossil fuels, minerals and soils. (In general, we may expect planning of resource sustainability to take place at a national level.)

The need for such global target setting is in fact now widely accepted. It forms the basis, to take the most notable example, of the 1987 Montreal Protocol on Substances that Deplete the Ozone Layer. The Protocol sets specific targets for reductions, by particular dates, in the production and consumption of the major ozone-destroying CFCs. It has been signed by over 60 countries, including all of the major industrialised ones, and was revised, with more stringent targets, in 1990. A similar agreement within the European Community, the 1988 Large Combustion Plant (LCP) Directive, sets complex and substantial reduction targets for sulphur dioxide and nitrous oxide emissions causing acid rain.[13]

Targets have also been proposed, by a number of international conferences and organisations, in relation to the greenhouse effect. The 1988 Toronto Conference on 'The Changing Atmosphere' called for a 20% reduction in carbon dioxide emissions worldwide by the year 2005. This was intended to achieve, it should be noted, not stabilisation of global climate, but a tolerable rate of change. Stabilisation would require a 50–80% reduction in global carbon emissions in this period, which is widely felt to be impractical.[14] Since then the European Commission has proposed a stabilisation of emissions by 2005; various individual countries have proposed other targets and timescales. A 'framework convention' on protection of global climate, similar to the one which preceded the Montreal Protocol on CFCs, is now being prepared under the auspices of the United Nations, with the hope (if not expectation) of binding protocols to follow.[15]

Getting international agreement on environmental targets, particularly for limiting greenhouse gas emissions, will be extremely difficult. All countries will have an incentive not to sign, since they can gain the benefits of the agreement (for example, reduced global warming) even if they don't participate. Moreover determining how a global limit is to be allocated between nations will provoke major arguments concerning the distribution of costs. In Chapter 15 we shall look at these questions in more detail, and how they might be solved.

For now it may be worth asking what should happen if international agreements for environmental targets – whether within the European

Community or on a wider scale – cannot be agreed. Should individual countries take unilateral measures? The case against is evident. If one country imposes regulations or taxes on its industries which are not imposed by other countries, the costs faced by domestic producers will rise in comparison with their foreign competitors. This fall in competitiveness may lead to reductions in export sales and increases in imports, with adverse consequences for jobs and incomes. Since many of the goods manufactured in industrialised countries and traded internationally are energy intensive (iron and steel products, machine tools, chemicals, etc.) increases in the price of energy caused by environmental taxation might have particularly significant effects.[16]

But this argument can be overstated. In the first place some environmental improvements may not actually cost money. Depending on how quickly new environmental controls come into force, and with what severity, they may actually lead to cost savings. This is especially true of many energy efficiency improvements and waste reduction measures.[17] Even where environmental measures do impose extra costs their impact on competitiveness may be small; certainly they may be outweighed by the impact of differential wage levels and interest rates or exchange rate fluctuations.

Perhaps more importantly, environmental measures can stimulate the development of new technologies which may not only increase resource productivity in their own right but may also give the country in question a technological lead in key environmental markets. These markets are likely to expand as other countries also raise environmental standards. In other words unilateral measures may in the long run improve rather than retard competitiveness. Several European countries, including Norway, Sweden and Germany, have taken unilateral measures, including some to limit carbon dioxide emissions, on this basis. Note that if unilateral measures are introduced, influential industries are forced to switch sides on the question of international agreements, becoming advocates (and lobbyists) in their favour rather than in opposition.[18]

Unilateral measures may also of course in themselves encourage other countries to impose similar measures, and may thus assist towards the formulation of international agreements. For these reasons, while clearly such agreements are desirable and should be strongly pursued, lack of progress towards them should not automatically be used as an excuse for inaction in any individual country.

11

Instruments for Environmental Protection

The four instruments

In the last chapter we outlined the four principal instruments by which economic activity can be constrained to meet environmental targets: voluntary mechanisms, regulation, government expenditure and financial incentives. In this chapter we shall explore these instruments in a little more detail. We shall focus on financial incentives, since these are in general the most unfamiliar, and their operation perhaps requires the most explanation. In Chapter 12 we examine the respective merits of regulations and incentives, which in many circumstances are the principal instruments available; and in Chapter 13 we explore the particular role of government expenditure. Chapter 14 suggests how consideration of social issues can be incorporated into environmental measures, and Chapter 15 looks at the international dimension. It isn't possible in a book of this length to propose definitive policies to deal with the myriad environmental problems facing the world today (even if these had been formulated). Rather, our purpose is the somewhat more modest one of suggesting the factors which might enter the debate.

Voluntary mechanisms

Voluntary mechanisms can be defined as all those actions unforced by law and unpersuaded by financial incentive, which individuals, groups and firms take to protect the environment. From voluntary recycling collections to organic vegetable growing on allotments, from green consumerism and consumer boycotts to trade union bargaining over occupational health, thousands of voluntary activities can and do contribute to an improved environment.

Often governments are entirely absent from these activities. But there are a number of ways in which encouragement can be given. First there is simple persuasion or exhortation. In some cases (such as the saving of water by households in a drought, or the prevention of litter in the countryside) this may indeed be the only practical tool available. In others, the small number of offenders and the coincidence of their own interests with those of the environment may make moral pressure sufficient. It is notable, for example, that the British government has not used any statutory powers to get the CFC manufacturers to cut production in line with the Montreal Protocol.[1]

Second, the provision of information can be a useful tool. Sometimes firms or consumers may simply be ignorant of cost-saving environmental measures. A UK Department of Trade and Industry report on waste minimisation, for example, has shown that many firms may be able to make substantial cost savings, and even find new sources of profit, by cutting down on waste. No additional incentives are required, only better knowledge of available technology, improved management methods and perhaps some degree of change in attitudes towards waste. Similarly, some households could make substantial cuts in their energy consumption by installing better domestic insulation (and could afford the initial costs) but are not aware of the possibility. In these instances, depending on the extent of the waste or energy saving target, information and persuasion can be useful, and even on occasion sufficient, instruments.[2]

Note that persuasion and the provision of information may themselves require use of other instruments. Firms may be forced to reveal the toxicity of chemicals or the content of pollution discharges by Freedom of Information legislation (and their doing so may then encourage others to take legal or campaigning action). They may be required to show energy efficiency data on electrical appliances by compulsory labelling. Persuading people to adopt energy conservation measures almost certainly requires government expenditure on advertising and educational campaigns.

The third type of encouragement governments can give to voluntary action is a change in the legal context. The United States' 'Superfund' legislation makes firms and landlords liable for the condition of their waste disposal sites even after they no longer use or have sold them. The threat of legal action has resulted in significant improvements in environmental care.[3]

The effectiveness of this threat can be amplified if firms can be taken to court not only by governments and other firms but by individuals and voluntary organisations. Effectively, the law can be used to give citizens 'environmental rights'. Several countries, including the United States, France, the Netherlands, Ireland and Brazil, allow their citizens to take violators of environmental standards to court directly. Both companies which do not comply with environmental regulations, and the government authorities which do not enforce them, can be prosecuted and compelled to repair the damage. Allowing such 'citizen suits' to be initiated not just by individuals directly affected by the environmental problem but also by pressure groups with an interest in the issue would give considerable extra backing to statutory environmental measures.[4]

In some cases it is possible to go further. In developing countries, in particular, an important instrument for environmental protection has been shown to be the transfer of ownership or control over environmental resources to local, poor families and communities. Whereas businesses may regard renewable resources such as fisheries and forests as expendable, since their time horizons are short and they can move elsewhere when the resource is exhausted, local people are likely to regard the environment as a source of long-term survival, which therefore needs protection. Communal traditions and ethics can often ensure that a resource is not over-exploited, where a private profit motive may not.[5] Use of this instrument, of course, need not be confined to the South.

Regulation

In general voluntary mechanisms will be most useful as reinforcements for other instruments, rather than on their own. By far the largest number of environmental protection measures come into the category of regulations. This is in a sense a catch-all term, encompassing any administrative measure taken by government which has the backing of law, but does not involve either a direct financial incentive or direct government expenditure.

Regulations come in a variety of forms. Some are exercised through the planning system, such as land use control and building codes (for example, on insulation standards). In the field of consumer goods, regulations include such things as energy efficiency standards for domestic appliances and the requirement that all new cars must be fitted with catalytic converters. For industrial polluters, regulations tend either to specify permitted emission levels (volume, concentration, timing) of different pollutants, or require that certain pollution control technologies or product specifications are used. Fishing quotas, which set maximum catches of different fish, are a form of regulation applied to resource depletion.

To the firm or consumer, regulations offer no legal choice. Pollution or resource use above the consented level or through use of unsanctioned technology (or whatever) is simply forbidden. The cost of non-compliance is judicial punishment: a fine or sometimes imprisonment. This means that enforcement and punishment are crucial. Where enforcement is difficult, or where the level of punishment is too low, the environmental target may not be achieved.

Regulation continues to be the most favoured method of pollution control throughout the world. The scope for regulation is enormous: Southern California's Air Quality Management Plan comprises 5,500 pages of regulations intended to reduce smog levels. They range from a prohibition on the use of barbecue lighter fuels to the compulsory adoption of 'car journey reduction plans' by all companies with over 25 employees. New York State has passed laws forcing people to separate household waste at source – with fines ranging from $25 to $500 for non-compliance. A police unit has been set up specifically to catch 'environmental criminals' who violate hazardous waste control laws.[6]

Government expenditure

There are two principal types of environmental expenditure: actions taken directly by government or state-owned bodies, and subsidies or grants provided by government to private organisations and households. These are generally categorised separately. Subsidies are usually classed as a form of financial incentive: they make an environmentally positive activity by a private firm or household cheaper. But often in practice it is only ownership which distinguishes a subsidy and direct government expenditure. If a precious habitat is on private land, government may protect it by offering the landowner a management subsidy. If the land is publicly owned the same measure will be described as direct government action.[7] Government expenditure directed towards private firms will be regarded as 'subsidy' if its take-up is voluntary (for example, general research and development grants for industry), but 'direct government action' if the programmes are centrally determined. There may be only a fine line between the two.

In this context it is the fact that the government is spending its own resources which is the significant feature. Regulations and financial incentives (as we have classified them) require polluters to pay for the environmental damage they cause. Both direct government actions and subsidies to private firms or households violate (or may violate) this 'polluter pays' principle. The cost of environmental protection is borne by the taxpaying community as a whole.

The principal arenas for government action are the utilities and general infrastructure. Public ownership has been widely accepted (at least until recently) where 'natural monopolies' exist, where there is a desire to keep natural resources in public hands or in cases of public goods. Moreover fields such as energy and water supply, the collection and treatment of waste, forest and river control and transport systems (including roads and public transport) offer the opportunity for large-scale changes in environmental impact. As we shall see later, it is precisely where large-scale changes are required that the other instruments may be insufficient, and where direct government action may therefore be necessary.

There are a number of different kinds of subsidy. Pollution abatement subsidies provide firms with incentives to reduce pollution. They may take the form of grants, soft loans or tax allowances. Subsidies can be offered either for a reduction in emissions below a set benchmark, or for research and investment in particular forms of pollution control technology. The first type are a poor tool: they encourage firms to maximise their discharges before the subsidy is introduced in order to raise their starting-point. Applied in conjunction with regulations or taxes, subsidies for research and development and for introducing new technology may be more appropriate, particularly to shorten the period in which a pollution target is reached or where firms might otherwise go out of business. In several countries, including Germany, France, Sweden and the Netherlands, such subsidies are funded out of pollution charges or are used to help firms comply with legal standards.[8]

Resource management subsidies may be provided to encourage good land management by private owners. In many countries agricultural producers are given grants or other subsidies to protect ecologically sensitive areas under their control. In the South, where vital environmental resources are often under the control of very poor people, subsidy is increasingly recognised as an important mechanism for environmental protection.[9] On a larger scale it will often be necessary for the North to subsidise poorer countries for the protection of globally important resources, such as tropical rainforests and wilderness areas.[10]

Another type of resource management subsidy is the support that may be given to collectors or producers of recycled or reused materials in order to encourage these activities. Such support is based on the recognition that the market price of non-virgin goods may be below the price which maximises the social and environmental benefits of their use. Subsidies to organic farmers have the same rationale.

Financial incentives

Just as subsidies reward environmentally positive behaviour, so financial incentives are designed to make environmentally damaging activities less attractive by making them more expensive. They thus use the price system to achieve environmental targets. (They are consequently sometimes known as 'market mechanisms'.)

Financial incentives can be understood as a way of literally 'internalising the externalities' of environmental damage. Such damage occurs, it can be argued, because firms and consumers don't pay the full costs of the things they make or buy. By raising the price of the damaging activity, say by levying a tax on it, they are made to pay the full cost. In theory, the tax levied on the activity or product should therefore equal the marginal (or additional) external cost it causes.[11]

Financial incentives are often associated with the techniques economists have developed to give environmental goods monetary values (see Chapter 17). If a money value could be placed on the external damage caused, the required tax could be calculated exactly. But this association is not necessary, and should not be a reason either for accepting or rejecting financial incentives. (Many environmentalists have appeared to oppose the use of incentives because they do not like the idea of placing monetary values on the environment.) An incentive can be applied without any valuation of the environmental damage it is intended to reduce. All that needs to be known is the relationship between the demand for the good or activity and its price. The tax is then levied at whatever rate will reduce demand by enough to achieve the environmental target set.

Excluding subsidies, there are essentially three types of financial incentive. *Taxes* and *charges* discourage undesirable behaviour by making it more expensive, simultaneously providing revenue to the government. *Tradable permits* make environmentally damaging activities illegal without a specially created right, which must be bought and can then be traded, thereby encouraging less damaging behaviour. *Refundable deposits* reward environmental care by returning the deposit and penalise damage by confiscating it.

Each of these types of incentive can be applied to the different stages of the industrial process: the extraction or management of resources, the inputs of production, the discharge and disposal of wastes, and consumption. Which stage is most appropriate depends on the nature of the environmental problem in question. In general, the earlier in the production process an incentive is applied, the easier it is to administer: there are usually fewer producers of a resource than there are users of it. So taxing the extraction of petroleum is a much simpler way of reducing carbon dioxide emissions than taxing car exhaust fumes. On the other hand, the later in the process the incentive is applied, the more accurately it can be 'targeted' at the (un)desirable activity. Taxing timber production in order to cut down on waste paper would not be very efficient. As we shall see below, administrative simplicity and efficient targeting may also have to be balanced against other principles such as the encouragement of public awareness (which suggests the use of consumer incentives) and equity.

Resources

Almost all financial incentives used currently – and most of the economic literature analysing them – are concerned with pollution. However a sustainable economy will also need to control the rate of resource depletion, both of renewable and non-renewable resources. Financial incentives will almost certainly be the most appropriate means of achieving sustainability in this field.

There are two principal methods. The first is a *resource depletion tax* (or 'severance' tax) levied on the extraction, harvest or import of the resource.[12] The tax is set at the rate which reduces extraction to the sustainable (or otherwise defined) level. By raising the price of all goods made with the resource, the tax encourages lower and more efficient use, conservation and (where possible) recycling. Although not related to depletion, resource taxes are already levied on certain raw materials, such as (in the UK) North Sea oil. It would be possible to apply them to other fossil fuels or to scarce metals.

The second method is a *resource depletion quota*. Here the annual output or harvest of the resource is fixed by the government (or equivalent authority) at the sustainable level. Extraction or import of the resource is illegal without sufficient permits. Ideally the permits are auctioned off to the highest bidder. Alternatively, where firms are already engaged in the industry, it may be more acceptable to give permits out in line with current production. In either case, the permits can then be traded in a competitive market. Since firms wishing to extract or import the resource (in the second case, above their initial allocation) have to buy permits as well as bear the costs of extracting the resource itself, they are effectively taxed on their output. Unlike depletion taxes, however, quotas ensure that the sustainable depletion rate is definitely adhered to, since the maximum output is fixed, and all fluctuation occurs in prices.[13]

Depletion quotas are particularly appropriate for renewable resources. They are used to control fishing catches, for example, in New Zealand. Here the permits are given out according to each fleet's current production. They are then bought back by the fishing authorities to reduce the total catch to the required level. This is effectively a subsidy rather than a tax, but it has the advantage of cutting output for the least cost, since the authorities buy permits back at the lowest price they can get. A similar system could be used for other renewable resources such as water and timber harvests, and could also apply to non-renewables.[14]

Pollution

The best known type of financial incentive to reduce industrial pollution is the charge or tax. There are two principal types.[15] Where it is possible to monitor discharges at the point of emission, *effluent charges* can be used. In a number of industrialised countries (among them France, West Germany, the Netherlands, Italy and Australia), firms pay charges according to the level of their polluting emissions to rivers and estuaries. In France sulphur dioxide emissions to the air are taxed. Solid and chemical waste is taxed in Belgium, Denmark, the United States and Australia; the Netherlands levies a charge on surplus manure. A number of countries, including the UK, levy noise pollution charges on aircraft, and the Netherlands has an industrial noise pollution tax as well.[16]

In theory pollution charges require that each firm's waste emissions are constantly measured. Moreover the rate of tax levied should be related not simply to the emission level but to the effect of those emissions on pollution. (In a river or estuary the effect of a given discharge can vary greatly according to the location of the factory, the time of day and year, water flows, etc.) In these ways the firm can be taxed in direct proportion to the damage it does to the environment. In practice, however, usually neither of these things occurs. 'Predetermined coefficients' (standard formulae agreed between the industry and the pollution control authority) are used to estimate emissions, with measurement only done for very large discharges. Little account is taken of variation in the recipient medium.

In fact many of the examples of effluent charges currently operating are levied at rates too low to provide incentives to better environmental behaviour. Their primary purpose, rather, is to raise revenue for government pollution control schemes. The money is either returned to firms as subsidies for pollution control equipment, or used to finance public treatment works and clean-up operations. One of the few to be geared towards changing behaviour is the Dutch water pollution charge. This appears to have had a considerable incentive effect. Emissions by the fourteen principal polluting industries fell by 50% between 1969 and 1975, a further 20% by 1980 and 10% to 1986.[17] If charge rates are high enough, the potential for cutting discharges is clearly substantial.

The second type of pollution tax is the *input charge*. Where waste discharges are widely dispersed, the responsibility of many thousands or even millions of polluters in many different locations, monitoring and taxing emissions directly may be very difficult. This is the case, for example, with the run-off of farm wastes containing concentrations of fertiliser nitrates, and with the emissions of carbon dioxide from cars, boilers and electricity generators.

In these instances it may be possible rather to tax the inputs which are the source of the pollution. Input charges can be placed, for example, on fertilisers containing nitrates, and fuels containing carbon. If the relationship between the input and the polluting output is fairly stable, this is likely to be an effective way of controlling the latter. Norway and Sweden levy charges in this way on the sulphur content of fuels to control acid rain emissions, and on pesticides as well as nitrate fertilisers.[18] (We shall return to the 'carbon tax' later.) Input charges can also be used to control pollution from toxic heavy metals such as mercury and cadmium, which tend to cause environmental damage however they are disposed of, and whose disposal tends to be very diffuse.

Another form of pollution control incentive is the *tradable pollution permit*. Operating on the same basis as resource depletion quotas, tradable pollution permits determine the total level of pollution by the allocation of 'permissions to pollute'. Pollution without the required number of permits is illegal. In currently operating systems the permits are usually given to firms according to their current discharges (a procedure quaintly known as 'grandfathering'), but they could in theory be auctioned.[19] Either way, they are then tradable between firms. For polluters with high costs of abatement it will be cheaper to buy permits than to reduce their emissions; polluters with low abatement costs will sell permits accordingly. Firms have a constant incentive to cut emissions, since this allows them to sell permits.

Tradable permits are now extensively used in the United States for air pollution control, with a variety of forms of 'emissions trading' allowed. Firms may trade permits with other firms in the same area ('offsetting'), or between their own discharge outlets ('netting' and 'bubbles'). They may also trade with themselves (as it were) over time, reducing emissions now in order to increase them later ('banking'). All trades are overseen by the Environmental Protection Agency. Limited use has also been made of tradable permits for water pollution control, for reducing the lead content in petrol and for reductions in CFC emissions.[20]

Tradable permits have one significant advantage over pollution charges. Unlike charges, permit systems can guarantee the achievement of particular pollution targets, because the authorities control the number of available permits. Moreover, if permits are leased rather than sold, the authorities are able to tighten the ambient targets by cutting the number of permits available. On the other hand, tradable permits have the disadvantage that they may allow very high discharges in some places, compensated by very low emissions elsewhere. This will often be unacceptable: they therefore usually have to operate with 'backstop' regulations setting maximum discharge rates. In general, the more closely pollution is controlled – by having different permits for different types of discharge in different places at different times – the 'thinner' trading is likely to be: this will reduce the incentive effect. Tradable permits are therefore most effective where there are a number of polluters, and for pollutants which are 'uniformly mixed', that is, which have the same environmental impact wherever they are discharged (for example, most sulphur, carbon and nitrous oxides).[21]

Consumption

The subsidies, charges and permits we have described so far apply to producers. Where pollution (or equivalent resource use) problems are caused more directly by consumer goods or activities, incentives can also be provided to change households' or firms' consumption behaviour.

Sometimes *consumer subsidies* are useful, particularly to encourage activities such as house insulation, where high initial costs prevent many people undertaking the investment even where they stand to make long-term savings. *Refundable deposits* on drink bottles and cans have a long history in most European countries and in several states in the US. They have been extremely successful in reducing waste and encouraging reuse and recycling. In Finland, for example, up to 90% of bottles are returned and the market share of non-returnable bottles is under 5%.[22] Deposits can also be applied to goods such as batteries, fridges and cars, whose uncontrolled disposal causes environmental problems.[23]

The principal consumer incentive, however, is likely to be the *consumption tax*. One type of consumption tax would be a modification of Value Added Tax, with higher rates charged for environmentally-damaging goods and lower ones for more benign products. However, since VAT is claimed back by industrial producers, charging it does not affect their behaviour. An 'environmental VAT' is therefore only appropriate for products which are mainly bought by households and are damaging in consumption or disposal (such as plastic bags).[24]

Where a consumption tax is intended to provide an incentive to both consumers and producers, it is more effective in the form of an excise duty, similar to the ones currently levied in most countries on tobacco and alcohol. Several European states levy environmental duties on lubricant oils, car fuels, non-returnable containers and cars, in the latter case differentiating between large and small engines.[25] We might call such a tax a Pollution Added Tax or PAT. Obviously, it must be levied on imports as well as on domestically-manufactured products.

The impact of PAT on consumer behaviour will depend to a large extent on the 'price elasticity of demand' of the taxed products.[26] The elasticity of demand for a product is a measure of the sensitivity with which demand reacts to a change in price. Products which are not essential, or which have close substitutes meeting the same needs, tend to be quite price elastic: a small rise in price will cause a large fall in demand, as consumers switch their purchasing behaviour. Demand for essential products with no close substitutes tends to be inelastic: since consumers have little choice, an increase in price hardly reduces demand at all.

Thus levying PAT on disposable toothbrushes would probably hit their sales quite hard, whereas an equivalent tax on, say, inorganically-grown potatoes would probably not (very few potatoes are grown organically). In many cases the effect of the tax will depend on the relationship between the taxed product and its substitute. Where the prices of the two products and the benefits they convey are very similar, taxing the environmentally-damaging one may cause a significant change in consumer behaviour. The experience of 'tax differentiation' of this kind between leaded and unleaded petrol (in comparison with the impact of higher petrol prices across the board) provides some evidence.

In these circumstances, it must be noted, the tax must be large enough to change the order of prices of the damaging and benign products. In the case of petrol, the prices of pre-tax leaded and unleaded were the same. This does not apply, however, in the case of batteries. Mercury-free batteries are less polluting but significantly more expensive than conventional batteries (which contain mercury). So the *level* of tax is crucial. A tax which raises the price of conventional batteries but keeps it below the price of mercury-free ones is unlikely to have very much effect. Since the two kinds of batteries are identical in performance, the consumer will have no incentive (other than the non-financial desire to protect the environment) to buy the benign product.[27] Only if the level of tax is sufficient to raise the price of the damaging product above the price of its substitute are consumers likely to make the switch.

If the tax is levied at such a rate, furthermore, the switch is likely to be total. Once the mercury-free battery is cheaper (and assuming that performance is indeed identical) consumers will have little incentive to buy the conventional type. In these circumstances, therefore, PAT would act more like a regulation than a financial incentive. Rather than rising rates of tax inducing a gradual reduction in demand, there would be very little reduction up to a certain point, and then almost a 100% fall thereafter. One might ask whether it would not be easier just to ban mercury batteries.

This problem will arise whenever the difference in (non-environmental) performance between the damaging good and its benign substitute is very small. Detergents perhaps offer another example. So long as phosphate-free detergents are more expensive than conventional ones (and no better at cleaning) few consumers will have a financial incentive to use them, even if the conventional ones are taxed. As soon as the tax is sufficient to change the order of prices, however, a large-scale switch can be expected.[28]

PAT will be more effective when there are differences other than price in the performance of the taxed and untaxed substitutes. Thus for example placing different duties on cars with differently sized engines can be expected to change behaviour in a more graduated fashion. As small cars have many advantages in their own right (such as being cheaper), any change in relative prices caused by a tax is likely to shift consumption towards them, and the greater the differential, the greater the shift likely. Similarly, since energy efficient appliances ultimately save consumers money, even a small change in price relative to conventional equipment is likely to induce some consumers to make the investment; and the cheaper conservation becomes, the greater the investment which can be expected.

All this assumes, of course, that it is easy to assess products for their 'environment-friendliness'. In fact the difficulties of comparing the environmental impact of different goods are immense. A crucial issue is how far back in the production chain the assessment goes: a product may involve little pollution in its own manufacture, but be made of materials which cause considerable degradation in theirs. For this reason, it may well be worth limiting the criteria for consumption taxes to environmental impacts caused *by the products themselves*, rather than the impacts of their manufacture. This will not eliminate the problems of assessment, but it may reduce them.

Six criteria might then be used:

(1) Pollution generated in use or on disposal. This would cover products such as petrol, CFC-using goods, detergents and batteries (while noting the comments made above).
(2) Energy consumption in use, for powered goods. Standards would need to be identified for fridges, washing machines and other appliances. Cars could be differentially taxed according to engine size or other features. Houses could attract differential mortgage tax relief according to their energy efficiency.

(3) Durability. This would cover products designed to be thrown away, such as disposable razors, those deliberately designed so as to be 'unrepairable', and products designed for long life.
(4) Recycled materials content. This would cover products made of recycled paper, wood, metals, etc.
(5) 'Recyclability' or 'reuseability'. This would cover goods such as bottles and containers designed for reuse.
(6) Biodegradability. This would be applied in particular to plastic products.

The first two might be described as 'negative' criteria, the last three as 'positive'. Durability is both: a product designed to be thrown away is particularly damaging; a long-lasting one particularly benign.

Administratively, it would be simplest to levy PAT only on the negative criteria. Most goods, without particular negative environmental impacts, would be zero-rated, but throwaway, non-biodegradable, other types of polluting and high energy consuming goods would all attract PAT, perhaps in varying bands according to the magnitude of the damage caused. The problem with this, however, is that, unless the 'damaging' and 'benign' goods were substitutes, it would not give any incentive to the latter (for example, long-lasting goods or those made of recycled materials).

Two mechanisms might provide such an incentive. It might be possible to rate goods not simply according to their own absolute impact, but according to their *relative* impact in comparison with a substitute good on the market. The more damaging good would then attract a positive PAT while the more benign one was zero-rated. If an 'even more environmentally benign' substitute came on the market, the PAT ratings of each of the existing goods would rise. This would encourage firms constantly to look for ways to reduce their PAT rating by improving their environmental impact – though it would no doubt generate much argument as to how goods should be compared.

Alternatively, benign goods could be encouraged through other means, such as a zero VAT rating. In the UK several goods such as food, books and children's clothes are already zero-rated on social grounds. As well as environmentally-benign goods, services such as repair and reconditioning could also be zero-rated. (It should perhaps be noted that in European Community countries this method would go against the grain of current proposals to harmonise VAT.)

The principal objection to PAT is that it could be administratively very cumbersome, with a large number of goods having to be assessed for environmental impact. Presumably the authorities would only have to seek out 'damaging' goods, as 'benign' ones would be drawn to their attention by the manufacturers. Firms would apply to have their goods lower-rated by proving 'environmental friendliness', in the same way that goods must currently be demonstrated to comply with design standards.

Apart from PAT, a variety of other forms of consumption tax can be devised, on consumption activities as well as goods. 'Road pricing' is an example: car drivers can be charged for driving in central urban areas where they cause congestion and pollution. This may be a standard charge (for example, a 'supplementary licence' required for a particular zone) or, using new technology, the charge can vary according to the time, district and traffic conditions.[29] Other forms of consumption activity tax include entrance charges for scenic areas which suffer degradation through overuse.

Consumption taxes have three significant advantages over other instruments of pollution control. Since they are levied on the final good in the market, they do not affect industrial competitiveness between nations. Imports are taxed in the same way as domestically-produced goods, while exports are not. They may therefore be easier for one country to introduce unilaterally than other measures. They are also able to distinguish between different end uses in a way that instruments applied earlier in the production process are not. Taxes levied on paper producers, for example, are likely to raise the prices of all types of paper use. Consumption taxes would enable a government, if it so wished, to differentiate between uses of paper regarded as of different value, say by making newsprint less expensive than packaging. Lastly, consumption taxes are more 'public' than controls applied to industrial producers. This is likely to stimulate public awareness of the environmental costs of consumption. On the other hand, the very 'obviousness' of consumption taxes may generate resentment at the price increases they cause!

Tax revenues

All of the taxes we have mentioned, along with auctioned tradable permits, generate revenue for the government. There is then an important issue of what happens to this revenue. It might be thought that there wouldn't be any, since the purpose of the tax is to reduce the pollution (or resource depletion) to the acceptable level, and at that level no tax would be payable. But this in fact is not how incentive taxes work. Even when the acceptable level is reached there is still a revenue, because the tax is paid on all the damaging activity, not just the proportion which exceeds that level.[30]

A number of uses (not mutually exclusive) might be made of this revenue. First, in the case of pollution charges, part of it could be returned to the polluting firms. Although this might seem strange, it is in fact merely a recognition of the observation just made, that polluters are charged more than it costs to reduce pollution to the acceptable level. Such redistribution occurs in most of the European systems of pollution charging, with the specification that redistributed sums must be spent on pollution control equipment.

Second, environmental tax revenues could be 'earmarked' by the state for expenditure on environmental protection and enhancement measures. Again this is done in the continental water charge systems, with funds going specifically to public investment in water treatment. Income from the Swedish taxes on fertilisers and pesticides is similarly used for research into more environmentally-sensitive agriculture.[31] Such earmarking or 'hypothecation' tends to be disliked by government treasuries, since it reduces the flexibility of expenditure, but it may be very important when the costs of meeting environmental standards are very high. In Britain, television and road fund licences provide existing precedents. Hypothecation carries the advantage that those paying charges can clearly see what they are paying for: this may assist public acceptance. We shall discuss the hypothecation of environmental taxes in more detail in Chapters 13 and 14.

Third, the revenues could be used to compensate people whose environments remain damaged by residual pollution. It is likely that however the 'acceptable' levels of pollution are decided, certain communities will face higher local costs than others, for example those living near chemical factories or landfill sites. It may be appropriate that they should be compensated, perhaps in the form of lower local taxes, or even in extreme cases as direct grants to households.

Fourth, revenues may be used specifically for income redistribution, either by increasing welfare benefits or by reducing the income tax paid by the poor (or both). Alternatively, revenues may be used to subsidise environmental improvements (such as energy efficiency) made by poor households. These measures would all go some way towards offsetting the regressive effects of higher prices likely to result from environmental taxes. We shall discuss this further in Chapter 14.

The fifth use of revenues is simply to add to the general public purse, without specific earmarking. If the revenues were large it would then almost certainly be necessary to reduce other forms of taxation. Any environmental tax can be made 'revenue neutral' – that is, can leave total government income unchanged – if other taxes, for example VAT or corporation tax, are reduced by equivalent amounts.

A number of environmentalists have indeed proposed that a larger proportion of government revenue should derive from environmental taxes.[32] Within the neoclassical framework it is generally argued that taxes on income and expenditure reduce economic efficiency, 'distorting' the choices that firms and households might otherwise make. By contrast environmental taxes improve efficiency, since they internalise what would otherwise be distorting externalities. Their revenues therefore have a beneficial impact not only when they are spent but in their collection. Given that all economic activities require energy, and the use of fossil energy at least is easily measured, some writers have suggested that a tax on energy should therefore become the principal source of government revenue, largely replacing other taxes.

This argument, however, needs to be approached with caution. In the first place, it is very unwise to make governments dependent for their revenue on an activity which one wants to reduce. It gives them a very strong incentive *not* to encourage its reduction. This phenomenon may be observed with respect to the taxation of tobacco, which is one of the easiest ways of collecting very large sums of money. For all their public pronouncements to the contrary, few governments really want people to give up smoking. Environmentalists who wish to cut energy consumption should be wary of giving governments strong arguments against doing so.

Secondly, it is widely accepted that the fairest basis for taxation is ability to pay. But energy and other kinds of resource consumption are not necessarily well correlated with income. Many firms may be very profitable, and individuals very rich, despite relatively small resource consumption. (Those in the financial sector provide the obvious examples.) Tax bills based on energy or resource use will then cease to reflect ability to pay; considerable social inequalities, as well as possibly undesirable shifts in economic activity, are likely to result.

A stronger case can be made for a more limited substitution of energy for labour taxation. At present, in the UK for example, companies are taxed (through National Insurance contributions) on the number of employees they have. If employers' NI contributions were abolished and replaced by a tax on energy use, the incentive for firms to employ people would rise, and energy conservation measures (rather than labour conservation ones!) would simultaneously be encouraged. Energy is actually less avoidable than labour and so would provide a stronger core of revenue. Since the process of automation effectively replaces labour with fossil energy use (part of it embodied in machines) replacing labour with energy taxes would seem particularly appropriate. Such a switch would have to be introduced gradually over a period, with a variety of schemes to ease adjustment, but both the social and environmental benefits might prove worth the cost.

12

Regulations versus Financial Incentives?

The 'polluter pays' principle

Having described the instruments which can be used to achieve environmental targets, we now need to ask which are most appropriate to use in which circumstances.

It can be said immediately that there will almost always be a role for voluntary mechanisms. The provision of information and encouragement of voluntary changes in behaviour, the extension of liability for environmental damage and the establishment of individual and collective 'environmental rights', are not substitutes for but complements to the more directive instruments. They will be useful whatever other mechanisms are employed. As society grows in general more aware of, and concerned about, the environmental crisis, we may indeed expect to see consequent changes in social behaviour, as the growth of 'green consumerism' perhaps shows. One obvious possibility, for example, is the development of a more collective consumerism, in which organised groups use their purchasing power in a political way to influence the environmental behaviour of companies.[1] Another is the emergence of a more environmentally-oriented trade unionism, in which concern for occupational and public health is placed higher up the bargaining agenda.[2] There is evidently considerable scope for the use of environmental rights as a means for citizens to enforce environmental standards.

Nevertheless, it must be recognised that the majority of environmental changes will come about primarily through the use of direct instruments of government policy. What then are the respective roles for regulations, financial incentives and government expenditure? As we noted in the last chapter, there is an important distinction between the first two instruments and the third. Both regulations and financial incentives make the polluter or degrader of the environment pay for the damage caused (or for preventing it), whereas government expenditure spreads the cost across the wider community. Public spending therefore violates the 'polluter pays' principle: those effectively forced to pay include many who may not be responsible for the

149

problem at all and others whose contribution to it may be smaller than their required tax contribution.

There is an exception. If government expenditure on a particular type of environmental improvement is funded wholly out of revenues raised by taxing those responsible for the damage, then the 'degrader pays' principle is maintained. In some cases, such as sewage and water treatment, it may be much more efficient for the government to remedy the problem than for each individual firm or household to do so. Then it will be perfectly reasonable to set a pollution charge and use the money received to pay for the treatment service. This is indeed commonly done in the case of sewage; most European pollution charges for emissions into rivers are also designed and used in this way. If, to take another example, government expenditure on protecting national parks were funded completely from the proceeds of entrance fees, there would equally be no violation of the degrader pays principle (though there no doubt would be violation of other principles, such as equality of access to the national heritage).

The polluter or degrader pays principle has been widely accepted since its formal definition by the Organisation for Economic Cooperation and Development (OECD).[3] It is intuitively attractive, embodying the idea that environmental externalities should be internalised by those who cause them. It may indeed be thought of in terms of property rights. If the degrader must pay to degrade, the 'ownership' of the environment is clearly vested in the community as a whole. Citizens have a right to enjoy an undegraded environment and polluters must pay for the privilege of using it. By contrast if the community must pay to preserve the environment, it effectively 'belongs' to the polluters, who can degrade it with impunity. There is evidently an important philosophical and political difference here.[4]

The principle also plays an important role in international trade relations. By accepting it, countries agree that they will not try to undercut one another's exports by subsidising polluters. If one state forces its companies to pay for their own pollution control, while another pays for it on their behalf (or simply allows the environment to be degraded), the firms from the second country will have a competitive advantage. The likely consequence then is that all countries will feel required to subsidise their exporters, leading to a 'beggar-my-neighbour' spiral of upward bidding which benefits only the companies. In the long run it is better if all countries make the polluter pay.

The polluter pays principle does not mean, it should be noted, that the consumer does not pay. It is sometimes supposed that making the polluter pay is a way of punishing companies *instead of* consumers. This is false. Almost always, if firms face added costs, they will pass at least some of these onto consumers in higher prices.[5] This should not be regarded as unfair, either. However unwitting, consumers of products whose manufacture degrades the environment are themselves effectively polluters. If they did not buy the products, the degradation would not occur. It is therefore reasonable that they should pay part of the cost of preventing or clearing up their externalities. It is the *victims* of degradation who should be spared the cost, not its causers.

The polluter pays principle should not always govern the choice of instrument, and in the next Chapter we shall discuss the circumstances under which government expenditure can be justified. But in general it is a useful presumption. This makes regulations and financial incentives the main tools of environmental policy. We may therefore ask, first, about their relative merits. What criteria might be used to choose between them?

Instruments and Ideology

There has been a long-running debate between those who favour regulations to control environmental behaviour (by and large, these have been the regulators themselves, as well as most environmentalists) and advocates of the incentive approach (mainly economists). In general this debate has been useful, with the existing system, principally based on regulations, subjected to intensive scrutiny on a number of different grounds. Unfortunately, one aspect of the debate has not been helpful, and it is as well to eliminate it before we go any further.

This is the claim that there is an intrinsic ideological difference between the regulatory and incentive approaches. Because environmental taxes use the mechanism of the market to change behaviour, they are often said to be the 'free market' solution to environmental problems, and therefore politically right-wing. In this view regulations, which use the law, are 'left-wing'.[6] This is nonsense. Both taxes and regulations operate within markets; they are both state interventions designed to influence the behaviour of otherwise autonomous firms and consumers. Neither has anything to do with the 'free market': on the contrary, if such a thing existed both would be seen as its enemy. Incentives and regulations are *both* designed to change the 'free' decisions which would be made in their absence.

The language used here is important. We have deliberately avoided the ambiguous term 'market-based mechanisms' which is often used for financial incentives. It is true that incentives *use* the workings of the market, unlike regulations. But this does not mean that only incentives work in markets, while regulations somehow abolish them. The label 'command and control', which economists and others now commonly use to mean regulation, is even more unhelpful. The intention is evidently to give the impression of a draconian bureaucracy coercing powerless firms and consumers. But this only goes to show that it is the label, not the instrument, which should not be used. There is in fact no particular reason why either regulations or incentives should be favoured a priori by left or right (or by economists); the choice between them should be made, more rationally, on how well they meet the objectives set.

Indeed there is little sense in choosing either one or the other approach in general. Different instruments will be appropriate for different circumstances; they can even be used together. This is in fact how incentives in practice are usually applied, with taxes or marketable permits being backed up by regulations setting maximum discharge rates or technological standards.

It is also unhelpful to compare regulations and financial incentives in terms simply of theoretical neoclassical models of economic behaviour, as is too often done. Not only do such models fail to represent the complexity of the real world, in which 'institutional' factors crucially affect corporate and consumer decision-making; they also ignore the wealth of evidence of actual experience which is now available. Empirical analysis of how different instruments have actually worked in practice is likely to provide more useful information than purely abstract argument.

We can identify five criteria by which regulatory and incentive instruments can be compared. First, we may ask about the instrument's *effectiveness*. How certainly does it achieve the environmental target set? How quickly? Is it flexible if circumstances change? Second, there is the question of *motivation*. Does the instrument provide a continuing incentive for firms and consumers to reduce their environmental impact? Does it encourage innovation in the development of less damaging technologies? Third, what is the instrument's *administrative cost* to the government authority which must implement it? Fourth, how *efficient* is it? By this is meant, how much does it cost the complying firms or consumers to meet the required standard? Other things being equal, the lower the cost the better. And last, how *politically acceptable* is the instrument likely to be? This will involve questions about liberty and fairness as well as more pragmatic considerations concerning the ease with which the instrument can be introduced.

One other criterion is also very important. This is the instrument's *distributional* impact. Who will bear the cost of the environmental improvement achieved? Will the poor or the rich pay proportionately more? These questions will obviously have a bearing on political acceptability. But they do not distinguish regulations and financial incentives in general. The distributional effects of any instrument will depend on its precise form and the conditions under which it is introduced. These issues therefore deserve more detailed discussion, which we shall reserve for Chapter 14.

Effectiveness

As the objective of a sustainable environmental policy is to meet ambient environmental targets, the most important criterion for any instrument is that it can achieve the targets set with a reasonable degree of certainty and speed. In this respect regulations and tradable permits generally score over taxes.

However environmental charges are designed, they cannot be guaranteed to meet the pollution or depletion target. For the charge-setting authority to be able to predict exactly how firms or households will react to different charge rates would require an immense amount of information on industrial costs and demand curves, which would be very expensive as well as difficult to collect. In any case economic actors may not behave in the way predicted because of inertia, ignorance or other 'institutional' factors. It is very unlikely therefore that any given charge will meet its target in the first instance. It is possible to adjust the charge annually until the pollution standard is reached ('iterating') but the cost to firms in doing so could be very high, especially if one year's charge has led to particular investment or sales decisions which are then invalidated. The uncertainty which iterating creates is also likely to impede investment.

By contrast, regulations and tradable permits can lay down the ambient standard that will be reached, and force prices to adjust in consequence. This will be particularly advantageous, it should be noted, when output is expanding. Under a tax regime (unless the tax rate is raised to compensate) expansion will cause pollution to increase, whereas a fixed permit allocation forces an improvement in environmental efficiency (pollution per unit of output) instead. (Not all regulations, of course, actually do set ambient standards: those based on technological criteria also allow pollution to increase when output expands.)

Taxes may be more effective than regulations in reaching an environmental target (other than zero) where it is consumers' rather than producers' behaviour which needs to be controlled. Given the number of users of consumer products – for example, paper – it is very difficult to design a regulation which reduces consumption without actually eliminating it altogether. By contrast, by changing its price a tax can change a product's consumption by variable amounts.

In two circumstances regulations are more effective than either taxes or permits. The first is when the environmental target for some activity or good is zero. Only regulation – an outright legal prohibition – can ensure that such a target is met. Taxing dangerous pesticides or imports of endangered species, for example, would almost certainly allow some level of activity, however low.

Second, if the goal of policy is to reduce an environmentally damaging activity quickly, regulations will generally be more useful. Incentives are likely to take longer to introduce, and reaction to them will usually be slower. The threat of illegality is generally more effective in changing behaviour in the short term than a rise in price. Where an incentive already exists, changing its level (the charge rate or number of permits) may or may not be easy, depending on the administrative system under which it operates. The flexibility of different instruments when circumstances change will depend on this.

Motivation

By contrast, financial incentives have a clear advantage over regulations in their motivational effect. Under a regulatory system firms and consumers usually have no incentive to reduce their damaging environmental behaviour below the permitted level. But in a tax or tradable permit system, all reductions cut the tax bill. Such instruments thus provide a continuing motivation to reduce damaging impacts, even below the target set.

In this sense financial incentives can be described as 'technology forcing'. At least in theory, they encourage firms constantly to innovate in pollution control techniques, both for their own emissions and in the consumer goods they make. Regulations actually tend to do the opposite. Not only do they provide no incentive to improve on the current or prescribed technology, but any innovations a firm might make are likely to be seized on by the regulatory authorities as a reason to raise environmental standards, thereby forcing higher costs. Rather than being developed, therefore, innovations may well be hidden.

In practice institutional inertia within firms makes innovation less likely than the theory suggests.[7] Nevertheless, this general advantage of incentives over regulation should not be underestimated. Technological innovation is the key to raising environmental efficiency. Although standards can be tightened when new technologies are developed, regulatory authorities rarely discover new processes and techniques themselves. It is therefore very important that firms are given incentives to do so.

Administrative cost

It is often supposed that financial incentives are simpler, and therefore cheaper to administer, than regulations. Instead of the complexities of framing laws and enforcing criminal penalties, taxes simply need collecting. This argument is mistaken. Taxes require laws too, and any complexity involved in drawing up regulations (for example, establishing allowable volumes, concentrations, location and timing of discharges, or setting standards for consumer goods) have to be mirrored in the schedules for taxation or design of permits. Financial incentives need as much monitoring and enforcement as regulation (tax evasion is as illegal as non-compliance with regulations); indeed, the measurement of emissions or 'pollution content' for taxation may be considerably more onerous. The additional information-giving and persuasive functions of regulators are just as necessary under tax systems, with the added function of tax collection. If the transactions allowed by tradable permits have each to be monitored by the regulatory agency (as in the US) the administrative costs can be particularly high.[8]

Almost certainly, therefore, the bureaucratic implications of incentives are as great, if not greater, than those of regulatory mechanisms. Of course, any change in a system is expensive; this certainly counts against incentives where they are not currently used. But it is worth noting that in this regard tradable permits would be easier to introduce than charges, since they are effectively the same as regulatory consents, merely adding the element of tradability to create the incentive effect.

Efficiency

Most environmental economists have regarded efficiency as the principal criterion for choosing between instruments; most policy makers and enforcers have not.[9] Nevertheless it is clearly an important objective. As the environmental crisis gets worse, sustainability – or even a lesser objective – is certain to require a considerable tightening of environmental standards. The costs of meeting them will correspondingly rise. Minimising these costs is likely to make the targets more acceptable. It will also save resources for other purposes. The more efficient the mechanisms used to reach a given target, the less prices will rise and the more society can spend on other objectives.

Where the cost of reducing environmental damage varies between firms, it is easy to prove theoretically that price incentives are more efficient than regulation.[10] In the case of pollution, for example, the least-cost solution arises where those for whom cutting emissions is relatively cheap cut them further than those for whom it is more expensive. Under a regulatory system this will not occur: all firms have to cut to a given standard (or introduce the same technology) irrespective of cost. But with pollution charges or tradable permits high-cost firms will prefer to pay the tax while low-cost firms will prefer to cut their emissions. The end result will be a lower total expenditure to meet the same standard.[11]

Studies of financial incentives in practice go some but not the whole way to supporting this conclusion. Since most current pollution charges are not primarily intended to provide incentives, evidence of their efficiency is thin. However the German system of water pollution charges was calculated (in advance of its introduction) to save about one-third of the costs of the previous regulatory system. Evidence from the tradable permit system used for air pollution in the United States suggests that, up to 1985, emissions trading had yielded savings of approximately $4.5 billion.[12]

But other evidence suggests that financial incentives may not always be more efficient than regulations. The efficiency case for incentives derives from the neoclassical theory which assumes that firms aim to maximise profit, and that they have access to perfect information on the options facing them. But these assumptions may not be correct.

For a number of reasons, particularly associated with the ignorance and inertia of management, firms often do not minimise their costs. Managers may not know their 'marginal cost' curves (that is, how their costs vary with output), may not appreciate how the charging system operates, and may be unaware of or not willing to invest in new pollution control techniques. If pollution charges are a small percentage of total costs, managers may also not regard this particular area of cost minimisation as a priority.[13]

Non-profit-maximising behaviour of this sort has been identified in a number of contexts. A study of sewage discharge fees in Britain, for example, showed that increases of up to 400% over a five-year period failed to induce changes in behaviour by the majority of firms, despite the fact that in some cases alternative technology was available which would have led to financial savings within a year. The main reason was lack of information; around a third of firms didn't even understand how the charging system worked![14] This indicates that at the very least price incentives need to be accompanied by information-giving and persuasion on the part of pollution inspectors. But it may also suggest that regulations, which enforce 'rational' (profit-maximising) economic behaviour, can actually cost less than the equivalent incentives.

Efficiency in the market for energy

This is perhaps most clearly demonstrated in the field of energy. Given the importance of this field, it is worth looking at the arguments in some depth.

It is often argued that the most efficient way of encouraging energy conservation is to raise its price. Energy could be taxed in a number of ways; one of the most widely canvassed is the so-called 'carbon tax', levied on fossil fuels in proportion to their carbon content. Since coal contains the most carbon per tonne, it would bear the tax most heavily, followed by oil and gas, which (in carbon terms) is the 'cleanest' fossil fuel. The aims of such a tax would be to encourage a lower general consumption of energy (especially through investment in energy efficiency measures) and to encourage 'fuel switching', in particular from coal and oil to gas, and from fossil to non-fossil sources.[15]

Neoclassical environmental economic theory suggests that such a tax would reduce carbon dioxide emissions at the lowest total cost to society, since those who could cut energy consumption most cheaply would do so rather than pay more for energy, while those facing higher reduction costs would find it more profitable to pay the extra. But this assumes that the market for energy is itself 'efficient'; that is, energy suppliers and consumers behave in such a way as to maximise their profits. Unfortunately, this is not the case.

First, energy conservation measures are undertaken by different economic actors at different 'discount rates'. In this context the discount rate is a measure of the timescale within which an investor wishes to recoup the cost of his or her investment. Cutting energy use usually requires some kind of investment in energy efficiency equipment or materials (for example, a more efficient machine or building insulation); this will have an up-front cost. Over time the investment will pay for itself, as it reduces day-to-day energy consumption. Whether it is worth making the investment then depends on how quickly the firm or household wishes to get its money back. Generally energy utilities have rather low discount rates: they are prepared to wait five to ten years, say, before an investment starts to earn net profit. But ordinary, smaller companies may require pay-back periods of only two or three years, while households, particularly poorer ones, may simply not have the cash to make the investments at all.

Clearly, the most efficient outcome for society as a whole will occur if as much energy efficiency investment as possible is the responsibility of the utilities, since with lower discount rates than firms and households they will invest in far more measures. Society will therefore save more money. But getting such investment undertaken by the utilities is not a matter of increasing the price of energy, as the carbon tax proposes. We know it isn't, because at the typical utility discount rate (10%) many energy efficiency investments are *already* profitable at the current price of energy. These investments include efficient appliances and lighting, cooking and heating improvements and small-scale and industrial combined heat and power (CHP) generation. In other words, if all these investments were the responsibility of the utilities instead of individual firms and consumers, they would already be undertaken. Indeed, it has been estimated that the UK could cut its projected carbon dioxide emissions for 2005 by approximately 170 million tonnes, or two-thirds of the Toronto target, by such measures – measures, that is, which at this discount rate wouldn't cost society anything at all.[16]

The reason the utilities do not make these investments is nothing to do with the price of energy. It is that the historical structure of the energy market has created a very small number of large utilities whose role is to supply energy, and whose profitability is increased by supplying ever more of it. The utilities are simply not structured to supply energy efficiency investments, even though these could be profitable. Indeed in Britain the way in which utilities are regulated effectively forbids them from doing so, being based on a pricing formula which precludes the possibility of recouping efficiency investment costs.[17]

This leaves such investments as the responsibility of individual firms and households. These actors not only have higher discount rates; they also have much more difficulty getting hold of the information and expertise required to make the appropriate investments. The market for energy supply has a limited number of products (types of energy available) and a very small number of suppliers, so it offers very simple choices for consumers. By contrast the market for efficiency investments (alternative appliances, insulation, CHP equipment, etc.)

is fragmented among a large number of suppliers with a great variety of products, about which unbiased consumer information is very difficult to obtain. It is hardly surprising that such investments are often not made.

The most efficient way to change these structural features of the energy market is not to increase the price, but to regulate the utilities so that they are forced to adopt the 'least cost' ways of providing energy – whether this is by saving watts or supplying them. This 'least cost planning' approach has been taken in several parts of Canada and the United States, with the result that as well as energy the utilities are now selling consumers a variety of energy conservation technologies. Indeed in order to overcome the problem of high consumer discount rates, insulation or new equipment is often installed free, with the cost recouped in the price of energy then supplied. The pricing formulae governing the utilities have been changed (again, by regulation) to enable the utilities to recoup their investment costs.[18]

The second obstacle preventing the market for energy from being 'efficient' is the so-called 'landlord–tenant' problem. In many cases the responsibility for undertaking energy conservation investments is separated from the responsibility for paying energy bills. Thus loft insulation, double glazing and so on are the responsibility of landlords, but it is their tenants who pay the bills. The landlord then has little incentive to make the investments, while the tenant often can't.[19] A similar separation occurs in the building design and construction stage. Architects, designers and builders are ideally situated to ensure the highest standards of energy efficiency, but often have no direct financial incentive to do so. Clearly, higher energy prices (from a carbon tax) would not alter this situation; regulations insisting on certain efficiency standards could do so. It is almost always cheaper to introduce efficiency measures in the construction phase rather than 'retrofitting'; and the universal nature of regulations increases the economies of scale for conservation equipment and installation, so reducing costs.

The third reason why the market for energy does not work as the neoclassical theory assumes is 'imperfect information', as we have already remarked. Neither firms nor households may know what savings can be made and how. It is true that the incentive to find out increases as the cost of energy rises; but it is also likely that various regulations could provide the information more cheaply. Such regulations might include compulsory energy labelling of appliances and compulsory 'energy audits' (assessments of energy use and conservation possibilities) for firms and on houses for sale. Regulations of these types are already in force in many parts of the US and in some European countries.

Lastly, even after all these measures have been implemented, there may still be a problem. This is that energy consumers may not behave 'rationally' according to the assumptions of the neoclassical theory. That is, even if they know about the available efficiency measures, they may not maximise their profits. Such 'irrational' behaviour may occur for a number of reasons. For many energy consumers, both firms and households, energy may constitute a small proportion of total expenditure, and therefore not be subject to detailed scrutiny. A large number of consumers pay bills by direct debit, so the amounts are effectively invisible. In many large companies and organisations, responsibility for making investments rests in one department while bills are paid elsewhere. And many consumers suffer simply from inertia, or the unwillingness to change one's behaviour even if it is in one's financial interest to do so.

Now again the introduction of a carbon tax would tend to reduce these instances of 'irrationality', as the cost of not maximising profit increased. But it might take quite an increase in price before behaviour changed sufficiently for all the profitable investments to be taken up. Such an increase in price might then actually lead to a much greater expenditure than would be incurred if consumers were forced to undertake the investments through regulation – for example, by setting minimum legal efficiency standards for all appliances. Effectively this would mean requiring consumers to act 'rationally' by removing the unprofitable options. Without detailed evidence we cannot know what the comparative costs would be of a carbon tax and the equivalent regulations; but if 'irrational' behaviour is widespread it is at least possible that regulation would be the cheaper, that is, the more efficient, instrument.[20]

These observations about structural obstacles, lack of information and consumer 'irrationality' apply to the current energy market. Clearly, if the appropriate regulations were introduced and the market became more efficient, the theoretical arguments for the efficiency of a carbon tax would become more relevant. Moreover, it is not necessarily the case that in other fields the advantages of regulations can be demonstrated in the same way.

These caveats however do not make the observations any less important. Given the growing interest in the carbon tax as potentially the key instrument of energy policy, they are vital to the assessment of its merits. They also make a wider point. This is that policy making must examine the actual conditions under which policies will be introduced, and not rely simply on theory. To be more precise, the lesson is that neoclassical theory, with its assumptions of efficient markets, fails to do justice to the institutional and human complexity of the world in which its recommendations must be applied. A more profound approach would serve policy makers better.

Political acceptability: liberty, licence and fairness

The last argument commonly heard in favour of financial incentives is that they are more libertarian than regulations. Whereas regulations force firms or consumers to do certain things, incentives merely encourage them to do so: they still have the freedom to choose. It is a moot point how far higher prices do in fact allow freedom to choose (or, perhaps more strictly, how valuable that freedom is if it can't be exercised); but there may be a subjective difference in how regulations and incentives are *perceived* which makes the incursions on freedom of the latter more acceptable. This may be particularly true for consumer goods, where the idea of banning certain categories of good (such as high grade paper, or large engine cars) may be regarded as unacceptably authoritarian.

This argument can, however, be turned on its head. One person's 'liberty' is another person's 'licence': it may actually be undesirable. It is sometimes argued by environmentalists, for example, that financial incentives are 'licences to pollute'. By taxing rather than outlawing pollution, polluters are allowed to carry on doing it – just so long as they pay for it. This is regarded as objectionable because it puts an explicit price on the environment, which many people feel debases its value – especially where pollution 'rights' can be traded as if the environment were a commodity.

The moral basis of this argument should be respected, but it is not helpful in practice. Price incentives are no more or less 'licences to pollute' than regulations. *Any* pollution standard above zero is effectively a licence to pollute up to that amount. (Regulations specifying permitted emissions are often called 'consents'.) In fact, far from giving polluters special 'rights' to pollute, incentive mechanisms actually reduce those rights in comparison with regulation.

This is because under a tax (or auctioned tradable permit), polluters pay not merely the cost of reducing pollution to the acceptable level (which is what they would pay under a regulatory system), but also an additional sum on top of this. The additional sum arises because the tax is paid on all the damaging activity, not just the proportion above the target level. This sum can be seen partly as a payment for the residual damage caused by the pollution at the target level, and partly as a 'rent' on the use of the environment.[21] The important point in this context is that the payment of the extra amount effectively *removes* rights that polluters enjoy under a regulatory system.

Since regulations only force the polluter to reduce pollution to the target level, pollution of the environment at that level is free: the polluter can be said to have a 'right' to do it. By contrast, a tax forces the polluter to pay for the cost of pollution at that level, and even charges a rent for use of the environment. In this sense 'property rights' over the environment pass from the firm to the community.[22] It could be argued that this is in many ways a much more 'Green' principle than that implied by regulation. Its tangible benefit is the increased revenue from the tax, which may be spent on further environmental improvement.

On the other hand, this additional payment is likely to generate considerable resistance on the part of current polluters to the introduction of environmental taxes. This is one reason why most of the European charge systems return some of the revenues to the taxed firms to subsidise the pollution control measures required to meet the target. In general such hypothecation of revenues is likely to increase the political acceptability of incentives. If voters, firms and consumers know that the additional taxes they are paying are going specifically to fund environmental improvement schemes, they are much more likely to support them. (Note that this resistance should not arise under a 'grandfathered' tradable permit system. Such permits cannot make firms worse off than they are under emissions regulations: if no trades take place, the systems are identical. If firms do trade, they will save money.)

The revenue gained from taxes and auctioned permits (but not grandfathered ones, since all the revenue from these accrues to the traders, not the government) is obviously a further argument in favour of these instruments. In particular, when the objective is to restrict the supply of a particular commodity, such systems may be preferred to regulations. This is because restrictions on supply inevitably raise prices, which leads to windfall profits being earned by the producers. If instead the product is taxed, this income accrues to the government. The difference may be observed in relation to current restrictions on the production of CFCs, which are significantly increasing the CFC producers' profits. It might be more sensible to tax CFCs to generate the same reduction in consumption *and* make the extra revenue. (Such taxes have been introduced in the US and Denmark.)

Where the restriction on supply is of a natural resource, such as a mineral, or timber, or even soil, the resource owner (if private) will probably regard regulations as more of a restriction on liberty than taxes. Most landowners are likely to feel that the institution of private property gives them the right to produce as much or as little as they want from their land, and that any restrictions on supply ordered by government in the name of sustainability are incursions on their freedom. They may accept by contrast that governments do have the right to tax them on their production. These arguments will no doubt be tested if environmental policy places depletion constraints on privately owned resources.

There is however another argument against the 'liberty' of financial incentives. Pollution taxes may be seen as inequitable, since they allow rich individuals and firms freedom to pollute simply because they can afford to, whereas poor people cannot. If the benefits of polluting are great, this creates (or worsens) 'environmental inequality'. Car use is an example. Personal mobility is already very unequally distributed, with many poor people not having access to cars at all. If environmental taxes were applied to cars or petrol, the gap between rich and poor would become even greater. Many people currently just able to afford to drive would be unable to; many others would be forced to reduce the distances and frequency of their travel. The rich however would be able to carry on polluting, albeit at greater cost. The polluter would be paying; but it might be thought fairer if everyone were forced to cut down equally. This might be achieved by the regulatory approach of, for example, cutting maximum speeds, reducing the number of parking spaces in cities or forcing commuters to share cars. The political acceptability of environmental instruments may well turn on distributional questions of these kinds. We shall return to them in Chapter 14.

Summary

The appropriateness of any particular instrument in any given circumstance will clearly depend on which of the above criteria are regarded as most important, and on the particular context and nature of the environmental damage to be prevented. However to assist consideration of the options it may be useful to summarise the arguments made. Table 12.1 sets out the three principal 'polluter pays' instruments – regulations, taxes and marketable permits – in terms of the various criteria given. '√' denotes a positive benefit in terms of the criterion, '?' indicates that the benefits cannot be determined in general.

Table 12.1: A comparison between regulation and financial incentives

Criterion	Regulation	Instrument Tax	Marketable permit auctioned	'grandfathered'
Ideology	?	?	?	?
Effectiveness				
on firms	√a		√	√
on consumers		√b		
if zero target	√			
if speed required	√			
flexibility	?	?	?	?
Motivation				
continual reduction		√	√	√
innovation		√	√	√
Administrative cost				
introduction c	low	high	high	medium
operation	?	?	?	?
Efficiency				
in inefficient market	√			
in efficient market		√	√	√
Political acceptability				
'liberty'		√	√	√
'licence'	√			
community 'rights'		√	√	
firms' resistance	√d			√
revenue		√	√	
fairness / equity	√			
Distributional impact	?	?	?	/ ?

a   If regulations are based on ambient standards
b   For non-zero consumption target
c   Assuming existing system is regulatory
d   Except in case of resources?

13

The Role of Government Expenditure

The costs of environmental change

Regulations and financial incentives are the principal tools of environmental policy because they make the polluter (or resource depleter) pay. The unbending application of this principle, however, is likely to cause problems when the costs of meeting environmental targets are very high, and it is in these circumstances that the use of government expenditure may be justified. If the degrader *cannot* pay, the ramifications of forcing him or her to do so may be more serious than anticipated. A firm may simply go out of business, for example – and its employees thrown out of work – if it is forced to pay high pollution charges or change its production processes. If there simply aren't any alternatives to a polluting activity, at least in the short term, a regulation or tax to reduce it significantly may cause a dramatic increase in prices or a serious shortage of products. A rise in the price of necessities such as food and energy, which are bought by everyone, will have a particularly damaging effect on the living standards of the poor.

The moral case for not making the poor poorer should hardly need stating. But even where the costs of environmental change fall on those more able to afford them, they should not be disregarded. Many of these costs are likely to be very high: meeting sustainability targets (or even less stringent ones) will inevitably require significant changes in current behaviour. Such high costs may simply make it impossible to win political support for the targets chosen. Unless government expenditure is allowed to cushion the effects of environmental change, a policy of sustainability is likely to find itself defeated before it is even attempted.

High costs and low elasticity

There are particular cases in which the required changes in behaviour will be very costly. These occur where it is difficult to switch to some alternative means of achieving the same end. If a product or industrial process has a comparably-priced and less damaging substitute, even a large reduction in environmental impact may be achievable without great cost. Thus it has been possible practically to eliminate CFC use in aerosols and packaging with only a small increase in prices, because cheap substitutes were available. But achieving a similar reduction in, say, petrol consumption would involve very large costs. A number of its uses are effectively necessities, and the present availability of substitute products or technologies (such as public transport for private cars) is in many cases limited.

Demand for petrol is said to be 'price inelastic'. The price elasticity of a product is the degree to which demand for it rises or falls when its price changes. A good is price elastic if a small rise in price induces a large fall in demand, and inelastic if the reverse applies. In general, the fewer substitutes a good has, and the more of a necessity it is, the more inelastic its demand will be. In such cases, only a very large tax will cut demand by the requisite amount. A regulation (say, a ban on certain uses) can do so, but only at the cost of considerable hardship, since consumers cannot easily switch to something else.

Petrol is in fact an instructive example. It has been estimated that the price of petrol in the UK would have to rise by 87% above its expected level in 2005 to reduce consumption by enough to meet the Toronto sustainability target (a 20% cut in carbon dioxide emissions from the 1988 level).[1] Regulations designed to achieve the same target might well require some form of petrol rationing. The costs of either approach would evidently be considerable, not just to private car users but to firms transporting goods by road, with a corresponding knock-on effect on prices (or the availability of goods) in general.

Unfortunately, some of the most important environmental problems involve products or activities with similarly inelastic demand, at least over the range of prices at which it is considered politically feasible to impose charges. Of the existing examples of effluent and product charges in European countries, for instance, few have had any significant impact on pollution levels. In Britain the introduction of trade sewage charges has faced some companies with 400% increases in discharge costs, yet has had almost no effect at all on polluting behaviour.[2]

Nitrate fertilisers provide another example. Their price elasticity is calculated at about 0.3: that is, if the price goes up by 1%, the volume of fertiliser bought will only go down by 0.3%. Once the relationship between fertiliser use and nitrate pollution is also taken into account, the result is an estimate that it would require a tax of 40% to cut nitrate concentrations in the water system by just 5%. The effect of such a tax either on farmers' profitability or (if they passed the extra cost on to consumers) on the price of food would be very considerable.[3] Since farmers evidently regard nitrate fertilisers as essential, any attempt to regulate a reduction in use, say by rationing, would inevitably lead to severe reductions in food supply.

Raising elasticity

An uncompromising advocate of the 'polluter pays' principle might argue that these low elasticities are short-term only. In time higher prices or shortages would force producers and consumers into alternative patterns of activity. Public transport and organic farming would become economic, and the development of new, less environmentally damaging technologies would be encouraged. But this is hardly an argument for the real world, where the short-term costs might simply defeat the policy before it got off the drawing board, quite apart from causing hardship in themselves.

Fortunately, low elasticity carries the seeds of its own solution. If a tax is imposed on an inelastic product or activity, consumption doesn't change much, but a great deal of money is raised in revenue. The polluter simply carries on doing much the same things as before but pays tax on them all. An additional 55p tax on petrol in Britain, for example, would cut petrol consumption by under 10%, but in doing so would raise over £3 billion per annum, which is around six times as much as the government subsidy to British Rail in 1990–1.[4] Similarly, a 40% tax on nitrate fertiliser would lead to a fall of only 5% in nitrate concentrations, but generate £142 million in revenue, or the equivalent of more than 10% of the subsidy given to British farmers in the same year.[5]

In conventional economic analysis, tax changes are generally assumed to be 'revenue neutral'; that is, the additional funds raised by environmental taxes are compensated for by reducing other kinds, such as VAT or income tax. But this is not necessarily the best way of using tax revenues. Where products or activities are price inelastic, it may be preferable to use the money collected to reduce the cause of the low elasticity – namely the difficulty for producers and consumers of switching to alternative methods of achieving the same end. If the elasticity of the damaging product or activity can be raised in this way, the tax rate required to achieve the environmental target is reduced. This in turn reduces the cost of the policy, which should make it more likely to be politically acceptable.

A number of different ways of using government expenditure to raise elasticity can be identified. First, where low elasticity arises from the high cost of installing improved technology, producers can be given subsidies to enable them to do so. Monies collected from water and air pollution charges in a number of European countries are given back to polluting firms for this purpose. So long as they are temporary, and well targeted (so that firms do not make windfall profits), subsidies of these kinds cushion the effects of severe pollution controls and speed up compliance with reduction targets.[6] Farmers could similarly be given subsidies to switch away from highly chemicalised farming methods towards a greater use of organic inputs. Such subsidies could be one part of a shift in financial assistance to agriculture, increasingly accepted as necessary, away from price support for intensive agrochemical-based farming.[7]

Second, government expenditure can support research and development into new materials, processes or technologies which will cause less environmental damage. The Swedish pesticide charge is used in precisely this way to fund research into alternatives to pesticides. A tax on, say, heavy metals could similarly be used to fund research into alternative materials and processes generating less hazardous waste. The effect on elasticity will of course be more long-term in these cases.

Third, government expenditure can be used to subsidise alternatives to current consumption patterns. Some of the most environmentally damaging behaviour occurs because consumers are 'locked in' to particular activities which in practice have few alternatives. Thus for example it is very difficult to avoid causing pollution from household wastes. Ideally wastes should be separated at source, both in dustbins and in sewage systems. Recyclable wastes should then go for recycling, while much of the remainder can be used as fuel for district heating. But consumers cannot achieve these changes on their own, even if they are charged or regulated. Government expenditure is required to build the sewage systems, organise the separate collection of wastes and their transport to recycling facilities, and construct the waste incinerators and heating systems.

The role of government in providing the 'infrastructure' for changed consumer behaviour in this way is even more obvious in the field of transport. The demand for petrol displays such low elasticity because there are so few alternatives available to car and lorry use. For many people, cars have become necessities, as residential patterns have become more dispersed, shops have shifted to out-of-town centres and public transport services have declined. Lorries take up an increasingly large proportion of total 'freight tonne kilometres' travelled because rail or water alternatives are simply not available – while average distances travelled per journey have become longer.[8]

The need to reduce petrol consumption is evident. As well as causing hydrocarbon and lead pollution, vehicle exhausts contribute 45% of nitrogen dioxide emissions (which cause acid rain), and are responsible for approximately 16% of all carbon dioxide emissions. CO_2 from the transport sector is expected to rise by 20–40% by 2005.[9] Yet low elasticity means it is not politically or economically feasible to achieve the reduction in transport fuel consumption required by sustainability targets simply by taxation or through regulation. There is no doubt that both are necessary: vehicle use must be made more expensive (by raising petrol prices, and perhaps by electronic road pricing) and more difficult (for example, through parking restrictions, lower speed limits, fuel efficiency laws and 'traffic calming' measures in cities). But at the same time motorists have to be given alternatives.

The first of these is public transport.[10] The technical means of providing cheap, quick and comfortable public transport systems are not in dispute. They include improved bus services and dedicated bus lanes, light railway and tram systems for commuters and shoppers in towns and cities; and the expansion (and reduction in price) of inter-city rail services for long-distance travellers. The provision of cheap taxis and car hire can also help.[11] But such systems cannot be achieved without substantial government investment in the transport infrastructure, and in many cases continuing subsidy. Similarly, a proportion of freight could be shifted to rail and water if new freight rail lines, improved signalling systems and trans-shipment points (where cargoes would be switched to light vans for local delivery) were established.[12]

The second alternative is private, but non-motor transport: walking and cycling. In the UK 41% of all urban car journeys cover a distance of under 5 kilometres: many of these are clearly unnecessary. But again public investment is needed to make walking and cycling safe and convenient, particularly by means of cycle lanes and measures to calm and remove traffic from urban streets.[13]

The third means of reducing private motorised transport is to reduce the need for it. Transport is not an end in itself: it is a means of getting from A to B. Over the longer term, by far the most important approach to reducing fuel consumption is to bring A and B closer together. Jobs need to be sited nearer to where people live, and cities made more habitable so that people want to live closer to their employment. There is scope through the use of information technologies to reduce the need for physical movement, both of people and goods. Both urban and rural communities need to be redesigned so that employment, shopping, leisure and other facilities are clustered where they are more easily accessible. Ultimately we shall need to look much more closely at the geography of industrial location and the patterns of international trade, so that transport of goods is reduced.[14]

To some extent such changes in the physical structure of industrialised societies will come about through higher transport prices: people and firms will choose to locate closer to their employers or customers, and higher prices will reduce the demand for goods traded long distances. But the role of government in planning the shape and interaction of land uses will inevitably be the crucial factor.

The exact details of an environmental transport policy are beyond the scope of this book. What is important to stress is that these measures requiring government expenditure are not simply ends in themselves. By providing alternatives to private vehicle use, they will also achieve the important task of raising the elasticity of demand for petrol. Petrol prices will almost certainly still need to be increased, but higher elasticity will reduce the required tax rate, which in turn should make it easier to win acceptance for the sustainability target. And of course the revenues from the tax can be used to finance the government expenditure.

Energy policy and the carbon tax

The problem of low elasticity – and therefore the need for government to help remove its cause – is perhaps raised most starkly in the field of energy. As we saw in the last chapter, a widely proposed mechanism to deal with global warming is the 'carbon tax'. The difficulty with the carbon tax, however, is that the demand for energy is generally price inelastic.[15] Moreover, since economic growth tends to raise energy consumption, merely to hold CO_2 emissions constant requires a rise in the real price of energy. So *reducing* emissions, say to the Toronto target (80% of their 1988 level by the year 2005), is likely to require a carbon tax to be levied at very high rates.

Various calculations have in fact been made. Nearly all of these suggest that meeting the Toronto target would demand extremely large energy price rises. One study for the UK suggests that by 2005 the tax on coal would need to be 351%, on oil 351% and on gas 132%. (These rates would be achieved by imposing an *ad valorem* tax on the value of energy sales and increasing it by about 10% every year.) Another study estimates the minimum tax rate to be over 200%, with the tax on coal at nearly 600% – and even then the target is not quite reached.[16] These figures should be regarded as estimates; they are clearly only as good as the models from which they are derived. But they do suggest the magnitude of the taxes needed by sustainability targets; and therefore the immense political problem any government would have in achieving them through this instrument alone.

But of course there is no need to use a carbon tax on its own. The revenues from such a tax would be very large: in the first study quoted, the rising tax would generate £1.2 billion in its first year and by 2005 would be raising £15.8 billion, which is about a fifth of the entire tax revenues of the British government in 1989–90. In order to compensate for these additional revenues, the model assumes that VAT would be progressively reduced: it falls to just 7.4% (from 15%) by 2005.[17]

But another way of using carbon tax revenues would be to increase the elasticity of energy demand – by subsidising, or otherwise encouraging, investment in energy efficiency. There are a number of reasons why energy demand is inelastic. But one of the most important is that, for many energy consumers, energy efficiency technologies (which range from more efficient refrigerators to building insulation) are expensive. There is also widespread ignorance about the savings in energy costs they can yield. So it takes a very large increase in energy prices before consumers begin to invest in them.

If improvements in energy efficiency were made significantly cheaper, however, and more information were provided on their potential benefits, energy consumers would be likely to invest in them when prices rose by much smaller amounts. The costs would be smaller and perceived gains larger. Thus the demand for energy would become considerably more elastic. This would in turn mean that much lower rates of carbon tax would be required to meet the emissions target. The more subsidy given to energy efficiency measures (and the more money spent on publicising them), the lower the required rates of tax would become.

But of course the revenue needed to increase the subsidies can only be raised (if the policy is to be 'self-financing') by higher tax rates, not lower ones. So there must be some compromise between the rising tax rate required to fund the subsidies and the falling tax rate the subsidies make possible. Somewhere in the middle we can identify what might be called the 'optimal' level of carbon tax. This is the rate which raises just enough revenue to subsidise the degree of energy efficiency which is required, at that rate, to achieve the target level of energy demand.[18]

By examining the reasons for low elasticity in more detail, we can in fact discover what this level of tax might be. We have already seen in the last Chapter that some of the reasons are related to the structure of the energy market; others to lack of information and consumer 'irrationality'. As we suggested there, many of these problems are best addressed by regulatory measures. In other cases the provision of information and education is appropriate, both to raise the general level of awareness of the benefits of energy conservation and to publicise specific options. Such measures require government spending on publicity materials, advertising, training and so on; revenues from a carbon tax could pay for these.

There are other, more directly 'economic' reasons for low elasticity.[19] First there is a simple lack of capital. Many energy efficiency technologies, both in the home and in industry, cost more than their less efficient counterparts. Over time – sometimes very quickly – the smaller quantities of energy they use lead to financial savings; but to realise these savings money must be found 'up front'. Many households and firms do not have access to the funds required. Even among those that do, many are unwilling to add to their debt burdens – or regard other investments as having higher priority when spending limited sums.[20]

A related problem is the high 'rate of return' or profitability expected by many firms and consumers. It is quite common for companies and financial investors to require that capital investment projects pay back their initial costs within three or four years, that is, to have rates of return of 25–30% or more. Many energy efficiency measures and similar investments in renewable energy sources or combined heat and power (CHP) plants cannot meet this requirement. Domestic consumers may have even higher expectations. Few explicitly work out the required profitability of their capital purchases (a new washing machine, say, or roof insulation) but observed behaviour suggests that effective rates of return may be as high as 40%, and for low income households rates up to 90% have been calculated.[21]

A third economic impediment to energy conservation is the fact that for many consumers energy costs constitute a rather small proportion of total expenditure. Well-off households, for example, may spend under

4% of their income on energy, while (outside heavy industry) the proportion for many firms will be even less. In these cases it may simply not be worth the effort (or for firms, the cost of energy management) to cut down – especially if in the latter case the cost can be passed on to customers. For poorer households, meanwhile, energy costs may be a much more significant proportion of total spending (up to 13%); but these are precisely those consumers who cannot afford to invest in reduction.[22]

These economic reasons for low energy elasticity suggest a considerable role for government subsidy. By providing grants, low interest loans, tax relief or product subsidies for investments aimed at cutting carbon emissions, governments can reduce their cost to consumers and thereby lower the threshold of energy prices at which they are taken up. Such subsidies should be available for improvements in the efficiency of energy supply, such as CHP, as well as for improvements in the efficiency of energy end use (such as insulation and higher-grade appliances). They should also be directed towards renewable energy technologies, such as wind, wave, tidal and solar power. In each case funds should be available for research and development into improved technologies (that is, to assist future emissions reductions) as well as current installation.

There is always a risk in providing subsidy that consumers and firms who would anyway have invested in the technology are given support they don't need. To some extent this 'deadweight' can be avoided in the design of the schemes: the size of grant for home insulation given to households, for example, can be varied according to income. But to some extent the problem simply has to be accepted as part of the price of the policy. A number of countries operate home and office insulation grants; some such as Denmark provide capital grants and soft loans for CHP; in the early 1980s California operated a tax credit scheme for wind energy. These schemes have had a significant impact on energy investment; there is evident scope for their application elsewhere. Additional incentives such as linking mortgage tax relief to the energy efficiency of homes and removing VAT from energy efficiency appliances are also possible.[23]

These various methods of increasing the elasticity of energy demand – both subsidies aimed at overcoming the economic sources of low elasticity, and informational activities to increase consumer knowledge – require government expenditure. Clearly it will be most cost-effective if the expenditure is aimed where it will have the greatest impact; that is, where the increase in energy efficiency achieved per pound of expenditure is largest.[24] This can be estimated by analysing the costs of different investments and the energy savings they can generate, and then setting these against the discount rates of those who would be responsible for investing in them (households, firms, energy supply companies, etc.). It should then be possible to work out how much needs to be spent to reduce energy consumption by the target amount – for example, the Toronto target.

Once this is done, we can then calculate the carbon tax rate which will be sufficient to raise the revenue required to pay for the government expenditure. But of course this initial rate will be too high, since by increasing the price of energy we shall anyway provide an incentive to investments in efficiency. Reducing the tax rate to take account of this, however, will also reduce the revenue raised. So we shall have to find the 'optimal' rate which just pays for the efficiency investments which in turn just yield the required energy demand at the taxed price.

Just such an exercise has in fact been performed for the UK.[25] The figures are necessarily very approximate, because they rely on a number of assumptions about the cost-effectiveness of different technological options (carbon emissions saved per pound of expenditure) and the discount rates of different actors. They also assume that many of the regulatory and information-providing measures proposed in the last chapter are implemented first, as the most cost-effective means of raising elasticity. These measures are assumed to achieve about 50% of the 'least-cost planning' options. The result is an estimated carbon tax to reach the Toronto target of 6.5% on coal, 5% on oil and 3.5% on gas. As we would expect, these rates are substantially lower than the ones which assume current elasticities and distribute their revenues elsewhere in the economy. More importantly, they are the sort of rates which can be considered politically feasible, particularly if brought in gradually over the period to 2005.

Exactly how the tax revenues would be collected and redistributed in subsidies and information programmes would need careful thought and planning. There is an obvious problem, for example, in that the revenues do not become available until the tax is levied, but until the revenues are spent the impact of the tax is very (and unnecessarily) severe. One way of avoiding this would be for the government to announce the tax a year or two in advance of its introduction, simultaneously initiate the various subsidy and information programmes, and then borrow money to pay for them against the future revenue stream. Given sufficient advertising and media coverage, considerable investment in energy efficiency might be stimulated in the pre-tax period.

Clearly, many details need to be worked out. But the essential principle is straightforward. Instead of insisting that a carbon tax perform all the uphill work against low elasticity of demand, the revenues from the tax can be applied directly to reducing the gradient.

14

Equity and the Integration of Social and Environmental Policy

The distributional impact of environmental policy

When the costs of environmental policy are high, there is clearly an important role for government expenditure in increasing the elasticity of damaging products and activities, and thereby making it easier for producers and consumers to change their behaviour. A second, equally crucial, function arises when these costs have adverse *distributional* impacts.

A great many environmental measures can be expected to raise prices. It is evident that in most cases it is less expensive to pollute or to degrade the environment than not to do so: what would otherwise be externalities must be internalised. Although some environmental measures (such as energy conservation) recoup their costs quite rapidly, and many others can be shown to save money in the long run, the short-term impact of environmental policy will almost always involve higher costs.

Both regulations and price incentives will cause prices to rise. But environmental taxes raise an additional distributional question, since as well as achieving the desired change in behaviour they generate revenue, which must be paid by someone. (Where, as theory suggests, regulations are less efficient than taxes – that is, where they involve higher total costs on polluters – this difference may be at least partially offset by the higher prices to which they will give rise.)

Economists tend to be most concerned about the distribution of price rises expressed as a *proportion* of each person's or household's income. If the extra costs to the poor constitute a greater proportion of their income than the extra costs to the rich, an environmental policy can be said to be socially 'regressive': it makes the relative gap between income classes greater.[1] But even if the rich pay proportionately more, for very poor people *any* increase in prices or taxes may cause hardship. In most industrialised countries (let alone in the South), poverty is serious enough without the imposition of additional burdens.

If regulations or taxes are imposed directly on consumers, it will be relatively easy to see how the costs are distributed. But the effect of environmental measures applied to firms is more difficult to predict. How far higher costs can be passed on in price rises will depend on the nature of the market in which a firm is operating. (In general, the more competitive the market, the smaller the amount which can be passed on.)[2] Moreover higher costs in one part of the economy may feed through the sales and purchases of different products into many other sectors.

For example, an energy tax (without accompanying subsidies) would have a particularly significant effect on firms in energy-intensive industries, such as iron and steel, plastics, transport, etc. This would then be reflected in the prices of these industries' products, which in turn would raise the costs of firms buying them. Iron and steel, plastics and transport are very widely used, so a large number of other industries would feel some impact of the original price rise (as well as paying extra for energy themselves). The effect on the prices of final products bought by consumers at the end of all these interactions would consequently be very complex.[3]

It is quite likely that the goods and services bought by richer people have a total percentage energy content much higher than those bought by the poor. So overall an energy tax might technically be described as 'progressive'. But since many poor people, particularly pensioners, already live in 'fuel poverty', unable to heat their homes adequately, the absolute effect of an increase in energy prices on those with the least income in society would be very severe.

We can estimate just how severe. By analysing the expenditure patterns of consumers over time, it is possible to see how households in different income bands react to a change in the price of a product. We can then use this information to estimate the distributional effect on consumption and expenditure of a product tax. This method has been used in Britain by the Institute of Fiscal Studies to assess the impact of a 15% rise in domestic fuel prices – equivalent to putting VAT on energy.[4]

The results show that the richest 10% (or decile) of households would spend about £2 per week more on energy, whereas the poorest 10% would spend just over £1. But since the richest group earn on average over fifteen times as much as the poorest, this is extremely regressive. As a proportion of household spending, the increase for the bottom decile would be four and a half times as much as for the top. Even more seriously, the poorest group would reduce their energy consumption by nearly 10%, whereas the richest would barely cut their consumption at all.[5]

This would be unfair under any circumstances, since the highest earning households consume over twice as much energy as the lowest, and are therefore much more responsible for global warming, yet the tax would impose nearly all the cost of reducing energy consumption onto the poor.[6] But it is particularly alarming in the context of widespread fuel poverty. The numbers of households in Britain characterised as 'fuel poor' approaches 6 million, that is, many of the

bottom 30% of the income range. The effect of being unable to afford
to heat one's home adequately is not just a colder home. It may well
involve increased debt and frequently leads to respiratory, allergic
and other diseases caused by damp. It has been calculated that in the
UK every 1°C drop in temperature below the winter average results in
an extra 8,000 deaths from cold-related ailments, including (but not
only) hypothermia.[7]

By forcing low-income households to cut their energy consumption
still further, a carbon tax would make all these problems worse.
Moreover, because pensioners tend to require more heat (being at
home more of the time) the effect on their energy consumption and
spending is proportionately more severe than for other types of
household.[8] Given the particular vulnerability of elderly people to cold-
related illnesses, an energy tax introduced on its own would raise
very serious questions of public policy.

Similar issues apply to the distributional effects of a rise in the price
of food. A number of environmental policies aimed at cutting
agricultural pollution – caused by nitrate fertilisers, pesticides and
farm slurry – are likely to raise food prices. Here the proportional falls
in food consumption and increases in amounts spent would be approximately equal across all income bands. Yet although not technically
'regressive' we might still be concerned about such price rises, since food
is a necessity, and for many poor people, particularly children and
pensioners, *any* reduction in food consumption and loss of disposable
income should be avoided. Indeed households with children would on
average pay more from such a tax than those without.[9]

By contrast, the distributional impact of an increase in petrol prices
would be socially progressive rather than regressive. Of the poorest 10%
of households, less than one in ten owns a car, whereas the average
number of cars among the richest decile is over 1.5 per household. So
on average, when calculated across the population as a whole, raising
petrol prices would be quite equitable: the proportional rise in costs
for the poorest decile would be only about one-fifth of the effect on
the richest.

On the other hand, an additional petrol tax would impose
considerable extra costs on poor car-owners in comparison with rich
ones. If set at, say, 55p per gallon, it is estimated that the tax would
cut the consumption of the poorest decile by over 10%, but that of
the richest by only 7.5%. Despite this fall, the tax paid by the poorest
group would still be larger as a proportion of their total spending. A
particular concern with such a tax might be the effect on people in
rural areas who have less access to public transport. Because they are
on average poorer, such people would cut their petrol consumption
more than those living in cities, and yet would still end up paying
a higher proportion of their total spending in tax. The loss in terms
of reduced mobility and access to facilities might be very
considerable.[10]

Compensation and integration

These distributional effects make it extremely important that environmental policies are assessed on more than simply their environmental consequences. Environmental protection needs to go hand-in-hand with social protection, so that the costs of meeting sustainability targets fall equitably. Inevitably this means that government expenditure must be used to cushion the impact on the poor.

There are essentially two ways in which such cushioning can be done. One is to design environmental policies without any consideration of distributional issues, and then compensate those who lose out through reductions in (other) taxes or increases in welfare benefits. The other is to integrate the social and environmental targets in the original design of the policies, ensuring from the start that the distributional effects are equitable.

The case for generalised compensation is very strong. Given the prevailing distribution of income and wealth in most industrialised countries, raising the income of the poor hardly needs environmental backing. But certainly if widespread and significant environmental policies are to be introduced, the burden on low-income groups is likely to be quite severe. It could be lightened either through reductions in the lower bands of income tax and improved pensions and welfare benefits, or through reductions in VAT or sales taxes.

Compensation will also be appropriate for certain specific policies. We noted that the principal impact of a rise in food prices was on households with children. Increasing the value of child benefits (including elements such as free school meals) would be a reasonably well-targeted means of offsetting the extra costs, and would have the advantage of administrative simplicity.[11]

On the other hand, compensation would not be particularly useful in the case of an additional petrol tax. The direct tax and benefit systems cannot easily identify poor rural car owners. It might be possible to offer some help to such groups by reducing the vehicle excise duty on small cars, but this would also have some perverse incentive effects on general car ownership.[12] It would also be of no help to those without cars. This is the poorest group of all, whose mobility, while not much reduced by the tax, is already likely to be the most limited. A more appropriate means of improving equity, therefore, would be to make alternatives available to car use: to expand and improve public transport services, to improve walking and cycling facilities and (over the longer term) to change land use planning so as to reduce the need for motorised transport. These are of course precisely the measures which we have already recommended to increase petrol elasticity. The more such measures are targeted at poorer people – for example, an emphasis on rail investment in rural areas and higher subsidies to rural bus services, and larger fare concessions – the more positive their distributional effect. The result would be an 'integrated' transport policy which met both environmental and social criteria.

A similar approach would be most appropriate with respect to energy. Trying to compensate the households which suffered worst from the effects of an energy tax would be extremely difficult. The current tax and benefit system identifies broad categories of people, such as pensioners, whom we might wish to help, but the *average* loss of a large group such as this conceals quite a significant variation in actual losses suffered by different households. Broad measures such as an increase in pensions, therefore, would tend to over-compensate some pensioners and under-compensate others. Indeed, since many of the poorest households receive means-tested benefits, which are calculated after the receipt of other income such as a pension or child benefit, increasing these would have no compensatory effect at all. The extra sum would simply be removed from the basic welfare payment received. It would be possible to target the poor more effectively through additions to means-tested benefits such as housing and one-parent benefit and 'family credit' (paid to low-income earners with children), but the take-up of such payments is poor. Many people made worse off by the tax would therefore not be reached.[13]

In any case, compensations of this sort are rather perverse. Their aim is to prevent poor households cutting their energy consumption, when cutting energy consumption is precisely what we wish them to do. What a social-environmental policy should be trying to avoid is not reductions in consumption, but reductions in *warmth*. It should be trying to increase energy efficiency, so that poorer households, like others, *can* reduce their energy consumption, but at the same time can increase their levels of comfort. The problem of fuel poverty is therefore not lack of income, but lack of capital. The fuel poor are cold because their homes are badly insulated and they tend to use very inefficient methods of heating (such as electric-bar fires) which cost a lot of money and provide little warmth. They do not have the money to invest in energy efficiency.[14]

Therefore the most appropriate means of avoiding the potentially adverse distributional impact of energy policy is by subsidising such investments. We have already argued that grants and subsidies should be available for energy efficiency investments such as home insulation and higher-grade products. If these are offered at 100% to the poorest households (with perhaps some contribution from landlords where possible), social as well as environmental criteria can be met. In many cases the most cost-effective way of doing this will be a general improvement programme for whole streets and municipal housing blocks, installing insulation and upgrading heating systems. It has been calculated that to raise the energy efficiency of all the households of the fuel poor in Britain (the 6.4 million dependent on state benefits for 75% of their income) such a programme would cost £16 billion, which could be achieved over a 15-year period at 450,000 homes and £1.1 billion a year. Clearly part of this could come from a carbon tax;

but since the effect would be a general improvement in living standards it might be felt appropriate to draw on general tax revenues as well.[15]

The employment implications of environmental policy

Price and tax increases are not the only consequences of environmental policies whose distributional effects are a cause for concern. It is evident that as companies react to regulations, incentives and other measures there will also be an impact on jobs. The assumption that stricter environmental protection causes unemployment has indeed been a principal source of the widespread suspicion of environmentalism to be found on the political left and in the trade union movement.

There is no doubt that there can be conflicts between employment and environmental objectives. In many cases protecting the environment clearly means desisting from activities which currently provide jobs and livelihoods. Banning asbestos use in buildings, for example, obviously has an impact on workers in asbestos manufacturing companies. There are some cases where environmental policies have involved whole plants closing down. A programme of air pollution reduction in Silesia in Poland is planned to result in the closure of 18 factories between 1988 and 1995, causing hundreds of redundancies. The closure of 155 plants in the United States allegedly due to pollution control regulations in the period 1971–83 was estimated to have cost 33,000 jobs.[16]

But these figures can be misleading. For one thing, it has been shown that many companies claiming to be shutting factories or laying workers off due to environmental regulations would have done these things anyway on economic grounds; the regulations tended only to accelerate the process (and perhaps provide an acceptable excuse).[17] More importantly, individual case studies of job losses ignore the job gains which environmental policies can engender elsewhere. To assess whether protecting the environment has a negative or positive impact on employment overall we need to look at the whole economy, not just individual sectors or firms.

In fact almost all studies of the employment effects of environmental policies show that in general they lead to a net gain in jobs. The Organisation for Economic Co-operation and Development (OECD) has collected together a number of macroeconomic studies carried out in industrialised countries, analysing both past policies and potential future ones. Almost all of these show a small but clear addition to employment. The effects depend on the structure of international trade (countries with domestic environmental industries do better than those without), and other factors such as the level of wages; the results vary in the short and longer term. But the overwhelming conclusion is positive.[18]

A study of the macroeconomic effects of doubling environmental investment in five European countries (to 2% of GDP) has similarly been carried out by the EC. This again shows a small net reduction in unemployment (of about 13,000 in the UK and Germany); this is larger if all countries act together. A simulation of a much more dramatic programme of environmental improvement in the Netherlands (with expenditure constituting 4% of GDP) shows a considerable cut in unemployment of 400,000 after five years, with a very small increase in the longer term. The long-term impact would be positive if other countries adopted similar environmental policies.[19]

It is not difficult to see why these results occur. Although environmental measures are likely to raise prices and taxes, they will also stimulate investment. In order to cut pollution discharges, firms will usually have to buy new waste treatment equipment. If a new manufacturing process will meet the standard more cheaply, they may buy new plant altogether. Simply raising energy efficiency will involve purchases of insulation materials, or new, upgraded machinery and appliances. All these expenditures will require other firms to produce (and install) the equipment or materials required, thus generating employment. Fields where job creation is particularly likely include recycling industries, the development and production of new materials, the establishment of new sources of energy supply (such as combined heat and power, and renewables), public transport, the treatment, collection and reclamation of waste, and others. Not just manufacturing but environmental services of all kinds (research and development, consultancy, education and training, monitoring and administration, etc.) can be expected to grow.

Some estimates of the job creation effects of environmental policies have been made. Many have involved relatively small (though by no means insignificant) numbers, but others show quite dramatic impacts. In the Netherlands, for example, a two-year 'Environmental Technology Production Plan' in 1980–2 is held to have led altogether to an additional 70,000 jobs, with about 50,000 of these in the production and installation of capital goods, and the remainder in conventional control programmes such as waste disposal and sewage works.[20] It is calculated that a programme of energy conservation in buildings in the UK would generate between 68,000 and 155,000 new jobs over a ten-year period (depending on the rate of return required of the investment). Of these about two-thirds would be direct: that is, in manufacturing and installing energy conservation equipment and materials. The remaining third would result from the 'multiplier' effect caused by the additional spending power of the workers employed, along with the extra consumption generated because people save money on heating bills. The figures take account of the small loss of employment in the energy supply industry.[21]

What is perhaps most significant about the employment potential of such a programme is that most of the the jobs created would be unskilled and semi-skilled, and they would be located especially in areas of high unemployment, where poverty tends to lead to low building insulation. So the programme would not only create jobs, but would create the kind of jobs that are most needed by the unemployed.

Moreover, if the programme were 75% financed by public expenditure, the 'cost per job' would be only about £10,000, which is 15% less than the equivalent figure for regional investment incentive policies.[22]

These kinds of figures provide some comfort to those worried about the effects of environmental policies on employment, but they do not remove the problem. Environmental policies may generate net employment growth, but this may still involve job loss in some industries, and for some people, even if such loss is more than matched by gains elsewhere. We do not know either that the gains will occur at the same time as the losses, or that the new jobs will be of the same type, and located in the same areas, as those replaced. If these conditions do not hold, environmental policies could lead to considerable personal suffering; and indeed, if countervailing measures are not taken, to considerable net unemployment, even if only in the short term.

There is an evident role for government here in planning the introduction of environmental policies so as to minimise these 'transitional' employment costs. A helpful first step would be for 'job audits' to be conducted for major policies to assess their likely employment effects. This would then enable mitigating programmes to be designed. As with measures to offset the adverse distributional impact of price increases, such programmes might be categorised as either 'compensatory' or 'integral'.

The basis of an integrated approach would be the provision of financial subsidies to firms facing particularly stringent environmental regulations or taxes, to reduce the cost of compliance and therefore the risk of job loss. Such subsidies would clearly have to be carefully targeted at firms in need, and to be available for discrete projects, not continuing revenue support. Such projects might include investment in new technology, retraining of employees, new marketing initiatives and research and development of new products.

For large firms needing not merely to invest in new technology but to diversify into less environmentally damaging sectors and products, government support might be more extensive. There are a number of industries – motor vehicles and chemicals are obvious examples – where environmental policies could result in extremely high unemployment unless alternative products can be developed and marketed. This suggests the development of planned, gradual 'conversion' strategies outlining how current damaging processes and outputs can be switched to environmentally acceptable alternatives. There is every reason for government to work directly with firms (including their trade unions) in the formulation of such strategies and to support their implementation. Measures might include grants for research and development, soft loans or tax credits for investment, export credits, and the opportunity to bid for public contracts. State support for industrial restructuring of this kind (though not particularly related to environmental policy) is of course already practised in a number of countries, most notably Japan. Its success there provides a useful model for integrated environmental policy.[23]

Where employment effects will be spread amongst a larger number of employers, on the other hand, compensatory programmes will be more appropriate. Three are likely to be particularly important. The first is a regional policy which gives support to investments made in depressed areas. It is probable that some of the industries most affected by environmental measures will be those which have already been worst hit by the industrial restructuring of the 1970s and 1980s, such as iron and steel, coal mining, chemicals and various kinds of engineering. In most countries, these industries are located in quite concentrated geographical areas (in Britain, notably, in Scotland, the North West, North East, West Midlands and South Wales), which have consequently suffered particularly high levels of unemployment. Some of the jobs created by environmental policies will belong in the same sectors (particularly engineering) but incentives may still be required to encourage companies to invest in depressed regions. It will be very important to ensure that environmental policies do not exacerbate already uneven patterns of geographical development.

Second, measures will be required to encourage and support retraining. Although studies show the net employment effect of environmental policies to be positive, they also warn that many of the jobs potentially available will require skills not possessed either by the currently unemployed or by those whose jobs may be threatened.[24] If unemployment – and delay in implementing environmental programmes – is to be avoided, retraining programmes will need to be established to enable workers to take up the new opportunities.

Third, governments can establish public environmental programmes which are themselves job-creating. A building insulation scheme, as already outlined, is an obvious candidate. Other infrastructural projects such as housing, sewer renovation and railway construction are also likely to be labour intensive. Significant numbers of jobs could be created in environmental improvement activities such as nature conservation, river clean-up and urban renewal. There is scope for further employment in waste collection, sorting and reclamation.[25]

Of course all these policies must be paid for. Ultimately some job creation programmes may pay for themselves through the multiplier effect, with a reduced need to pay unemployment benefits and higher income tax receipts. But even for these, in the short term, money needs to be found. Here again it may be possible to use the revenues from environmental taxes, in addition to general government income. One proposal, for example, might be to levy a small surcharge on corporation tax for certain, particularly damaging (but also highly profitable) industries, such as energy and chemicals. The revenues could then be used to set up an 'environmental dislocation fund' to pay for compensatory programmes. Of course money may well also have to be diverted from other areas of expenditure. There can be no illusions that either environmental policies, or measures to alleviate their adverse effects, will come cheap; or that difficult choices can be avoided.

15

Global Environmental
Economic Policy

Equity and the international economy

This book is primarily about environmental policy in industrialised
countries. But we have already noted that sustainability is meaningless
if it does not apply on a global basis. There are two principal aspects
to this. First, much environmental degradation in the South is the
consequence, through international trading relationships, of economic
activity in the North. Sustainability therefore has to address the issue
of resource flows between the industrialised and developing worlds.
Second, a number of environmental problems, such as the greenhouse
effect and the depletion of the ozone layer, affect all countries.
Ultimately this means that they must be tackled through some kind
of international agreement.

As we saw in Chapter 3, industrialised countries are currently
'exporting unsustainability'. Sometimes this is very starkly obvious, as
when toxic wastes are shipped to Third World countries for disposal.
But it occurs on a much more widespread basis through the normal
mechanisms of international trade. Environments in the South are often
degraded in the process of producing primary commodities for export
to the North. Fishing grounds are depleted, forests destroyed, soil
eroded, wilderness areas despoiled. Even degradation caused by
subsistence farming can often be traced back to the displacement of
traditional communities onto more fragile, marginal land by landowners
and governments oriented towards export.[1] Meanwhile manufactured
goods exported by Third World countries are kept cheap (in part) by
waiving the environmental standards which would apply in the North.
This has the effect of forcing Southern factory workers, neighbouring
communities and local ecosystems to pay the cost – in ill-health and
ecological damage – which the Northern consumer avoids.[2]

Even if policies are implemented which maintain environmental
capacity in the North, therefore, sustainability cannot be said to be
achieved so long as such degradation continues in the Third World.
There is clearly a crucial international dimension to environmental
economic policy *even for Northern countries considered alone*; that is,

without considering the equally reasonable demand of equity that the Third World should be assisted simply because it is poor.

This is an important conclusion. From the point of view of industrialised countries, measures which assist the South to achieve sustainable development will frequently look like 'aid' in one form or another. Given current inequalities, most actions designed to enhance Southern environments will involve costs to the North. But it seems much more appropriate to regard transfers to the South as *compensations* for environmental damage than simply as charitable gifts to alleviate poverty. If the reason that environments in the South are degraded is because of past and present demands placed on them by the North, the 'degrader pays' principle suggests that those who benefited should pay the costs. 'Aid' is then simply a way of internalising transnational externalities.

This is particularly true when global environmental issues such as the greenhouse effect and ozone depletion are considered. Here the inequality between North and South is not simply a question of wealth: that poor countries cannot afford to cut down their emissions of carbon dioxide and CFCs to the same degree as industrialised ones. It is that the global commons (such as the atmosphere) have not been equally damaged by all countries. If they are thought of as waste sinks of finite size, it is the North which has filled almost all the space in them so far. A reasonable principle for common resources is that all nations should have the opportunity to benefit equally from them. But if this is so, the poor countries should not have to reduce their emissions at all. At the very least, if they are to be encouraged to do so by the North, the North should pay the cost.

Internalising North–South externalities

There are essentially two mechanisms by which the industrialised countries can finance the repair and prevention of environmental degradation in the South. The first and most important is through an increase in the prices of primary commodities and manufactured goods imported from the Third World.

It is evident that prices currently paid by Northern countries for primary commodities do not reflect their environmental costs. The huge fall in commodity prices during the 1980s, along with an increase in First World protectionism, has indeed led to a considerable worsening of the terms of trade for Third World countries. A vicious spiral has been set up in which lower prices require higher production levels to earn the same amount of foreign exchange, but the extra supply merely adds to the downward pressure on prices. Meanwhile the natural resource base is further degraded. So the divergence between price and environmental costs has actually grown.

As almost all Northern governments have long since concluded in relation to their own agricultural production, the only way in which commodity prices can be raised is to remove them from the free market. In practice this means the negotiation of commodity agreements between North and South which stabilise prices at sustainable levels of production. Only if prices are stable and high will Third World countries be able to take marginal land out of cash crop production, reduce soil erosion, hold forestry and fishery yields to their sustainable level and reduce the destruction rate of habitats. Such agreements should include a reduction in Northern protectionism; and ideally would also provide aid for Third World economies to diversify away from reliance on a small number of commodities and to increase the level of commodity processing.

'Sustainability agreements' of these kinds – which could be negotiated both through multilateral trade forums such as the General Agreement on Tariffs and Trade (GATT) and bilaterally between nations – would undoubtedly involve costs for Northern countries. Larger funds would be required for commodity 'buffer stocks', commodity prices would be higher, and there might be job losses in currently protected industries. But such agreements are an essential basis for sustainable development. Third World environments cannot be protected unless more of the costs of using them are reflected in the prices charged for their outputs.[3]

There is also clearly a role for Northern countries in placing greater environmental controls on transnational corporations (TNCs) operating in the Third World. Needing investment and technological know-how, and competing with one another to gain it, many Southern countries find themselves in very weak positions in negotiating with large foreign companies. This is one cause of low environmental standards. A system of regulations or a code of conduct for TNCs which restricted access to Northern markets unless certain environmental standards were applied in the South could be a useful instrument here. Such regulations would almost certainly have to be applied by economic blocs such as the EC. Again, a cost would have to be paid in higher import prices.[4]

The second North–South financing mechanism is aid. In recent years there has been a wider recognition in Northern aid policies of the importance of environmental criteria. Criticisms of the environmental impact of projects funded by the World Bank, for example, have led to a partial reassessment both of individual projects and of overall policies. The stricter measurement of environmental impact is likely to lead to a redirection of aid away from large infrastructural projects which cause extensive environmental damage (such as giant dams) towards sectoral programmes specifically aimed at the sustainable use of natural resources. A sectoral programme might cover for example soil conservation, or the sustainable harvesting of fisheries, forests or water resources, the managed depletion of non-renewables, the conservation of habitats and species, energy efficiency and the development of renewable supply sources, or pollution control. A number of countries have adopted sustainability plans of these kinds, often in conjunction with financing packages from international agencies.[5]

Such plans will then usually be most appropriately implemented by smaller-scale projects in particular areas. The history of development planning, as well as the principle of equity, indicates the paramount importance of involving poor and indigenous groups (such as forest-dwellers) in both the design and implementation of plans and projects. Indeed environmental protection frequently requires challenging market-based ownership rights over natural resources such as fishing grounds, forests and agricultural land. Sustainable management of these resources has been shown in many cases to be best achieved by giving control over them to local, poor communities, whose livelihoods depend on them, and who therefore have a long-term interest in their conservation.[6]

Environmental conditionality and international debt

Where programmes for sustainable development have been drawn up and adopted by countries of the South, aid to finance them will be welcome and uncontroversial. But Northern governments are increasingly coming under pressure to apply environmental conditions to aid programmes even where these are opposed, or not regarded as a high priority, by recipient governments.

Such opposition or lack of interest may arise because environmental protection precisely involves measures such as indigenous control or land reform which challenge established interests. But it may also occur because conservation is seen not as a part of, but as an obstruction to development. This is especially true of some of the most urgent measures urged on the South by Northern environmentalists, such as protection of rainforests and wetlands. In many cases, it is argued, these areas are being destroyed in order to free land for agriculture or industrial development needed by rapidly growing populations. In others habitat and wildlife protection may simply not be regarded as the highest priority in countries racked by poverty and hunger. For Northern countries to demand that aid is used for these ends can then appear merely a way of keeping people in poverty. It is (quite reasonably) seen as hypocritical for the North to try and prevent Southern countries exploiting their own natural resources for economic growth when such exploitation – of Southern resources as well as their own – is precisely how Northern nations developed and became wealthy themselves.

The issue of 'environmental conditionality' in Northern assistance to the South has arisen in particular in the field of international debt. It can hardly be doubted that debt reduction and cancellation are crucial prerequisites for sustainable development. As we saw in Chapter 3, debt not only reduces the funds available in Third World countries for environmental improvement and development, it actually contributes to degradation, since many countries are only able to meet their commitments by over-exploiting their natural resources for export.

However there is no guarantee that, if Northern banks or governments simply reduce debt, the benefits will go either to the environment or to the poor. They may simply be absorbed by the governments and businesses whose debt it is, with the resultant increase in disposable income benefiting mainly the wealthy – and indeed often leaving the country altogether. To prevent this, a number of proposals have been made, and in some cases carried out, linking debt reduction to environmental conservation. In so-called 'debt-for-nature swaps', for example, non-governmental organisations such as the World Wide Fund for Nature have bought up part of a Third World nation's debt, in return for which the country's government has then committed itself to spending the money saved on the preservation of an area of tropical rainforest or other wilderness region. Such swaps have been carried out in Ecuador, Costa Rica, Bolivia, the Philippines and elsewhere.[7]

Debt-for-nature swaps carried out by non-governmental organisations in this way can necessarily make only a marginal contribution to debt reduction, since the funds that can be raised are very small in comparison with the total sums owed. But it is now widely argued that governments should in the same way make official debt reduction schemes conditional upon the implementation of conservation programmes. Proposals of this kind have been drawn up, for example, to offer Brazil (one of the world's most indebted nations) a substantial debt reduction in return for protection of the Amazonian rainforest. A few small official swaps have already been carried out by European governments, for example in Zambia, where aid funds have been used to buy back debt to finance a preservation programme for the black rhino.[8]

Such conditionality is however widely seen by governments and organisations in the South as a kind of blackmail (or 'gringo greenmail', as one Brazilian president put it),[9] by which 'imperialist' industrialised countries attempt to dictate to sovereign nations what their development priorities should be. It is especially resented in relation to debt, since the huge sums now owed are widely regarded as illegitimate, the result of the dramatic rise in interest rates in the 1980s which the Northern nations themselves caused. Debt reduction should therefore be unconditional. If the moral argument that North–South transfers are merely compensations for past environmental damage is accepted, the idea of attaching strings is evidently unfair: even straightforward aid is a payment for goods received and should be given as such.

Since it is indeed unlikely that funds released by unconditional debt reduction or aid would automatically go towards conservation projects, there is clearly a potential contradiction between the acceptance of this argument and the needs of environmental protection. In practice this contradiction can be mitigated in two ways. The first is to negotiate debt reduction, like aid, through programmes which benefit the poor as well as the environment. It is after all mainly the poor in the Third World who have borne the debt burden, through lower living standards and the degradation of the natural environments on which they depend. And it is harder for Southern governments to argue against 'conditionality' which clearly reduces poverty. Population planning programmes, which are widely recognised in North and South as necessary to tackle both poverty and environmental damage, might be particularly appropriate mechanisms.[10]

Second, Northern governments must ensure that environmental conditionality is not simply a means of imposing new requirements on existing aid budgets, but that it *increases* the total resources available to the South. Debt reduction must be negotiated on the basis of equity in relation to the sums originally owed and current ability to pay; but must then be matched by additional assistance funds for sustainable development programmes. Such funds, it should be noted, should come not only from government budgets but from the commercial banks with outstanding Third World debts. Many banks have now effectively written off these debts in their accounts. This allows them to claim tax relief without actually easing the burden for their debtors. Such relief should be clawed back unless debt is actually reduced by the amounts set aside.[11]

Although it may seem unlikely in the present climate that industrialised countries will increase aid funds, there are in fact good reasons why support for environmental policies in the South is in Northern countries' own interest. Indeed in some instances the argument over conditionality may be turned on its head.

First, in matters of global environmental degradation, the North is as dependent on the South as vice versa. If the rich countries of the world want to protect themselves against global warming, for example, they cannot do so alone. While the contribution to the greenhouse effect of the very poorest countries may be negligible, this cannot be said of the larger 'newly-industrialised' and 'middle-income' nations such as Brazil, India, Indonesia and China. With their significant and growing industrial sectors and large populations, these countries have the potential to undermine any agreements reached between the Northern nations on carbon dioxide, CFC and other greenhouse gas reductions. Moreover, those such as Brazil possessing large areas of remaining forest have a crucial role to play in the implementation of policies to absorb carbon dioxide as well as ones to limit its production.

This interdependence gives the South a degree of potential bargaining power over the North which it has rarely had in the past. As has already been demonstrated in the negotiations over the Montreal Protocol on reducing CFCs, large Southern nations can refuse to agree to global environmental measures unless they are compensated for doing so. For countries such as China and India, with heavy coal consumption and significant growth plans (China's stated intention is to provide every household with a refrigerator), the cost of CO_2 and

CFC limitation is very large. So far from Northern countries imposing environmental conditionality on aid to the South, the prospect here is that Southern countries will impose aid conditionality on environmental protection for the North. It is certainly unlikely that Third World countries will agree to any international convention on global warming unless very substantial aid is provided to enable them to comply. Such aid will especially be demanded in the form of 'technology transfer', enabling Southern countries to use the most modern and environmentally efficient technology available in the North without paying extensive royalty fees.[12]

The second, connected reason why aid to the South is likely to benefit the industrialised countries is that environmental degradation carries an evident risk of causing international political instability. Competition for increasingly scarce resources is already generating disputes both within and between countries, as conflicts over both oil and water resources in the Middle East and elsewhere have demonstrated. Further desertification and rising sea levels caused by the greenhouse effect could create particular havoc, with international migration – and the consequent creation of refugees – on an unprecedented scale. Northern nations will not be able to insulate themselves from these events. Indeed, it is being widely suggested that traditional notions of international security based on a balance of arms and territorial agreements should be augmented by new concepts of 'environmental security' based on equitable distributions of, and access to, natural wealth.[13]

Interestingly, these reasons for increasing environmental assistance themselves suggest where the additional funds could be raised. Operating on the principle that the source of revenue should be related to the problems for which it is required, two kinds of international aid 'hypothecation' (earmarking) could be established.

The first would be an international 'greenhouse levy', imposed on countries in proportion to their emissions of CO_2, CFCs and other greenhouse gases. Such a levy could be recouped by national governments through a carbon charge and by taxing the windfall profits of CFC producers resulting from output restrictions. These measures could raise substantial sums: a carbon levy equivalent to raising the price of coal by just 1% would raise $2.4 billion a year if applied worldwide; in Europe alone it would raise $300m. It is estimated that a CFC tax could raise around $20 billion over a decade. The revenues from such levies would then be placed in a 'global environmental trust fund', managed by a UN agency, which would be specifically used to assist Southern countries to combat the greenhouse effect. A number of proposals for such a fund and its use have been made.[14]

The second source of funds would be a diversion of government budgets away from military expenditure. World military spending currently absorbs approximately $900 billion every year, much of which evidently exacerbates rather than diminishes international political tension. Redirecting just a proportion of this spending towards measures designed to improve 'environmental security' (such as population planning, soil conservation, energy efficiency, water management and afforestation) could have a very large impact both on the environment in the South and on potential international stability. Particular efforts could be made to switch research and development funds, around 30% of which in the US and the UK are currently devoted to defence, towards environmental and social ends.[15]

Interestingly, such a diversion of military expenditure, if carefully introduced, would almost certainly bring economic benefits to industrialised countries. There is strong evidence that military expenditure creates fewer jobs and has a smaller multiplier effect than alternative investments. In general there is clearly significant scope for environmental policies in the Third World to generate markets for Northern products, particularly in biotechnology, energy efficiency and supply, pollution control and other advanced technologies.[16] It is likely that such benefits would to some extent offset the costs of international environmental assistance.

Such assistance will not of course be readily given. The sums required are very large: the World Resources Institute has estimated that as much as $50 billion extra per annum may be required to finance environmental protection in the South over a decade, which is approximately twice as much as current aid budgets.[17] The obstacles in the way, both political and economic, are clearly very large. But it is increasingly apparent that the alternatives are not pleasant either. It is to be hoped that this will provide sufficient motivation, in both South and North, to make progress.

International environmental agreements[18]

In Chapter 10 we argued that a process of international environmental target-setting was required for pollutants and resources acting at a global scale, such as CFCs and carbon dioxide, tropical and other forests and habitats of particular importance. We pointed out that several international agreements had already been signed, such as the 1987 Montreal Protocol on Substances that Deplete the Ozone Layer, and the European Community's 1988 Large Combustion Plant (LCP) Directive on sulphur dioxide and nitrous oxide emissions causing acid rain. A 'framework convention' on the greenhouse effect, centring on target reductions in carbon dioxide emissions, was in preparation.

But the difficulties in getting international agreement on environmental targets, particularly for limiting greenhouse gas emissions, should not be underestimated. In this respect it has to be said that the Montreal Protocol may not be the best guide. Only a small number of nations are involved in CFC production. The costs of phasing CFCs out are substantially less than the costs of reducing greenhouse emissions, with substitutes for several major uses readily available. Moreover, in the end it has proved actually to be in the interests of the major CFC-manufacturing companies to ban the substances, since this effectively gives them a monopoly in the production of substitutes.[19] These conditions are unlikely to apply in the case of CO_2 emissions or for other global environmental treaties.

There are two principal obstacles in the way of such agreements. One is the 'free rider' problem. Since a country which does not comply with the treaty will gain the benefits (in the greenhouse gas case, reduced global warming) generated by the actions of those that do, what incentive does it have to comply? One answer to this is that the agreement will not exist unless at least a certain number of countries participate; and the more countries do so the greater the benefits will be. By complying itself, and thereby encouraging other countries to comply, each country can help gain greater benefits; to this extent cooperative behaviour can be 'self-enforcing'.[20] Indeed in these circumstances the moral pressure of the international community in generating the agreement may exert an influence over individual countries' behaviour not readily reducible to financial self-interest.[21]

But even if this process encourages many countries to sign a treaty, there are still likely to be other, more obvious 'compliance mechanisms' needed – both to encourage the participation of countries which may still be tempted to free ride and to 'punish' violations of the agreement by signatories. (If a participating country is allowed to get away with non-compliance, the agreement will soon break down.) For violations, 'fines' could be levied, to be paid into a global environmental fund; such a system would reinforce the incentives to comply. For non-signatories, various kinds of political sanctions could be applied, or tariff walls could be constructed against the country's exports, or certain types of aid such as technology transfer could be refused. This would obviously require the establishment of a global agency responsible for monitoring and enforcement of the treaty, such as perhaps the United Nations Environment Programme. Although sanctions such as these are not easy to impose, they are not unknown.[22] In the end no sovereign country can be forced to behave as other countries wish; but in an interdependent world the ability to ignore the rest of the international community completely is limited too.

The second problem is that of allocation within the global target. From the point of view of the climatologist, the important part of an international greenhouse treaty will be the total level of global emissions allowed. But for the national political leader the real issue will be how much carbon dioxide (or other gases) his or her country will be permitted to discharge. How will each country's allocation of the total emissions limit be decided?

There are several possible formulae. One is a uniform percentage reduction target – say, every country to reduce emissions by 20%. This is the approach taken by the Montreal Protocol on CFCs. Some variation to take account of different countries' circumstances is possible: the Montreal Protocol allows developing countries to take ten years longer than industrialised countries to reach the target. In the case of carbon dioxide, different percentage reduction targets might be set for perhaps four or five 'bands' of countries at different levels of national income. Developing countries, which have low emissions per capita and which need to increase energy consumption in the process of industrial development, might be set emissions increase limits rather than reduction targets.

The problem with even a modified formula of this sort, however, is that the energy consumption of different countries varies very greatly, with the result that equal percentage targets will actually have very unequal effects. The cost of reducing emissions depends on each nation's current levels of energy efficiency – that is, energy consumption per unit of GNP. For a country such as Japan, which is already relatively efficient, a 20% cut in consumption will cost far more than the same reduction for a country such as the United States, whose consumption per unit of GNP is almost twice as great. Such an agreement would quite reasonably be opposed by the Japanese on the grounds that it would effectively penalise them for having already achieved a high level of efficiency and would reward the US for its lack of progress so far.[23] They could point out, moreover, that it would be economically inefficient, since it might actually cost the US less to reduce emissions by 25% than it would for Japan to achieve a 15% cut; yet the US would only be required, and the Japanese would be forced, to cut by 20%.

Further resistance would arise because countries are differently endowed with fuel resources. China, for example, has large reserves of coal but almost no oil or (as yet discovered) gas. It will therefore find it much harder to cut emissions than, say, the USSR, which has extensive oil and gas supplies. (One way of reducing carbon emissions is by 'fuel switching', since gas and oil have a much lower carbon content than coal.)[24] Moreover, poorer countries will point not just to current but to historical emissions. The industrialised countries have been using up the assimilative capacity of the atmosphere for many years already; fairness suggests not an equalisation of present but of total emissions over time.[25]

These variations in the 'energy economies' of different countries suggest that different targets might have to be set for different countries. This is the approach taken by the EC's Large Combustion Plant Directive. But the problem with this is the enormous difficulty of negotiating such an agreement, with countries trading off their individual costs against each other. The LCP Directive provides an instructive example. Only twelve countries were involved in the negotiations, all at reasonably similar levels of economic development. Yet negotiation of the Directive took five years of almost full-time bargaining. At this rate of progress, negotiation of a greenhouse treaty would almost certainly be overtaken by the climatic and political events it was trying to forestall. Moreover, it should be noted, this approach induces an unhelpful psychology among the negotiators, with each constantly looking, not for opportunities to cut emissions, but for the additional costs of doing so.[26]

An alternative is available to both the uniform target and country trade-off approaches. This is to set emission 'allowances' for every country according to some neutral concept of entitlement, and then allow countries to trade their allowances with one another.[27] The obvious basis for neutral entitlement would be population: the global carbon emissions target would be divided by the world's population, and then each country allocated its proportionate allowance. Such an allocation would have the great advantages of simplicity and fairness, resting on a principle against which it is difficult to argue, namely that each person in the world should have an equal entitlement to use the atmosphere's assimilative capacity.[28]

Equalising per capita allocations, of course, would leave developing countries with much larger allowances than they currently need, and industrialised countries with much smaller ones. This is where the second part of the mechanism comes in. In order to gain the carbon 'permits' they would require, industrialised countries would be forced to buy them from developing nations. There would be no centrally fixed price: this would be determined in each case by the trading countries. Clearly, such a system would give both rich and poor nations a strong incentive to become as energy efficient as possible: in the case of industrialised countries, in order to minimise the number of permits they were required to buy; for developing countries, to maximise the income from unwanted permits. In theory at least this should in turn induce an 'efficient' (or least-cost) global use of energy. Countries able to save energy more cheaply than they could buy permits would do so, while others with higher costs of saving would buy permits instead.[29]

For a number of reasons permits would need to be valid for a limited period only. After perhaps two years they would be reissued, with a new total limit based on current scientific evidence of global warming, and new allocations according to population changes. This would prevent permits being bought up by rich countries, thereby forcing developing countries to buy back permits (probably at a higher price) when needed in the future. It would also correctly require countries to make continuing rather than one-off payments for continuing use of the atmosphere. Such time-limited permits would therefore effectively be leased rather than sold.

A system such as this would have the merit, from the point of view of fairness, of entailing a significant transfer of resources from North to South. Industrialised countries would be forced to acknowledge their greater historical use of the common atmospheric resource, and their greater current capacity to cut energy consumption, by compensating poorer countries. This transfer of resources could take the form of money, or any other tradable commodity. Or it could be limited to specific environmental technologies and development assistance – most particularly, the transfer of technologies designed to raise energy efficiency in the South. This would ensure that at each stage the mechanism helped to reduce environmental degradation. It would overcome one of the principal objections developing countries are likely to have to any global agreement, namely that they are unable to cut energy consumption because the industrialised world charges such high prices for the technological know-how to do so. And it would overcome one of the objections likely to come from the North, namely that such an agreement would have nothing in it for them. New markets would be opened up for energy and environmental technologies, assisting Northern employment and investment.

This is not to say that industrialised countries will easily be persuaded to sign an agreement of this kind. Clearly, payments to the South will add to the cost of emissions reductions. But it is frankly unlikely that a greenhouse agreement of *any* kind will be signed by Southern countries unlesss it involves compensation by the North. As India and China have already shown in the case of the Montreal Protocol, an agreement which involves substantial current costs in return for uncertain future benefits is simply not worth making to a poor nation unless some form of compensation is paid. Neither country would sign the Protocol until a fund was established to transfer CFC-substitution technology to developing countries, thereby cutting the cost to them of meeting the Protocol's targets.

Interestingly, the Montreal Protocol sets a precedent not only for such compensatory payments (in the form of North–South technology transfer) but also for trading permits between countries. The Protocol specifically allows countries to trade up to 10% (and after 1998 15%) of their quota with other countries, if this will reduce the overall cost of CFC reduction.

The exact form of any international greenhouse agreement – indeed, whether one is signed at all – will clearly depend primarily on the attitude of the rich countries of the world whose emissions must be reduced the most, notably the United States and the nations of the European Community. But the capacity of at least the larger developing countries to undermine any agreement to which they are not signatories will give them some kind of bargaining power; and the principle of equal per capita entitlements then seems a rational starting point. There is evidently considerable scope for negotiation: for example, equal entitlements could be established as the goal, and a gradual programme agreed to reach it over a number of years. This would allow higher entitlements to industrialised countries in the first few years, gradually reducing to equality.[30] A large number of other aspects of the scheme – monitoring and enforcement mechanisms, who could deal in permits (companies as well as governments?), what technologies and development assistance programmes would be allowed as trading 'currencies', allowances for afforestation programmes, and so on) would also of course need detailed agreement.

Part IV
Measurement

16

Making Environmental Decisions (1): The Limits of Cost-Benefit Analysis

The rationale and method of cost-benefit analysis

Most of the decisions made by individual firms and consumers can be held within sustainability constraints by the use of the various instruments described in Chapter 11. When the environmental effect of each individual decision is of itself small, the state need only be concerned with the macroeconomic total. Another mechanism is required, however, for major investment projects whose environmental effects are very large. Projects such as new factories and power stations, new roads or railway lines, new industrial complexes or urban settlements, require decisions to be made directly by governments. Such projects are likely to be very expensive, and may have far-reaching impacts on land use and habitats, pollution and health, visual, recreational and other forms of amenity, resource consumption, etc.

Where such projects are in the public sector, governments necessarily have to make decisions. But even where they are privately funded, environmental protection may require the state to decide whether they should be allowed or not (and in what form). This already happens where extra land is required: new buildings are subject to planning controls. Environmental policy may now be forced to extend the scope of project appraisal further into the private sector, to wherever investment decisions have major environmental effects for which existing taxation and regulation policy is inadequate. Society as a whole may want to decide: are the benefits of the project worth its costs – including its environmental costs?

Similar sorts of decisions will occur in setting local environmental standards. We noted in Chapter 8 that the concept of sustainability would not of itself necessarily generate standards for localised pollution which met the economists' criterion of optimality (maximum benefit over cost). It might be that the sustainability constraints, which are primarily aimed to protect future generations, would be less strict than the local population would like. A local river might be ecologically stable at current pollution levels, for example, but not swimmable. If local people would like it to be swimmable, it would seem reasonable to ask what the cost of making it so would be. Some mechanism would then need to be found for deciding whether this cost was worth paying. We might also describe this as a decision on an environmental protection 'project'. Such projects are likely to be proposed (even after sustainability constraints have been met) for a variety of local environmental issues: local pollution levels, the use and appearance of natural land and the built environment, the enhancement of habitats and other environmental features, etc.

One way of making all these sorts of decisions is simply through the interplay of political forces. If the 'roads lobby' is more powerful than the 'nature conservation lobby', then the road gets built. If governments are linked to the nuclear industry, nuclear power stations are constructed however strong the economic and environmental arguments against them. Pollution levels are set by whatever the polluting industry claims it can achieve. In practice this is often exactly what happens; and only the naive or the utopian can hope that political decision-making can ever be free of politics.[1] Nevertheless many people, particularly economists, have claimed that a more rational and objective way of making such decisions is possible. They claim that the costs and benefits of a project can be weighed up in a systematic way. Instead of politicians or experts simply dictating what is good for people, account can be taken of the expressed interests and preferences of all those affected by the decision.

The method devised by economists for systematic decision-making in this way is *cost-benefit analysis*, or CBA. CBA starts from a simple premise, namely that an investment project should only be undertaken if all its benefits outweigh all its costs. Given several alternative forms of a project (or competing projects) the one for which the difference between benefits and costs is greatest should be chosen. Now clearly costs and benefits can only be added and subtracted in this way if they are expressed in the same units; so CBA attempts to place monetary values on them, money being a convenient 'measuring rod' of value. Since the costs and benefits of a project will occur over a period, future ones are subjected to a discount rate which converts them into their 'present value'.[2]

An example can illustrate. Imagine we are faced with a decision on whether or not to build a new bypass around a village. The basic financial costs of the road include purchase of the land and the costs of construction. On top of these there will be various kinds of environmental costs: the loss of some habitats, greater noise and a deterioration of the view for local residents, extra pollution, and so on. The benefits of the road will similarly accrue to a number of different groups of people. Road hauliers will gain from faster journeys, reducing the cost to consumers of the goods they transport. There will be fewer lorries driving through villages, resulting in lower air pollution and noise and fewer accidents. What cost-benefit analysis tries to do in these circumstances is, first, put monetary values on those costs and benefits which don't already have them, and then add up all the costs and benefits to see which total is greater. Since it is held that people are impatient, and since if the road were not built the money could be put into a bank where it would earn interest, future benefits and costs are 'discounted'. If the 'net present value' of the bypass is then positive, the project is held to be worth undertaking.

In practice, as they are actually carried out, many cost-benefit analyses do not add up all the costs and benefits in this way. Environmental effects are often left out, because the environment – not being 'bought' for a price – doesn't obviously have a monetary value. For example, in Britain new trunk roads are assessed using a combination of CBA and a separate 'environmental impact assessment' (EIA).[3] In the CBA are included the benefits of time savings, accident saving and changes in vehicle operating costs. These are given monetary values using a variety of statistical methods. Thirteen different environmental effects are then assessed in the EIA: noise, visual impact, air pollution, effects on agriculture, ecological impact and others. Since these effects are not given monetary values, the final decision is made by some judgement of the relative weight of the monetary conclusion reached by the CBA in comparison with the non-monetary indicators of the environmental impact assessment. Many commentators have observed that in practice the environmental effects are accorded little importance; government decision-makers are much more impressed by a project with high net present value despite major environmental costs than by one with significant environmental benefits but a smaller financial return.[4]

It is for this reason that many environmental economists have in recent years argued that the environmental effects of projects *should* be included in the cost-benefit analysis – by giving them monetary values. They argue that since it is inevitable that decisions are made on financial grounds, the only way of properly protecting the environment is to express its value in the same terms as other costs and benefits. The environment is very highly valued, they argue; many people would be willing to pay substantial sums of money to protect it. If this is so it should be possible to discover how much they are willing to pay, and thus to estimate how much a particular feature of the environment is 'worth' in monetary terms. This value can then be put into the cost-benefit analysis. Since it will almost always be positive, doing this will result in a higher level of environmental protection than otherwise. Moreover, it will reflect how much people actually value the environment, not the arbitrary and subjective level of concern of a politician or bureaucrat.[5]

It is not just 'use values' which can be included in the CBA, either. As well as estimating how much people are willing to pay for directly 'consuming' different aspects of the environment, modern environmental economists have attempted to discover people's 'option', 'bequest' and 'existence' values as well: that is, the value placed on the possibility of being able to use the environment in the future, on being able to bequeath it to the next generation, and on the simple existence of the environment irrespective of use.[6] In this way, they argue, the full value of the environment can be included in decision-making.

Two different questions arise from the environmental economists' approach. There is the overall issue of whether cost-benefit analysis as a technique is a legitimate way of making decisions. Does it take into account all the factors we would wish to be considered? There is then the question of whether it is possible to value the environment in monetary terms. Even if the CBA procedure is acceptable in theory, some people have argued, it is not actually possible to carry it out, because the environment cannot be measured by money. None of the methods devised by environmental economists to discover the environment's 'value' actually generate meaningful numbers. We shall address the overall question of whether CBA is a legitimate way of making decisions in the remainder of this chapter. The issues surrounding monetary valuation will be discussed in the next.

Applying sustainability constraints to CBA

The first and perhaps most obvious objection to CBA as a way of making decisions is that it does not take into account the interests of all those people affected (quite apart, it might be added, from the interests of other living beings). As we argued in Chapter 6, any attempt to value the environment will exclude two categories of 'distant' people: those living overseas and those living in the future. Both may be affected by a decision subjected to a CBA; but neither will be included in its calculus. In theory some attempt could be made to discover the valuations of people living overseas, but in practice this would be extremely difficult, especially for people living in the South who are unlikely to be able to express their preferences in monetary terms, and for whom direct comparison with people living in the North cannot be made.[7] Future generations' valuations, of course, are necessarily excluded.

For anyone concerned about sustainability – about the interests of future people – this limitation of CBA immediately invalidates its claims to legitimacy as a decision-making procedure. The whole basis of sustainability was a rejection of the 'valuation' approach to environmental protection, with its implicit bias against distant people; CBA is a concrete expression of that approach.

This does not mean, however, that there is no place at all for cost-benefit procedures. The interests of future people, and those overseas, can be taken into account in individual decisions by the same means used at the level of the whole economy, namely by applying sustainability constraints. Set for each environmental function at the level which maintained minimum environmental capacity, such constraints would ensure that no project was undertaken which harmed the interests of future (or overseas) people. Thus, for example, road projects would have to fall within constraints on habitat diversity and carbon dioxide levels. If a proposed road would destroy a protected habitat, or would lead to traffic generating more than the prescribed CO_2 emissions for the transport sector, it would be prohibited – even before any consideration were taken of its costs and benefits to present, local people. Similarly, if a new factory were projected to raise pollution levels in the water table or upper atmosphere above their sustainability targets, cost-benefit analysis would be redundant – the project would be rejected before any monetary valuation were attempted.

As at the level of the whole economy, sustainability constraints applied to CBA would thus protect the minimum interests of future people first, before current decision-makers' preferences were valued. Note that in order to stay within the sustainability constraints a project could include ancillary measures to offset its primary environmental effects. For example, if the protected habitat could be recreated on another site (at the same level of diversity and richness), or if the additional CO_2 emissions could be absorbed by the planting of trees, the new road proposal could go forward to CBA. The inclusion of such 'shadow projects' within the proposed investment would enable it to comply with the sustainability constraint.[8] Of course, the costs of the shadow projects would have to be included in the costs of the original investment as measured by the CBA. The shadow projects would also have actually to be undertaken: they could not remain simply 'notional' compensations for environmental damage as often envisaged in welfare economics.[9]

If CBA were undertaken within such a framework of sustainability constraints, it would be more precise to speak of it being a form of 'cost-effectiveness' analysis. The constraints would act as policy targets, and then the point of the valuation exercise would be to determine the least costly way of meeting these targets. This sort of procedure is familiar in the field of engineering design, where safety standards are set on objective grounds (not according to the 'value' of accidents) and then the most cost-effective method of meeting them is chosen.

A framework of sustainability constraints is a more sensible way of protecting the interests of future generations than changing the discount rates used in cost-benefit analysis. There has been a long-running argument between environmentalists and economists on this subject.[10] Environmentalists have argued that high discount rates contribute to environmental degradation, since they devalue future returns in comparison with present ones, and many environmental effects occur over the long term. Thus, for example, the cost of decommissioning a nuclear power station will fall 20 or 30 years into the future, whereas the financial benefits of electricity generation are immediate. On the other hand, an afforestation project is expensive now, while its environmental benefits do not emerge until the trees are mature.

In both cases the use of high discount rates in a CBA (for example, the 5–7% currently demanded by the UK Treasury in public sector projects) discriminates against future generations. Many environmentalists have therefore argued that discount rates should be reduced where environmental interests are involved. (To some extent the UK Treasury agrees: its discount rate for forestry projects is 3%.)[11]

There is no question that many of the arguments for discounting the future value of the environment are spurious. As we saw in Chapter 7, discounting does indeed weight decisions against the interests of future people. It is quite wrong to argue that, because such people will be richer, the marginal benefit of a given environmental feature will be less than it is presently: if environmental degradation continues (or if people became more environmentally aware), it may well be greater. Moreover, just because it is possible to give the environment a monetary valuation does not mean that it therefore grows like a sum of invested capital, allowing us to discount its future size into present value.

Nevertheless, reducing discount rates within the CBA procedure (even to zero) is not the best way of protecting the environment. This is because, whether discounting occurs or not, the procedure is still based on financial not environmental criteria. It is the 'bottom line', expressed in money units, that counts. The environment can only be taken into account if it too is valued in monetary terms, since no other values are allowed. But then this places the whole burden of environmental protection onto monetary valuation, a concept and a technique which (as we shall show below) remains fraught with difficulty. If, as we shall claim, monetary valuation doesn't in fact capture the full value of the environment, even refusing to discount altogether might not lead to sustainable levels of environmental protection. Indeed, since in most large-scale projects the major financial costs occur before the benefits, a lower discount rate would tend to encourage higher levels of investment, with concomitantly higher environmental costs. This would make the potential undervaluation of the environment by monetary techniques even more serious, increasing the disparity between financial benefits and environmental costs. This would reduce the likelihood that sustainable levels of environmental protection would be achieved.

By contrast the use of sustainability constraints guarantees such levels, by imposing them on the decision-making process. The interests of future generations are safeguarded directly, by defining them in environmental terms and making their protection the first stage of the decision-making procedure. Altogether the direct use of sustainability constraints is simpler and more practical.[12]

Equity and political judgement

Ths second objection to cost-benefit analysis as a decision-making procedure rests on its utilitarian foundation. In its basic form, CBA adds up all the costs and benefits of a project without discrimination as to whom they affect. One pound or dollar of benefit is assumed to have the same value to a rich person as to a poor one; one pound or dollar of cost to be as harmful. The simple addition and subtraction of monetary figures takes no account of concepts such as justice or rights: decisions are based on the 'greatest net benefit of the greatest number', whoever gets harmed on the way.

The justification for this disregard for considerations of equity is sometimes known as the 'compensation test'. Since almost all projects will have winners and losers, one would never invest in anything if everyone had to gain from the decision. Therefore CBA decrees that a project should go ahead if the gain to the winners is greater than the loss to the losers, since this would mean that the winners could compensate the losers and still be better off, with no one then being worse off.[13] In reality of course the compensation rarely happens, so the losers still lose. Indeed the rule is seldom strictly observed, since just one loser claiming that nothing would compensate him or her would blow the entire calculation to pieces. Such infinite claims of loss are usually ignored, breaking the compensation test but making decisions possible.[14]

This point was illustrated recently in Germany. By law all residents living within a 45° angle from the top of a proposed building must give their consent before construction is permitted. In 1989 one Frau Kraus, a resident of Frankfurt, refused to do so. She was offered 10 million Deutschmark (over £3 million) by the property developers but declined to take it. She claimed the new building would block out the sunlight and spoil her neighbourhood, and no amount of money would be sufficient compensation. Because of the law the project was effectively vetoed; but a cost-benefit analysis would more likely have simply ignored her infinite valuation.[15]

For those concerned about equity, the utilitarian basis of CBA renders it inadequate as a decision-making procedure. Many people, for example, would wish to weight the gains and losses made by the poor more highly than those of the rich. Many would wish to ensure that people's or communities' rights over their own environments were not infringed (though there would no doubt be disagreement over what constituted a 'right'). Since these considerations are moral issues, subject to conflicting values, they cannot be accommodated within a cost-benefit framework which seeks apparently objective numerical answers. They require moral or political judgements.[16]

This again does not mean, however, that there is no place for CBA, only that CBA itself is not sufficient for decision-making. That the ultimate decision on a project must be political, not simply computational, is not a reason to abandon systematic estimation of costs and benefits altogether. It is still helpful to identify what these costs and benefits are and (as far as is possible) their magnitude. By identifying on whom they fall, and keeping the effects on different groups of people separate, judgements of equity are indeed made easier. Costs and benefits can be added up within each group without adding up all the groups' valuations together. For example, a CBA on a new industrial development in a scenic area could list separately the effects on local residents, tourists, potential employees, potential consumers, and so on, dividing each group into income bands. Although the final decision on the overall effect of the project would still have to be made through moral or political judgement (perhaps via a public enquiry) the CBA could provide the information on which the judgement would be based.

Such a process is indeed how advocates of CBA generally claim it should be used. The objection to CBA in practice then becomes a political one, that decision makers do not in fact take equity considerations sufficiently into account in their judgements, relying too much on the simple CBA totals.

Are environmental values 'commensurable'?

The third general objection to cost-benefit analysis is that it attempts to do what cannot be done, namely to weigh up 'incommensurable' values. One cannot say that, for example, a human life is worth more than the preservation of a scenic view, or that the lives of wild animals are more valuable than the maintenance of indigenous hunting cultures. These values are incommensurable: like apples and pears they cannot be added to or subtracted from one another. Yet this is exactly what CBA attempts to do, converting all values into monetary units and then comparing them as if they were simply commodities cashable at the local pawn shop. To proponents of this objection, the incommensurable nature of environmental and other non-marketed values (such as human life, community, culture and so on) makes the whole process futile – if not actually dangerous.[17]

But what does it mean, to say that environmental or other values are 'incommensurable'? In one sense this idea seems clearly mistaken. We often compare alternative states of the world, without being able to measure them. We say, for example, that the loss of liberty involved in banning racist literature is worth it for the additional security and harmony it brings to society. Yet we cannot 'measure' liberty and security on a common scale. Similarly, we acknowledge that allowing cars on urban streets entails more accidents, yet judge that (within a certain limit, perhaps) such accidents are a tolerable price for the benefits of mobility and comfort those cars bring. There is no unit, however, in which human life and mobility can both be expressed.

Note that even if no one explicitly says that the extra accidents are 'tolerable', this is the implicit conclusion that can be drawn from the fact that cars *are* allowed, when the larger number of accidents is a predictable consequence. Whoever agrees that cars should be allowed effectively makes that valuation. In the real world we have to make choices, and these choices must express some comparison between alternative states of affairs, such that one is judged to be 'better', or 'more valuable' than another. If the building of a bypass would reduce the number of accidents but entail the loss of a scenic view or a stretch of green land, our decision on whether to support the new road would entail some valuation, even though not measurable, of fewer accidents as against the loss of amenity and habitats. Unless we are to toss a coin, this is the only way a decision can be made. In some cases the decision may be very hard: we may not be able to judge which state of affairs is preferable. But in others our valuation may be clearer: if the area of green land was small, of no particular beauty and could be replaced elsewhere, perhaps.

It is crucial to recognise that the statement 'this state of affairs is more valuable than that' need *not* imply that it is worth more in monetary terms. Some writers have objected to statements of this kind on the grounds that they appear to reduce the alternatives (such as accidents and green space) to commodities which can be exchanged.[18] But this is not what is meant. Neither of the alternatives need be measurable by money, and therefore 'saleable', for some comparison between them to be made. No amount of money measures the value of a human life; therefore one life is not worth one-tenth of ten lives. But this does not mean that the health service should not allocate scarce resources so as to save ten lives rather than one.[19] 'Value' in this context is simply a relative (or 'ordinal') term expressing a ranking between alternative states of affairs; it does not require any connection with money at all, nor any other sort of ('cardinal') scale of measurement.

It is therefore not true to say that environmental and other non-marketed values are 'incommensurable', in the sense that no comparison may be made between them. But there is another meaning of this term for which such a claim might be made. Cost-benefit analysis, after all, doesn't simply seek to rank alternative options. It actually *does* wish to put monetary values on environmental and other non-marketed goods; to say that a human life is worth £500,000 and the preservation of the Colorado wilderness $93.2 million per annum.[20] For most opponents of commensurability, it is this which is illegitimate. Comparison in general may be possible, but it cannot be done by expressing values on a monetary scale. Things like human life and the environment simply aren't comprehensible in such terms.

This claim, if upheld, would destroy the cost-benefit approach, since CBA precisely does rely on different values being commensurable through monetary valuation. So far we have argued that CBA cannot be *sufficient* as a decision-making procedure, because it cannot take account of the values of sustainability and equity. But if sustainability constraints are applied and it is recognised that distributional judgements must be made, there could still be a place for a cost-benefit approach in weighing up alternatives. If monetary valuation of the environment is not possible, however, even this limited place will be forfeit. To see whether it is possible or not, we shall have to examine how economists have tried to find monetary values for environmental goods.

17

Making Environmental Decisions (2): Monetary Valuation of the Environment

Methods of monetary valuation

When people hear that economists have represented a particular environmental feature by a sum of money, it is often assumed that the figure has been plucked out of the air, and merely reflects the economist's subjective estimation. But this is not what economists have tried to do at all. Their goal has been to discover how much *the public* values the environment, by measuring their willingness to pay for it. In this sense, the economist will argue, the method is actually quite democratic. It tries to find out what people want, rather than simply ignoring them and letting politicians (or whoever) make decisions.

Finding out what people want in relation to the environment is not easy, however, because there are not generally markets for environmental goods. As we saw in Chapter 3, they are usually 'public goods' which are free and available to everyone. So economists have devised two broad approaches to measuring what people would be willing to pay for the environment if a market did exist.[1]

In the first, the 'revealed preference' approach, consumer behaviour with respect to goods *associated* with the environment is analysed, and the value of the environment is inferred from it. Demand for a given environmental feature is 'revealed' by demand for the associated good. In the second, the 'hypothetical preference' approach, consumers express their environmental valuations directly, but not in real situations. Rather they are placed in hypothetical situations where they can pay for a particular environmental feature (or receive compensation for losing it) and are then asked how much it is worth.

The revealed preference approach has been widely used to measure the value of air and noise pollution and scenic views near people's homes. It rests on a simple proposition, namely that the price of a good is related to its characteristics. In the case of a house, these characteristics include the quality of the local air, noise levels and amenity. It is assumed that if two houses were on offer, identical except that one

204

were under an aircraft flight path, the price of the houses would differ by the value people placed on peace and quiet. By analysing the prices of houses of a similar size, age, location, etc., but with differing levels of air quality, noise and visual amenity, it is therefore possible, economists claim, to isolate the value which house buyers put on the environmental features.[2]

Similar sorts of calculations have been performed to identify the value that workers place on health and safety risk in the workplace. Here it is assumed that wage levels are correlated with a variety of characteristics of employment. The economist's task is then to compare similar jobs with differing levels of danger, and isolate the element of the wage associated with the extra risk.[3]

Another widely-used revealed preference method, that of 'travel cost', aims to discover the value of recreational areas such as nature parks to which people have to travel. Since it costs both money and time to visit such areas, it is possible to infer their monetary value (economists claim) by investigating how far visitors travel, how much they pay, how many times they visit, etc.[4]

These revealed preference methods can be used where consumers are making real decisions about goods or services associated with the environmental features whose values are in question. But they are of little help where real behaviour cannot be observed. If we are trying to find out, for example, what value people would place on an environmental improvement (such as a reduction in traffic) or on the survival of a rare species (such as the grizzly bear or blue whale), there is no associated good whose demand will reveal people's preferences. So economists have decided to ask them directly.

There are two principal hypothetical preference methods. The first, 'contingent valuation', uses surveys to ask people how much they would be willing to pay to secure a given environmental improvement, or not to suffer its loss. For example, respondents might be asked how much they would be willing (and able) to pay to reduce lead pollution levels in the air by a given amount, or to preserve a particular scenic view. Often they are given a series of possible prices; the highest one they are willing to pay is taken as their 'bid'. Sometimes the procedure is reversed, and respondents are asked what is the smallest amount of money they would accept in compensation for the loss of a valued feature, such as a view or local habitat.[5]

The second method, 'stated preference', is a little more complex, and has been much less widely applied. Here, the questionnaire describes various possible alternative situations, each having a different combination of attributes. For example several different transport options might be offered, each involving a different length of journey, degree of comfort, waiting time, price and environmental impact. Respondents are then asked to rank the alternatives. By varying the combination of attributes in the different options, it is possible to discover the element of the price which respondents are willing to pay for a given environmental impact (or for any other attribute).[6]

Each of these methods of finding monetary values for the environment has generated results. For example, a 1% increase in air pollution around Los Angeles has been estimated to cause a 0.22% reduction in property prices, that is, $220 for a $100,000 house. The impact of aircraft noise on house prices around Gatwick Airport has been calculated as 1.46% per unit of NNI (noise and number index), or a reduction of £1,460 on the value of a £100,000 home.[7] The recreational value of a forest visited by tourists in Scotland using the travel cost method was found to be £1,068,160 per annum.[8] The same method generated a value of $1.85 to $2.59 per visitor per day for a particular landscape in the Jemez mountains area of New Mexico threatened by a planned geothermal energy project. Interestingly, this site produced an average 'willingness to pay' of $2.54 per household in a parallel contingent valuation exercise.[9]

Contingent valuation has generated figures for several different kinds of environmental feature. For example, visitors to a river in Pennsylvania bid an average of $12.26 to make the water fishable and a further $29.64 to make it swimmable.[10] Respondents to an American survey who had no intention of ever seeing grizzly bears in the wild were nevertheless willing to pay an average of $24.00 a year to ensure their preservation – this 'existence value', incidentally, being more than the 'use value' generated by both bear hunters ($21.50) and tourists ($21.80).[11] A Norwegian exercise in which respondents were asked to pay a hypothetical income tax to prevent acid rain damage to freshwater fish stocks generated an average bid of 800 krone (about £80) per person per annum. Multiplied by the Norwegian population of 3.1 million, this gave a national annual value of 2.5 billion krone at 1980 prices (£250 million) or about 1.5% of the Gross National Product.[12]

Monetary values such as these are clearly useful. Showing how much Norwegians are willing to pay to preserve their freshwater fish provides good ammunition for environmentalists (Norwegian ones, at least) seeking to curb the production of acid rain. Placed in cost-benefit analyses, monetary figures can be compared directly to the projected financial benefits of an investment project, avoiding the need to judge between 'incommensurables'. Since such values are always positive, they will raise the financial hurdles over which investment projects must pass, and correspondingly make conservation measures easier to justify. For example, the benefits of visibility in the Grand Canyon have been estimated as up to $7.4 billion per annum, compared to conservation costs of only $3 billion.[13] Calculations of 'existence value' are particularly helpful, acknowledging the benefits which everyone, not just direct users, gets from the environment.

But usefulness does not equal accuracy. The fact that it is possible to generate monetary values by these various methods does not mean that the numbers produced actually do represent the value people put on the environment. Critics of monetary valuation tell environmentalists to beware. These methods may generate some useful results, it is said, but they can equally easily 'undervalue' what conservationists regard as important environmental assets. Thus, for example, survey respondents may not realise a particular habitat's ecological significance, and so may place a low monetary value on it. Or a project may cause environmental benefits to a rich group of people but costs to a poor group: their respective valuations may simply reflect ability to pay. In these cases environmentalists might wish to override the results of the CBA. But if they have accepted the results of similar exercises elsewhere when it suited them, critics warn, they will find themselves (as it were) without a leg to stand on.

The problems of monetary valuation

Criticisms of monetary valuation in fact fall into two categories. In some cases the problems are merely technical. It can be accepted that there *is* a monetary value to be found, but for one reason or another the techniques available are unable to discover it with much accuracy. But in other cases the problems lie deeper. It is not 'accuracy' which is at issue, but the whole idea that meaningful monetary values exist at all.

The technical problems of the monetary valuation methods are considerable. It is very difficult, for example, to isolate particular characteristics of houses and correlate them with prices. A large amount of sometimes inaccessible information must be collected, all the possible characteristics must be identified, variables moving together must be separated. Results can be sensitive to the particular equations used to relate characteristics to price. The whole exercise assumes that people make relatively free choices as to where they live, when this is not necessarily the case at all. Each of these problems makes it harder to achieve accurate results; together they may considerably reduce the legitimacy of the figures generated. Similar problems arise in the 'wage risk' and 'travel cost' methods.[14]

But just because it may not be possible to identify the values being sought does not mean that they do not exist. It does seem reasonable to suppose that environmental features make a difference to house prices, and that the amount people pay to visit recreational sites reflects at least a minimum valuation. After all, it is real behaviour which is being analysed, with real monetary expenditures. Even if in practice we may not trust the results achieved – and even if they will only ever be a *partial* valuation of the environmental feature in question – the revealed preference approach is at least meaningful in conception.

This cannot be so obviously said, however, of the hypothetical preference approach. Here we are not dealing with real behaviour: the figures are generated in specially contrived situations, some of them not at all similar to situations found in real life (bidding for cleaner water, for instance). Moreover many of the environmental goods whose value is sought by these methods are quite unlike other goods which consumers are accustomed to 'purchasing' (grizzly bear preservation being a case in point). In these circumstances the question arises of whether the results obtained are meaningful at all.

Researchers in this field have acknowledged that it has problems. They have indeed been assiduous in identifying, and trying to eradicate, the various different kinds of 'bias' which might distort the values found.[15] They have looked, for example, for evidence of 'strategic bias': survey respondents deliberately understating their willingness to pay for a public environmental good because they know that they can 'free ride' if everybody else pays; or deliberately overvaluing because they won't actually be asked to pay up. In some cases 'social norm bias' is suspected: if people believe that it is socially responsible to be concerned about the environment, they may feign a high willingness to pay.

Various kinds of bias arising from the design of surveys have been identified. 'Starting-point bias' is said to occur if the payment level at which bidding starts influences the final value given. Respondents may well feel that the first bid they are offered indicates an 'acceptable' range. 'Information bias' results if the amount of information which respondents are given about the good they are valuing or the cost of protecting it changes their willingness to pay for it. 'Payment vehicle bias' occurs if the method by which respondents are asked to pay for the environmental feature affects their valuation. For example, the preservation of a nature reserve might be paid for by an entrance fee, an increase in income tax or annual payments to a trust fund. Respondents may feel that one method is more appropriate or practical than another, and give their valuations accordingly.

Another sort of bias arises from the sample of people who answer the questionnaire. If the result is to be relevant, the sample must be representative of the population as a whole. Yet people who answer surveys (response rates are often under 50%) frequently belong to better-educated social groups. Moreover they are likely to be those who are particularly concerned about the environmental feature in question; this will exaggerate the value the population as a whole places on it. The treatment of non-responses and of 'outlying' (far from the average) bids can make a considerable difference to the final result.

Finally, researchers have asked if there is 'hypothetical market bias'. Since all these exercises are artificial, do the results bear any relation to what would happen in the real world? There, people engage in repeated transactions, learning from their experiences and modifying their behaviour accordingly; they can compare their valuations with those of other people and the values of other goods. These conditions are absent when one-off hypothetical questions are asked. Are the answers then just hypothetical too?

Those who have carried out hypothetical preference exercises have both tested for these various kinds of bias and formulated ways of reducing them. For some types, such as strategic bias, there is little evidence in practice. For others, such as starting-point bias, the evidence is considerable.[16] By setting out models of 'best practice' in the design of the exercises, practitioners hope to keep bias to a minimum, and therefore to produce reasonably accurate results. They claim that accuracy can be checked by comparing the values generated in hypothetical preference exercises (particularly contingent valuation) with those achieved by the revealed preference approach. Such comparisons show fair but not uniform results: sometimes the values are quite close, in other cases less so.[17]

Unfortunately, however, this test of 'accuracy' begs several questions. In the first place, of course, it depends upon the reliability of the revealed preference results with which the hypothetical ones are being compared. If these are not accurate, proximity to them is no virtue. But more importantly, it cannot be assumed that because contingent valuation generates 'accurate' values in one set of cases – those that can be compared directly with revealed preference examples – it therefore does so in another set, namely those for which such comparison is impossible. It is, after all, in cases where the revealed preference approach is not available that hypothetical methods are useful. If contingent valuation were only ever applied to environmental goods whose monetary value could also be estimated by revealed preference, it would not be particularly interesting; leaving aside questions of cost and simplicity, etc., we might as well use the latter approach. The method gains its usefulness – its advocates claim – from the fact that it can discover the values, including the option and existence values, of environmental goods such as wild animals and inaccessible land areas for which no revealed preferences can be identified.

But *these* are precisely the cases where the 'best practice' conditions do not apply. Contingent valuation has the fewest biases, researchers have found, where respondents understand and are familiar with the commodity to be valued, where they have some prior experience with its monetary valuation, and where the hypothetical market is 'realistic'.[18] These conditions are naturally met best in situations where revealed preference is also possible: where, for example, people are used to thinking about paying for lower air pollution or for a scenic view through differences in house prices. By the same token they do not apply where the revealed preference approach is unavailable, precisely *because* it is unavailable. Comparing the results of contingent valuation exercises with revealed preference ones for the same environmental goods therefore tells us very little about the 'accuracy' of such exercises in relation to other kinds of goods for which such comparisons cannot be made. Unfortunately, these latter goods are the very ones for which contingent valuation is said to be useful.

In effect what this means is that there are two different sorts of contingent valuation exercise. Those which fulfil the best practice conditions *could* be described as reasonably 'accurate', because their results conform to similar revealed preference values. These exercises, however, are not especially useful, since the revealed preference approach is also available. (There is no harm, of course, in trying both methods; and there may be practical difficulties with the revealed preference approach.) The other kind of exercise is more useful, since it attempts to measure the value of environmental goods which revealed preference is unable to; but in these cases we have no idea whether the results achieved are 'accurate' or not.

What do monetary values mean?

In fact the objections to the hypothetical preference approach are more serious than this. Its practitioners speak about 'accuracy' and 'bias', but it is by no means clear what these terms actually mean. A value is only accurate, and a technique biased, if there is some 'true value' against which they are being measured. Yet we have no way of knowing what this true value is. Indeed, in many cases of environmental goods it may be questioned whether there is such a thing as a 'true monetary value' at all. Interestingly, several of the types of bias researchers have identified suggest just this conclusion.

Take 'starting-point bias'. In a number of contingent valuation exercises the choice of starting point for bids has had a very large effect on the values people have given for the environmental good in question.[19] Researchers have tried to overcome this by using 'payment cards' presenting a range of possible bids to respondents. But a deeper question is raised by this form of 'bias' which cannot be solved through better techniques. The huge disparity in bids suggests that, when first presented with the question, respondents may have *no idea* what an environmental good is worth to them in money terms. Having had no experience of paying for the environment in this way, and therefore no sense of its monetary value, respondents are quite unable to give a considered figure. It is only, then, a suggested starting bid that enables them to make any sense of the question at all.

This is in fact a highly plausible explanation. If asked, for example, how much one was willing to pay to preserve the American bighorn sheep the reply 'I have no idea' seems quite reasonable. If a figure were suggested one might think 'this must be approximately what is considered "normal"' and then choose something a bit higher or a bit lower, but this figure could be almost anything and one would behave in the same way. The resulting 'valuation' would be practically meaningless.

A similar conclusion may be reached from 'information bias'. Significantly different results have been generated when the amount of information respondents are given is changed; when, for example, the total cost of the environmental improvement or the ecological importance of a site are mentioned, or when the value of other respondents' bids is given. The concept of 'bias' suggests that it could be eliminated – but what is the 'correct' information which respondents should be given?[20] Even more crucially, how can they be expected to understand what the effect would be of a major environmental change? Altering the scenery of a local area, or changing global pollution levels, or reducing the numbers of a rare species, could have both uncertain and far-reaching effects on people's lives which it may be extremely difficult to *imagine*, let alone put into monetary terms. When an environmental change is actually only a change in *risk* (say, increased health risks from pollution) it may be particularly hard to come to any rational judgement on how much it is worth. In these circumstances, where lack of 'information' actually means a quite understandable difficulty in comprehending the change being valued, figures produced by the hypothetical exercise may have little meaning at all.

These comments suggest, not that the values generated by hypothetical methods are 'inaccurate', but that no determinate monetary values exist at all. There may simply be no figure which corresponds to the value people put on the environment – because people don't know what it is. To be sure, they will give a value if pressed, but this is no nearer being the 'true' one than any other, as will be revealed if the conditions under which they are asked are varied.

'Payment vehicle bias' suggests a similar conclusion. It has been found that different methods of payment induce quite different results. But this makes it hard to claim that there is a 'true' value of the environmental good in question, from which any particular result is 'biased'. Which is the correct one? Researchers have indeed had to acknowledge that there are in fact several different values, each corresponding to a different payment vehicle.[21]

Prices, incomes and market values

The indeterminacy of monetary values may not simply be an empirical matter, a question of observed behaviour. Important philosophical issues are raised by the hypothetical preference approach to valuation. This approach is based on the idea that a thing's value is discovered when it is placed in a market. That is, it equates value with *price*, generated by the interaction of supply and demand. Given this concept of value, the hypothetical exercises are an explicit attempt to replicate the conditions in a market, facing the respondents with an environmental good and asking them to say how much they would be willing to pay for it, just as if it were a commodity in a shop. The more like a real market the exercise conditions are made, the more 'accurate' the results are claimed to be. This is the basis of the notion of 'hypothetical market bias', which is said to occur when the conditions are *not* much like a real market. 'True' values are obtained, the theory goes, when the invented market is as lifelike as possible.

There is no doubt that price is one way of valuing things. For most ordinary commodities which are traded in markets and consumed individually (that is, whose value is appreciated solely by the purchaser), price indeed seems a reasonable means of valuation. It is in turn, and more importantly, a practical method of deciding what should be produced and by whom it should be consumed.[22] But it is not the only way in which things can be valued; and it is not obvious that what is appropriate for toothbrushes and ice cream must necessarily be right for such things as beautiful landscapes and rare species. Public environmental goods such as these are not 'commodities', since they are not traded in markets, and they are not consumed individually – their value is appreciated collectively. It is therefore not enough to argue that simply because other types of goods are valued in markets, so these goods should be also. However like real markets the hypothetical ones are designed to be, they may not be the appropriate means of valuation.

There are two strong objections to valuation in markets. The first is that the values obtained depend upon the incomes of the consumers. This is true of all prices; it is particularly obvious in hypothetical exercises where respondents are specifically asked about their 'willingness to pay'. Clearly one's willingness to pay for a good is constrained by one's ability to do so. Yet it does not seem fair to say that because one is unable to pay therefore one doesn't actually desire the good. On the contrary, the welfare gain that one might make by a particular environmental change – say, a reduction in air pollution – might be greater the lower one's income. Poorer people tend to live in more polluted neighbourhoods and have less access to the countryside. So they might value a reduction in pollution levels more highly than richer people: their gain in welfare (which is ultimately what economists seek to measure) might be greater.[23] But of course in a hypothetical market it is likely to show up as less, since they are less able to pay for it. This is indeed what evidence from such exercises indicates.[24]

The problem of measuring value by willingness to pay is illustrated vividly when the method is applied to environmental issues in the Third World. How much would the Yanomami Indians of the Amazon be willing to pay to protect the tropical rainforests which sustain not only their livelihoods but their social and spiritual culture? Given that they have very little or no money income, it would clearly be absurd to say that the 'value' of the rainforest to them could be measured in this way. It would be equally absurd to say that because their 'bids' would be very low, the much higher willingness to pay of the logging companies and cattle ranchers should be allowed to override them. This is an extreme example, but the same situation would arise wherever a poor group of people were asked to defend their environment by monetary valuation against the higher bids of richer agents wishing to exploit or degrade it.[25] The unequal bargaining position in the market of rich and poor people makes a critical difference to the valuations generated; this hardly seems an appropriate way for society to value the environment, still less to make decisions about it.

It is possible for the results of contingent valuation exercises to be adjusted for the distribution of income. In the 'aggregation procedure' by which individual bids for an environmental good are added up to give its total value, the bids of poorer people can be weighted more highly than those of richer people. But this is very rarely done; and indeed it removes the principal point of the monetary valuation approach. The purpose of this approach, after all, is to find some kind of (apparently) 'objective' way of valuing the environment, which takes into account people's actual preferences and does not simply impose those of the decision-makers. But this is exactly what the weighting of preferences does. It says that some people's preferences (those of the poor) are more important than others, and that decisions should take this into account. But how much extra weight is given to poor people's preferences can only reflect a value judgement on how environmental costs and benefits should be distributed. There is not much difference between doing this and imposing decision-makers' preferences directly. A degree of objectivity might be gained by the initial valuation process, but this is almost entirely cancelled out by the subsequent weighting procedure.

What this shows, of course, is that no method can be 'objective'. If no weighting is done, so that all bids are simply counted equally, an implicit value judgement is made that one pound or dollar gives the same amount of welfare to a poor person as to a rich one, and that the inequality of bargaining power in the market is of no consequence in judging environmental valuations. If these claims are denied, and poor people's preferences are given extra weight, the choice of weighting must involve a value judgement on the importance of equity considerations in environmental decision-making.

What is at root here is the conflict between a simple economic model of the 'optimal' decision, which maximises benefits over costs without concern as to who experiences them, and an alternative view in which moral considerations such as justice are allowed to influence the outcome. Many people would say that the Amazonian rainforest should be protected because the Yanomami and other Indians have a right to live in it; the issue of how the rainforest is used should not be decided by weighing up their costs with other people's benefits. We have already noted that the cost-benefit approach cannot be more than an aid to decision-making, since it cannot take such distributional questions into account. What is now evident is that this failure is actually bound up in the monetary sums which CBA presents to the decision-maker. If environmental goods are given values based on willingness to pay, with no weighting in the aggregation procedure, a bias against the poor is inbuilt, even before questions over who should experience the costs and who the benefits are judged. So long as the distribution of income is unequal, the costs and benefits themselves are inequitably valued.

The second objection to valuing the environment by inventing markets for it is that this is inappropriate for public goods which are consumed collectively by society as a whole (or parts of it) rather than individually. In a market consumers behave as individuals; they are motivated by self-interest. Consumption in markets is something each individual or household does by itself, for itself. This is not to denigrate consumers or their behaviour; it is almost impossible to act in any other way for most of the many hundreds of different purchase decisions which we all have to make. We cannot hope to make these decisions with other people, or even to know how they are behaving, let alone to know what the overall outcome of everyone's purchases might be.

It has long been recognised, however, that market behaviour with respect to *public* goods is problematic. This is because once such goods (for example, a lighthouse or the police) are provided, people cannot be excluded from consuming them. If asked to pay for them in a market, people will therefore tend to 'free ride': the value obtained will be less than the real value of the good to them. Now as we have seen, researchers conducting contingent valuation exercises have tested for such 'strategic bias', and concluded that it is rare. But the notion of such a 'bias' is again based on the assumption that, so long as such 'cheating' is eliminated, the market will reveal the 'true value' of the good.

This assumption, however, can be challenged. When making private decisions about public goods, people face a kind of 'prisoner's dilemma'. They know that the good will only be secured if other people also pay for it; but they don't know what other people are prepared to pay. And of course everyone is in the same position. So each may hedge his or her bets, and give a lower value than they would if they could be sure that everyone else was also prepared to pay. This latter, higher value would be discovered if the respondents were allowed to discuss their bids with each other: they could come to an agreed collective decision. But such sharing of information is precisely one of the sources of so-called 'strategic behaviour' which the researchers have attempted to eliminate. Moreover some researchers have attempted to make the exercises as 'realistic' as possible by introducing real money which respondents can lose or gain. But this of course is likely only to make people even more cautious about committing themselves before they know what other people are doing.

The researchers reason that in a real market people don't know how other people are behaving, and deal in real money. So therefore the hypothetical exercises should be the same. But this just begs the question of whether the market is the right place for public goods to be valued. If it is correct that people might value the environment differently if they could make collective decisions, discussing the issues with each other and agreeing to be bound by the result, why is this not the correct way of discovering the environment's value rather than the market method?

There is a good case for saying that it is a 'more realistic' way. Contingent valuation tries to replicate conditions in a market, but public goods can't be sold in markets. Decisions about them have to be made collectively, usually by public authorities; this is after all what CBA is for. Shouldn't collective decisions involve collective valuation? Rather than standing in for the market, it might be considered more appropriate if valuation methodologies for public environmental goods tried to be proxy for the *political* process. It is after all in the political arena not the market that decisions on major environmental issues are decided.

In the political process we get the opportunity to discuss the issues with other people (and through this to change our minds); the consequences of everyone's actions can be made clear; and collective decisions can be enforced through collective payment (taxes), so avoiding prisoner's dilemma and free-rider problems.[26]

There is ample evidence to show that people's valuations in the political arena are different from their market ones – that is, that their behaviour as *citizens* is different from their behaviour as *consumers*. For example, in opinion polls (which are proxies for democratic choice) substantial majorities of people say that they wish to protect the environment, and are willing to pay higher taxes and prices to do so. But as consumers they continue to buy goods and services which cause serious environmental degradation. This may be partly to do with ignorance, or lack of choice. But it is equally explicable in terms of the prisoner's dilemma of market consumption. To put it succinctly: since no one knows whether, if they use less electricity, everyone else will also, and since if everyone doesn't there is no point in their not doing so, they don't. If, however, everyone were forced to cut their electricity consumption by higher prices or taxes, the same people might accept this as the price of doing something about global warming. In the one case, as consumers, people's behaviour is individualistic and self-interested; in the other, as citizens, it has at least the opportunity to acknowledge wider interests and values, including in this case those of future generations.

That 'citizen' valuation may be different from 'consumer' valuation has in fact been illustrated in a hypothetical exercise using the stated preference method to measure the value of different transport options.[27] Because they were cheaper, one-person-operated (OPO) buses were preferred to buses with conductors. But when it was pointed out that OPO meant that the conductors would be made redundant, this completely changed the valuations given. In a market people do not have information on the wider costs of their decisions in this way, and they do not take other people's interests into account. Hypothetical preference researchers speak of this being 'information bias'. But this is not 'bias': it is a quite different sort of valuation being made. Who is to say that the market method is the 'correct' way of valuing the environment and the collective method wrong?

Non-monetary values

So far we have made two claims against the hypothetical preference approach to monetary valuation. First we argued that monetary values may be indeterminate, because people don't know what they are. Then we suggested that in any case valuing the environment by market methods may be inappropriate; this builds in inequalities of income, and fails to allow people to judge value collectively, as citizens, rather than simply individually, as consumers.

There is an even more fundamental criticism which can be made. The hypothetical preference approach presupposes that environmental goods do have monetary values; the question is simply whether they can be found. But in some cases people may actively *refuse* to put a monetary value on the environment.

This is one interpretation, for example, of so-called 'non-response bias'. There are no doubt a variety of reasons why people do not respond to surveys. But one of them may well be a rejection of the whole idea of valuing the environment in monetary terms. There is indeed evidence of such behaviour.[28] Such refusals to 'play the game' are sometimes simply excluded from the calculation, or else they are represented by zero valuations. But this seems quite wrong. Some non-respondents might well value the environmental good in question very highly. What they are unwilling to do is to put this in monetary terms. Their behaviour could therefore be seen as an expression of *non-monetary* valuation. There may indeed be many people for whom the environment cannot be valued in money. Rare species or beautiful landscapes, such people will say, are 'priceless'. If this is a widespread attitude, trying to find monetary values for them will therefore be futile.

Many economists believe that no goods can rationally be described as 'priceless'. This would imply, they argue, that their price was infinite; that we would use up the entire wealth of the world (and more) to save the white rhino or the Grand Canyon. Since this is obviously not the case, and since there must therefore be some maximum figure we would be willing to pay, the value of such goods must be expressible in money terms. It is acknowledged that many people do not like to think in this way; that money can somehow appear to 'devalue' the natural world. But money is just a 'measuring rod', economists say, a way of comparing alternatives. Since environmental protection involves making choices, the way we spend our money effectively does represent the monetary value we put on the environment. If I am unwilling to spend, say, a hundred pounds on saving the rainforest, this must mean that its preservation is worth less than that sum to me – whether or not I myself am thinking about its value in those terms.[29]

But this is not the only way to understand the term 'priceless'. If we say that a human life is 'priceless', this does not mean that we would spend an infinite sum to save it. It means that it cannot be exchanged; that there is nothing which would replace it if it were lost. In particular there is no sum of money which can make up for someone's death. Where resources are scarce, the 'value of a life' is often expressed in money terms – governments have to decide how to allocate health service budgets; people choose life assurance sums. But no one supposes that these figures represent the 'worth' of the lives concerned. By the same token, it does not seem unreasonable for some environmental goods to be regarded as 'priceless'. Aspects of the environment which are unique (like landscapes) and whose loss would be irreversible (like species) seem particularly likely candidates for such non-monetary valuation.

Again, contingent valuation exercises appear to support the existence of such valuation, even while being based on its denial. The difference between the economists' understanding of 'priceless' and the non-monetary version concerns the direction of payment. The economist notes that people are not willing to pay infinite sums to save a life and concludes that therefore life must have a monetary value. The objector notes that no amount of money will compensate for the loss of a life, so its value must be infinite. This difference between 'willingness to pay' (WTP) for a good and 'willingness to accept compensation' for it (WTA) is precisely the issue which has caused most puzzlement in the contingent valuation literature. Economic theory predicts that WTP and WTA for the same good will be approximately equal. But in fact they are found in most cases to be considerably different, with WTA always the larger – sometimes having values as much as five or six times higher.[30]

A variety of explanations for this divergence have been suggested. One of the most plausible is that people place a much higher value on what they have already got than on something they might potentially gain – even if it is the same thing. So the compensation required by people in one neighbourhood for losing their peace and quiet is much higher than the sum people in another area would be willing to pay to reduce their noise level by the same amount. But another explanation is also available. This is that the higher WTA figures effectively represent non-monetary valuations. Since the exercises in which these values are generated does not permit a formal non-monetary valuation, this is how such valuations emerge.

Consider a contingent valuation exercise in which one is asked how much one is willing to pay for preservation of the African elephant. Many people might find this difficult to answer; it would surely depend on their income, the expected behaviour of other people, and so on. But they might be able to choose from a range of given values. Consider then being asked how much it would take to be compensated for the elephant's extinction. Many people would surely find the question absurd, if not offensive. They would want to answer 'nothing': the existence of elephants does not have a monetary value. But since this answer, in the terms of the exercise, would tend to *reduce* rather than increase the value of the elephant, a high figure (from amongst those offered) would be given. So WTA would exceed WTP.

We do not know whether this is in fact the sort of reasoning that generates the divergence.[31] But the idea that non-monetary valuation might be revealed by WTA is surely reasonable. Consider what would happen if a researcher conducted a contingent valuation exercise to test people's WTP and WTA for famine or disease; that is, for the loss of human life. Willingness to pay would presumably be finite: people only have a certain amount of money, and, however much they care about other people, they are understandably not willing to spend their entire income on charity.

But what would 'willingness to accept' be? Most people would surely be disgusted by the idea of receiving compensation for other people's deaths, however much was offered. This feeling of disgust is quite different from the feeling of 'not enough' which one gets when monetary compensation *is* acceptable, but merely insufficient. Disgust is surely an expression of the fact that the compensation is not merely insufficient but *inappropriate*. Whether people would in these circumstances refuse to give a WTA at all, or (fearing that this would reduce the total valuation) would give a very high figure, is less important here than the recognition that some things may simply not be valued in monetary terms. If this is so, it does not seem unreasonable that the survival of the African elephant or the preservation of the tropical rainforests should be amongst those things similarly granted values 'beyond price'.

The orthodox economist might have a reply to this argument. He or she might say that, since in the real world protecting the environment always does cost money, there always is a figure (WTA or WTP) which represents the monetary value of the environment. If, for example, it were found that the cost of preserving some rare mammal species came to one million dollars a year, it might well be felt that the cost was not worth the benefit. In this case it would be clear that, so far from being 'priceless', the species was worth less than a million dollars.

But this in fact proves nothing in relation to monetary valuation. The question here is, what would the money be spent on otherwise? If it were to be spent on nuclear weapons, many people would say that the preservation of the animal was more important. If the alternative was spending the money on famine relief, they might argue the reverse. The valuation here is not with respect to money, since no amount of money *per se* can compensate for the loss of the species. The valuation is a straightforward judgement between alternative states of affairs, in which a monetary valuation adds nothing to the ease of the decision. The loss either of the species or of people in a famine would be a tragedy. If we found that we would have to choose between them this wouldn't imply that either is worth less than a million dollars. It would simply be a reflection of the awful fact that a decision has to be made, and that therefore one must be regarded as more valuable than the other. In these circumstances, finding people's willingness to pay for each alternative *in the abstract* would be of no help in making the judgement.

Cost-benefit analysis reconsidered

These observations bring us back to the cost-benefit method which introduced this discussion. It will be recalled that the starting-point for monetary valuation techniques was the requirement that all values in CBA should be put on a common scale of measurement. The question then was whether this was possible: whether or not environmental values (among others) were 'commensurable' in this sense.

The most important conclusion we have reached, perhaps, is that different features of the environment are different in this respect. It seems true to say that unique and irreplaceable public goods, like human lives, do not have meaningful monetary values; they are not exchangeable for money. For many other environmental features, trying to find determinate monetary values is impossible, because people don't know what they are; and in any case the market-based methods used may be regarded as inappropriate for public goods consumed collectively.

It is likely that most environmental goods fall into one of these categories. There may be some aspects of the environment, however, which *are* commensurable on a financial scale. Where an environmental feature involves relatively small and localised changes, where it is easily understood by its consumers, and where, most importantly, there is a strong sense in which it is consumed individually, monetary valuation may be meaningful. This is probably true, for example, for localised air or noise pollution, for a particular local view and for some recreational areas. These are the types of goods whose values may be measured by revealed preference methods or sometimes by hypothetical preference techniques. The values found will only ever be minimums (only some aspects of the environmental good are measured, and there will always be additional people affected outside the sample constituency); and it must always be recognised that monetary valuations are based on the prevailing distribution of income. Nevertheless it does seem reasonable to say that these kinds of environmental goods are sufficiently comparable to commodities to be valued in the same way.

Taken together, however, these conclusions must inevitably deflate the more extravagant ambitions of cost-benefit analysis. The hope that CBA provided a method by which all the conflicting values involved in environmental decision-making could be transformed into commensurable numbers and slotted into a universal calculus must be disappointed. It is now clear that, even though some environmental goods may be valued in money terms, many of the most important are not commensurable in this way. Effects on irreplaceable and large-scale environmental goods, like those on human life, must be judged directly. In this process a systematic setting-out of costs and benefits to different groups is extremely useful, and to this extent the underlying cost-benefit procedure has a role to play. But there can be no mathematical short-cut to the 'correct' solution. The difficulty of making choices between different sorts of values does not alter the recognition that ultimately such choices must be a matter of judgement, not computation.

This conclusion turns the argument away from the economic and philosophical questions about valuation to the political ones about whose judgements are involved. The environmental movement has tended to be deeply distrustful of the decision-making process, not least where CBA is practised, on the grounds that government departments and agencies are able to manipulate supposedly impartial procedures to get the results they want. For example a study of CBAs for land drainage schemes in the UK (often involving considerable ecological damage) identified 16 techniques by which assessments were biased in favour of drainage. Appraisals of trunk roads using the joint CBA and environmental impact assessment framework do not appear to have had any effect on the volume of road building at all.[32]

Does this mean that environmental decision-making must simply end up as the battle of political forces which we identified as one possibility at the beginning of the last chapter? Political power cannot be wished away. But this should not prevent a more considered approach being developed – or pressure being applied for it to be institutionalised in decision-making procedures. There is not space here to describe such an approach in detail.[33] But some elements of it may be identified.

First, sustainability constraints need to be established as the essential framework within which decisions are made. Second, objectives need to be defined for the particular projects in question. For transport schemes, for example, policy priorities need to be decided: these might be (as now) time savings for business travel and industrial freight, or they could be accessibility and safety for urban residents. Third, a presumption needs to be entrenched *against* development. At present (in the UK) the onus is on objectors to developments to prove that they are damaging; it should be on developers to show that they are beneficial. It is currently possible for rejections of planning permission to go to appeal; it should be equally possible for permissions granted to be challenged. Fourth, when appraising investment projects such as transport or energy generation schemes, *all* the possible options to meet the objectives should be considered. Too often enquiries deal with only the officially favoured option, which makes rejection appear more damaging than it need be.

Fifth, environmental impact assessments need to be performed for all projects above a certain size or with suspected adverse environmental effects. These assessments should be carried out by independent authorities, and should be of all impacts from 'cradle to grave'. Sixth, for each project or option, a 'planning balance sheet' needs to be drawn up, setting out in a systematic way the costs and benefits to each group of people and to other aspects of the environment. Where monetary values are available, including values of small-scale environmental effects, these should be included; other effects, including loss of human life and major environmental changes, should be described without monetisation. The value people place on non-monetary effects may be gauged through opinion polls and simulated exercises in which people can discuss the proposed changes and suggest alternatives.[34] Seventh, the entire decision-making procedure must be public, with freedom of information and all interested parties allowed (and financially assisted if necessary) to present evidence. Last, a judgement must be made through the political process as to the best option for meeting the objectives set out.

Exactly what institutional structures should carry out project appraisals along these lines is open to question. It may be, for example, that an 'inquisitorial' public enquiry on the French model may prove more helpful than the 'adversarial' British approach.[35] The scale on which a decision is made (local, regional, national, international) will vary in different circumstances. These suggestions will not make environmental decision-making any less subject to conflict. What they may offer is a reasonably considered and open approach to mediating such conflict within the sustainability framework. This is the most, in the real world, that can be asked.

18

Measuring Success

Objectives and indicators

For the past 150 years, since the end of the first industrial revolution, Western society has had little doubt about its economic goals. The purpose of the economy is to create wealth. Economic progress can therefore be measured by the size of the national income, along with the base of capital or wealth from which it is generated. Economies are successful when wealth and income rise, allowing higher consumption and therefore higher standards of living. Economic growth, it is assumed, makes people better off.

These claims have been taken by most people as practically self-evident. It is true that there have been disagreements about the nature and distribution of the national income. Those on the left have emphasised that wealth and consumption need not be private, pointing out that public services (from street cleaning to museums) make as valuable a contribution to living standards as private expenditure. They have argued too that the distribution of income is as important as its creation. But neither caveat challenges the basic view of economic progress as the expansion of monetary wealth. Indeed, many socialists have stressed that it is only by generating wealth that public services can be provided and poverty relieved.[1] Governments of all shades in practically all countries have been committed to the achievement of economic growth.

Yet it is precisely this accepted view of economic success which a concern for the environment throws into question. If the creation of wealth causes environmental damage, should it automatically be counted as progress? Is an economy with a high growth rate of national income and a high growth rate of degradation necessarily performing better than one with lower rates of both? If not, is economic growth society's most appropriate goal?

These questions are essentially about economic *objectives*. But they can very quickly turn into debates about *indicators*; that is, about the statistical measures of economic behaviour. If economic progress is defined as the growth of national income, society can only tell whether or not it is progressing if national income can be measured. So the indicators which do this – Gross National or Domestic Product (GNP or GDP) – assume considerable significance.[2] GNP, GDP and their annual growth rates serve to measure the economy's performance. These indicators are both the principal means of judging one country's economic progress over time, and of comparing the economic success of different countries.

Arguments over objectives are consequently often expressed as arguments over indicators. The substance of the Green case is that society should not seek higher income levels if this involves environmental damage. But given that national income is measured by GNP, this is equivalent to saying that GNP is the wrong indicator of economic performance. A successful economy, environmentalists argue, should be defined as one which does not experience environmental degradation. But GNP, as a purely monetary statistic, doesn't record degradation. So GNP cannot be maintained as society's chief indicator of economic success.

The environmental critique of GNP

The Greens' argument against GNP and its growth rests on two separate but connected observations about the effect of environmental degradation. Degradation directly reduces the *current* well-being or welfare of the population, through pollution and loss of aesthetic amenity. It also reduces the capacity of the economy to produce *future* welfare, through the depletion of resources, loss of absorptive capacities and impairment of life support services. Both of these effects might reasonably be said to reflect badly on the performance of the economy. Yet because they don't have monetary measures, neither is recorded in national income.

Indeed, environmental degradation has a rather perverse relationship to GDP. In cases of pollution, for example, national income clearly overstates the actual level of welfare. If GNP is to be used as a measure of how well-off people are, it would seem sensible to subtract something to reflect the loss of amenity, damage to health and other ill-effects which the pollution causes. Yet the effect of pollution, if anything, is the reverse. If people are less healthy and need more medical care, or if buildings have to be cleaned more often, economic activity increases, which adds to national income. Indeed, the more pollution there is, the higher will be these 'defensive expenditures' (that is, expenditures on things which defend people against the effects of the pollution). If society makes a concerted attempt to control and repair pollution damage, for example by investment in pollution control equipment and clean-up programmes, the contribution to GNP will be even greater.

It is not true to say, as some Greens have done, that 'pollution increases GNP'. The extra anti-pollution or defensive expenditure could have been spent on something else, leaving the final level of national income unchanged. But those alternative goods and services might have made a net contribution to welfare, whereas spending on pollution control and repair simply uses up resources to keep welfare exactly where it was to start with. GNP becomes less reliable as a measure of welfare.

The failure of national income to measure the depletion of natural resources is perhaps even more serious. As we showed in Chapter 1, the environment is an essential foundation of economic activity: it may be considered a part of the 'capital' from which the economy derives its income. Yet it is not recorded as such in the national income accounts.

It is one of the first principles of accounting that economic success must be measured by the stock of capital as well as the flow of income. There is little virtue in high income if it is achieved simply by running down reserves or productive capacity. This way lies long-term ruin: when the capital runs out, there will be no income at all. The national income accounts acknowledge this in respect of human-made capital (factories, machines, etc.), by subtracting from GNP an allowance for 'depreciation'. This is the sum which, if reinvested in productive capacity, would maintain the capital stock intact. The result is known as 'Net National Product' (NNP; or its counterpart Net Domestic Product). NNP is actually very rarely used, partly because it is very difficult to estimate the appropriate figure for depreciation, and partly because depreciation is assumed to be roughly constant from year to year, so that its effect on the growth of GNP can safely be ignored. But in theory at least NNP is intended to be a measure of 'sustainable income': the amount that can be earned indefinitely, since capital remains constant. In strict accounting terms, sustainable income is 'true' income: the amount available for consumption after the sum required to maintain capital has been set aside.[3]

But in fact, environmentalists point out, NNP isn't such a measure, since no allowance is made for the depreciation of 'natural capital' – despite the fact that this capital is also being run down, in some cases very rapidly. On the contrary, so far from environmental degradation leading to a subtraction from GNP, it tends to increase it. When a forest is felled for timber, for example, GNP includes all the income earned, but NNP records no loss in future productive capacity. Similarly, when high levels of agricultural production cause soil erosion, GNP rises, but NNP remains unchanged, despite the depletion of the natural capital base.

This mismeasurement of sustainable income can have a particularly damaging effect for countries in the South for whom a large proportion of output comes from natural resources. Rapid depletion of these resources causes high GNP growth, which is taken to mean economic success. But if no allowance is made for the reduction in income which must inevitably follow when the resources are exhausted, such 'success' can only be illusory and short-lived.[4]

Environmentalists' criticisms of the conventional national income measures are therefore not simply academic debating points. Of themselves indicators such as GNP and NNP are only tools. But choice of the wrong tool – measuring the economy's performance by the wrong indicators – may lead to wrong policies being adopted, and wrong judgements being made about how successful such policies are. Countries may decide to exhaust their natural resources in the belief that this will lead to a long-term increase in consumption. Reductions in welfare caused by pollution, urban congestion and loss of amenity may simply go unrecognised, and therefore untackled, because policy-makers have assumed that living standards are measured simply by national income. It is this influence on the making and evaluation of economic policy which has made GNP an object of such opprobrium in the Green movement.[5]

Of course one response to these arguments is to return to the primary issue of objectives. If governments do not believe that environmental degradation matters, because welfare and sustainable income are *not* the goals of economic policy, the Green case will cut no ice. But let us assume (not unreasonably) that both current and future welfare are considered important objectives. What effect does the environmental critique then have on the choice of economic indicators? For many Greens, the answer is self-evident. The way in which national income is calculated should be changed so that it includes the effects of environmental degradation. Specifically, three kinds of adjustment have been proposed.[6]

First, 'defensive expenditures' (such as pollution control equipment and medical expenditure on pollution-related illnesses) should be subtracted from GNP in its current form. Such expenditures are not net additions to welfare: as 'regrettable necessities' they should be regarded as the costs of consuming other goods and services rather than benefits in their own right.

Second, any residual damage to the environment which reduces welfare and has not been made good by defensive expenditure should be valued and also removed from current GNP. If only defensive expenditures are subtracted GNP would clearly be higher the more pollution was left untreated. To prevent this, any pollution which remains should also cause a reduction in GNP.

Third, Net National Product should include an allowance for the depletion of natural capital as well as the depreciation of human-made capital. The point of NNP is to measure the potential for future income. It does not do this if no recognition is made that exhaustion of and damage to the economy's natural resource base is effectively a form of capital consumption. Unless new investment is undertaken, environmental damage reduces the possibility of earning future income. (Note that if both the second and third adjustments are made, there is a risk of double counting, since some aspects of the environment that provide welfare, such as forests, are also aspects of 'natural capital'.)

If national income were adjusted in these ways, the environmentalists argue, it would act as a more accurate indicator of the overall performance of the economy and therefore as a better guide to the conduct of policy. Environmental costs would be properly accounted for, both in the measurement of current welfare (through the first two subtractions) and in that of future sustainability (through the third). Growth of an 'Environmentally adjusted Net National Product' would then be a genuinely acceptable economic objective.

The role of economic indicators

We shall examine the practicalities (and indeed the theoretical problems) of making such adjustments to national income below. To many economists, however, the whole argument is ill-founded. For them, the environmentalists' desire to change the calculation of national income simply misunderstands what GNP is for. It is not a measure of welfare; and its growth is not the only or even the principal objective of economic policy.

To the economist, GNP is a measure of annual economic activity – and as such it serves its purpose very well just as it is. Of itself a high level of economic activity shows neither 'success' nor 'failure': many other indicators are also required to judge the performance of an economy. These include, for example, the rate of inflation, employment and unemployment, the balance of payments, the exchange rate, the interest rate, the size of the public sector borrowing requirement and the rate of money supply. They could also include the rate of environmental degradation if so desired. All these may be just as important as the rate of GNP growth, and their increase or decrease may be at least as if not more pressing an objective of policy.

To most economists, the importance of GNP lies rather in its central role in the theoretical underpinning of macroeconomics. Without knowing the level of activity and its rate of change, economic analysis would be almost impossible. Indeed, the measurement of GNP was originally undertaken (in more or less its current form) because J.M. Keynes and his colleagues needed a more accurate estimate of the size of national income in order to conduct Britain's economic policy in the Second World War.[7] GNP is moreover one of the easier indicators to manipulate in the short term, through policy measures such as public spending changes or controls on the money supply, so it is an important means of affecting other indicators.

For these reasons, most economists will argue, adjusting the calculation of national income by introducing non-monetary elements such as environmental degradation would be of no help at all; indeed, it would fatally compromise its usefulness. GNP measures precisely what it is intended to. The Greens' wish to change it is simply misplaced.

So who is right, the environmentalist or the economist? The answer, of course, is both, for GNP plays two quite different roles in public life, and much of the debate about it rests on a confusion between them. In one role GNP is simply a tool for *understanding* how the economy works; it is an objective measurement without moral content. In the other GNP is a means of *evaluating* the performance of the economy, carrying the subjective judgement that higher national income – and, in particular, a faster rate of growth – is an indication of economic success. In this latter role (but never in the former) GNP often stands in for a measurement of welfare, since welfare itself is impossible to measure, but income and welfare are assumed to be closely correlated.

Any economic or social indicator can play both these roles, and both may be valid; the problem lies simply in their not being distinguished. In day-to-day economic analysis, economists are right to say that GNP is merely a tool for understanding, and is not regarded as a means of evaluation. But environmentalists are equally right to argue that this is precisely how GNP is used in longer-term judgements – particularly by politicians, for whom a period of several years' growth is generally regarded as the highest pinnacle of economic achievement. In the short term other indicators such as the balance of payments and inflation may also reflect important objectives of policy; but ask a politician *why* he or she wants to keep the balance of payments in balance or the inflation rate down and the reply will almost certainly be that they are necessary to maintain long-term growth.

Once these two roles have been distinguished, the environmentalists' desire to change the calculation of national income can be more sensibly considered. And it is fairly clear that the two roles actually require *different* indicators. As a measurement of annual marketed economic activity GNP is reasonably accurate and extremely useful; it should be left alone.[8] But as an indication of economic performance, neither GNP nor NNP is adequate. GNP clearly doesn't measure welfare, and NNP doesn't measure sustainable income. For these purposes, the environmentalists are right to argue that new indicators are needed. But such indicators should not change the calculation of GNP; they should simply be used instead of it (or alongside it) in its evaluative role. GNP should be retained for economic analysis; it should be supplemented by other indicators in the judgement of economic success.

The case for adjusting GNP

These arguments reduce the grander claims of the environmentalists' proposals, but they do not undermine them. On the contrary, it is precisely the role of evaluative indicator which 'adjusted GNP' is designed to play. The environmentalists' case is that GNP cannot measure economic performance because it does not take account of environmental degradation; to make it do so, various subtractions have to be made. An 'environmentally adjusted' GNP then *would* be an appropriate measure of economic success.

This seems a reasonable argument, but it is important to note the implicit assumption here. This is that GNP is the best starting point to measure economic performance, even if various subtractions have to be made from it. After all, one response to the inadequacy of GNP might have been to abandon it altogether for evaluative purposes and start again with a different indicator or set of indicators. It is easy to see why the environmentalists have not done this. In the first place, GNP is a measure of income, and it will generally be agreed that income should be an important component of any performance measure. Moreover, incorporating environmental measurement into national income avoids the problem of comparing unlike indicators. If environmental changes are recorded in non-monetary terms, politicians and the electorate must somehow judge whether, for example, a rise in GNP and a fall in environmental performance constitutes a net loss or gain: being expressed in different units there is no easy means of comparison.[9] If both objectives are counted in one indicator, on the other hand, the problem disappears and judgement is (apparently) made easier.

Perhaps most importantly, however, the point of adjusting GNP is to challenge it. GNP is an influential indicator. It is widely used to measure economic success: its rate of growth is announced monthly and features prominently in news broadcasts and economic analysis. Politicians and economists are accustomed to measuring performance by it. In these circumstances, the environmentalists reason, merely proposing a new, separate indicator will not have the desired effect of dethroning GNP. It has to be replaced directly, by saying not merely that it is inadequate, but that it is inadequate by such-and-such an amount, which they have calculated and can then subtract from it. GNP has to be shown to be *wrong*, not merely insufficient.

These are strong arguments. If adjusting GNP can be done successfully and a meaningful indicator generated, there will clearly be a good case for doing this. The issue then is, *can* such adjustments be done successfully? How meaningful is adjusted GNP? To answer these questions, we need to examine in more detail the three subtractions it is proposed should be made: those for defensive expenditures, residual pollution and natural capital depletion.

Defensive expenditures

Intuitively the notion of 'defensive expenditure' is very appealing. If a production process causes environmental degradation, any measures taken to clean up the damage (or to prevent it happening) make no contribution to 'added value'. That is, the extra spending enhances neither the value of the product nor that of the environment. All it does is to leave the environment exactly as it was before production started, and the product itself unchanged. It therefore seems sensible to subtract the spending from GNP, since no addition to welfare has occurred.

Two errors are often made in discussion of defensive expenditures. The first is to describe them as 'external costs of production'.[10] At first sight this seems plausible: they seem to be part of the social price that must be paid to gain the benefits of other, intrinsically desired goods and services. But if defensive expenditures really were costs, there would be no justification for subtracting them from GNP. Other costs of production aren't subtracted; they are simply incorporated in the price of the final product, which is part of GNP. The difference is that other costs of production *do* add value to their products, which is why they get included in GNP; the whole point about defensive expenditures is that they don't add value, which is why they shouldn't.

The second error is to suppose that only defensive expenditures made by households and governments (that is, by 'final consumers') should be subtracted from GNP.[11] This is held to be the correct procedure because defensive spending by firms (such as on pollution control equipment) is *already* subtracted as 'intermediate' expenditure. (Intermediate expenditures are products bought by other firms, not by final consumers.)

But this simply misunderstands the way in which GNP is calculated. Intermediate expenditures, including defensive ones, are not subtracted from GNP. They are just not counted twice. This is avoided by one of two methods of calculating GNP: either by counting only goods and services bought by final consumers, or by counting only the 'value added' produced by each firm. Value added equals the value of output minus intermediate expenditures, which is where the notion of 'subtraction' arises. But this subtraction does not exclude such expenditures from GNP; they are incorporated in it in the value of final output.

If we want to subtract defensive expenditures, therefore, it doesn't matter whether they are carried out by households, governments or firms. If a firm cleans up its own pollution, the extra cost will appear in the price of its output. If the same expenditure is undertaken by consumers or governments, it will appear as a separate item in the national accounts. Either way it should be subtracted if GNP is intended to measure welfare.

But here we run into the first problem with the concept of defensive expenditures. Can we isolate them out? A programme to clean up a river is easily identified, as is a piece of 'end-of-pipe' technology added to existing equipment. But much pollution control is now done 'integrally', as part of the basic manufacturing process. Imagine that a company buys a new machine which is both more productive and less polluting than the last one. It is also more expensive. What proportion of the purchase price should be counted as a 'defensive' expenditure?

It may be said that integral pollution control means that pollution is effectively not being caused, so there is no defensive expenditure. But the cost to the firm of installing the less polluting machine is higher than it would have been if there were no requirement to control pollution. These costs are passed on to the customer in prices, so are recorded in GNP. The fact that the expenditure is undertaken earlier in the process, and incorporated within other budget headings, makes no difference to its categorisation; the problem is simply how to identify how much it is.

In practice, this problem could no doubt be overcome (if not solved) by using a variety of conventions and estimates.[12] But much more difficult issues are raised when the concept of defensive expenditure is applied to other areas of welfare. It will be widely accepted that spending on pollution control, other environmental protection programmes and the treatment of pollution-related illnesses is defensive. But adjusting GNP for these expenditures alone cannot plausibly be claimed to lead to a figure for welfare, since many other types of spending have essentially the same defensive nature. Many Greens have therefore wanted to broaden the definition.

The most ambitious typology of defensive expenditures has been constructed by the German economist Christian Leipert. To the directly environmental expenditures he adds another four categories.[13] These are, first, expenditures induced by the spatial concentration of production and urbanisation, such as the increased costs of commuting, housing and recreation; second, expenditures to protect against the increased insecurity and risks of industrial society, such as spending on crime prevention, accident prevention and national defence; third, expenditures caused by car traffic growth, such as on catalytic converters and medical spending on road accident surgery; and fourth, expenditures arising from poor living and working conditions and 'unhealthy consumption and behavioural patterns', such as the costs generated by smoking, alcohol, drug addiction, industrial accidents and mental illness due to unemployment. All of these expenditures, Leipert argues, repair damage to welfare that would have been enjoyed in the absence of various kinds of industrial production.

Leipert has attempted not only to identify but actually to measure these defensive expenditures for the German economy.[14] The rationale for doing so is evident. Greens want to ask if all the extra output generated by industrialised economies in the last 40 years of rapid modernisation and urbanisation has actually made people any better off. Of course, they will argue, people are richer. But much of people's money is spent on defensive expenditures protecting them from the unwanted costs of industrial society. Nobody wants to have to commute for an hour to get to work, to pay large sums for house insurance because crime rates are so high, to be taxed for the medical costs of treating drug addicts – or for environmental protection programmes. These are not parts of 'net product', the goods and services which people really want. They are the regrettable necessities which we must pay for in order to be able to consume the goods and services that we really do want without experiencing losses of welfare in other areas. To measure 'net product' – the value of the things which genuinely contribute to welfare – all these expenditures should therefore be subtracted from GNP.

The argument is seductive. But it rests on an assumption which on closer inspection is very difficult to sustain. This is that it is possible to identify a state of the world prior to, or existing in the absence of, the industrial production which gives rise to the defensive expenditures. Thus for example we can only measure the level of ill-health caused by economic activities if we have first estimated how much ill-health there would be without those activities. Similarly the costs of policing necessitated by the higher crime levels of urban life can only be gauged in relation to some base line of non-urban or pre-urban crime. In the case of the environment, where the relationship between economic activity and degradation is fairly clear, estimating the 'pre-industrial' level of environmental quality is just about possible: a base line of zero pollution and plausible levels of other features (such as forest cover) can be used. But for spending in the fields of health, crime, accidents, transport, housing, etc., any base line must be competely arbitrary, if not actually meaningless. It is not at all evident that the question, 'How much crime (or alcoholism, etc.) would there be if society were less urbanised?', makes any sense at all.

Of course one way of avoiding this problem would be to say that *all* expenditures on health care, crime prevention and so on are defensive, not simply those induced by economic activity. This might seem reasonable: no one wants to have to spend money on antibiotics or insurance. But two results would follow. The first is that we would have to subtract the entire total of health spending from welfare, effectively denying that any of it brings positive (net) benefits. This however is patently false: few people would prefer to live in a society which didn't provide medical care, even if the industrial causes of ill-health were also absent. There are many such societies in the South.

The second result would be that the concept of defensive expenditure would be redefined. Instead of defensive expenditures protecting people from a loss of welfare which in the absence of some economic activity they would have experienced (clean air, good health, lack of crime) they would be recording 'regrettable necessities' of all kinds. Defensive expenditures would simply become the costs of achieving some particular level of welfare, whether or not that welfare might have been achieved anyway if it hadn't been for an economic activity.

But if *this* is done, practically anything can be classified as a defensive expenditure, since nothing is really wanted for its own sake, but only for the service it provides. A telephone then becomes a defensive expenditure, on the grounds that it is really just a cost of communicating with people. We don't really want a telephone *per se*; what we want is to talk to our friends and associates. We would be much better off if we could do this personally, without spending money on a phone. Almost all travel would become defensive: how much nicer it would be if we could simply arrive on holiday without all that hassle. That is certainly not a net part of welfare. Indeed a lot of education would probably have to be subtracted from welfare as well: it is well known that much of the time spent in education is merely a cost of getting employment.[15] With this definition of defensive expenditure, it becomes impossible to distinguish between 'final' goods and services desired for their own sakes and things which are simply the costs of acquiring them.[16]

It should be stressed again that environmental defensive expenditures suffer much less from these criticisms than the other kinds listed. Because the link between environmental damage and economic activity is very close, it *is* possible (though not easy) to distinguish costs which would not have been necessary if the activity hadn't occurred, including some obviously pollution-related medical expenditures. It would indeed be extremely useful if these costs were recorded in the national accounts, to show just what proportion of GNP is being absorbed merely repairing damage caused by other parts of GNP. And such a figure should certainly be given prominence, to deflate the claims of GNP as a measure of net product.

But subtracting this amount from GNP would not lead to a figure for welfare. If it is accepted that welfare is not simply represented by income (this being the basis of the concept of defensive expenditure) it cannot plausibly be argued that crime, ill-health, accidents and so on do not also affect it. But if they do, simply adjusting GNP for environmental expenditures cannot be sufficient. We seem caught in a bind: for consistency and completeness we need to subtract all defensive expenditures; but there is no meaningful way of identifying what most of these are. We can plausibly identify environmental expenditures; but then all we have achieved is an 'environmentally-adjusted GNP', not a figure for welfare.

The problem of monetary valuation

In fact we have not even achieved an environmentally-adjusted GNP. To get this we shall also have to make the second and third subtractions proposed. We shall have to take off any residual degradation that remains after defensive expenditures have been undertaken: if we did not do this we would end up with the absurd result of GNP being higher (that is, economic performance being judged better) when nothing is done about pollution than when something is done. And if we are to take account not only of current welfare losses but of potential future ones, we shall also want to subtract an allowance for the depletion of natural capital. (We shall need to make sure that aspects of the environment which contribute both to welfare directly and to 'natural capital' are not counted twice.)

But here we encounter an even more difficult problem. In order to incorporate environmental degradation in GNP, the environment must be valued in monetary terms. Any additions or subtractions must be made in the same units: this is, we pointed out, one of the reasons why adjusting GNP is attractive. But as we have already seen, monetary valuation of the environment is extremely problematic. Using the techniques we examined in the last chapter, at least, the figures obtained cannot be guaranteed for accuracy, and in many cases may not actually be meaningful at all. Adjustments to GNP derived from these methods would clearly be open to serious objections.

Certainly Greens who oppose the use of monetary valuation in cost benefit analysis are in danger of self-contradiction if they advocate the same techniques for environmental adjustments to GNP.

This argument might seem fatal to the 'adjusted GNP' case. If environmental degradation cannot meaningfully be measured in money terms, there seems no way in which adjustments to GNP can be made. But the injury is in fact not quite so bad. The crucial requirement here is to distinguish between the two types of adjustment proposed. Much of the debate about adjusting GNP has assumed that subtracting for damage to current welfare and for depletion of natural capital should be done simultaneously. By this means, it is claimed, we can arrive at a single figure for 'sustainable welfare'.[17]

But the two kinds of subtraction are in fact quite different. In the first place, they have different justifications. Subtracting an allowance for depreciation of natural capital merely takes the concept of Net National Product to its logical conclusion: an environmentally adjusted NNP can reasonably be said to measure what NNP is supposed to, namely 'sustainable income'. But adjusting GNP for current environmental losses will only lead to a true figure for welfare if GNP is itself a reasonable proxy for welfare *except* in an environmental sense, so that the adjustment makes good the difference. But this should certainly not be accepted without argument: as we have already seen, welfare will widely be felt to include other factors such as health and crime which are not simply included in income; and (as we shall suggest below) may involve other indicators besides.

Even more importantly, however, the two kinds of subtraction involve different types of monetary valuation. In order to estimate the contribution made to welfare by an environmental good or service, we should need to know how valuable it is: how much benefit people gain from it. This is what the techniques of monetary valuation discussed in the last chapter attempt to measure, with (in many cases) such unconvincing results. So adjustments to GNP to take account of current environmental losses are certainly open to the objection that they depend upon unreliable valuation methods.

Subtractions to measure the depletion of natural capital, however, are not of this kind. When depreciation of capital is calculated, it is not the 'benefit value' of the capital which needs to be known. Rather, it is its 'replacement value': how much it would cost to make good the capital worn out. This need not equal the value in terms of benefit at all. It is no use a company allowing in its accounts a proportion only of the current worth of a machine as depreciation; when the machine is replaced, a new model will be required. It is the purchase price of this which depreciation must cover. Similarly, to calculate the depreciation of natural capital we do not need to know the value of the environmental good or service lost, only how much it would cost to replace it. And *this* is not nearly so problematic to discover. It is after all not a question of trying to give the environment *itself* a money value, whether by asking people their willingness to pay for it or by observing associated behaviour. It is simply a matter of working out what would need to be done to repair the damage and then calculating the money cost of this.

This is not to say that finding out how much it would cost to repair or replace 'damaged' environmental features is easy. There are a host of problems. It may actually be very difficult to identify what policies are required, particularly if the consequences of the damage are far-reaching (such as in global warming). Conventions would probably need to be established on the average cost of repair of different types of damage, even though in actual situations the real cost might differ substantially. Where degradation is permanent, such as in the depletion of non-renewables, special techniques would be required to calculate the cost. (If the value of the quantity depleted were simply subtracted from GNP, the entire benefit of the resource would be erased.)[18]

But these problems are not of the same type as those discussed in the last chapter. They make it difficult to estimate the monetary value of replacement costs; they do not (in most cases) render valuation itself meaningless.[19] For this reason some environmental economists and statisticians have shown considerable interest in the concept of an environmentally-adjusted NNP, or 'sustainable income'. Although they accept that the figure calculated may not be very accurate, it is (they claim) at least meaningful. And for this reason it will provide a more useful guide to economic performance – and therefore to policy – than GNP or NNP as conventionally defined.[20]

Sustainable income

Unfortunately, however, sustainable income is not as helpful an indicator as its supporters have argued. Indeed, far from providing a guide for policy makers, it may positively mislead them.

The first problem is that of irreversible environmental damage. In these cases there is no repair or replacement cost. Where a depleted resource has a market value (such as with fossil fuels or minerals), some monetary figure may be given. Sometimes, such as where a natural habitat is destroyed, the concept of the 'shadow project' can be used: depreciation can be valued by estimating the cost of creating an 'identical' habitat elsewhere. This would not be a true reflection of the loss, but it would conform to the idea of 'replacement' cost and would offer some working figure. But even this method is not available for resources which cannot be 'replaced' in any way. When a species is made extinct or a beautiful landscape destroyed, an irreversible depletion occurs which nothing can make good. No doubt some monetary figure could be derived from the techniques outlined in the last chapter. But this would be subject to all the problems we have already identified; and in any case it would not reflect the concept of 'depreciation' which is the basis of sustainable income.

The second problem is perhaps even more serious. This is that the concept of sustainable income is not, as it may appear to be, a measure of sustainability. Indeed it is not even a measure of environmental performance. It cannot be assumed that if sustainable income is rising, environmental quality is improving. One reason for this is that merely maintaining current environmental capacities may not be enough to secure sustainability, since the stock of some kinds of natural capital is already so low. Sustainable income is concerned, not with the sustainable level of environmental capital, but simply with maintaining last year's level.[21]

But an even more fundamental reason is that subtracting the depreciation of natural capital from conventional NNP is an accounting practice only. It is intended to show how much income would be left if sufficient investment were made to keep environmental capacities intact. But this does not mean that such investment actually *is* made. No accounting techniques can guarantee that policies for sustainability are actually carried out. Of course, if they are not, degradation is likely to get worse, and this will be reflected in a growing divergence between GNP and adjusted NNP over time. But sustainable income itself can grow *even if degradation increases*. This will occur if in any year growth of GNP is greater than growth of depreciation, that is, if the 'environmental efficiency' of GNP is rising, but not by enough actually to cause environmental improvement.

This is illustrated in Table 18.1. GNP grows at 5% per annum. Depreciation of human-made capital remains constant at 10% of GNP. Environmental degradation starts at 10% of GNP and gets worse at a rate of 2% per annum. So environmentally-adjusted NNP rises.

Table 18.1: Sustainable income and environmental degradation

	Year 1	Year 2	Year 3	Year 4
GNP	1,000	1,050	1,102	1,157
less depreciation of human-made capital	100	105	110	116
less environmental depreciation	100	102	104	107
equals Environmentally-Adjusted NNP (EANNP)	800	843	888	934

The problem here is that sustainable income takes environmental degradation into account only after it has measured GNP. It is therefore at least as influenced by changes in GNP as it is by changes in environmental quality: if the former are larger, they will have a bigger impact on it. Sustainable income is thus not an environmental indicator: its movement does not show environmental quality to be improving or declining. Even less is it a measure of sustainability, since an economy can be unsustainable – *and moving away from sustainability* – even while EANNP rises. It is an income measure, one which better (though not properly) reflects the long-term ability of the economy to generate financial flows.[22] As such it should be used, not to assess environmental performance, but to deflate the claims of GNP. For this purpose it could play a useful role, acting as a salutary reminder to those obsessed by GNP growth that 'true' income is income which can be sustained over time. If we wish to measure environmental performance or sustainability, however, we shall have to look elsewhere.

Physical indicators

It seems that the environmentalists' project of adjusting GNP is doomed to failure. Defensive expenditures either cannot be identified, or (if they are extended beyond the environmental sphere in order to generate a figure for overall welfare) turn out to be meaningless. The problems of monetary valuation undermine any attempt to measure the loss of welfare caused by residual degradation. And although the concept of sustainable income is (just about) coherent, it isn't actually a measure of sustainability, or indeed of environmental performance, at all.

But disappointing though these conclusions may be, they are not a cause for despair. As we observed at the beginning, the environmentalists' proposals rest on the assumption that alternative indicators to measure economic success should be based on GNP. But if this assumption is abandoned, other possibilities become available. As far as indicators of environmental performance are concerned, withdrawing the requirement that the environment should be measured in monetary terms is extremely helpful.

After all, this is specifically not how we have defined sustainability. In Chapter 7 we rejected the idea that future generations could be compensated for the loss of environmental goods and services through investment in human-made capital, arguing that much of the natural environment was not 'substitutable'. Sustainability was therefore defined not in monetary but in straightforward physical terms, as the maintenance of environmental capacities.

As we showed in Chapter 9, these capacities must be measured in their 'own' units: in parts per billion of air pollution, in acreages of forest, in volume and quality of soil, and so on. If we now wish to measure the performance of the economy in relation to the environment, these units remain perfectly adequate. If air pollution has gone up, if the acreage of forest has fallen, if there is less soil and it is of lower fertility, we can say that the economy's 'environmental performance' has declined, and we are moving away from sustainability. If these indicators show improvements, the economy's performance has improved, and we are moving closer to sustainability. No monetary valuation is required, simply the physical indicators of environmental capacity.

Two countries, Norway and France, have developed fairly comprehensive environmental accounts on this basis, and others are doing so. These accounts record, in appropriate physical units, the stocks and flows of different environmental features. In the Norwegian accounts these are classified as 'material' resources (non-renewables, renewables and continuing resources) and 'environmental' resources (air, water, soil and space). For material resources, the stock accounts show the current reserves; the flow accounts show extractions and additions, along with the materials' end uses by economic sector. For the 'environmental' resources the stock or 'status' accounts show the ambient levels of pollutants in different media; the flow or 'emission' accounts record discharges of wastes. These accounts also measure different categories of land use, and shifts from one category to another. The accounts are presented on a geographical basis where appropriate. The French system uses similar categories and also includes rather more complex information on the linkages between the environmental features and economic activities.[23]

Physical environmental accounts such as these are clearly essential if we are to make sustainability operational in the ways discussed in Chapter 8. Without accurate and systematic information about the state of and changes in the environment (which many countries, perhaps surprisingly, lack) it is impossible to set sustainability targets and to direct policy to meet them. As we showed in Chapter 10, and as the Norwegian and French systems recognise, both 'primary' (stock) indicators measuring ambient environmental conditions, and 'secondary' (flow) indicators measuring the economic activities which affect them (such as waste discharge rates) are required. Moreover, if national accounts are to measure the economy's full environmental impact, damage done (and improvements made) to foreign and global environments by national activities must also be recorded.[24]

Physical environmental indicators are therefore the basis of any measurement of environmental performance. But on their own they are unlikely to be sufficient. This is because the wide variety of indicators involved, nearly all in different units, makes it very difficult to evaluate an economy's success. If all the indicators are moving in the same direction, there will be little problem. But it is much more likely that some indicators will show improvement, some deterioration. In these circumstances making a judgement on the overall 'environmental performance' of the economy will be very difficult.

In one respect this does not matter. If our aim is sustainability (or any other degree of environmental improvement), we do not need to know how the economy is performing *overall*. What we need to know is the level of and change in each environmental feature, measured separately. It is this information which will enable policy to be directed towards meeting sustainability targets, themselves expressed separately for each element of environmental capacity. In their role as aids to understanding, therefore, separate physical environmental indicators are perfectly sufficient.

But in another respect the problem of multiple indicators does matter. In their role as criteria for evaluation, economic indicators are not simply neutral academic tools. They are weapons in public debate. Indicators such as GNP growth get announced on television and in the newspapers; they are used by politicians and pressure groups to demonstrate how well or badly the economy is performing. In this context a large set of environmental indicators expressed in different physical units is no use at all. It is hardly likely that newscasters will describe all the different stock and flow accounts for all the different elements of environmental capacity at the same time as announcing the monthly inflation rate. (They do not do so in Norway or France.) If environmentalists wish to present an overall assessment of the economy's performance, one or two 'headline indicators' which can directly rival GNP and other conventional measures are almost certainly needed.

One way of doing this is to distil the large set of physical indicators into a small number of 'environmental indexes'. An index is a combination of two or more indicators. It overcomes the problem of 'non-commensurability' (that is, of different physical indicators being expressed in different units) by relating each physical measurement to a number on a common scale. This works in much the same way as the scoring system in an athletics decathlon. Since it is impossible to add the length of a long-jump to the time of a 100-metres sprint, each possible score in each decathlon event is given a number of points. The points achieved in each event are then added together to give the competitor's total score.

So in an environmental index, different levels of each physical indicator would be given a points 'score' (with 0 being the best possible environmental condition), and then all the scores would be added up to give the total index number. Clearly, the lower the index number, the better the overall environmental performance. Indexes could be constructed for broad elements of environmental quality, such as air pollution, water pollution, land use, etc. As single numbers, such indexes could be announced and published at the same time as other economic indicators such as inflation, unemployment and GNP. They would enable comparisons in environmental quality to be made both over time and between different countries.

Indeed, it would be possible to construct a single 'environmental index' covering all elements of environmental quality. Such an index was attempted for Canada in the mid-1970s, and has been proposed for Britain.[25] The key problem here would be the 'weighting' given to the different elements to acknowledge their differing importance. The weights could be allocated according to expert opinion (as in the Canadian case). But this would leave the index open to the charge that it was not properly objective. So alternatively they could be determined by opinion surveys, showing how important each element was felt to be by the public. (This is proposed in the British example.) But this might underestimate crucial environmental features of which the public was ignorant, and might make the index subject to the vagaries of media attention to particular environmental problems. There is no doubt much room for discussion on whether and how a single index should be designed. But any method is likely to raise the public profile of environmental performance; and this is, after all, the point.

Or rather, it is part of the point. It is important to know how the economy is performing in an environmental sense. But the real value is in knowing what can then be done about it. Better indicators here are only half the battle. Our understanding of the environmental economy must be developed at the same time, so that the indicators are connected to policy instruments through which they can be affected. As we said in Chapter 10, we shall need new economic theories and models if environmental performance is not simply to be observed, but determined.

Indicators of welfare

We come then to the final question left unanswered. At the start of this chapter we noted that economic growth was widely assumed to make people better off, but that the environmental critique of GNP threw this assumption into doubt. We have since seen that adjusting GNP for environmental damage, whether through the concept of defensive expenditures or through the valuation of losses, cannot provide an adequate measure of welfare. What then can?

A complete answer is obviously beyond the scope of this book. But the arguments of this chapter perhaps suggest how the question should be approached. Welfare is not a simple concept encapsulated by any particular indicator; it is made up of many things.

Income is clearly one of these. Environmental quality is another. We have suggested that health conditions and levels of crime might also be recognised as contributing factors. Many people will want to add the levels of employment and unemployment, which can affect people's standard of living independently of the income they receive. They may also want to include the amount of (voluntary) leisure time enjoyed. Others will argue that public services such as education and recreational facilities (which people do not consume individually, and which are therefore not related directly to private income) should also appear in their own right.

There will also be a strong case for recognising not just income (and therefore expenditure) but the goods and services which people consume but do not pay for. A great deal of production occurs outside the 'formal' economy in which goods and services are exchanged: housework, do-it-yourself, voluntary work, childcare, care of elderly people, and so on. The products generated by these 'informal' activities are often the same as the products generated by marketed production; they also contribute to welfare. Finally, many people will want to say that for a country as a whole the *distribution* of income is as important as its sum. The more unequal a society, it might be said, the less valuable the income it generates.

There are no doubt other factors which might be included. Many people will have their own view on what makes a society better off. But the point is that each of these factors makes some contribution, and each has its own measure. They are not all expressed in one indicator. To be sure, it would be possible somehow to 'value' each of them in monetary terms, and add (or subtract) them all together to get an overall figure for 'net product', in just the way that the environmentalists have wanted to do with GNP. Various attempts have indeed been made to do this, generating adjusted GNP figures called the 'Measure of Economic Welfare' (MEW), 'Net National Welfare' (NNW) and the 'Index of Sustainable Economic Welfare' (ISEW), among others.[26] But if it is felt that meaningful results cannot be obtained when only environmental adjustments are made, the problems are multiplied when the process is undertaken for all these other factors.

In the first place, so many assumptions have to be deployed in order to convert each indicator into a monetary variable that the exercise effectively becomes arbitrary. The final figure is so sensitive to the assumptions made that it ceases to carry any 'objective' status at all. Moreover, after each addition or subtraction is carried out, the resulting number becomes less and less an indicator of anything which can actually be recognised and defined. It is difficult to see what the figures for MEW, NNW and ISEW are actually measures *of*.[27] But perhaps most importantly, it isn't clear what role the overall number plays. Because so many factors are incorporated into it, the only way of analysing it, particularly its changes over time or comparisons between different countries, is to break it back down into its individual components. Simply to say that 'welfare' has gone up or down tells us nothing about which aspects of welfare have changed – and therefore what can be done about them. But of course if to be useful we need to go back to the original indicators, why bother with the overall number at all?

The problem here surely lies in the desire to have a single indicator which can measure welfare. Such a desire is understandable: if there is only one, we shall have no trouble knowing whether it is going up or down, and the challenge to the single indicator GNP will be strongest. But the attractiveness of the idea cannot hide the meaninglessness of its execution. Welfare is *not* a unitary concept, and cannot be expressed in one indicator. Economic performance must be assessed using a variety of indicators, each showing in its own terms one aspect of what is considered important. It is true that in many cases these will move in opposite directions, making it difficult to say whether, 'overall', society is getting better or worse off. But this problem is not erased by the use of a single indicator, it is simply hidden within its calculations. It is much better that the changes in the different indicators are out in the open, where they can be seen. We can all then make our own judgements on whether any given change from one year to another represents progress or not; and economic policy can be decided accordingly.[28]

19

The Standard of Living and the Quality of Life

A return to the cave?

In both industrialised and developing countries, one question above all is likely to be asked of the Green economic programme. What effect would it have on the standard of living? The principal source of opposition to environmentalism has long been the belief that, in the somewhat rhetorical words of two American economists, it would mean 'a return to regulated caveman culture'.[1] Protecting the environment to the extent that Greens demand, it is feared, will require substantial falls in consumption; effectively, this view claims, sustainability would spell the end of the post-war era of high living standards to which Northern societies have become so attached and to which Southern nations so understandably aspire.

There are some Greens for whom this fear is of little concern. Unimpressed by what they see as the spiritual emptiness and psychological alienation of the 'consumer society', they regard a fall in living standards as something to be welcomed, not feared. But whether or not one sympathises with this view, it surely misses the point. It is not the Greens' perception of a reduction in consumption which counts. It is the rest of society's. If people in general fear that sustainability will cause a substantial fall in their living standards they are unlikely to vote for it; and if they do not vote for it, it will not happen. In democratic societies the Green programme will not be implemented without popular support, and a significant determinant of this is likely to be the impact of the programme on people's level of consumption. Few governments have been elected on a promise to cut the standard of living.

Many Greens will want to counter this argument with another. The claim that a prospective fall in living standards will make sustainability unattractive presupposes that the alternative to it is a rise in living standards. This is clearly the assumption made by the opponents of environmentalism. But, Greens will argue, it does not represent the choice facing industrialised societies at all. When the full effects of environmental degradation are experienced, society will be

242

forced to accept a fall in consumption whatever policies are adopted. In these circumstances the Green programme may lead to a higher standard of living than the only available alternatives, even if this standard is effectively a fall from current levels.

This is certainly a foreseeable scenario at some point in the future. If environmental damage is not checked, there may well come a time when the depletion of resources, limits to absorptive capacity and impairment of life support services enforce a reduction in current consumption irrespective of policy choices. But it is evidently not the situation facing industrialised societies today. Despite the seriousness of the environmental crisis, it *is* still possible for economic policies to raise consumption in the short term. And given that elections tend to be fought on fairly short-term economic horizons, this means that there clearly is a trade-off which can be made between higher living standards and sustainability – *if* sustainability means, as its critics maintain, that living standards must be reduced. The original question is therefore valid. Is this what it does mean?

Unsurprisingly, to answer the question we must define its terms. We have so far spoken as if 'the standard of living', 'consumption' and some notion of how 'well-off' a person is are interchangeable ways of saying something whose meaning is perfectly clear. But this is by no means obviously the case. Indeed, asking if environmental protection will reduce living standards is necessarily problematic. The answer almost certainly depends on how the concept is defined.

Definitions of the standard of living

In popular discussion, 'the standard of living' is often equated with disposable income. If people have more money to spend (after allowing for inflation), they are assumed to be better off. This view, however, takes account only of private consumption. It ignores the fact that many of the things which make people well-off are consumed collectively. These things fall into two categories.

First are public services (education, health care, pensions, street cleaning and so on) which are paid for out of taxes. These services also make a contribution to welfare. Comparison between disposable income in the UK and US, for example, would not give an accurate picture of relative living standards, since in the US most people's health care is bought privately, whereas in the UK it is paid for through taxation. Public services must clearly be included in any overall assessment.

Secondly, aspects of welfare which are not bought or sold at all – such as the environment – also need to be included. Most people will feel that their standard of living has declined if, other things being equal, the air in their neighbourhood becomes more polluted, or the local park is replaced by a motorway. They may make the same judgement if crime rates rise, or their sense of living in a cohesive and peaceful community diminishes. These things obviously bear some relation to public expenditure, since environmental protection, policing and community services are provided by government. But the correlation is not straightforward. A higher level of public spending on the environment does not guarantee that environmental quality will rise; this depends on the countervailing rate of degradation. Similarly, crime rates are not simply determined by the police budget. Public expenditures and these 'non-purchased' factors are therefore linked but not the same.

Collective consumption of both these types contributes to what may be described as 'the quality of life'. This term is often used imprecisely, to denote the less tangible, perhaps less material aspects of living standards. But here we shall use it quite strictly, to mean that component of the standard of living which individuals cannot (or at least do not) consume privately from their disposable income. In our definition, the quality of life is simply the sum of all the things which people consume collectively, whether through public expenditure or not purchased at all. Part of the quality of life, such as the level of crime, is indeed intangible or non-material; but part (such as the number of trees in a neighbourhood) is perfectly material. It is just not individually bought.[2]

Recognising that what makes people well-off consists of both individual and collective consumption allows us to formulate a very simple definition of the standard of living. *The standard of living equals real disposable income plus the quality of life.* (By 'real' is meant the level of disposable income expressed in terms of the quantity of goods and services it can buy, taking inflation into account. This definition will apply also to the terms 'living standards' and 'welfare' and the notion of how 'well-off' a person is; 'consumption' we shall confine to more specific uses.) It follows that only if *both* disposable income and the quality of life are rising or falling will it be clear what is happening to living standards. If there is divergence the consequence will not be certain.

But this of course merely begs the question of how the quality of life is measured. Measuring disposable income is relatively easy. But measuring collective consumption is not. Things which are not bought at all do not have prices; and though they may have their own indicators, such as the level of air pollution or crime rate, these are not easily placed on a common scale. (Some of these things, such as a sense of community, may not have objective indicators at all.)

Even public expenditures, which can be measured in monetary terms, cannot simply be compared with one another or with private expenditure. This is because what matters in the concept of living standards is the welfare people get from consumption, not simply the sums being spent. When people spend their own money we may generally assume that the level of welfare gained correlates fairly closely with the amount spent: this is presumably how people decide what to spend their money on.[3] But when governments spend money this assumption can no longer be sustained, since people are not in direct control over what is provided on their behalf. It therefore does not follow that a given sum of spending always makes the same contribution to welfare.

This is particularly important when public and private expenditures are being compared. For example, public health provision is generally found to be more efficient than private: that is, a smaller sum is spent on administration and more on care.[4] But if this is true the same amount of money spent in the public and private health systems is likely to yield different contributions to the standard of living.

Similarly, if a sum of government income previously used for, say, road repairs is 'given back' to taxpayers in the form of tax cuts, the value it generates will depend on how people compare the benefits of better-maintained roads as against the consumer goods, or whatever, they buy with the extra disposable income. Since private individuals *can't* spend the money on road repair (which is a collective good) it cannot automatically be assumed that the private consumption is worth the same amount to them as the public consumption it replaced. On the other hand, the very fact that it *is* private may convey extra value: for some people simply being able to choose how to spend the money may be a benefit itself.

Another problem also arises here. This is that public and private expenditures often lead to a different *distribution* of benefits. Welfare expenditures, for example, in general aim to benefit poorer people, taking taxes from the more affluent to do this.[5] If such spending is cut to reduce taxes, one set of people will gain and another will lose. The effect of such a change on the overall standard of living is then a matter of judgement. And of course different people are likely to have different judgements. Note that in these circumstances the affluent need not feel that 'the standard of living' has risen, even though the benefits they experience have increased. It is quite possible for people to make evaluations about the standard of living of society as a whole independently of how well-off they personally feel themselves. Either a changed distribution of consumption or a shift in the things on which it is spent may lead one to conclude that overall living standards have risen or fallen.

These observations lead to an important conclusion. The standard of living is a subjective notion which cannot be reduced to objectively measurable indicators such as income or expenditure, whether private or public. Indeed welfare is an inherently personal concept: each individual will regard a given pattern of consumption – their own and others' – differently. In this sense the standard of living induced by an economic programme such as the one described in this book cannot simply be 'read off' from the policies it contains, even if the consequences of these policies could be accurately predicted. The standard of living depends just as much on the people who experience it as it does on the policies which generate it.

Disposable income and the quality of life

In the short term at least it is quite possible that environmental protection measures will stimulate economic growth. As we have seen, the need for new products, new industrial processes and new infrastructure may well lead to an increase in national income. However this does not necessarily mean that real disposable incomes will rise. First, much of the additional expenditure will push prices up, as firms try to recoup higher production costs and new investment programmes. Even if nominal incomes rise, therefore, real incomes may not. Second, taxes are likely to be higher. Many environmental programmes will require public expenditures which will have to be paid for; consumption taxes may also be used directly. So even if gross income rises, disposable income may not.

The overall impact of environmental protection programmes on disposable income will depend on the balance between these negative effects and the generalised impact of growth. It is possible that in the short term the latter may be larger. But over the longer term a reduction in real disposable income is to be anticipated. In the first place, continued GNP growth within the sustainability constraint cannot be guaranteed: we do not know what will prove possible but it is evident that the environmental restrictions on growth will become more severe. Since the environment is in general consumed collectively and without payment, greater expenditure on protecting it can be expected to lead to a smaller amount of income being available for private consumption.

Let us assume for the sake of argument then that a programme for sustainability will reduce real disposable incomes. What effect would this have on the standard of living? To answer this we need to know what happens to the money that is removed from private consumption and spent instead on environmental protection. Who benefits from it?

First and most obviously, environmental expenditures may go towards improving the current environment of the people whose disposable income is reduced. Here a straight purchase is effectively made: the lost income pays for various improvements to the quality of life, such as lower pollution, more green space, a wider variety of habitats, less urban congestion, less risk of ill-health, and others. There is a simple transfer from private to collective consumption.

If this were the only use to which the reduction in disposable income was put, the effect on the standard of living would be a simple matter. Given our definition (real disposable income plus quality of life) the standard of living would depend on whether or not the improvements to the quality of life were felt to be worth more than the income forgone. However not all the reduction in disposable income is likely to benefit the people whose income is reduced. Some of the environmental improvements will be experienced by future generations. These will be the major beneficiaries, for example, of policies to reduce global warming, soil erosion, hazardous waste and so on. Assuming that such people's welfare is not fully reflected in the welfare of people living now, these expenditures will be 'lost' to the present generation. The reduction in income suffered now brings no equivalent benefit.

Similarly, some of the extra environmental spending may go towards improving the environment overseas. Policies to reduce acid rain emissions in the UK and US will benefit Scandinavian countries and Canada probably more than the UK and US themselves. Expenditures aimed at reducing desertification in Africa and rainforest destruction in the Amazon will make only a marginal (direct) contribution to welfare in the North, though possibly a major one in the recipient countries. These expenditures will therefore again be 'lost' in terms of the spending nation's standard of living.[6]

Many environmental policies will of course have some effect on all three types of welfare ('current local', 'future' and 'distant'). Cutting petrol consumption, for example, may be geared primarily towards reducing future global warming; but it will also cut acid rain deposits in other countries and improve the quality of present urban air. There is therefore rarely a straightforward choice between the beneficiaries of environmental expenditure. Nevertheless it must be accepted that trade-offs can be made; and if this is so it is evident that the more redistributive an environmental programme is, the greater the likely adverse impact on the standard of living. The more money is spent on protecting the environment for future generations and for people living overseas – particularly in the South, to which sustainability demands a genuine redistribution of resources – the less will be available for improvements to the current quality of life in the North.

We may conclude that the impact of environmental programmes on the standard of living will depend on two factors: first, on the extent to which the programmes redistribute environmental benefits to future and distant people; and second, on how the disposable income forgone is valued in comparison with the better quality of life obtained in return.

The appreciation of the quality of life

Is it likely that people will value improvements to the quality of life more than the disposable income they will lose? This obviously depends on how much incomes fall and what improvements are made. In some cases improvements to the quality of life may be more than the sum of their parts. That is, the benefit of a public good to each individual may be greater than the income he or she forgoes to achieve it. It may take only a small increase in taxation, for example, for major environmental improvements to be made – say, to the appearance and 'greenness' of urban neigbourhoods. These may be worth much more to local people than the disposable income lost. On the other hand, where price elasticities are low, the reverse may be the case. As we have seen, it may take major price increases to cause relatively small environmental changes, for example in petrol consumption. In such cases the effect on overall living standards may depend on the instruments of policy employed.

It will also depend, as we have already noted, on the distribution of costs and benefits. If environmental improvements benefiting poorer people are funded primarily through tax increases levied on the more affluent, many people may feel that living standards in general have increased.

The evaluation of disposable income losses against quality of life gains is also likely to depend on people's levels of awareness. In general we may assume a high degree of consciousness about changes in personal income. Some environmental improvements may also be relatively obvious – a reduction in traffic congestion or the cleaning up of beaches, for instance. But others may be largely hidden. Most people may be unaware of a reduction in hazardous waste production or the increase in numbers of a threatened butterfly species, despite the fact that, if they *were* aware of these things, they might regard them as of greater value than the marginal reduction in income required to pay for them. In cases of pollution, where the principal issue is the risk to health, the amount of information people have on the possible danger will obviously be crucial to their judgement of the value of reducing it. In these circumstances the publicity which attaches to environmental improvements may be as important a factor as the improvements themselves.

Another problem here is that people may not be aware of what might have happened to the environment had the protective policy not been introduced. In many cases, after all, such policies will not so much improve the environment as prevent (or perhaps just slow down) its further degradation. The quality-of-life benefits gained will then need to be judged not in their own right but in comparison with the degradation that would have occurred otherwise. If people are not aware of this, the value of the policy may go unrecognised.

A final point may be made. This is that people's appreciation of the quality of life is not fixed. Increasing affluence, for example, may lead to a shift of priorities from material consumption to more qualitative contributions to welfare – this is the assertion made by one of the most famous theories of human needs.[7] It may also be that as various aspects of the environment become more scarce or more degraded their value increases. The greater the despoilation of the countryside, for example, the more willing people may be to pay for its preservation. Or it may simply be the case that the attitudes of a society change as people become more aware of environmental degradation and as the influence of political or cultural movements (such as the Green movement) increases. Any of these changes – or their opposites – could lead to different evaluations being made of changes in the quality of life, and therefore of living standards.

These observations suggest that not only is the perception of the standard of living in any given situation inherently subjective, it is also amenable to change. This is an important conclusion to which we shall return.

The value of disposable income

So far we have shown that the impact of a Green economic programme on the standard of living would depend on how improvements to the quality of life were valued against the loss of disposable income. But this is in fact only half the picture. For the value of the disposable income remaining may also change.

As we saw in Chapter 9, the least painful way of meeting sustainability targets is to increase environmental efficiency; that is, to reduce the amount of environmental impact per unit of GNP. This can be done in essentially two ways. The first is by changing the nature of products: altering their design, their manufacturing processes, the materials they are made of, etc. In many instances it may well be possible to reduce environmental impact quite considerably through these methods. For example, CFCs in aerosols have largely been substituted by what are believed to be less harmful propellants. Similarly, new materials such as ceramics and optical fibres look set to replace metals in many industrial uses, increasing both energy and resource efficiency.

The second way of increasing environmental efficiency is to change the range of products being consumed. Thus public transport, cycling and walking might take over some of the functions for which cars are currently used. The volume of consumer durables might fall, being replaced by a greater consumption of, say, educational, health or arts services. (Sometimes the distinction between the two methods of increasing efficiency may be blurred: if alcohol-driven cars replaced petrol ones, for example, this might be interpreted either as an increase in the efficiency of cars or as a replacement of one product with another. It matters little.)

These changes will in turn have a number of effects on the standard of living. In some cases all that will happen is that the improvement in its efficiency will cause the price of a product to rise. Thus fridges without CFCs and biodegradable detergents will cost more; but as far as the consumer is concerned the product itself will remain largely unchanged. Such price rises will reduce the level of real disposable income, as we have already discussed. In other cases the price of a product may rise, but at the same time the product itself may be improved. Thus for example installing fibre optic cables in place of conventional cables increases the amount of information which can be carried as well as causing less pollution in manufacture and use. In these circumstances it cannot simply be said that real incomes have fallen, since consumers may well feel that the additional benefits are worth the extra costs. In still other cases, environmental improvements may actually save consumers money, as with energy efficient light bulbs and longer-lasting consumer durables. Here real incomes may effectively rise, despite price increases.

In general however price rises can be expected to reduce real income: what economists call the 'income effect'. In addition they have a 'substitution effect'. As the relative prices of products change, consumers shift their patterns of consumption, buying more of the thing that has become relatively cheaper and less of that which has become more expensive. Thus one reaction to a rise in the price of petrol will be an increase in the proportion of household income which is spent on it. But equally likely is that people will start using their cars less, spending their money instead on other things as the relative value of car travel declines. One of the substitute products will no doubt be public transport, particularly if petrol price rises are accompanied by improvements in bus and train services. But they may also choose to spend more money on home or local entertainments and less on distant holidays; or more on bicycles and less on cars. In this way environmental policies will begin to alter the range of products sold at a given level of disposable income.

In the short term it may reasonably be assumed that such changes in the patterns of consumption will be experienced as reductions in living standards. If people had wanted to use public transport more, or to spend more of their time off in the garden and less abroad, they would have done so before such behaviour was induced by the environmental policy.

But over the longer term this assumption may need to be revised. After all most people's pattern of consumption is influenced strongly by social norms, and their evaluation of it governed to a large extent by comparison with others. If car use were restricted for everyone, and public transport services were improved, people might find that using buses and trains was not really the hardship they had anticipated; once they had got used to it, the loss might hardly be felt at all. Indeed, some might even find that cycling to work and to the shops was positively pleasurable. (There would of course be fewer cars on the road, and less pollution.)

Similarly, increases in the prices of consumer goods might in the short term be perceived as a reduction in living standards. But over time people might come to value more the things they bought instead: sports and leisure activities, books, evening classes, live entertainment or whatever. Meat and other farm prices might rise, but home-grown vegetables might quite quickly be recognised as healthier and more satisfying anyway. It is even possible that people might find that they didn't actually need to spend so much money to feel well off. It is a commonplace that many of the products that cram homes in the Northern hemisphere are superfluous to needs: while they are there for the taking it is difficult to avoid consuming them but if the options changed – and changed for everyone, so that the Joneses were not able to sneak ahead – they would not much be missed.

We do not know if this will happen; it may well be that any reduction in private car use and the ability to change one's hi-fi system every two years will prove utterly traumatic to Northern societies. But the possibility that it might happen – that people's perception of what constitutes a high standard of living may change – illustrates a crucial point.

This is that the same measure of living standards may be achieved by a number of different patterns of consumption. People may judge themselves equally well-off in two situations where the goods and services they are actually consuming are quite different. Or put another way, environmental policies might change the *constitution* of the standard of living without changing its *level*.

The politics of consumption

This is, surely, the Green ideal. There can be no question that sustainability demands a reduction in the current environmental impact of the average citizen of the industrialised world. If we go on as we are, catastrophe beckons. But few people will want this necessary change to be experienced as a reduction in living standards – not least because the citizens concerned may then refuse to vote for it. On the contrary, the ideal must be that environmental impact is brought within the sustainability constraint while people in general feel no worse off. This will be possible – to summarise the arguments of this chapter – if the increases in efficiency brought about by environmental policies are of three types.

First, they must noticeably improve the quality of life, sufficiently for people to value the improvements more highly than the loss of disposable income required to pay for them. Second, they must generate new and improved products which are not simply better for the environment but more highly valued in other ways, or which actually save consumers money, for example through energy efficiency or durability. Third, they must lead to shifts in the patterns of consumption which people come to regard as at least no worse than the patterns they replace.

The concept of the standard of living may be thought of as a relationship between supply and demand. So long as the supply of goods and services keeps pace with people's demand for them, the standard of living will not decline: people's expectations will be matched by the availability of the things they want. The environmental crisis, however, entails a reduction in the supply of resources: if humankind is to avoid catastrophe, we must reduce our impact on the natural world to a level consistent with the maintenance of environmental capacities. Reducing supply in this way must then inevitably involve a reduction in living standards – *unless* demand for resources also declines. Such a reduction in demand is possible, as we have seen, both through technological change and changes in tastes. The more it occurs, the less will be the reduction in living standards. If the fall in the demand for resources matches the reduction in sustainable supply, the standard of living can be maintained even as sustainability is achieved.

Can this be done? The timescale of change will surely be crucial. Changes in the constitution of living standards cannot be effected overnight. The technological advances and investments required to increase environmental efficiency will be considerable; it will take time for them to be developed. To change people's valuation of more environmentally-benign patterns of consumption will require changes in tastes and culture which are unlikely to happen quickly.

Both of these types of change will of course be encouraged by environmental protection measures, as damaging activities are made more expensive and benign ones cheaper. In this sense the very act of reducing the available supply of environmental resources may lead to reductions in demand.[8] The ideal scenario would then be that the reductions occur at about the same pace: that demand for use of the environment falls (through both technological advance and changes in tastes) at approximately the same rate as the environmental protection measures which restrict supply are introduced. In this way the cost of the sustainable development policy in terms of reduced current living standards will be minimised.

We might describe this as the 'knife-edge path' to sustainable development. We can fall off either side. If environmental protection measures lead to a reduction in the supply of resources more quickly than changes in technology and tastes reduce the demand for them, living standards will be perceived to fall and the policy may not be adopted. If on the other hand we restrict the rate of supply to the rate at which demand falls, and this is too slow, we risk environmental catastrophe. Staying on the path will surely require immense political skill as well as carefully designed economic policies.

That new technological advances will increase environmental efficiency cannot be doubted. Many people will however be more sceptical about the likelihood that the tastes and culture of industrialised societies will be able to change enough to accommodate the required reduction in environmental impact. Will people really be willing to regard a reduction in car use as *not* a reduction in their living standards? Will they really be happy to forgo the constant expansion of material possessions in favour of a more sustainable lifestyle? It will be acknowledged that environmental policies will bring considerable benefits: reduced pollution, better health, more beautiful countryside, less traffic congestion, pleasanter urban neighbourhoods, reduced fears for the future. But whether people will really feel these improvements compensate for the changes in lifestyle which must occur to achieve them remains an open question.

The apparent attachment of Western societies to the consumer culture – and the infectious way this has spread to the countries of Eastern Europe and the South – makes it perhaps difficult to be optimistic. But the important point here is surely not how *likely* such a change in culture might be. Whether or not the change occurs is not a matter of fate, outside the control of human agency. Cultures and tastes are made, they do not spring innate from our genes. And they are influenced by a whole range of social and political factors which can themselves be changed and developed by political parties, pressure groups, voluntary organisations, individual behaviour and cultural activity.

In this sense achieving the Green Economy will not ultimately prove a question of economics. As we have seen in this book, the causes of the environmental crisis are fairly clear. Sustainability provides an objective both morally defensible and capable of being translated into policy. A range of instruments are available to hold the economy within sustainability constraints. But a Green economic programme will not be introduced unless industrialised societies manifest the desire and the will to change. Describing the requisite policies is therefore only the first part of the task at hand. The second – perhaps the more important – is to encourage those political and cultural changes which will enable them to be put into practice.

It remains to be seen whether the Green programme can gain popular support. We do not know what it would take to encourage people to value the quality of life more highly; to give more weight to the interests of future generations and distant people and wildlife; to appreciate less materialistic forms of consumption. But that is not the point. For those concerned about the environmental crisis, the task is surely to find out.

Notes

Introduction

1. World Commission on Environment and Development, *Our Common Future* (Oxford: Oxford University Press, 1987), p. 5.
2. See F. Capra, *The Turning Point* (New York: Simon and Schuster, 1982); H.E. Daly and J.W. Cobb, *For the Common Good* (Boston: Beacon Press, 1989); P. Ekins (ed), *The Living Economy* (London: Routledge and Kegan Paul, 1986); H. Henderson, *Creating Alternative Futures: The End of Economics* (New York: Putman, 1978) and *The Politics of the Solar Age: Alternatives to Economics* (New York: Doubleday, 1981); S. McBurney, *Economics into Ecology Won't Go* (Bideford: Green Books, 1990); N. Singh, *Economics and the Crisis of Ecology*, 3rd edn (London: Bellew, 1989).
3. See David Pearce's defence in his Inaugural Lecture, *Sustainable Futures: Economics and the Environment*, University College, London, 5 December 1985, pp. 8–10.
4. A good textbook in the neoclassical tradition is D.W. Pearce, *Environmental Economics* (London: Longman, 1976). The seminal work is probably W. Baumol and W. Oates, *The Theory of Environmental Policy*, 2nd edn (Cambridge: Cambridge University Press, 1988).
5. D.W. Pearce, A. Markandya and E.B. Barbier, *Blueprint for a Green Economy* (London: Earthscan, 1989). Interestingly, the Pearce Report is not a simple neoclassical text. Its initial discussion of sustainability and the concept of 'constant natural capital stock' does not fall within the neoclassical tradition, being based on an ethical concern for the interests of future generations. However the remainder of the book ignores these arguments and follows the neoclassical line. In his public statements Pearce himself has been a leading advocate of the orthodox approach, though he has also on occasion argued for the 'constant natural capital stock' view.
6. It is used there explicitly instead of, say, a more Marxist explanation of the causes of environmental degradation, which would emphasise the need of capitalist corporations to expand their markets and the relationships of power and dependence between rich and poor nations. This is because of its greater clarity to the reader not versed in either school. Neither the neoclassical nor the Marxist explanation is 'correct'; they are, rather, two alternative perspectives on the same phenomenon. For a subtle and persuasive Marxist account see M. Redclift, *Development and the Environmental Crisis: Red or Green Alternatives* (London: Methuen, 1984) and *Sustainable Development: Exploring the Contradictions* (London: Methuen, 1987).

7. In this sense the book could be said to belong in the 'institutionalist' tradition. See G.M. Hodgson, *Economics and Institutions* (Cambridge: Polity Press, 1988). Other recent critics of the neoclassical school include Daly and Cobb, *Common Good*; A. Etzioni, *The Moral Dimension: Towards a New Economics* (New York: Free Press, 1988); M.A. Lutz and K. Lux, *Humanistic Economics* (New York: Bootstrap Press, 1988).

8. See Capra, *Turning Point*; Daly and Cobb, *Common Good*; Ekins, *Living Economy*; J. Robertson, *Future Wealth* (London: Cassell, 1990).

9. See in particular the work of Richard Norgaard, 'Coevolutionary Development Potential', *Land Economics*, 60 (2), 1984; 'Environmental Economics: an Evolutionary Critique and a Plea for Pluralism', *Journal of Environmental Economics and Management*, 12 (4), 1985, pp 382–94; *The Scarcity of Resource Economics*, paper presented to the American Economics Association, New York, 1985; 'Sustainable Development: A Co-Evolutionary View', *Futures*, 20 (6), 1988. A useful historical perspective is provided by J. Martinez-Alier, *Ecological Economics: Energy, Environment and Society* (Oxford: Basil Blackwell, 1987).

10. See Sandy Irvine's critique of the present author's approach: 'No Growth in a Finite World', *New Statesman and Society*, 23 November 1990.

11. See R. Bahro, *From Red to Green* (London: Verso, 1984); E. Callenbach, Ectopia (London: Pluto Press, 1978); J. Robertson, *The Sane Alternative*, 2nd edn (Ironbridge: James Robertson, 1983) and *Future Wealth*.

12. Wilde, *The Soul of Man Under Socialism* (1891), quoted in K. Kumar, *Prophecy and Progress: The Sociology of Industrial and Post-Industrial Society* (Harmondsworth: Penguin, 1978).

13. This contrasting of feasible and Utopian ideas is taken from A. Nove, *The Economics of Feasible Socialism* (London: Allen and Unwin, 1983), pp. 11, 15–20, 238–9.

14. J. Porritt, 'Re-aligning the Vision', in F. Dodds (ed), *Into the Twenty-First Century* (Basingstoke: Greenprint, 1988), p. 203.

15. An example would be the response of the petrochemical and motor industries to the proposals made during the 1970s and 1980s to reduce lead in petrol. See D. Wilson, *The Lead Scandal* (London: Heinemann, 1983), pp. 121–40.

16. These questions are discussed (in different contexts) in, for example, R. Bahro, *Socialism and Survival* (London: Heretic, 1982), *From Red to Green* and *Building the Green Movement* (London: GMP, 1986); M. Bernstam, *The Wealth of Nations and the Environment* (London: Institute of Economic Affairs, 1991); A. Bramwell, *Ecology in the 20th Century* (New Haven and London: Yale University Press, 1989); F. Capra and C. Spretnak, *Green Politics* (London: Hutchinson, 1984); A. Dobson, *Green Political Thought* (London: Unwin Hyman, 1990); T. O'Riordan, *Environmentalism* (London: Pion, 1980); T. Paterson, *The Green Conservative* (London: Bow Publications, 1989); D. Pepper, *The Roots of Modern Environmentalism* (London: Croom Helm, 1984); J. Porritt, *Seeing Green* (Oxford: Basil Blackwell, 1984); Redclift, *Development and the Environmental Crisis*; M. Ryle, *Ecology and Socialism* (London: Hutchinson, 1989); F. Sandbach, *Environment, Ideology and Policy* (Oxford: Basil Blackwell, 1980); H. Stretton, *Capitalism, Socialism and the Environment* (Cambridge: Cambridge University Press, 1976); J. Weston (ed), *Red and Green* (London: Pluto Press, 1986); R. Williams, *Socialism and Ecology* (London: Socialist Environment and Resources Association pamphlet, undated).

17. See (among many others) G. Bird (ed), *Third World Debt: The Search for a Solution* (Aldershot: Edward Elgar, 1989); M. Caldwell, *The Wealth of Some Nations* (London: Zed Press, 1977); S. George, *A Fate Worse Than Debt* (Harmondsworth: Penguin Books, 1988); P. Harrison, *Inside the Third World* (Brighton: Harvester, 1980); T. Hayter, *The Creation of World Poverty* (London: Pluto Press, 1983); B. Jackson, *Poverty and the Planet: A Question of Survival* (Harmondsworth: Penguin, 1990); J. Schatan, *World Debt: Who Is To Pay?* (London: Zed Books, 1987).

1: The Economy and the Environmental Crisis

1. This analogy is taken from R. Riddell, *Ecodevelopment* (Farnborough: Gower, 1981), p. 40.

2. World Resources Institute, *World Resources 1990–1* (New York/Oxford: Oxford University Press, 1990), pp. 322–3. The resource lifetime is calculated by dividing the 1988 reserves by the 1988 world production level. Clearly if annual production rises or falls, the lifetime will change. 'Reserves' include only that part of the measured and indicated 'reserve base' which it is currently economic to extract. Including all the reserve base would extend the lifetimes to 230 years for iron ore and 2,380 years for aluminium.

3. Ibid.

4. Much substitution is already going on. See J.E. Tilton, *Materials Substitution* (Washington DC: Resources for the Future, 1983); D. Deadman and R.K. Turner in R.K. Turner (ed), *Sustainable Environmental Management: Principles and Practice* (London: Belhaven Press; Boulder, CO: Westview Press, 1988), pp. 67–101.

5. World Resources Institute, *World Resources 1990–1*, p. 145. These figures are computed from 1988 production levels and reserves. It should be noted that proved reserves are increasing.

6. World Resources Institute, *World Resources 1990–1*, pp. 180, 340; N. Myers (ed), *The Gaia Atlas of Planet Management* (London: Pan, 1985), pp. 82–3; World Resources Institute, *World Resources 1988–9*, (New York: Basic Books, 1988), p. 156. 'Maximum sustainable yield' (MSY) is defined as the maximum number of fish which can be harvested year after year without depleting the natural breeding stock. The nine fisheries above this level are calculated on the FAO's lower estimates of MSY. Loss of whales as a mere resource is not of course the only reason to lament their near-extinction.

7. Myers, *Gaia Atlas*, pp. 141, 152; World Resources Institute, *World Resources 1988–9*, pp. 291–2. This defines desertification as a loss of productivity of 25% or greater. See A. Grainger, *The Threatening Desert: Controlling Desertification* (London: Earthscan, 1990).

8. Myers, *Gaia Atlas*, p. 40; World Resources Institute, *World Resources 1988–9*, p. 2. The effect on food production is analysed by L.R. Brown and J.E. Young, 'Feeding the World in the Nineties', in L.R. Brown et al, *State of the World 1990* (New York: W.W. Norton/London: Unwin Hyman, 1990), pp. 59–78.

9. World Resources Institute, *World Resources 1990–1*, p. 102; Myers, *Gaia Atlas*, p. 42. See D. Poore, *No Timber Without Trees: Sustainability in the Tropical Forest* (London: Earthscan, 1989).

10. C.M. Peters, A.H. Gentry and R.O. Mendelsohn, 'Valuation of an Amazonian Rainforest', *Nature*, 339, 29 June 1989, pp. 655–6.
11. Myers, *Gaia Atlas*, p. 148.
12. Myers, *Gaia Atlas*, pp. 147, 149. See also N. Myers, *The Primary Source: Tropical Forests and Our Future* (New York: W.W. Norton, 1984).
13. For an account of the destruction of the Amazonian rainforest and the effect on the people living in it, see S. Hecht and A. Cockburn, *The Fate of the Forest* (London: Verso, 1989).
14. Note that 'pollution' is defined here as wastes *causing harm*. Wastes themselves are not pollutants unless ecological or health damage is done. This is explored further in Chapter 8.
15. H.F. French, 'Clearing the Air', in Brown et al, *State of the World 1990*, p. 104; S. Postel, 'Controlling Toxic Chemicals', in L.R. Brown et al, *State of the World 1988* (New York: W.W. Norton, 1988), p. 121.
16. French, 'Clearing the Air', in Brown et al, *State of the World 1990*, pp. 106–9; Myers, *Gaia Atlas*, p. 118.
17. Myers, *Gaia Atlas*, p. 86. See also World Resources Institute, *World Resources 1990–1*, pp. 181–8.
18. Myers, *Gaia Atlas*, pp. 86, 153.
19. For an account of the environmental economists' concept of existence value, see D.W. Pearce and R.K. Turner, *Economics of Natural Resources and the Environment* (Hemel Hempstead: Harvester Wheatsheaf, 1990), pp. 129–140. See also Chapters 7 and 17 in this book. For a discussion of humankind's 'need' for contact with nature, see K. Thomas, *Man and the Natural World* (London: Allen Lane, 1983).
20. The phrase 'environmental bankruptcy' comes from L. Timberlake, *Africa in Crisis* (London: Earthscan, 1985). Although the environmental causes of famine are important, it should not be thought that they are overriding. Famines are more strictly the result of economic factors, particularly a divergence between the price of food and the incomes of the poor. See A. Sen, *Poverty and Famines: An Essay on Entitlement and Deprivation* (Oxford: Clarendon Press, 1981).
21. E.O. Wilson, 'Threats to Biodiversity', *Scientific American*, 261 (3), September 1989, p. 60; World Resources Institute, *World Resources 1990–1*, p. 8. See also W.V. Reid and K.R. Miller, *Keeping Options Alive* (Washington DC: World Resources Institute, 1989); N. Myers, *The Sinking Ark* (Oxford: Pergamon Press, 1979) and *A Wealth of Wild Species* (Boulder, Co: Westview Press, 1983).It should be noted that 'Genetic erosion' occurs not only when species are made extinct but when they are reduced in numbers, since the greater the number the greater the variety of genetic types.
22. R.R. Jones and T. Wigley (eds), *Ozone Depletion: Health and Environmental Consequences* (New York: John Wiley, 1989).
23. *Guardian*, 12 July 1989; S. Boyle and J. Ardill, *The Greenhouse Effect* (London: Hodder and Stoughton, 1989), pp. 47–8.
24. World Meteorological Organisation/United Nations Environment Programme Intergovernmental Panel on Climate Change/J.T. Houghton, G.J. Johnson and J.J. Ephraums (eds), *Climatic Change: the IPCC Scientific Assessment* (Cambridge: Cambridge University Press, 1990), p. xi. A useful brief survey of the evidence on the greenhouse effect can be found in World Resources Institute, *World Resources 1990–1*, pp. 11–31. Readable accounts include Boyle and Ardill, *The Greenhouse Effect*; S. Schneider, *Global Warming: Are We Entering the Greenhouse Century?*

(San Francisco: Sierra Club Books, 1989); F. Pearce, *Turning Up the Heat* (London: Bodley Head, 1989).

25. An estimate made by Sir Crispin Tickell, the then British Ambassador to the United Nations: *Guardian*, 6 June 1989.

2: Whose Environment?

1. The first argument used to be commonly heard on the Left, though it is becoming a rare species now. More recently it has been spotted on the Right, used for example by Conservative ministers in the British Government after the European elections in 1989 to explain their opposition to the environmental movement's demands. The second argument is still quite common amongst Greens. See, for example, J. Porritt, *Seeing Green* (Oxford: Basil Blackwell, 1984), p. 226.
2. Department of the Environment, *Digest of Environmental Protection and Water Statistics* (London: HMSO, 1990), p. 79. The poll in fact shows a divergence between the views of people in different social classes on 'national' and 'global' environmental issues. Levels of concern about problems such as sewage on beaches, radioactive waste and loss of wildlife is fairly uniform. Respondents in unskilled occupations (social class V) show less concern than those in 'higher' social classes about issues such as ozone depletion, the greenhouse effect and tropical rainforest destruction.
3. M. Redclift, *Sustainable Development: Exploring the Contradictions* (London: Methuen, 1987), pp. 159–170. See also W.M. Adams, *Green Development: Environment and Sustainability in the Third World* (London: Routledge, 1990); C. Conroy and R. Litvinoff, *The Greening of Aid: Sustainable Livelihoods in Practice* (London: Earthscan, 1988); P. Harrison, *The Greening of Africa* (London: Earthscan/Paladin, 1987).
4. S. Hazarika, *Bhopal: The Lessons of a Tragedy* (New Delhi: Penguin, 1987), pp. 34–5.
5. For readable accounts of the environmental crisis in the South see B. Jackson, *Poverty and the Planet: A Question of Survival* (Harmondsworth: Penguin, 1990); A. Gupta, *Ecology and Development in the Third World* (London: Routledge, 1988). See also note 3 above.
6. See H.J. Leonard, *Pollution and the Struggle for the World Product* (Cambridge: Cambridge University Press, 1988).
7. J.L. Simon and H. Kahn, *The Resourceful Earth: A Response to Global 2000* (Oxford: Basil Blackwell, 1984); J.L. Simon, *The Ultimate Resource* (Oxford; Martin Robertson, 1981).

3: The Invisible Elbow

1. This is a common view on the Right, and among some 'non-political' environmentalists. For the former position, see J. Simon and H. Kahn, *The Resourceful Earth: A Response to Global 2000* (Basil Blackwell, 1984). For the latter, J. Elkington, *The Green Capitalists* (London: Victor Gollancz, 1987).
2. Modern ecology can be dated from the formation of the British Ecological Society in 1913 and the Ecological Society of America in 1915, both of which were instrumental in setting up the first protected national parks

for the conservation and study of ecosystems. C.S. Elton's pioneering work *Animal Ecology* was published in 1927 (London: Sidgwick and Jackson, 1927). Rachel Carson's famous book *Silent Spring* (Harmondsworth: Penguin, 1982) first alerted the world to the dangers of agricultural chemicals in 1962.

3. For a good account of the politics of technological choice, see D. Dickson, *Alternative Technology and the Politics of Technical Change* (London: Fontana, 1974).

4. Though some economists have tried to give these things monetary values – see Chapter 17.

5. See Garrett Hardin's famous essay 'The Tragedy of the Commons', *Science*, 162, 13 December 1968, pp. 1243–8, reprinted in H.E. Daly (ed), *Toward a Steady-State Economy* (San Francisco: W.H. Freeman, 1973), pp. 133–48. The prisoner's dilemma is discussed in this context by M. Taylor, *Anarchy and Cooperation* (Chichester: John Wiley, 1976).

6. The most famous exponent of this view is Ronald Coase, whose seminal paper 'The Problem of Social Cost' (*Journal of Law and Economics*, 3, October 1960, pp. 1–44) argued that if property rights could be assigned to the environment, degradation would become simply a private matter of bargaining between the polluter and the polluted. This view is discussed succinctly in D. W. Pearce and R. K. Turner, *Economics of Natural Resources and the Environment* (Hemel Hempstead: Harvester Wheatsheaf, 1990), Chapter 5.

7. Though he or she would still be likely to 'discount' the future. This is discussed later.

8. M. Redclift, *Sustainable Development: Exploring the Contradictions* (London: Methuen, 1987), pp. 150–7; J. McNeely and D. Pitt (eds), *Culture and Conservation: The Human Dimension in Environmental Planning* (London: Croom Helm, 1985).

9. Even the noted free-market economist Friedrich Hayek recognised this: F. Hayek, *The Road to Serfdom* (London: Routledge & Kegan Paul, 1962), p. 29.

10. This can also be understood in terms of risk. The risk to the individual from investing in the future is greater than to society as a whole. Even if the landlord dies or goes bankrupt, the resources will still exist for use by others, but he or she has to pay for the whole of the investment. It can be shown that under most conditions (even in monopoly) private producers using genetic material (drug companies and others) will wish to conserve less than the 'socially optimum' volume of natural habitats, despite their obvious interest in preserving raw material supplies. They simply do not value the future enough. See G.M. Brown and J. Swierzbinski, 'Endangered Species, Genetic Capital and Cost-Reducing R & D', in D. Hall, N. Myers and N.S. Margolis (eds), *Economics of Ecosystem Management* (Dordrecht, the Netherlands: Dr W. Junk Publishers, 1985).

11. We leave to one side here the question of whether inequality is integral to a market forces system; that is, whether such a system could exist without major inequalities. Since in reality there *is* inequality, this is (in this context) rather academic.

12. World Commission on Environment and Development, *Our Common Future* (Oxford: Oxford University Press, 1987), p. 33; World Resources Institute, *World Resources 1988–9* (New York: Basic Books, 1988), p. 336.

13. P. Brown, 'Britain, the Dump of Europe', *Guardian*, 31 August 1988 and 'Europe's Toxic Waste Timebomb Ticks Away', *Guardian*, 16 May 1989.
14. See S. Hecht and A. Cockburn, *The Fate of the Forest* (London: Verso, 1989); C. Secrett, *Rainforest* (London: Friends of the Earth, 1986).
15. See T. Hayter, *The Creation of World Poverty* (London: Pluto Press, 1983); B. Jackson, *Poverty and the Planet: A Question of Survival* (Harmondsworth: Penguin, 1990); L. Timberlake, *Africa in Crisis* (London: Earthscan, 1985); M. Redclift, *Sustainable Development: Exploring the Contradictions* (London: Methuen, 1987).
16. For readable accounts of the debt crisis, see G. Bird (ed), *Third World Debt: The Search for a Solution* (Aldershot: Edward Elgar, 1989); S. George, *A Fate Worse than Debt* (Harmondsworth: Penguin, 1988); J. Schatan, *World Debt: Who is to Pay?* (London: Zed Books, 1987).
17. B.J. Cummings, *Dam the Rivers, Damn the Poor* (London: Earthscan, 1990).
18. Hecht and Cockburn, *Fate of the Forest*.
19. World Resources Institute, *World Resources, 1988–9*, p. 16.
20. N. Myers, *The Gaia Atlas of Planet Management* (London: Pan, 1985), p. 48; B. Ward and R. Dubos, *Only One Earth* (Harmondsworth: Penguin, 1972), p. 176.
21. World Commission on Environment and Development, *Our Common Future*, pp. 98–9.

4: Capitalism, Industrialism and Green Politics

1. J. Elkington, *The Green Capitalists* (London: Victor Gollancz, 1987), p. 250.
2. Elkington himself acknowledges that pollution control is almost always a net cost to a firm: Elkington, *Green Capitalists*, pp. 208–10.
3. Elkington, *Green Capitalists*, pp. 135–7; 'Equinox', Channel 4 TV, 3 September 1987. In fact it may be true that the major CFC producers only eventually agreed to controls because they found that they could make profits from the restrictions on supply. Smaller competitors are effectively prevented from entering the market for substitutes because of the high costs of innovation. See S. Barrett, *Ozone Holes, Greenhouse Gases and Economic Policy*, London Business School, 1989, pp. 12–14.
4. D. Wilson, *The Lead Scandal* (London: Heinemann, 1983), pp. 121–40. Similar resistance to controls is still displayed by pesticide manufacturers. See E. Goldsmith and N. Hildyard (eds), *Green Britain or Industrial Wasteland?* (Cambridge: Polity Press, 1986), pp. 136–42.
5. A cogent critique of green consumerism is S. Irvine, *Beyond Green Consumerism* (London: Friends of the Earth, 1989).
6. 'Communism' is used here to mean the economic system of the Soviet Union and Eastern Europe prior to 1989. Many Marxists, among others, will want to retain this term for a different sort of society altogether, arguing that the Soviet system was nothing like what Marx meant by communism. They are right, but the usage employed here is of such common currency that in this context it seems reasonable to adopt it. For the sake of simplicity, we shall continue to speak of communism in the present tense. Whether or not communism can be said still to exist even in the Soviet Union the arguments are unchanged.
7. J. Porritt, *Seeing Green* (Oxford: Basil Blackwell, 1984), p. 44.
8. See for example R. Bahro, *Building the Green Movement* (London: GMP, 1986); E. Goldsmith, *The Great U-Turn: Deindustrialising Society* (Bideford:

Green Books, 1988); F. Capra and C. Spretnak, *Green Politics* (London: Hutchinson, 1984); P. Kelly, *Fighting for Hope* (London: Chatto and Windus, 1984); S. McBurney, *Ecology Into Economics Won't Go* (Bideford: Green Books, 1990); Porritt, *Seeing Green*; T. Roszak, *Person/Planet: The Creative Disintegration of Industrial Society* (London: Victor Gollancz, 1979); W. Schwarz and D. Schwarz, *Breaking Through* (Bideford: Green Books, 1987); J. Seabrook, *The Myth of the Market* (Bideford: Green Books, 1990); T. Trainer, *Abandon Affluence!* (London: Zed Books, 1986).

9. For an even more radical 'Deep Ecology' view, see A. Naess, 'The Shallow and the Deep, Long-Range Ecology Movement', *Inquiry*, 16, 1973; R. Sylvan, 'Deep Ecology', *Radical Philosophy*, 40 and 41, 1985; M. Tobias (ed), *Deep Ecology* (San Diego, CA: Avant Books, 1984). The Deep Green position is succinctly reviewed by M. Redclift, 'Economic Models and Environmental Values: A Discourse on Theory', in R.K. Turner (ed), *Sustainable Environmental Management: Principles and Practice* (London: Belhaven Press/Boulder, CO: Westview Press, 1988).

10. See B. Komarov, *The Destruction of Nature in the Soviet Union* (London: Pluto Press, 1978); C. Ziegler, *Environmental Policy in the USSR* (London: Frances Pinter, 1987).

11. For a discussion of Marxist ideology in relation to nature, see A. Schmidt, *The Concept of Nature in Marx* (London: New Left Books, 1971); H. Enzenberger, 'A Critique of Political Ecology' in *New Left Review* 84, 1974; and the journal *Capitalism Nature Socialism: A Journal of Socialist Ecology*. A succinct review is again to be found in Redclift, 'Economic Models', in Turner, *Sustainable Environmental Management*.

12. For a discussion of how the Soviet system works (or worked) in general see A. Nove, *The Soviet Economic System*, 3rd edn (Boston, MA: Allen and Unwin, 1986). For an illuminating debate into the environmental efficiency of centrally planned and market-based economic systems see R. McIntyre and J. Thornton, 'On the Environmental Efficiency of Economic Systems', *Soviet Studies*, April 1978, and C. Ziegler, 'Soviet Environmental Policy and Soviet Central Planning: a reply to McIntyre and Thornton', *Soviet Studies*, January 1980, and their further discussion in *Soviet Studies*, January 1981 (McIntyre and Thornton) and April 1982 (Ziegler).

13. On the creation of demand, there is none better than J.K. Galbraith's classic work, *The New Industrial State* (Harmondsworth: Penguin, 1969).

5: Sustainable Development

1. D.H. Meadows et al, *The Limits to Growth* (London: Pan, 1972).
2. See for example H.S.D. Cole et al (ed), *Thinking About the Future: A Critique of 'The Limits to Growth'* (London: Chatto and Windus, 1973).
3. Gross National Product is one way of measuring national income. Another is Gross Domestic Product (GDP). GNP includes all income earned by the nationals of a country, whether the relevant production takes place in that country or abroad. GDP measures all the income earned within the country's borders.
4. The environmental impact coefficient could incorporate cumulative damage if the concept of 'environmental consumption' was not simply one of the flow of use but also took account of stock levels.

5. Organisation for Economic Cooperation and Development, *OECD Environmental Data Compendium 1989* (Paris: OECD, 1989), p. 227, p. 311. On materials intensity in general, see R. Auty, 'Materials Intensity of GDP', *Resources Policy*, 11 (4), 1985; D. Deadman and R.K. Turner, 'Resource Conservation, Sustainability and Technical Change', in R.K. Turner (ed), *Sustainable Environmental Management* (London: Belhaven Press/Boulder, CO: Westview Press, 1988), pp. 80–1.

6. T. Barker and R. Lewney, 'A Green Scenario for the UK Economy', in T. Barker (ed), *Green Futures for Economic Growth* (Cambridge: Cambridge Econometrics, 1991), pp. 14–27.

7. A.S. Manne and R.G. Richels, 'Global CO_2 Emission Limits: An Economic Cost Analysis for the USA', *Energy Journal* 11, Spring 1990; R.E. Marks et al, 'The Cost of Australian Carbon Dioxide Abatement', *Energy Journal* 11, Spring 1990; S. Glomsrod, H. Vennemo and T. Johnsen, *Stabilisation of Emissions of CO_2*, Discussion Paper No. 48, Central Bureau of Statistics, Oslo, 1990.

8. Barker and Lewney, 'Green Scenario', in Barker, *Green Futures*, p. 7.

9. Ibid., pp. 27–37.

10. L. Timberlake, *Africa in Crisis* (London: Earthscan, 1985), p. 7.

11. J. Elkington, *The Green Capitalists* (London: Victor Gollancz, 1987), pp. 186–9.

12. This is an argument against the 'steady state economy' theories developed in particular by Herman Daly. Daly defines a steady state economy as one in which there are 'constant stocks of artifacts and people'. But it is not clear what artifacts are or (as with resources in the more conventional zero-growth argument) how they are counted. See 'The Steady-State Economy: Toward a Political Economy of Biophysical Equilibrium and Moral Growth' in H.E. Daly (ed), *Toward a Steady-State Economy* (San Francisco: W.H. Freeman, 1973); *Steady State Economics* (San Francisco: W.H. Freeman, 1977) and Daly's paper in P. Ekins (ed), *The Living Economy* (London: Routledge and Kegan Paul, 1986), pp. 13–14.

13. International Union for the Conservation of Nature and Natural Resources, *World Conservation Strategy* (Gland, Switzerland: IUCN, 1980).

14. World Commission on Environment and Development, *Our Common Future* (Oxford: Oxford University Press, 1987), p. 43.

15. See for example: W. Clark and R. Munn (eds), *Sustainable Development of the Biosphere* (Cambridge: Cambridge University Press, 1986); E. Barbier, *Economics, Natural Resource Scarcity and Development* (London: Earthscan, 1989); R. Goodland and G. Ledoc, 'Neoclassical Economics and Principles of Sustainable Development', *Ecological Modelling* 38, 1987; R. Norgaard, 'Sustainable Development: A Co-Evolutionary View', *Futures* 20 (6), 6 December 1988; D. Pearce, A. Markandya and E.B. Barbier, *Blueprint for a Green Economy* (London: Earthscan, 1989); J. Pezzey, *Economic Analysis of Sustainable Growth and Sustainable Development*, World Bank, Environment Department, Working Paper No. 15, Washington DC, May 1989; M. Redclift, *Sustainable Development: Exploring the Contradictions* (London: Methuen, 1987); R. Repetto, *World Enough and Time* (New Haven: Yale University Press, 1986); M. Tolba, *Sustainable Development – Constraints and Opportunities* (London: Butterworths, 1987); R.K. Turner, 'Sustainability, Resource Conservation and Pollution Control: An Overview' and T. O'Riordan, 'The Politics of Sustainability', both in Turner, *Sustainable Environmental Management*.

16. *Our Common Future: A Perspective by the United Kingdom on the Report of the World Commission on Environment and Development* (London: Department of the Environment, 1988).

17. For example, the then British Secretary of State for the Environment, Chris Patten, in a speech to the Confederation of British Industry on 20 November 1989 used the terms 'sustainable growth' and 'green growth'. The former has now gained academic respectability: see T. Barker, 'The Environment and Economic Growth' in T. Barker (ed), *Green Futures for Economic Growth* (Cambridge: Cambridge Econometrics, 1991), p. 8. 'Sustainable growth' can be a confusing term, however, since it is also used by orthodox economists and politicians to mean economic growth which can be sustained for three or four years or until the next general election, whichever is the sooner.

18. See for example, H.E. Daly and J.D. Cobb, *For the Common Good* (Boston: Beacon Press, 1989).

6: Valuing the Environment

1. See M. Redclift, *Sustainable Development: Exploring the Contradictions* (London: Methuen, 1987), especially Chapters 5–8.

2. In Britain the most well-known advocate of this approach is David Pearce, co-author of the influential 'Pearce Report' for the British Government: D.W. Pearce, A. Markandya and E.B. Barbier, *Blueprint for a Green Economy* (London: Earthscan, 1989). In some of his writings, however (including the first part of the *Blueprint*), Pearce adopts the 'sustainability' approach developed in the next chapter.

3. The original 'deep ecology' view was put by Arne Naess, in 'The Shallow and the Deep, Long-Range Ecology Movement', *Inquiry* 16, 1973, pp. 95–100. The philosophical arguments have been developed by a number of writers. See for example P.W. Taylor, *Respect for Nature* (Princeton, NJ: Princeton University Press, 1986).

4. Environmental economists call these respectively 'option', 'bequest' and 'existence' values. See note 8.

5. This is discussed further in Chapter 17.

6. See D.W. Pearce and R.K. Turner, *Economics of Natural Resources and the Environment* (Hemel Hempstead: Harvester Wheatsheaf, 1990), pp. 129–40.

7. There is an interesting philosophical question as to whether my future self should be regarded as being the same person as myself today. This need not detain us here. See D. Parfit, *Reasons and Persons* (Oxford: Oxford University Press, 1984).

8. The Grand Canyon is valued in W. Schulze et al, 'The Economic Benefits of Preserving Visibility in the Grand Canyon', *Natural Resources Journal* 23, 1983. Grizzly bears are valued in D. Brookshire et al, 'Estimating Option Prices and Existence Values for Wildlife Resources', *Land Economics* 59 (1), 1983.

9. Indeed one well-known result in environmental economics is that extinction of a species can be 'optimal'. See C. Clark, *Mathematical Bioeconomics* (New York: John Wiley, 1976). See also Pearce and Turner, *Economics of Natural Resources*, Chapter 17.

7: Sustainability

1. P. Singer, 'Not for Humans Only: The Place of Nonhumans in Environmental Issues'; R. Routley and V. Routley, 'Against the Inevitability of Human Chauvinism', both in K.E. Goodpaster and K.M. Sayer (eds), *Ethics and Problems of the 21st Century* (Notre Dame, IN: University of Notre Dame Press, 1979).
2. Singer, 'Not for Humans'.
3. See for example P.W. Taylor, *Respect for Nature* (Princeton, NJ: Princeton University Press, 1986).
4. A. Naess, 'The Shallow and the Deep, Long-Range Ecology Movement', *Inquiry* 16, 1973, pp. 95–100.
5. This is acknowledged by Singer, 'Not for Humans', p. 203.
6. A. Leopold, *A Sand County Almanac* (Oxford: Oxford University Press, 1949), pp. 224–5.
7. This possibility is acknowledged by advocates of the Land Ethic: see J. B. Callicott, 'Animal Liberation: A Triangular Affair', *Environmental Ethics* 2, 1980, p. 326.
8. See B.G. Norton, *Why Preserve Natural Variety?* (Princeton, NJ: Princeton University Press, 1987), p. 179.
9. J Rawls, *A Theory of Justice* (Cambridge, MA: Harvard University Press, 1971). His method has been widely criticised; see for example N. Daniels, *Reading Rawls* (Oxford: Basil Blackwell, 1975); P. Pettit, *Rawls: A Theory of Justice and Its Critics* (Cambridge: Polity Press, 1990). Talbot Page has developed the Rawlsian approach specifically as an environmental ethic in a number of places. See for example his *Conservation and Economic Efficiency* (Baltimore: Johns Hopkins University Press, 1977), and 'Intergenerational Justice as Opportunity', in P. Brown and D. Maclean (eds), *Energy and the Future* (Totowa, NJ: Rowman and Littlefield, 1983).
10. Some philosophers would argue that people who don't exist cannot be harmed; since the people who will live in the future will not know any other conditions than the ones they will inherit, they cannot be said to be wronged by the actions of the present generation. This is not the position taken here, however. For a discussion of this 'person affecting principle', see J. Glover, *Causing Death and Saving Lives* (Harmondsworth: Penguin, 1977), pp. 66–9, and on potential people in general, pp. 60–73. See also J. Feinberg, 'The Rights of Animals and Unborn Generations', in W. Blackstone (ed), *Philosophy and the Environmental Crisis* (Athens, GA: University of Georgia Press, 1974).
11. It is also discussed by M. Sagoff, *The Economy of the Earth* (Cambridge: Cambridge University Press, 1988).
12. For a longer discussion of the discounting issue, see D.W. Pearce and R.K. Turner, *Economics of Natural Resources and the Environment* (London: Harvester Wheatsheaf, 1990), pp. 211–25. The chapter in the Pearce Report (D.W. Pearce, A. Markandya and E.B. Barbier, *Blueprint for a Green Economy* (London: Earthscan, 1989), pp. 132–52) is less clear.
13. See J.L. Simon, *The Ultimate Resource* (Oxford: Martin Robertson, 1981); J.L. Simon and H. Kahn, *The Resourceful Earth: A Response to Global 2000* (Oxford: Basil Blackwell, 1984).
14. C.S. Holling, 'The Resilience of Terrestrial Ecosystems: Local Surprise and Global Change', in W.C. Clark and R.E. Munn (eds), *Sustainable*

Development of the Biosphere (Cambridge: Cambridge University Press, 1986), pp. 292–317.

15. On the issue of population growth, see P.R. Ehrlich and A.H. Ehrlich, *The Population Explosion* (London: Heinemann, 1990).

8: Making Sustainability Operational

1. Useful reviews of the ecological effects of agrochemicals may be found in S. Postel, 'Controlling Toxic Chemicals', in L.R. Brown et al, *State of the World 1988* (New York: W.W. Norton, 1988), pp. 118–24, and L.R. Brown and J.E Young, 'Feeding the World in the Nineties' in L. R. Brown et al, *State of the World 1990* (New York: W.W. Norton/London: Unwin Hyman, 1990), pp. 59–68.

2. See D.W. Pearce and R.K. Turner, *Economics of Natural Resources and the Environment* (Hemel Hempstead: Harvester Wheatsheaf, 1990), Chapter 18.

3. Pearce and Turner, *Economics of Natural Resources*, pp. 262–70.

4. Ibid., pp. 292–5. For more detailed discussion of mineral scarcity, see H. Barnett, 'Scarcity and Growth Revisited' in V.K. Smith (ed), *Scarcity and Growth Reconsidered* (Baltimore: Johns Hopkins University Press, 1979); D.C. Hall and J.V. Hall, 'Concepts and Measures of Natural Resource Scarcity, with a Summary of Recent Trends', *Journal of Environmental Economics and Management*, 11 (3), 1984. A good review of the field is J. Rees, *Natural Resources: Allocation, Economics and Policy*, 2nd edn (London: Routledge, 1990), Chapters 2–5.

5. For example, 62% of vehicles in Brazil run on alcohol fuel: C. Flavin, 'Slowing Global Warming', in Brown, *State of the World 1990*, p. 26.

6. See Pearce and Turner, *Economics of Natural Resources*, pp. 299–301.

7. Short-term reversible increases might be acceptable in terms of sustainability, if not for those experiencing them now.

8. T. O'Riordan et al, 'On Weighing Gains and Investments at the Margin of Risk Regulation', Working Paper, School of Environmental Sciences, University of East Anglia, Norwich, 1985. See also R.K. Turner (ed), *Sustainable Environmental Management* (London: Belhaven Press/Boulder, CO: Westview Press, 1988), pp. 17–19.

9. Postel, 'Controlling Toxic Chemicals' in Brown et al, *State of the World 1988*, pp. 129–36.

10. If perceptions of risk change (either because a waste material is found to be more dangerous than previously thought, or because society becomes more 'risk-averse') the demands of sustainability will change accordingly.

11. This conclusion supports moves towards self-reliance for Southern countries. See J. Galtung, P. O'Brien and R. Preiswerk (eds), *Self Reliance* (London: Bogle L'Ouverture, 1980); S. Amin, *Delinking* (London: Zed Books, 1989).

12. C. S. Holling, 'The Resilience of Terrestrial Ecosystems: Local Surprise and Global Change', in W.C. Clark and R.E. Munn (eds), *Sustainable Development of the Biosphere* (Cambridge: Cambridge University Press, 1986), pp. 292–317.

13. The matrix is derived from R. Costanza, 'What is Ecological Economics?', *Ecological Economics*, 1 (1), 1989, pp. 1–7.

14. This approach is developed by Richard Bishop, 'Endangered Species and Uncertainty: the Economics of a Safe Minimum Standard', *American Journal of Agricultural Economics*, 61 (5), 1978. Interestingly, such a 'precautionary' approach to environmental policy would be sensible even if we had no prior commitment to preservation arising from arguments for intergenerational equity. Even if we were prepared to discount the future, the risk of irreversibility or other significant degradation would often make it rational to conserve rather than degrade the environment; that is, to pay the costs of environmental protection in advance of the problem occurring rather than waiting until afterwards to clear it up. (If the degradation is irreversible, such as in species loss, clearing it up may not be an option at all.)

This is because, in conditions of uncertainty, inaction may itself increase the value of the environment. Where there is a general tendency towards environmental loss, the aesthetic and instrumental benefits of individual aspects of the environment are likely to rise over time. Moreover postponing exploitation allows greater information to be gathered about, say, the medicinal or food properties of a rare species. Extinction would wipe this value out forever, with possibly large losses. Delay further allows the introduction of improved technology or new development plans, which might make the environmental damage altogether unnecessary.

These arguments, known in their mathematical form as the Krutilla-Fisher algorithm, suggest that in a cost-benefit analysis the benefits of environmental exploitation (or the costs of protection) must be very large for irreversibility or major damage to be risked. See J. Krutilla and A. Fisher, *The Economics of Natural Environments* (Washington DC: Resources for the Future, 1985) and R. Porter, 'The New Approach to Wilderness Preservation Through Benefit Cost Analysis', *Journal of Environmental Economics and Management*, 9, 1982.

9: Environmental Efficiency, Entropy and Energy

1. The diagrams could be refined by drawing two sustainability boundaries, corresponding to the 'minimal' and 'maximal' definitions. (Though as we have noted, parts of these would touch.) And of course a more accurate picture would not represent environmental impacts by a perfect circle, but rather by an irregularly shaped line, some of which would be inside the sustainability boundary and some outside. Not all current environmental impacts are unsustainable.

2. An interesting account of the technical advances which might achieve sustainability in the year 2030 are given in L.R. Brown, C. Flavin and S. Postel, 'Picturing a Sustainable Society', in L.R. Brown et al, *State of the World 1990* (New York: W.W. Norton/London: Unwin Hyman, 1990), pp. 173–90.

3. World Commission on Environment and Development, *Our Common Future* (Oxford: Oxford University Press, 1987), pp. 98–9. If average consumption rose by 50%, to 9,000 calories daily, the population carrying capacity comes down to 7.5 billion.

4. L.R. Brown and J.E. Young, 'Feeding the World in the Nineties', in Brown, *State of the World 1990*, pp. 65–8. See M. Mantegozzini, *The Environmental Risks of Biotechnology* (London: Frances Pinter, 1986); P. Wheale and

R. McNally, *Genetic Engineering: Catastrophe or Utopia?* (Hemel Hempstead: Harvester Wheatsheaf, 1988).

Ecologists use the concept of 'carrying capacity' to define the maximum population of a given species which a particular ecosystem can support. Some environmentalists have wanted to apply this concept also to human beings. But this is not so simple. In the first place 'carrying capacity' cannot refer to population alone, since human beings (unlike other animals) can live at different levels of consumption, and within an average level different people will consume unequal amounts. If average global consumption were at current North American levels the 'carrying capacity' of the earth would clearly be less than if it were at current African levels. Moreover, whereas for other animals technology (the capacity to extract resources from the environment) is a constant, human society is able to improve it. So we cannot simply say that, at such-and-such average per capita consumption level, the biosphere can support this or that number of people. It depends on how productive the environment is, which in turn depends on the technology we use to cultivate it. Moreover social and cultural variables are also involved. Different human societies have different ways of organising themselves and their environments and different values in respect of them. These too will affect the 'carrying capacity'. For an exploration of the concept of carrying capacity in relation to human society, see P.M. Fearnside, *Human Carrying Capacity of the Brazilian Rainforest* (New York: Columbia University Press, 1986).

5. 'Weather Watch', *Guardian*, 23 May 1990.

6. See *Industry and Environment*, 'Low and Non-Waste Technology', 9 (4), 1986; D.W. Pearce and R.K. Turner, 'The Economic Evaluation of Low and Non-Waste Technology', *Resources and Conservation* 11 (1), 1984; S.P. Maltezou, A.A. Metry and W.A. Irwin, *Industrial Risk Management and Clean Technology* (Vienna: Verlag Orac, 1990).

7. See for example E. Dammann, *The Future in Our Hands* (Oxford: Pergamon Press, 1979); D. Elgin, *Voluntary Simplicity* (New York: William Morrow, 1981); E. Fromm, *To Have or To Be?* (London: Jonathan Cape, 1978); F. Hirsch, *Social Limits to Growth* (London: Routledge and Kegan Paul, 1977); H. Marcuse, *One Dimensional Man* (London: Sphere Books, 1968); E.J. Mishan, *The Costs of Economic Growth* (Harmondsworth: Penguin, 1969); T. Roszak, *Where the Wasteland Ends* (London: Faber and Faber, 1973); E.F. Schumacher, *Small Is Beautiful* (London: Blond and Briggs, 1973); J. Seabrook, *The Race to Riches* (Basingstoke: Green Print, 1988).

8. T. Roberts and R. Porter (eds), *Energy Savings from Waste Recycling* (London: Elsevier Applied Science Publishers, 1985).

9. It is true of course that both the raw material and waste disposal space is saved. But then society needs to decide which is more valuable, saving the resource and the space or not contributing to the greenhouse effect. In the case of glass recycling, for example, sand and limestone are saved, but these are not in short supply and are almost certainly less valuable than a reduction in carbon dioxide emissions – if we found that recycling indeed had a higher net energy consumption than using virgin materials.

10. See N. Mortimer, 'Energy Analysis and Renewable Energy Sources', *Energy Policy* 19 (4), 1991; R. Peckham and K. Klitz, 'Energy Requirements of North Sea Oil by Secondary and Tertiary Methods', WP-79-7, IIASA, cited by M. Slesser, *Enhancement of Carrying Capacity Options*, Part II: Introductory Guide (Pitlochry: Resource Use Institute, 1990), p. 18.

11. See K. Boulding, 'The Economics of the Coming Spaceship Earth', in H. Jarrett (ed), *Environmental Quality in a Growing Economy* (Baltimore: Johns Hopkins University Press, 1966), reprinted in H. Daly (ed), *Toward a Steady-State Economy* (San Francisco: W. H. Freeman, 1973).

12. The most notable exception among economists is Nicholas Georgescu-Roegen, who in his seminal 1971 essay 'The Entropy Law and the Economic Problem' (reprinted in Daly, *Toward a Steady-State Economy*) noted that the discovery of means by which to transform solar energy into motor power directly 'will represent the greatest possible breakthrough for man's entropic problem'. His book *The Entropy Law and the Economic Process* (Cambridge, MA: Harvard University Press, 1971) is a complete study of this field. The implications of entropy for economic activity have also been discussed in several places by Herman Daly and Richard Norgaard. See for example, their exchange in *Land Economics*, 62 (3), 1986, pp. 319–22 and pp. 325–8. Norgaard's article 'Coevolutionary Development Potential', *Land Economics*, 60 (2), 1984, pp. 160–73, is an important contribution to a debate little recognised, let alone understood, by orthodox economists.

13. All use of energy generates thermal pollution (heat). Some kinds of continuing energy sources may also have significant environmental effects of other kinds, such as disruption of visual amenity and noise (as in the case of wind turbines), destruction of habitats (tidal barrages) and so on. There are no environmentally costless energy sources. Moreover all sources also generate pollution (to different degrees) in their manufacture.

14. It is true that the goal of development in the Third World should not be equated with that of economic growth, but there can be no doubt that growth will result from it.

10: Sustainability Planning

1. Known as 'BATNEEC'. It should be noted that UK policy towards water pollution control has for some time been based on ambient standards, though prior to European Community intervention these standards were not formally laid down. It also needs to be said that much of the failure of pollution control policy in the UK has been due to lack of enforcement rather than the structure of the system. For a good account of recent pollution control policy in industrialised countries, including the BATNEEC principle, see N. Haigh and F. Irwin, *Integrated Pollution Control in Europe and North America* (Washington, DC: The Conservation Foundation/London: Institute for European Environmental Policy, 1990). A standard general text in F. Sandbach, *Principles of Pollution Control* (Harlow: Longman, 1982).

2. *Independent on Sunday*, 27 January 1991.

3. This debate between ambient standards and emission standards is still unresolved within the European Community. See N. Haigh, *EEC Environmental Policy and Britain*, 2nd edn (Harlow: Longman, 1989), pp. 13–23.

4. Such a law has been passed in Orange County, California.

5. See for example, T. Barker and R. Lewney, 'A Green Scenario for the UK Economy' in T. Barker (ed), *Green Futures for Economic Growth* (Cambridge: Cambridge Econometrics, 1991), pp. 11–38. See also the Dutch National

Environmental Policy Plan (NEPP), which includes the results of a comprehensive macroeconomic modelling exercise of an 'NEPP scenario': *To Choose or to Lose: National Environmental Policy Plan* (The Hague: Ministry of Housing, Physical Planning and Environment, 1989), pp. 248–54, and the European Community's Task Force on the Environment and the Single Market, *'1992': The Environmental Dimension* (Brussels: Commission of the European Communities, 1990).

6. It was even conceded by the free market economist and philosopher Friedrich Hayek, *The Road to Serfdom* (London: Routledge and Kegan Paul, 1962), p. 29.

7. *To Choose or to Lose.* On the Japanese and French economic planning systems, see C. McMillan, *The Japanese Industrial System*, 2nd edn (Berlin: de Gruyter, 1985), particularly Chapter 4; S. Estrin and P. Holmes, *French Planning in Theory and Practice* (London: Allen and Unwin, 1983).

8. We leave to one side here the altogether more complex question of how democratic the state is: a comment is made on this in the Introduction. Another Green argument is that sustainability should be achieved by reducing the *scale* of society: creating smaller, more self-reliant economic regions between which trade is reduced. There is no doubt that reducing trade, which is extremely energy-intensive, will be one of the measures necessary to cut energy use. A greater reliance on visible local resources might also induce more of a concern for their sustainability. But the question still needs to be asked: *how* is society to be decentralised and reduced in scale? Too often Green writers either ignore this question or merely urge that it happen through spontaneous and voluntary lifestyle change. But this is wholly unrealistic. Economic scale will be reduced when economic conditions make trade unprofitable and self-reliance a more secure strategy than resource dependence. To create these conditions various instruments need to be used: regulations, financial incentives, government expenditures, and so on. These instruments are not alternatives to reducing scale, or to any other method of reducing environmental impact: they are the means to achieving it. For the Green argument on scale, see among others N. Albery and M. Kinzley (eds), *How to Save the World* (Wellingborough: Turnstone Press, 1984); I. Illich, *Energy and Equity* (London: Calder and Boyars, 1974); L. Kohr, *The Breakdown of Nations* (London: Routledge and Kegan Paul, 1987); K. Sale, *Human Scale* (London: Secker and Warburg, 1980); E. F. Schumacher, *Small is Beautiful* (London: Blond and Briggs, 1973).

9. Again, this raises the issue of how far systems of representative democracy do place 'decision-making power' in the hands of electorates. Again, we cannot discuss this here. See D. Held, *Models of Democracy* (Cambridge: Polity Press, 1987).

10. For an accessible account of European environmental policy see Haigh, *EEC Environmental Policy*; N. Haigh and D. Baldock, *Environmental Policy and 1992* (London: Institute for European Environmental Policy, 1989).

11. For an analysis of the impact of transnational corporations see N. Hood and S. Young, *The Economics of Multinational Enterprise* (Harlow: Longman, 1979); N. Harris, *Of Bread and Guns: The World Economic Crisis* (Harmondsworth: Penguin, 1983).

12. See Haigh and Baldock, *Environmental Policy*, pp. 16–20. For a wider analysis of democracy within the EC see J. Palmer, *1992 and Beyond* (Luxembourg: Commission of the European Communities, 1989).

13. The Montreal Protocol is described in S. Boyle and J. Ardill, *The Greenhouse Effect* (London: Hodder and Stoughton, 1989), pp. 43–5. The Large Combustion Plant Directive is described in Haigh, *EEC Environmental Policy*, pp. 224–7.

14. This is the estimate made by the US Environmental Protection Agency: D. Lashoff and D. Tirpak (eds), *Policy Options for Stabilising Global Climate*, EPA Draft Report to the US Congress, February 1989, cited in M. Grubb, *The Greenhouse Effect: Negotiating Targets* (London: Royal Institute of International Affairs, 1989), p. 7. The Intergovernmental Panel on Climate Change estimated a reduction of 'over 60%' in net emissions (sources minus sinks): World Meteorological Organisation/United Nations Environment Programme/J.T. Houghton, G.J. Jenkins and J.J. Ephraums (eds), *Climate Change: The IPCC Scientific Assessment* (Cambridge: Cambridge University Press, 1990), p. xi.

15. The possible form of a 'framework convention' is discussed in Grubb, *Greenhouse Effect*, pp. 10–11; and by W.A. Nitze, *The Greenhouse Effect: Formulating a Convention* (London: Royal Institute of International Affairs, 1990).

16. R. Freeman, 'Environmental Costs and International Competitiveness' in Barker, *Green Futures*, pp. 69–84.

17. See for example T. Jackson, *Energy Policy in a Warming World* (London: Friends of the Earth, 1991, forthcoming); J.S. Hirschhorn and K.U. Oldenburg, *Prosperity Without Pollution* (New York: Van Nostrand Reinhold, 1991).

18. Grubb, *Greenhouse Effect*, pp. 51–2. See also the papers by Freeman and Pezzey in Barker, *Green Futures*. Note that there may be some problem with the imposition of unilateral measures by countries within the European Community. See Haigh, *EEC Environmental Policy* and Haigh and Baldock, *Environmental Policy*.

11: Instruments for Environmental Protection

1. This is mainly because it has proved in the interests of the companies to cut production. See S. Barrett, *Ozone Holes, Greenhouse Gases and Economic Policy*, London Business School, July 1989. It is arguable that production might have been cut more quickly if regulations or incentives had been applied.

2. Department of Trade and Industry, *Cutting Your Losses* (London: DTI, 1989). It has to be said, however, that purely informational and persuasion-based approaches have had only limited success in reducing either waste or energy consumption. The energy example is discussed further in Chapter 13.

3. D. Farer, 'Superfund Law Cleans Up the States', *The Law Society's Gazette*, 3 October 1990, pp. 18–20.

4. See J. Cameron, 'Environmental Public Interest Litigation' in D. Vaughan (ed), *EC Environmental and Planning Law* (London: Butterworths, 1991); L. Bulatao, 'Citizen Suits and Association Suit Provisions in Environmental Statutes and National Constitutions: Examples From Across the Globe', Centre for International Environmental Law, Kings College, London, 1990.

5. J. McNeely and D. Pitt (eds), *Culture and Conservation: The Human Dimension in Environmental Planning* (London: Croom Helm, 1985); J.A.

McNeely, *Economics and Biological Diversity* (Gland, Switzerland: International Union for Conservation of Nature and Natural Resources, 1988).

6. Southern California Association of Governments, *Air Quality Management Plan* (Los Angeles: SCGA, 1989); G. Lean, 'Sunshine State Plans a Green Future', *Observer*, 3 September 1989; A. Lloyd et al, 'Air Quality Management in Los Angeles: Perspectives on Past and Future Emission Control Strategies', *Journal of the Air and Waste Management Association* 39 (5), May 1989, pp. 696–703; D. Weston, 'Eco Law', *Eco News* 46, Aug/Sep 1989.

7. The distinction between regulation and government expenditure may sometimes similarly be a question merely of ownership. If sewage treatment and electricity supply companies are publicly owned, for example, their activities will involve public spending. If they are privately owned, governments may force them to behave in exactly the same ways through regulation.

8. J.B. Opschoor and H.B. Vos, *Economic Instruments for Environmental Protection* (Paris: Organisation for Economic Cooperation and Development, 1989), pp. 74–82.

9. McNeely, *Economics and Biological Diversity*. It should be noted that the system of subsidies to farmers to protect habitats operated in the UK has been subjected to fierce criticism by environmentalists. See J.Blunden and N. Curry, *A Future for Our Countryside* (Oxford: Basil Blackwell, 1988); J.K. Bowers and P. Cheshire, *Agriculture, the Countryside and Land Use: An Economic Critique* (London: Methuen, 1983).

10. See Chapter 15.

11. At the 'optimum' level of pollution (where marginal cost equals marginal benefit). See D.W. Pearce and R.K. Turner, *Economics of Natural Resources and the Environment* (Hemel Hempstead: Harvester Wheatsheaf, 1990), Chapter 6.

12. Proposed by Talbot Page in H.E. Daly (ed), *Economy, Ecology, Ethics* (San Francisco: W.H. Freeman, 1980), pp. 317–20.

13. H.E. Daly, *Steady State Economics* (San Francisco: W.H. Freeman, 1980).

14. L.G. Anderson, 'Property Rights in Fisheries: Lessons from the New Zealand Experience', Working Paper 89–22, Political Economy Research Center, Bozeman, MT, 1989. One problem with depletion quotas is that they can prove an encouragement to monopoly, if large companies can buy up significant quantities of permits.

15. There are in fact several different ways of categorising environmental taxes and charges: see Opschoor and Vos, *Economic Instruments*, pp. 14–15; Pearce and Turner, *Economics of Natural Resources*, p. 172. Administration and enforcement charges, which the OECD and Pearce and Turner include, are not incentives in the same sense as the others, since they do not vary with pollution caused, only with the cost of administering its control. Note that we use the terms 'tax' and 'charge' interchangeably. Strictly speaking, a tax is administered through the fiscal (general tax-collecting) system, a charge through the environmental administrative system. This distinction does not affect how the levy itself works; but is important in the discussion of what is done with the revenues generated. See below, and Chapters 13 and 14.

16. Opschoor and Vos, *Economic Instruments*, pp. 33–55.

17. Ibid., pp. 42–3.

18. Ibid., pp. 55–66.

19. Auctioning permits forces the polluters to pay more than if they are 'grandfathered' (granted). Grandfathering benefits existing firms in the market in comparison with newcomers (who must buy permits) and may thus be seen as anti-competitive. The theoretical differences between the two systems are analysed in J. Pezzey, 'Market Mechanisms of Pollution Control: "Polluter Pays", Economic and Practical Aspects' in R.K. Turner (ed), *Sustainable Environmental Management: Principles and Practice* (London: Belhaven Press/Boulder, CO: Westview Press, 1988), pp. 190–242. See also T.H. Tietenberg, *Emissions Trading: An Exercise in Reforming Pollution Policy* (Washington, DC: Resources for the Future, 1985).

20. Opschoor and Vos, *Economic Instruments*, pp. 88–100. See also R. Liroff, *Reforming Air Pollution Regulation: The Toil and Trouble of EPA's Bubble* (Washington DC: Conservation Foundation, 1986); Tietenberg, *Emissions Trading* and 'Economic Instruments for Environmental Regulation', *Oxford Review of Economic Policy* 6 (1), Spring 1990, pp. 17–33. The effective use of tradable permits for CFC reduction is specifically permitted by the Montreal Protocol: see S. Barrett, *Ozone Holes*.

21. There may also be a problem that permits will either be bought up by a monopolist or the small number of polluters in a particular area will make trading 'thin' or non-existent, thus reducing the cost savings accruing from the system. Permits may also be 'hoarded' against the possibility that future emissions may rise or pollution standards tighten. See Pezzey, 'Market Mechanisms' in Turner, *Sustainable Environmental Management*, pp. 231–2; N. Hanley, S. Hallett and I. Moffatt, 'Why is More Notice Not Taken of Economists' Prescriptions for the Control of Pollution?', *Environment and Planning A*, 22, 1990, pp. 1421–39; Tietenberg, *Emissions Trading*.

22. Opschoor and Vos, *Economic Instruments*, pp. 83.

23. Similarly, oil tankers and other carriers of potentially hazardous materials can be required to deposit a 'bond' returnable only on proof of safe discharge of wastes. See Opschoor and Vos, *Economic Instruments*, pp. 82–8.

24. It is possible to make VAT non-deductible on some goods but this would add considerable administrative complexity to the system.

25. See Opschoor and Vos, *Economic Instruments*, pp. 55–66, 69–74.

26. This is of course true of all taxes. See any introductory economics textbook, for example P.A. Samuelson and W.D. Nordhaus, *Economics*, 13th edn (New York: McGraw-Hill, 1989), pp. 434–5.

27. Though he or she will have an incentive to cut battery use in general – for example to use mains electricity.

28. Brand names may make a difference here, since much purchasing is influenced by name as much as by price and quality. But it is surely likely that in these circumstances firms will make their existing brand-name products environmentally benign, as they have done with aerosols. Note that there are some consumers who will defy this argument: those who will buy 'ecological' detergents and batteries even if their price is higher than environmentally damaging alternatives. The number of these consumers is likely to rise as the difference in price between the two types of products declines. For these people, the environmental effect of the good is effectively an aspect of its 'performance': for them different tax rates will affect behaviour differently.

29. See P. Hewitt, *A Cleaner, Faster London: Road Pricing, Transport Policy and the Environment* (London: Institute for Public Policy Research, 1989).

30. See Pezzey, 'Market Mechanisms' in Turner, *Sustainable Environmental Management*, pp. 204–10.
31. Opschoor and Vos, *Economic Instruments*, p. 62.
32. See for example E.U. von Weizsäcker, 'Global Warming and Environmental Taxes', paper given to International Conference on Atmosphere, Climate and Man, Torino, Italy, January 1989; F. Bradbury, *The Joules of Wealth* (Ross-on-Wye: Hydatum, 1988).

12: Regulations Versus Financial Incentives?

1. This has already been done with some success by Friends of the Earth and others over specific individual issues, such as whale and fur products and CFC-using goods. In Japan the Seikatsu Club has demonstrated the potential of a consumer organisation which mobilises its members' purchasing activities to pressurise companies into ethical behaviour: in 1988 it had 150,000 family members, a turnover of £160 million and (consequently) some influence. See P. Ekins, 'Growing Concern', *Guardian*, 13 January 1988. Ekins' pamphlet *Sustainable Consumerism* (London: New Economics Foundation, 1989) explores this possibility a little further.
2. The most notable example of an 'environmental trade unionism' in an industrialised country is probably the Australian 'Green Bans' movement of the early 1970s, in which building workers refused to work on environmentally damaging development projects. See S. Joseph, 'Green as a Class Issue', *New Ground* 10, Summer 1986, pp. 14–15. See also N. Bryson, 'Trade Unions and the Environment', *New Ground* 17, Spring 1988, pp. 6–7.
3. Organisation for Economic Cooperation and Development, *The Polluter Pays Principle: Definition, Analysis and Implementation* (Paris: OECD, 1975).
4. See J. Pezzey, 'Market Mechanisms of Pollution Control: "Polluter Pays", Economic and Practical Aspects', in R.K. Turner, *Sustainable Environmental Management: Principles and Practice* (London: Belhaven Press/Boulder, CO: Westview Press, 1988), pp. 190–242.
5. How much depends on the price elasticity of demand for the product. This is simply explained in D.W. Pearce, A. Markandya and E.B. Barbier, *Blueprint for a Green Economy* (London: Earthscan, 1989), p.159.
6. See for example D. Miller, 'The Market Solution to Reduce Pollution', *Independent on Sunday*, 29 July 1990.
7. J. Rees, 'Pollution Control Objectives and the Regulatory Framework', in Turner, *Sustainable Environmental Management*, pp. 170–89.
8. T.H. Tietenberg, 'Economic Instruments for Environmental Regulation', *Oxford Review of Economic Policy* 6 (1), Spring 1990, p. 30.
9. See Rees, 'Pollution Control Objectives' in Turner, *Sustainable Environmental Management*, pp. 176–9; N. Hanley, S. Hallett and I. Moffatt, 'Why Is More Notice Not Taken of Economists' Prescriptions for the Control of Pollution?', *Environment and Planning A*, 22, 1990, p. 1425.
10. See for example D.W. Pearce and R.K. Turner, *Economics of Natural Resources and the Environment* (Hemel Hempstead: Harvester Wheatsheaf, 1990), pp. 94–6. But note that *in theory*, an equally low-cost regulatory system could be designed. This would simply require the central pollution control authority to know in detail about each firm's production cost curves. With such information it could calculate the regulations which

would need to be applied to each firm to achieve the efficient collective result.

11. It should be noted, however, that the cost advantage of financial incentives over regulation diminishes as the target level of pollution is tightened. If firms are required to reduce their emissions by very large amounts, the possibility of low-cost measures declines, and firms will face more similar costs, for example in introducing wholly new technology. The technology-forcing role of financial incentives, however, would have added advantage in these circumstances.

12. G.M. Brown, Jr. and R.W. Johnson, 'Pollution Control By Effluent Charges: It Works in the Federal Republic of Germany, Why Not in the United States?', *Natural Resources Journal* 24, 1984, p. 942; R. Hahn and G. Hester, 'The Market for Bads', *Regulation*, 3/4, 1987. See also A. Krupnick, 'Costs of Alternative Policies for the Control of Nitrogen Dioxide in Baltimore', *Journal of Environmental Economics and Management*, 13, 1986, pp. 189–97.

13. Rees, 'Pollution Control Objectives' in Turner, *Sustainable Environmental Management*, p. 184.

14. M. Pearson and S. Smith, *Taxation and Environmental Policy: Some Initial Evidence* (London: Institute for Fiscal Studies, 1990), p. 37.

15. The carbon tax has been discussed in many places. A good review is in M. Grubb, *Energy Policies and the Greenhouse Effect* (Aldershot: Gower, 1991). We discuss the tax in greater detail in Chapters 13 and 14.

16. T. Jackson and S. Roberts, *Getting Out of the Greenhouse* (London: Friends of the Earth, 1989).

17. T. Jackson, *Energy Policy in a Warming World* (London: Friends of the Earth, forthcoming), draft pp. 16–17.

18. R. Williams, 'Innovative Approaches to Marketing Electric Efficiency', in T. Johansson, B. Bodlund and R. Williams (eds), *Electricity: Efficient End-Use and New Generation Technologies and Their Planning Implications* (Lund, Sweden: Lund University Press, 1989). In general the most efficient system involves the actual supply of energy efficiency services to the consumer being undertaken by 'third party' companies, with the utilities paying them in return.

19. In theory the landlord could charge a higher rent for an insulated dwelling, but rents are not usually sensitive to such considerations.

20. A counter argument can be put on equity grounds (anticipating the discussion in Chapter 14). Energy efficiency standards are likely to be inequitable, since poor people have higher discount rates. This means that, if given a choice, they would prefer to spend more money on daily energy consumption than on an up-front efficiency investment. The strength of this argument partly depends on how great the investment costs are.

21. See Pezzey, 'Market Mechanisms', in Turner, *Sustainable Environmental Management*, p. 205.

22. Ibid., pp. 204–6.

13: The Role of Government Expenditure

1. T. Barker and R. Lewney, 'A Green Scenario for the UK Economy' in T. Barker (ed), *Green Futures for Economic Growth* (Cambridge: Cambridge Econometrics, 1991), p. 25. Price elasticities are likely to be different in

the short and long term. See P.B. Goodwin, *Evidence on Car and Public Transport Demand Elasticities, 1980–88*, Transport Studies Unit, Oxford University, June 1988. There is evidence that transport behaviour exhibits major shifts at certain 'threshold' prices. See P.R. White, 'Man and His Transport Behaviour: User Response to Price Changes: The Application of the Threshold Concept', *Transport Reviews* 4 (4), 1984, pp. 367–86.

2. M. Pearson and S. Smith, *Taxation and Environmental Policy: Some Initial Evidence* (London: Institute for Fiscal Studies, 1990), p. 37. The one exception appears to be the effluent charges levied in the Netherlands, which have resulted in a significant reduction in water pollution. See J.B. Opschoor and H.B. Vos, *Economic Instruments for Environmental Protection* (Paris: Organisation for Economic Cooperation and Development, 1989), pp. 42–3.

3. London Economics, *The Effects of Taxes on Fertiliser*, 1990. The price of food is of course also affected by the Common Agricultural Policy.

4. P. Johnson, S. McKay and S. Smith, *The Distributional Consequences of Environmental Taxes* (London: Institute for Fiscal Studies, 1990), p. 27; Department of Transport, *Report 1991* (London: HMSO, 1991), p. 54.

5. London Economics, *The Effects of Taxes*; Friends of the Earth, *How Green is Britain?* (London: Hutchinson Radius, 1990), p. 67.

6. Opschoor and Vos, *Economic Instruments*, pp. 74–82.

7. See J. Blunden and N. Curry, *A Future for Our Countryside* (Oxford: Basil Blackwell, 1988); D. Harvey, *The CAP and Green Agriculture* (London: Institute of Public Policy Research, 1991).

8. Department of Transport, *Transport Statistics: Great Britain 1979–89* (London: HMSO, 1990), p. 23.

9. S. Boyle, L. Taylor, I. Brown, *Solving the Greenhouse Dilemma* (London: Association for the Conservation of Energy, 1989), p. 9. (Motor vehicles also cause urban congestion, very high numbers of accidents and arguably immense disruption to communities.)

10. 'Public' transport is actually something of a misnomer. On purely environmental grounds the key attribute is that transport is 'collective' rather than publicly owned (though public ownership may be required or desirable on economic and social grounds).

11. For an innovative approach to urban transport policy see J. Roberts, *User Friendly Cities* (London: TEST, 1989); M.J.H. Mogridge, *Travel in Towns* (London: Macmillan, 1990); T. Elkin and D. McLaren, *Reviving the City* (London: Friends of the Earth, 1991), pp. 49–82.

12. Steer Davies and Gleave Ltd, 'Turning Trucks Into Trains', report prepared for Transport 2000, 1987.

13. J. Button, *How to Be Green* (London: Century Hutchinson, 1989), p. 181; Roberts, *User Friendly Cities*; Mogridge, *Travel in Towns*.

14. See S. Owens, *Energy, Urban Form and Planning* (London: Pion, 1986).

15. UK Department of Energy, *Report of the Working Group on Energy Demand Elasticities*, Energy Paper No 17 (London: HMSO, 1977). It is not just the simple price elasticity of individual fuels which needs to be taken into account but the 'cross-elasticities' of substitution between different fuels. See S. Barrett, 'Memorandum to the House of Commons Select Committee on Energy', London Business School, 1989, pp. 5–7; T. Barker and R. Lewney, 'A Green Scenario for the UK Economy', in T. Barker (ed), *Green Futures for Economic Growth* (Cambridge: Cambridge Econometrics, 1991), p. 10. Elasticities also change over time. See 'World Status: Energy Taxation?', *Energy Economist*, February 1990, p. 16.

16. Barker and Lewney, 'Green Scenario', in Barker, *Green Futures*, pp. 14–27; P. Capros, P. Karadeloglou and G. N. Mentzas, *Carbon-Tax Policy and its Impacts on CO$_2$ Emission*, National Technical University of Athens, 1990. See also S. Barrett, 'Pricing the Environment: The Economic and Environmental Consequences of a Carbon Tax', *Economic Outlook*, London Business School, February 1990, pp. 24–33.
17. T. Jackson, *Energy Policy in a Warming World* (London: Friends of the Earth, forthcoming), draft p. 50; Barker and Lewney, 'Green Scenario', in Barker, *Green Futures*, p. 24.
18. This is not 'optimal' in the orthodox sense, meaning the point where marginal cost equals marginal benefit.
19. In addition to the reasons given here, the current structure of tariffs and taxation in the UK (for example, VAT is levied on efficiency equipment but not on energy supply) also impedes energy efficiency. See Jackson, *Energy Policy*, draft p. 8.
20. E. Jochem and E. Gruber, 'Obstacles to Rational Electricity Use and Measures to Alleviate Them', *Energy Policy* 18 (4), May 1990, pp. 340–50.
21. H. Chernoff, 'Individual Purchase Criteria for Energy Related Durables: The Misuse of Lifecycle Cost', *Energy Journal* 4 (4), 1983; J.A. Hausman, 'Individual Discount Rates and the Purchase and Utilization of Energy-Using Durables', *Bell Journal of Economics* 10, 1979, pp. 33–54, cited in S. Barrett, *Memorandum*, p. 2. The latter study suggested that the poorest households had effective discount rates of 89%.
22. Johnson, McKay and Smith, *Distributional Consequences*, p. 9.
23. International Energy Agency, *Energy Conservation in IEA Countries* (Paris: International Energy Agency and OECD, 1987), pp. 130–45.
24. T. Jackson and S. Roberts, *Getting Out of the Greenhouse* (London: Friends of the Earth, 1989); T. Jackson, *Energy Policy*. Strictly speaking energy efficiency here should mean the 'environmental efficiency' of energy sources as explained in Chapter 9: alternative sources of supply, such as renewables, should also be included in the analysis.
25. T. Jackson and M. Jacobs, 'Carbon Taxes and the Assumptions of Environmental Economics' in Barker, *Green Futures*, pp. 49–67.

14: Equity and the Integration of Social and Environmental Policy

1. Strictly speaking, it might be argued, both the costs and benefits of a measure should be taken into account. Some policies, such as reductions in air pollution, may give greater benefits to the poor than to the rich, if the poor currently live in more polluted areas. Others, such as actions taken to protect the countryside, may be appreciated more by richer people, who live in the country or who visit it more often. In order to assess the overall distributional impact of the policy, we would need to compare its costs and benefits for different income groups. If higher income groups experienced higher net benefits (or lower net costs) than lower income groups, the policy should be regarded as inequitable. See for example R. Dorfman, 'Incidence of the Benefits and Costs of Environmental Programmes', *American Economic Review*, Papers and Proceedings, 1977, pp. 333–40; D. Pearce, 'The Social Incidence of Environmental Costs and Benefits', in T. O'Riordan and R.K. Turner, *Progress in Resource Management and Environmental Planning* 2, 1980, pp. 63–87;

H.M. Peskin, 'Environmental Policy and the Distribution of Benefits and Costs', in P.R. Portney (ed), *Current Issues in US Environmental Policy* (Baltimore: Johns Hopkins University Press, 1977).

In practice we shall be concerned only with the costs of policy, not its benefits. This is partly because it is in fact very difficult to estimate the benefits of environmental improvement in monetary terms. (This is discussed in Chapter 17.) But more importantly it is because we have explicitly rejected the approach to environmental protection which is based on a simple cost-benefit calculation. Many of the benefits of sustainability measures are intended to accrue to future generations or people overseas. Sustainability targets are not derived by simply assessing the benefits which people living here and now will get from them; therefore the crucial question is who will pay for sustainability rather than who will benefit from it.

2. See D.W. Pearce, A. Markandya and E.B. Barbier, *Blueprint for a Green Economy* (London: Earthscan, 1989), p. 159.

3. These effects can be analysed through the use of 'input-output tables' showing the movements of resources between industrial sectors. See S. McKay, M. Pearson and S. Smith, 'Fiscal Instruments in Environmental Policy', *Fiscal Studies* 11 (4), November 1990, pp. 8–11; H.D. Robison, 'Who Pays for Industrial Pollution Abatement?', *Review of Economics and Statistics* 67 (4), 1985, pp. 702–6.

4. P. Johnson, S. McKay and S. Smith, *The Distributional Consequences of Environmental Taxes* (London: Institute for Fiscal Studies, 1990), pp. 6–19.

5. Ibid., p. 16.

6. Note that if the level of UK carbon dioxide emissions required for the Toronto target were allocated equally between all households, the poorest 30% of households would contribute precisely the number of tonnes (41 million per annum) they do presently. That is, the poor are contributing their 20% savings already through deprivation, and on equity grounds should not be required to cut consumption any further. See B. Boardman, *Fuel Poverty and the Greenhouse Effect* (London: Neighbourhood Energy Action/Heatwise Glasgow/National Right to Fuel Campaign/Friends of the Earth, 1990), pp. 9–10.

7. M. Curwen and T. Devis, 'Winter Mortality, Temperature and Influenza: Has the Relationship Changed in Recent Years?', *Population Trends* 54, 1988, cited in Boardman, *Fuel Poverty*, p. 6.

8. Johnson, McKay and Smith, *Distributional Consequences*, pp. 16–17.

9. Ibid., p. 34. Food prices are of course determined principally by agricultural subsidies.

10. Ibid., pp. 27–8. The figure of 55 pence was chosen because (before the 1991 Gulf War) it would have restored petrol prices to their highest historical level. It should be noted that the poorest people in rural areas do not have access to cars.

11. Although note that Child Benefit itself is removed from Income Support. Also, because a rise in food prices changes the relative prices of other goods, extra compensatory income is unlikely to be spent entirely on food.

12. This measure is suggested by Johnson, McKay and Smith, *Distributional Consequences*, pp. 48–9.

13. Johnson, McKay and Smith propose one combination of benefits which would provide (subject to take-up) some measure of compensation: *Distributional Consequences*, pp. 41–5.

14. Ibid., pp. 10, 17; Boardman, *Fuel Poverty*, p. 7.

15. Boardman, *Fuel Poverty*, pp. 11–12.
16. International Labour Organisation, *Employment and Training Implications of Environmental Policies in Europe* (Geneva: ILO, 1989), pp. 6, 12.
17. Ibid., p. 6.
18. Organisation for Economic Cooperation and Development, *The Impact of Environmental Policy on Employment*, Background Paper, Conference on Environment and Economics, Paris, 1984.
19. Task Force on the Environment and the Internal Market, *'1992': The Environmental Dimension* (Brussels: Commission of the European Communities, 1990) pp. 8–10. The results depend on how the environmental investment is financed. See also *To Choose or to Lose: National Environmental Policy Plan* (The Hague: Ministry of Housing, Physical Planning and the Environment, 1989), pp. 248–54.
20. International Labour Organisation, *Employment and Training Implications*, pp. 7–8.
21. Environmental Resources Ltd, *Jobs and Energy Conservation* (London: Association for the Conservation of Energy, 1983), p. 7.
22. Ibid., pp. 7–8.
23. See for example K. Smith, *The British Economic Crisis* (Harmondsworth: Penguin, 1984), Chapter 12.
24. International Labour Organisation, *Employment and Training Implications*, pp. 30–9.
25. Ibid., pp. 9–15.

15: Global Environmental Economic Policy

1. See for example T. Hayter, *The Creation of World Poverty* (London: Pluto Press, 1983); M. Redclift, *Sustainable Development: Exploring the Contradictions* (London: Methuen, 1987); L. Timberlake, *Africa in Crisis* (London: Earthscan, 1985); B. Jackson, *Poverty and the Planet: A Question of Survival* (Harmondsworth: Penguin, 1990).
2. The World Commission on Environment and Development calculates that the exports of developing countries to OECD member countries in 1980 would have incurred $14.2 billion dollars' worth of pollution control costs had they been required to meet the environmental standards then prevailing in the United States. *Our Common Future* (Oxford: Oxford University Press, 1987), pp. 83–4. The Commission points out, moreover, that pollution is not the only form of environmental damage caused by these products.
3. See T.A. Oyejide, 'Primary Commodities in the International Trading System' in J. Whalley (ed), *Developing Countries and the Global Trading System* (London: Macmillan, 1989), pp. 91–111. It should be noted that GATT is far from an ideal structure for assisting developing countries. See R. Chakravati, *Recolonisation: GATT, the Uruguay Round and the Third World* (London: Zed Books/Penang, Malaysia: Third World Network, 1990).
4. See N. Hood and S. Young, *The Economics of Multinational Enterprise* (Harlow: Longman, 1979), Chapter 6.
5. World Resources Institute, *Natural Endowments: Financing Resource Conservation for Development* (Washington, DC: WRI, 1989), pp. 17–20; C. Conroy and R. Litvinoff (eds), *The Greening of Aid: Sustainable Livelihoods in Practice* (London: Earthscan, 1988).

6. Conroy and Litivinoff, *The Greening of Aid*; Redclift, *Sustainable Development*, pp. 150–70. One of the most notable examples of aid-assisted sectoral environmental planning, the Tropical Forestry Action Plan, has been severely criticised precisely because few countries have involved local people either in the drawing-up of the national plan or in its implementation. See M. Colchester and L. Lohmann, *The Tropical Forestry Action Plan: What Progress?* (Penang, Malaysia and Sturminster Newton: World Rainforest Movement and the *Ecologist*, 1990).

7. World Resources Institute, *Natural Endowments*, p. 8.

8. The Brazilian proposal was made by Karl Ziegler. See S. Wavell, 'Gringo Greenmail Puts Nature on the Balance Sheet', *Sunday Times*, 14 May 1989.

9. Wavell, 'Gringo Greenmail'.

10. It should not be thought, however, that the 'imperialist' argument is overcome by this tactic. The argument relies on making a distinction between the people of a country (who deserve compensation) and their government (which doesn't) which few industrialised nations would allow for themselves.

11. Oxfam, *Submission to the Treasury and Civil Service Select Committee on Management of Third World Debt*, December 1989.

12. M. Grubb, *The Greenhouse Effect: Negotiating Targets* (London: Royal Institute of International Affairs, 1990), pp. 23–5. Precisely how much bargaining power developing countries have is open to dispute. First, it has to be recognised that the chief obstacle to an international agreement is currently the United States, which is by far the largest single producer of global pollutants; if the US does not sign up, no other country has any effective bargaining power at all. Second, it is possible that some of the poorest countries will suffer more from global warming than industrialised ones (for example, through coastal flooding), increasing their desire to secure an agreement.

13. L.R. Brown and E.C. Wolf, 'Reclaiming the Future', in L.R. Brown (ed), *State of the World 1988* (New York: W.W. Norton, 1988), pp. 182–8; P. Eavis and M. Clarke, *Security After the Cold War* (Bristol: Saferworld Foundation, 1990).

14. See for example Grubb, *Greenhouse Effect*, p. 27; World Resources Institute, *Natural Endowments*.

15. L.R. Brown, *State of the World 1988*, p. 186; Eavis and Clarke, *Security After the Cold War*, p. 8.

16. Eavis and Clarke, *Security After the Cold War*, p. 18.

17. World Resources Institute, *Natural Endowments*, pp. 3–5.

18. This section borrows heavily from the work of Michael Grubb, notably *The Greenhouse Effect: Negotiating Targets*.

19. S. Barrett, *Ozone Holes, Greenhouse Gases and Economic Policy*, London Business School, July 1989, pp. 12–14.

20. S. Barrett, 'The Problem of Global Environmental Protection', *Oxford Review of Economic Policy* 6 (1), 1990, pp. 68–79.

21. Barrett cites the example of the UK House of Commons Environment Committee in 1984, arguing for Britain to join the '30% Club' of European countries pledged to cut acid rain-causing emissions; their reasoning appeared to be that if 'other European nations are reducing their emissions, so we should too.' 'Problem of Global Environmental Protection', p. 74.

22. The Nuclear Non-Proliferation Treaty, for example, includes a provision allowing the International Atomic Energy Authority to suspend all assistance to countries violating the treaty's verification procedures.
23. Grubb, *Greenhouse Effect*, p. 18. The figures are calculated on a Purchasing Power Parity basis to remove exchange rate distortions. Such a formula has indeed already been rejected by the Japanese (Ibid., p. 20, note 41).
24. Ibid., p. 19.
25. K. Smith, *Global Warming and the Natural Debt* (Hawaii: Environment and Policy Institute, East West Centre, 1989). The argument is not quite as simple as supposed, since in earlier historical periods the awareness of the need to reduce emissions and the technology to do so was absent or less powerful.
26. Grubb, *Greenhouse Effect*, pp. 21–2. Such reaction is indeed already occurring.
27. This proposal has been made by Grubb, *Greenhouse Effect*, pp. 33–41.
28. It would however ignore the 'historical equity' argument referred to earlier. Grubb argues (p. 37) that it would be possible to base the allocation on adult population only, if it were felt that using the whole population would provide an incentive to maintain high population growth.
29. See D.W. Pearce and R.K. Turner, *Economics of Natural Resources and the Environment* (Hemel Hempstead: Harvester Wheatsheaf, 1990), Chapter 10; and Chapter 12 in this volume.
30. A gradual movement towards equality of this sort has been proposed in the *Princeton Protocol on Factors that Contribute to Global Warming*, Woodrow Wilson School of Public and International Affairs, Princeton University, 1988.

16: Making Environmental Decisions (1)

1. For revealing analyses of the politics of decision-making in particular fields, see for example C. Sweet, *The Price of Nuclear Power* (London: Heinemann, 1983) and M. Hamer, *Wheels Within Wheels: A Study of the Road Lobby* (London: Routledge and Kegan Paul, 1987). For a general review see J. Rees, *Natural Resources: Allocation, Efficiency and Policy*, 2nd edn (London: Routledge, 1990), Chapter 9; F. Sandbach, *Environment, Ideology and Policy* (Oxford: Basil Blackwell, 1980).
2. Cost-benefit analysis is described more fully in a number of textbooks; for example D.W. Pearce and C.A. Nash, *The Social Appraisal of Projects* (London: Macmillan, 1981); E.J. Mishan, *Cost Benefit Analysis*, 4th edn (London: Allen and Unwin, 1988).
3. The method is commonly known as the Leitch framework, after the chairman of the committee which introduced it: Sir George Leitch, *Report of the Advisory Committee on Trunk Road Assessment* (London: HMSO, 1977).
4. S. Atkins, *Unspoken Decrees: Road Appraisal, Democracy and the Environment* (London: London Wildlife Trust, 1990).
5. The case is cogently made out in the 'Pearce Report': D.W. Pearce, A. Markandya and E.B. Barbier, *Blueprint for a Green Economy* (London: Earthscan, 1989), pp. 55–7.
6. These concepts are explained more fully in D.W. Pearce and R.K. Turner, *Economics of Natural Resources and the Environment* (Hemel Hempstead: Harvester Wheatsheaf, 1990), pp. 129–37. Economists now

tend to interpret option value (or, strictly, option price, which is option value plus expected consumer surplus) as a measure of direct user benefits where supply of the good is uncertain. They have also identified the phenomenon of 'quasi-option value', which is the value of preserving options for future use given some expectation of the growth of knowledge (for example, of the medicinal value of tropical rainforest species).

7. In theory, distant people could be included in monetary valuations by enlarging the constituency of which the sample is taken to be representative. At present, the total value of an environmental good is calculated by multiplying the average values given by individuals in the sample by the population of the area affected by the good. (Monetary valuation methods are discussed in more detail in the next chapter.) This population could in theory be a geo-region or the entire world, but the figures would become pretty meaningless, since it is hard enough knowing if a sample is representative of its own neighbourhood, let alone of several billion people.

8. This 'shadow project' principle is now practised in the Netherlands: see L.H. Klaassen and T.H. Botterweg, 'Project Evaluation and Intangible Effects: A Shadow Price Approach', *Etudes du Cémagref* 7, 1983, cited in C. Nash and J. Bowers, 'Alternative Approaches to the Valuation of Environmental Resources' in R.K. Turner (ed), *Sustainable Environmental Management: Principles and Practice* (London: Belhaven Press/Boulder, CO: Westview Press, 1988), p. 121.

9. One of the basic concepts in welfare economics is the 'Hicks-Kaldor compensation test', which proposes that a given change can be regarded as an improvement in overall welfare if the gainers from the change could compensate the losers and still be better off – even if the compensation is not in fact carried out. See Pearce and Nash, *Social Appraisal*, Chapter 3.

10. The debate is reviewed in Pearce, Markandya and Barbier, *Blueprint*, pp. 132–52. A similar but rather clearer account is given in Pearce and Turner, *Economics of Natural Resources*, pp. 211–25.

11. The effect of discounting on the environment is not in fact always damaging. Where environmental costs are experienced before financial benefits (such as, for example, in the destruction of a scenic area to build an undersea tunnel with a long construction period and uncertain long-term benefits) the use of discounting makes environmental protection more likely, not less. (In the decision to build the Channel Tunnel, of course, no attempt was made to put monetary values on the environmental costs.)

12. It also means that only the discounting of the environment is avoided; discounting of financial returns, to which fewer objections can be made, is still allowed.

13. This is called a 'potential Pareto improvement' and is the result of the Hicks-Kaldor compensation test – see note 9.

14. D.W. Pearce, *Cost-Benefit Analysis* (London: Macmillan, 1971), p. 77.

15. *Daily Telegraph*, 18 September 1989, quoted in J. Adams, 'Unsustainable Economics', *International Environmental Affairs* 2 (1), Winter 1990, p. 16.

16. This is of course recognised by academic advocates of CBA, who would not be so unwise as to claim that it provided 'objective' answers. However in practice the computational method of analysis is frequently held to give it an objectivity denied to more qualitative judgements. Note also

that more sophisticated CBA procedures can give additional weighting to poorer people's preferences. This is discussed further in Chapter 17.

17. See for example R. Grove-White and O. O'Donovan, 'An Alternative Approach', in R. Attfield and K. Dell, *Values, Conflict and the Environment* (Oxford: Ian Ramsey Centre, 1989).

18. Ibid., p. 79.

19. Alternatively, if the choice is between killing one person and saving ten, the wrong of killing may override the tragedy of avoidable but unintentional death.

20. £500,000 is the value of a life used in the British trunk road CBA procedure. The Colorado wilderness was valued at $93.2 million per annum by R. Walsh, J. Loomis and R. Gillman, 'Valuing Option, Existence and Bequest Demands for Wilderness', *Land Economics* 60 (1), 1984, pp. 14–29.

17: Making Environmental Decisions (2)

1. There is a third approach to monetary valuation, 'alternative cost', which does not attempt to measure willingness to pay. Alternative cost measures the cost of repairing the environmental damage of a project. The alternative cost of traffic noise, for example, might be the cost of installing double glazing; that of a road, the cost of recreating lost habitats. This method may be useful if the alternative or 'shadow project' is undertaken, but it does not strictly measure the environment's value. First, alternative projects rarely compensate for the original damage in full. Second, the cost of replacement does not give an indication of how valuable the original environmental feature was. Restoring the *status quo ante* (say, zero pollution levels, from slightly higher but still non-harmful levels) may be very expensive without much benefit being gained. Alternative cost is discussed in R. Hueting, *New Scarcity and Economic Growth: More Welfare Through Less Production?* (Amsterdam: North Holland, 1980). Since the Roskill Commission on the Third London Airport valued a medieval church at its replacement value the alternative cost approach has had few advocates. Commission on the Third London Airport, *Report* (London: HMSO, 1971).

2. For a survey of this method (usually called 'hedonic pricing'), see Per-Olov Johansson, *The Economic Theory and Measurement of Environmental Benefits* (Cambridge: Cambridge University Press, 1987).

3. Ibid.

4. Ibid.

5. Ibid. See also R. Cummings, D. Brookshire and W. Schulze (eds), *Valuing Environmental Goods: An Assessment of the Contingent Valuation Method* (Totowa, NJ: Rowman and Allanheld, 1986); and R.C. Mitchell and R.T. Carson, *Using Surveys to Value Public Goods: The Contingent Valuation Method* (Washington DC: Resources for the Future, 1989).

6. For a survey of this method see MVA Consultancy, Institute for Transport Studies (University of Leeds) and Transport Studies Unit (University of Oxford), *The Value of Travel Time Savings* (Newbury: Policy Journals, 1987).

7. D.W. Pearce, A. Markandya and E.B. Barbier, *Blueprint for a Green Economy* (London: Earthscan, 1989), pp. 66–9.

8. N. Hanley and M. Common, *Estimating Recreation, Wildlife and Landscape Benefits Attached to Queen Elizabeth Forest Park*, Final report to Forestry

Commission, Edinburgh, 1987, quoted in N. Hanley, 'Valuing Non-Market Goods Using Contingent Valuation', *Journal of Economic Surveys* 3 (3), 1989, p. 249.

9. M. Thayer, 'Contingent Valuation Techniques for Assessing Environmental Impacts: Further Evidence', *Journal of Environmental Economics and Management* 8 (1), March 1981, pp. 27–44.
10. V.K. Smith and W. Desvouges, *Measuring Water Quality Benefits* (Boston: Kluwer Nijhoff, 1986), pp. 170–4.
11. D. Brookshire, L. Eubanks and A. Randall, 'Estimating Option Prices and Existence Values for Wildlife Resources', *Land Economics* 59 (1), February 1983.
12. J. Strand, 'Valuation of Freshwater Fish as a Public Good in Norway', Institute of Economics, Oslo University, 1981, cited in D.W. Pearce and R.K. Turner, *Economics of Natural Resources and the Environment* (Hemel Hempstead: Harvester Wheatsheaf, 1990), p. 140.
13. W. Schulze et al, 'The Economic Benefits of Preserving Visibility in the National Parklands of the South West', *Natural Resources Journal* 23, July 1983, pp. 149–73.
14. A good summary of the problems is given in Pearce, Markandya and Barbier, *Blueprint*, pp. 82–90. See also Johansson, *Economic Theory and Measurement*.
15. Surveys of the different types of bias include Cummings, Brookshire and Schulze, *Valuing Environmental Goods*, and Mitchell and Carson, *Using Surveys*. See also S. Edwards and G. Anderson, 'Overlooked Biases in Contingent Valuation Surveys', *Land Economics* 62 (2), 1987, pp. 168–78.
16. On strategic bias, see Cummings, Brookshire and Schulze, *Valuing Environmental Goods*, pp. 21–6, 206–7. Generally it is found that only economists free ride. (See R. Rowe, R. D'Arge and D. Brookshire, 'An Experiment on the Economic Value of Visibility', *Journal of Environmental Economics and Management* 7 (1), March 1980, pp. 1–19; and, in another context, G. Marwell and R. Ames, 'Economists Free Ride, Does Anyone Else?', *Journal of Public Economics* 15, 1981, pp. 295–310.) It should be noted that the stated preference method, unlike contingent valuation, is difficult to bias strategically. On starting-point bias, see also K. Boyle, R. Bishop and M. Welsch, 'Starting Point Bias in Contingent Valuation Bidding Games', *Land Economics* 61 (2), 1985, pp. 188–94.
17. Cummings, Brookshire and Schulze, *Valuing Environmental Goods*, p. 125. The range of overlap between contingent valuation results and those of other methods was found to be ±60%. This is a standard range of error in estimates of demand functions, but would still lead to huge disparities in the total value of the environmental goods when aggregated across large populations. Used in cost-benefit analysis the differences could be crucial.
18. N. Hanley, 'Valuing Non-Market Goods', p. 250. In *Valuing Environmental Goods*, pp. 230–1, Cummings, Brookshire and Schulze set out a list of eleven 'reference operating conditions' whose fulfilment will lead to the largest measure of accuracy.
19. Boyle, Bishop and Welsch, 'Starting Point Bias'; C. Seller, J. Stoll, and J.-P. Chevas, 'Validation of Empirical Measures of Welfare Change: A Comparison of Non-Market Techniques', *Land Economics* 61 (2), 1985, pp. 156–75.
20. Rowe, d'Arge and Brookshire, 'Economic Value of Visibility', pp. 1–19. See also Cummings, Brookshire and Schulze, *Valuing Environmental*

Goods, pp. 33–4, 59–60; Mitchell and Carson, *Using Surveys*, pp. 216–7. The latter argue that there is no such thing as information bias, simply differently described goods being valued.

21. Cummings, Brookshire and Schulze, *Valuing Environmental Goods*, pp. 209–10. There is in fact another form of indeterminacy which arises from the very notion of people paying to secure environmental improvements. In some circumstances people may feel this is unjust: if for years, for example, they have had to put up with increasing noise levels without anyone ever offering them compensation, asking them to pay to secure noise reductions may be regarded as unfair. On the other hand if they are asked to pay for their environment not to be made worse, this may be felt to be tantamount to blackmail. To the respondent, the procedure appears to give the prospective polluter the right to pollute, with the victims forced to pay to save what in the past they have regarded as theirs by right. The apparent injustice of the exercise may severely affect respondents' willingness and ability to value the environmental change in the way the exercise requires. See P.G. Hopkinson, C.A. Nash and N. Sheehy, 'How Much Do People Value the Environment? The Development of a Method to Identify How People Conceptualise and Value the Costs and Benefits of New Road Schemes', paper prepared for the 3rd International Conference on Survey Methods in Transportation, Institute of Transport Studies and Department of Psychology, University of Leeds, 1990.

22. This is, of course, the long-standing debate about the efficiency and justice of markets, which cannot be rehearsed here. See Chapter 10.

23. This begs the question, of course, about how welfare is measured, but this assumption (of 'declining marginal utility') is intuitively plausible and is generally accepted in welfare economics.

24. N.D. Hanley, 'Using Contingent Valuation to Value Environmental Improvements', *Applied Economics*, 20 (4), 1988, pp. 541–50. Another study, D. Brookshire, B. Ives and W. Schulze, 'The Valuation of Aesthetic Preferences', *Journal of Environmental Economics and Management* 3 (4), 1976, pp. 325–46, found a smaller difference in valuations between different income groups.

25. It is true that the rainforest can be shown to have a higher value when the potential for renewable crops and Northern citizens' existence values are taken into account. This is argued, for example, by D. Pearce, *An Economic Approach to Saving the Rainforest*, London Environmental Economics Centre, August 1990. But it does not alter the basic case. There are other parts of the natural environment where these special conditions of the rainforest do not apply.

26. This suggests that, in so far as the contingent valuation method is used, taxes are the best payment vehicle.

27. P. Goodwin, 'Problems of Women's Mobility and Employment in the One Person Operation of Buses', in M. Grieco, L. Pickup and R. Whipp (eds), *Gender, Transport and Employment* (Aldershot: Gower, 1987), pp. 141–2.

28. R. Gregory, 'Interpreting Measures of Economic Loss: Evidence of Contingent Valuation and Experimental Studies', *Journal of Environmental Economics and Management* 13 (4), 1986, pp. 325–37. See also M. Sagoff, 'Some Problems with Environmental Economics', *Environmental Ethics*, Spring 1988.

29. This argument is made, for example, by Pearce, Markandya and Barbier, *Blueprint*, pp. 53–4.

30. Cummings, Brookshire and Schulze, *Valuing Environmental Goods*, p. 35.
31. It is suggested by Gregory, 'Interpreting Measures of Economic Loss'.
32. J. Bowers, 'Cost-Benefit Analysis in Theory and Practice: Agricultural Land Drainage Projects', in R.K. Turner (ed), *Sustainable Environmental Management: Principles and Practice* (London: Belhaven Press/Boulder, CO: Westview Press, 1988), pp. 265–89; S. Atkins, *Unspoken Decrees: Road Appraisal, Democracy and the Environment* (London: London Wildlife Trust, 1990).
33. An attempt is made in R. Attfield and K. Dell, *Values, Conflict and the Environment* (Oxford: Ian Ramsay Centre, 1989), pp. 47–69.
34. Interesting experiments in participative and interactive planning have been conducted in the UK by Tony Gibson and the Neighbourhood Initiatives Foundation. See M. Duckenfield, 'Planning for Real', *New Society*, 2 August 1979.
35. See Attfield and Dell, *Values, Conflict*, pp. 51–2.

18: Measuring Success

1. See for example Anthony Crosland's seminal social democratic text *The Future of Socialism*, 2nd edn (London: Jonathan Cape, 1964).
2. GNP, it will be recalled, measures all the income earned by a country's citizens, at home and abroad; GDP all the production generated within a country's borders. For the purposes of the present discussion the differences are unimportant. We shall use GNP because it is the better known term.
3. This definition of 'true income' was first given by Sir John Hick, *Value and Capital*, 2nd edn (Oxford: Oxford University Press, 1946), p. 172.
4. A comparison between GNP and environmentally adjusted NNP is made in R. Repetto et al, 'Wasting Assets: Natural Resources in the National Income Accounts' (Washington, DC: World Resources Institute, 1989), cited in D.W. Pearce, A. Markandya and E.B. Barbier, *Blueprint for a Green Economy* (London: Earthscan, 1989), pp. 112–14.
5. See for example J. Porritt, *Seeing Green* (Oxford: Basil Blackwell, 1984), pp. 35–6, 69, 121–2; P. Ekins (ed), *The Living Economy: A New Economics in the Making* (London: Routledge and Kegan Paul, 1986), pp. 32–8.
6. See for example H.E. Daly, 'Toward a Measure of Sustainable Social Net National Product' in Y.J. Ahmad, S. El Serafy, E. Lutz (eds), *Environmental Accounting for Sustainable Development* (Washington, DC: World Bank, 1989), pp. 8–9.
7. D. Patinkin, *Anticipations of the General Theory?* (Oxford: Basil Blackwell, 1982).
8. Note however that GNP only measures *marketed* economic activity. Unmarketed production, such as housework, do-it-yourself, childcare, voluntary work, gift work and barter are not included. GNP cannot therefore be used as a measure of production or economic value. Since much unpaid work is done by women, GNP has a particular tendency to underrate women's contribution to the economy. See V. Anderson, *Alternative Economic Indicators* (London: Routledge, 1991, Chapter 3); M. Waring, *If Women Counted* (London: Macmillan, 1989).
9. This assumes that there are no fixed sustainability targets against which to measure performance, in which case the change in GNP would be secondary.

10. This is done by Daly, 'Sustainable Social Net National Product' in Ahmad, El Serafy and Lutz, *Environmental Accounting*, p. 8; and by C. Leipert, 'From Gross to Adjusted National Product', in Ekins, *The Living Economy*, p. 132.

11. See Pearce, Markandya and Barbier, *Blueprint*, pp. 105–6.

12. S.W. Blades, 'Measuring Pollution Within the Framework of the National Accounts', in Ahmad, El Serafy and Lutz, *Environmental Accounting*, pp. 26–31.

13. C. Leipert, *Die Heimlichen Kosten des Fortschritts: Wie Umweltzerstörung das Wirtschaftswachstum Fördert* (Frankfurt: S Fischer, 1989). See also his summary in Ekins, *The Living Economy*, pp. 132–40.

14. He finds, interestingly, that between 1970 and 1988 defensive expenditures have been growing faster than GDP, although not sufficiently fast actually to cause an adjusted GDP to fall. Leipert, *Heimlichen Kosten*, pp. 126–7.

15. L. Thurow, 'Education and Economic Equality' in D.M. Levine and M.J. Bane (eds), *The 'Inequality' Controversy: Schooling and Distributive Justice* (New York: Basic Books, 1975); see H.E. Daly and J.B. Cobb, *For the Common Good* (London: Green Print, 1990), pp. 403–4.

16. And of course, even if we could identify the 'costs' of real welfare, this would not be a reason for subtracting them from GNP, since other costs are not subtracted.

17. See Daly, 'Sustainable Social Net National Product' in Ahmad, El Serafy and Lutz, *Environmental Accounting*, p. 8; Daly and Cobb, *Common Good*, pp. 401–55; Pearce, Markandya and Barbier, *Blueprint*, p. 108.

18. This can be overcome by calculating the 'user cost' of a non-renewable resource. This is clearly explained in S. El Sarafy, 'The Proper Calculation of Income from Depletable Natural Resources' in Ahmad, El Serafy and Lutz, *Environmental Accounting*, pp. 10–18. The method is criticised in Daly and Cobb, *Common Good*, pp. 437–9.

19. Except in the case of irreversible loss such as species extinction. See below.

20. E. Lutz and S. El Sarafy, 'Recent Developments and Future Work' in Ahmad, El Serafy and Lutz, *Environmental Accounting*, pp. 88–91; Pearce, Markandya and Barbier, *Blueprint*, pp. 107–15.

21. An alternative approach would be to identify sustainability targets and work out the cost of achieving them, and then subtract this from current income. This is advocated by R. Hueting, 'Correcting National Income for Environmental Losses: Toward a Practical Solution' in Ahmad, El Serafy and Lutz, *Environmental Accounting*, pp. 32–9.

22. Because there is no guarantee that income earned from the depletion of non-renewables is reinvested in future income-generating projects; it may simply be consumed.

23. The French system is documented in some detail by J. Theys, 'Environmental Accounting in Development Policy: The French Experience', in Ahmad, El Serafy and Lutz, *Environmental Accounting*, pp. 40–53. Both the French and Norwegian systems are described more simply in Pearce, Markandya and Barbier, *Blueprint*, pp. 96–104.

24. This is not easy, and it is not done in either the French or Norwegian systems.

25. C. Hope and J. Parker, 'Environmental Information for All: The Need for a Monthly Index', Management Studies Group, University of Cambridge, 1990; H. Inhaber, 'Environmental Quality: Outline for a National Index for Canada', *Ekistics* 243, 1976, pp. 102–8, cited in Hope and Parker.

26. The Index of Sustainable Welfare is described, and the others are reviewed, in Daly and Cobb, *Common Good*, pp. 76–84, 401–55.
27. See Anderson, *Alternative Economic Indicators*, Chapter 4.
28. In order to limit the number of indicators to which publicity is given, indexes like those for environmental quality proposed here, and perhaps for other aspects of quality of life, might be used. Interesting work on quality of life indexes has been done by the University of Glasgow Quality of Life Group. See for example A.M. Findlay, R.J. Rogerson and A.S. Morris, 'Quality of Life in British Cities in 1988', *Cities* 10, 1988, pp. 268–76; R. Rogerson et al, *Quality of Life in Britain's Intermediate Cities* (Glasgow: Quality of Life Group, Glasgow University, 1989).

19: The Standard of Living and the Quality of Life

1. H.S. Burness and R.G. Cummings, 'Thermodynamic and Economic Concepts As Related to Resource-Use Policies: A Reply', *Land Economics*, 62 (3), 1986, p. 323.
2. Thus the 'quality' of life cannot strictly be contrasted with anything called the 'quantity' of life.
3. It is a common assumption in economics that consumers maximise their 'utility' or satisfaction. Though there is considerable debate as to what this actually means (utility is not measurable) it is generally wise to accept it in terms of economic policy, since it is tantamount to saying that in normal private consumption people should have the liberty to choose what they will buy with their own money. However we shall have reason to relax the assumption later, when asking whether a given amount of disposable income always has the same value.
4. R. Robinson, *Competition and Health Care: A Comparative Analysis of UK Plans and US Experience* (London: Kings Fund Institute, 1990).
5. Though it should be noted that the welfare state as a whole is not redistributive, at least in Britain. See J. Le Grand and R.E. Goodin (eds), *Not Only the Poor: The Middle Classes and the Welfare State* (London: Allen and Unwin, 1987).
6. It is true that aid to the South also has a variety of benefits to the North, and that to some extent the welfare of people overseas is included in the welfare of people at home.
7. A.H. Maslow, *Motivation and Personality* (New York: Harper and Row, 1954), and other works. The application of Maslow's theory of needs to economics is discussed in M. A. Lutz and K. Lux, *Humanistic Economics: The New Challenge* (New York: Bootstrap Press, 1988).
8. This suggests a reverse form of Say's Law, that supply creates its own demand.

Bibliography

Adams, J. *Transport Planning: Vision and Practice* (London: Routledge and Kegan Paul, 1981).
—— *London's Green Spaces: What Are They Worth?* (London: London Wildlife Trust/Friends of the Earth, 1989).
—— 'Unsustainable Economics', *International Environmental Affairs*, 2 (1), 1990.
Adams, W.M. *Green Development: Environment and Sustainability in the Third World* (London: Routledge, 1990).
Agarwal, A. *Politics of Environment*, in Centre for Science and Environment, *The State of India's Environment 1984–5* (New Delhi: Centre for Science and Environment, 1985).
Ahmad, Y.J., El Serafy, S. and Lutz E. (eds), *Environmental Accounting for Sustainable Development* (Washington, DC: World Bank, 1989).
Albery, N. and Kinzley, M. (eds), *How to Save the World* (Wellingborough: Turnstone Press, 1984).
Amin, S. *Delinking* (London: Zed Press, 1989).
Anderson, L.G. 'Property Rights in Fisheries: Lessons from the New Zealand Experience', Working Paper 89–22, Political Economy Research Center, Bozeman, MT, 1989.
Anderson, V. *Alternative Economic Indicators* (London: Routledge, 1991).
Arrow, K.J. and Fisher, A. 'Environmental Preservation, Uncertainty and Irreversibility', *Quarterly Journal of Economics*, 88 (2), 1974.
Atkins, S. *Unspoken Decrees: Road Appraisal, Democracy and the Environment* (London: London Wildlife Trust, 1990).
Attfield, R. and Dell, K. *Values, Conflict and the Environment* (Oxford: Ian Ramsey Centre, 1989).
Auty, R. 'Materials Intensity of GDP', *Resources Policy*, 11 (4), 1985.
Ayers, R.U. and Kneese, A. 'Production, Consumption and Externality', *American Economic Review*, lix, June 1969.
Bahro, R. *Socialism and Survival* (London: Heretic, 1982).
—— *From Red to Green* (London: Verso, 1984).
—— *Building the Green Movement* (London: GMP, 1986).
Barbier, E.B. *Earthworks: Environmental Approaches to Employment Protection* (London: Friends of the Earth, 1981).
—— *New Approaches in Environmental and Resource Economics* (London: New Economics Foundation/International Institute for Environment and Development, 1988).
—— *Economics, Natural Resource Scarcity and Development* (London: Earthscan, 1989).
Barbier. E.B. and Pearce, D.W. *Thinking Economically About Climate Change*, London Environmental Economics Centre, 1989.

Barker, T. (ed), *Green Futures for Economic Growth* (Cambridge: Cambridge Econometrics, 1991).

Barker, T. and Lewney, R. 'A Green Economic Scenario for the UK Economy', in T. Barker (ed), *Green Futures for Economic Growth* (Cambridge: Cambridge Econometrics, 1991).

Barnett, H. 'Scarcity and Growth Revisited', in V.K. Smith (ed), *Scarcity and Growth Reconsidered* (Baltimore, MD: Johns Hopkins University Press, 1979).

Barnett, H. and Morse, C. *Scarcity and Growth: The Economics of Natural Resource Availability* (Baltimore, MD: Johns Hopkins Universtiy Press, 1963).

Barney, G.O. *The Global 2000 Report to the President of the US* (Oxford: Pergamon Press, 1980).

Barrat-Brown, M. *Models in Political Economy* (London: Penguin, 1985).

Barrett, S. *Ozone Holes, Greenhouse Gases and Economic Policy*, London Business School, July 1989.

—— 'The Problem of Global Environmental Protection', *Oxford Review of Economic Policy*, 6 (1) 1990.

—— 'Pricing the Environment: The Economic and Environmental Consequences of a Carbon Tax', *Economic Outlook*, London Business School, February 1990.

—— *Memorandum to the House of Commons Select Committee on Energy*, London Business School, May 1990.

Barry, B. 'Justice Between Generations', in P. Hacker and J. Raz (eds), *Law, Morality and Society* (Oxford, Clarendon Press, 1977).

Bartelmus, P. *Environment and Development* (London: Allen and Unwin, 1986).

Baumol, W. and Oates, W. *Economics, Environmental Policy and the Quality of Life* (Englewood Cliffs, NJ: Prentice Hall, 1979).

—— *The Theory of Environmental Policy*, 2nd edn (Cambridge: Cambridge University Press, 1988).

Becker, R.A. 'Intergenerational Equity: The Capital-Environment Trade-off', *Journal of Environmental Economics and Management*, 9 (2), 1982.

Beckerman, W. *In Defence of Economic Growth* (London: Jonathan Cape, 1974).

—— *Pricing for Pollution*, 2nd edn (London: Institute for Economic Affairs, 1990).

Bernstam, M. *The Wealth of Nations and the Environment* (London: Institute of Economic Affairs, 1991).

Bird G. (ed), *Third World Debt: The Search for a Solution* (Aldershot: Edward Elgar, 1989).

Bishop, R. 'Endangered Species and Uncertainty: The Economics of a Safe Minimum Standard', *American Journal of Agricultural Economics*, 61 (5), 1978.

—— 'Option Value: an Exposition and Extension', *Journal of Environmental Economics and Management*, February 1982.

Blackstone, W. (ed), *Philosophy and the Environmental Crisis* (Athens, GA: University of Georgia Press, 1974).

Blunden, J. and Curry, N. *A Future for Our Countryside* (Oxford: Basil Blackwell, 1988).

Boardman, B. *Fuel Poverty and the Greenhouse Effect* (London: Neighbourhood Energy Action/Heatwise Glasgow/National Right to Fuel Campaign/Friends of the Earth, 1990).

Bookchin, M. *Post-Scarcity Anarchism* (London: Wildwood House, 1974).

—— *Toward an Ecological Society* (Montreal: Black Rose Books, 1980).

Bowers, J. 'Cost-Benefit Analysis in Theory and Practice: Agricultural Land Drainage Projects', in R.K. Turner (ed), *Sustainable Environmental Management:*

Principles and Practice (London: Belhaven/Boulder, CO: Westview Press, 1988).

—— *Economics of the Environment: The Conservationists' Response to the Pearce Report* (Newbury: British Association of Nature Conservationists, 1990).

Bowers, J. and Cheshire, P. *Agriculture, the Countryside and Land Use: An Economic Critique* (London: Methuen, 1983).

Boyle, K., Bishop, R. and Welsch, M. 'Starting Point Bias in Contingent Valuation Bidding Games', *Land Economics*, 61 (2), 1985.

Boyle, S. and Ardill, J. *The Greenhouse Effect* (London: Hodder and Stoughton, 1989).

Boyle, S., Taylor, L. and Brown, I. *Solving the Greenhouse Dilemma* (London: Association for the Conservation of Energy, 1989).

Bradbury, F. *The Joules of Wealth* (Ross-on-Wye: Hydatum, 1988).

Bramwell, A. *Ecology in the 20th Century* (New Haven, CN: Yale University Press, 1989).

Brennan, A. *Thinking About Nature* (London: Routledge, 1988).

Brittan, S. 'The Green Power of Market Forces', *Financial Times*, 4 May 1989.

Brookshire, D. and Coursey, D. 'Measuring the Value of a Public Good: An Empirical Comparison of Elicitation Procedures', *American Economic Review*, September 1987.

Brookshire, D., Eubanks, L. and Randall, A. 'Estimating Option Prices and Existence Values for Wildlife Resources', *Land Economics*, 59 (1), 1983.

Brookshire, D., Ives, B. and Schulze, W. 'The Valuation of Aesthetic Preferences', *Journal of Environmental Economics and Management*, 3 (4), 1976.

Brown, E., Conaty, P. and Kunz, C. *Fuelsavers: A Feasibility Study* (Birmingham: Community Energy Research/Birmingham Settlement Money Advice Services/Birmingham Settlement Research Unit, 1990).

Brown, Jnr, G.M. and Johnson, R.W. 'Pollution Control By Effluent Charges: It Works in the Federal Republic of Germany, Why Not in the United States?', *Natural Resources Journal*, 24, 1984.

Brown, Jr., G.M. and Swierzbinski, J. 'Endangered Species, Genetic Capital and Cost Reducing R&D', in D. Hall, N. Myers and N.S. Margolis (eds), *Economics of Ecosystem Management* (Dordrecht, The Netherlands: Dr. W. Junk Publishers, 1985).

Brown, L.R. et al, *State of the World 1988* (New York, NY: W.W. Norton, 1988).

—— *State of the World 1989* (New York, NY: W.W. Norton, 1989).

—— *State of the World 1990* (New York, NY: W.W. Norton/London: Unwin Hyman, 1990).

Brown, P. and Maclean, D. (eds), *Energy and the Future* (Totowa, NJ: Rowman and Littlefield, 1983).

Brown, T. 'The Concept of Value in Resource Allocation', *Land Economics*, 60 (3), 1984.

Brundtland in the Balance: A Critique of the UK Government's Response to the World Commission on Environment and Development (London, Friends of the Earth and others, 1989).

Bryson, N. 'Trade Unions and the Environment', *New Ground*, 17, Spring 1988.

Buchanan, J. 'External Diseconomies, Corrective Taxes and Market Structure', *American Economic Review*, March 1969.

Bulatayo, L. *Citizen Suits and Association Suit Provisions in Environmental Statutes and National Constitutions: Examples From Across the Globe*, Centre for International Environmental Law, Kings College, London, 1990.

Burness, H.S. et al, 'Thermodynamic and Economic Concepts as Related to Resource-Use Policies', *Land Economics*, 56 (1), February 1980.

Burness, H.S. and Cummings, R.G. 'Thermodynamic and Economic Concepts as Related to Resource-Use Policies: Reply', *Land Economics*, 62 (3), 1986.

Button, J. *How to Be Green* (London: Century Hutchinson, 1989).

Caldwell, M. *The Wealth of Some Nations* (London: Zed Press, 1977).

Callenbach, E. *Ectopia* (London: Pluto Press, 1978).

Callicott, J. B. 'Animal Liberation: A Triangular Affair', *Environmental Ethics* 2, 1980.

Camerson, J. 'Environmental Public Interest Litigation', in D. Vaughan (ed), *EC Environmental and Planning Law* (London: Butterworths, 1991).

Capra, F. *The Turning Point* (New York, NY: Simon and Schuster, 1982).

Capra, F. and Spretnak, C. *Green Politics* (London: Hutchinson, 1984).

Capros, P., Karadeloglou, P. and Mentzas, G.N. *Carbon-Tax Policy and its Impacts on CO_2 Emission*, National Technical University of Athens, 1990.

Carroll, J.E. *International Environmental Diplomacy* (Cambridge: Cambridge University Press, 1988).

Carson, R. *Silent Spring* (Harmondsworth: Penguin, 1982).

Chakravati, R. *Recolonisation: GATT, the Uruguay Round and the Third World* (London: Zed Books, 1990).

Chambers, R. *Rural Development: Putting the Last First* (Harlow: Longman, 1983).

Chambers, R. *Sustainable Livelihoods: An Opportunity for the World Commission on Environment and Development*, Institute of Development Studies, University of Sussex, 1986.

Chernoff, H. 'Individual Purchase Criteria for Energy Related Durables: The Misuse of Lifecycle Cost', *Energy Journal*, 4 (4), 1983.

Christensen, P.P. 'Historical Roots for Ecological Economics – Biophysical Versus Allocative Approaches', *Ecological Economics*, 1 (1), 1989.

Ciriacy-Wantrup, S.V. *Resource Conservation* (Berkeley, CA: University of California Press, 1963).

Clark, C. *Mathematical Bioeconomics* (New York, NY: Wiley, 1976).

Clark, W. and Munn, R. (eds), *Sustainable Development of the Biosphere* (Cambridge: Cambridge University Press, 1986).

Clawson, M. *Methods of Measuring Demand for and Value of Outdoor Recreation*, RFF Reprint No. 10 (Washington, DC: Resources for the Future, 1959).

Coase, R. 'The Problem of Social Cost', *Journal of Law and Economics*, 3, October 1960.

Colchester, M. and Lohmann, L. *The Tropical Forestry Action Plan: What Progress?* (Penang, Malaysia and Sturminster Newton: World Rainforest Movement and the *Ecologist*, 1990).

Cole, H.S.D. et al, *Thinking About the Future* (London: Chatto and Windus, 1973).

Collard, D., Pearce, D. and Ulph, D. (eds), *Economics, Growth and Sustainable Environments* (London: Macmillan, 1988).

Commission on the Third London Airport, *Report* (London: HMSO, 1971).

Common, M. 'Poverty and Progress Revisited', in D. Collard, D. Pearce, and D. Ulph (eds), *Economics, Growth and Sustainable Environments* (London: Macmillan, 1988).

—— *Environmental and Resource Economics* (Harlow: Longman, 1989).

Commoner, B. *The Closing Circle* (New York, NY: Knopf, 1971).

Conroy, C. and Litvinoff, R. *The Greening of Aid: Sustainable Livelihoods in Practice* (London: Earthscan, 1988).

The Conservation and Development Programme for the UK, *A Response to the World Conservation Strategy* (London: Kogan Page, 1982).

Costanza, R. 'What is Ecological Economics?', *Ecological Economics*, 1 (1), 1989.

Cotgrove, S. *Catastrophe or Cornucopia: The Environment, Politics and the Future* (Chichester: John Wiley, 1982).

Crosland, A. *The Future of Socialism*, 2nd edn (London: Jonathan Cape, 1964).

Cummings, B.J. *Dam the Rivers, Damn the Poor* (London: Earthscan, 1990).

Cummings, R., Brookshire, D. and Schulze, W. (eds), *Valuing Environmental Goods: An Assessment of the Contingent Valuation Method* (Totowa, NJ: Rowman and Allanheld, 1986).

Daly, H.E. 'The Steady-State Economy: Toward a Political Economy of Biophysical Equilibrium and Moral Growth', in H.E. Daly (ed), *Toward a Steady-State Economy* (San Francisco, CA: W.H. Freeman, 1973).

—— (ed), *Toward a Steady-State Economy* (San Francisco, CA: W.H. Freeman, 1973).

—— *Steady State Economics* (San Francisco, CA: W.H. Freeman, 1977).

—— (ed), *Economy, Ecology, Ethics* (San Francisco, CA: W.H. Freeman, 1980).

—— 'Thermodynamic and Economic Concepts as Related to Resource-Use Policies: Comment', *Land Economics*, 62 (3), 1986.

—— 'The Economic Growth Debate: What Some Economists Have Learned But Many Have Not', *Journal of Environmental Economics and Management*, 14 (4), 1987.

Daly, H.E. and Cobb, J.W. *For the Common Good* (Boston, MA: Beacon Press, 1989/London: Green Print, 1990).

Dammann, E. *The Future in Our Hands* (Oxford: Pergamon Press, 1979).

Daniels, N. (ed), *Reading Rawls* (Oxford: Basil Blackwell, 1975).

Dasgupta, P. *The Control of Resources* (Oxford: Basil Blackwell, 1982).

—— 'The Environment as a Commodity', *Oxford Review of Economic Policy*, 6 (1), 1990.

Dasgupta, P. and Heal, G. *Economic Theory and Exhaustible Resources* (Cambridge: Cambridge University Press, 1979).

Deadman, D. and Turner, R.K. 'Resource Conservation, Sustainability and Technical Change', in R.K. Turner (ed), *Sustainable Environmental Management: Principles and Practice* (London: Belhaven Press/Boulder, CO: Westview Press, 1988).

Department of Energy, *Report of the Working Group on Energy Demand Elasticities*, Energy Paper No. 17 (London: HMSO, 1977).

Department of the Environment, *Controlling Pollution: Principles and Prospects: The Government's Response to the Tenth Report of the Royal Commission on Environmental Pollution*, Pollution Paper 22 (London: HMSO, 1985).

—— *Our Common Future: A Perspective by the United Kingdom on the Report of the World Commission on Environment and Development* (London: Department of the Environment, 1988).

—— *Digest of Environmental Protection and Water Statistics* (London: HMSO, 1990).

Department of Trade and Industry, *Cutting Your Losses* (London: Department of Trade and Industry, 1989).

Devall, B.B. 'The Deep Ecology Movement', *Natural Resources Journal*, 20, 1979.

Dickson, D. *Alternative Technology and the Politics of Technical Change* (London: Fontana, 1974).

Dobson, A. *Green Political Thought* (London: Unwin Hyman, 1990).

Dodds, F. (ed), *Into the Twenty-first Century* (Basingstoke: Greenprint, 1988).

Dorfman, R. 'Incidence of the Benefits and Costs of Environmental Programmes', *American Economic Review*, Papers and Proceedings, 1977.

Dower, N. (ed), *Ethics and Environmental Philosophy* (Aldershot: Avebury, 1989).

Downing, P.B. and White, L.J. 'Innovation in Pollution Control', *Journal of Environmental Economics and Management*, 13 (1), 1986.

Eavis, P. and Clarke, M. *Security After the Cold War* (Bristol: Saferworld Foundation, 1990).

Eckholm, E.P. *Down to Earth* (London: Pluto Press, 1982).

Edwards, S. and Anderson, G. 'Overlooked Biases in Contingent Valuation Surveys', *Land Economics*, 62 (2), 1987.

Ehrlich, P.R., Ehrlich, A.H. and Holdren, J.P. *Ecoscience: Population, Resources, Environment*, 3rd edn (San Francisco, CA: W.H. Freeman, 1977).

Ehrlich, P.R. and Ehrlich, A.H. *The Population Explosion* (London: Heinemann, 1990).

Ekins, P. (ed), *The Living Economy* (London: Routlege and Kegan Paul, 1986).

—— 'Growing Concern', *Guardian*, 13 January 1988.

—— *Sustainable Consumerism* (London: New Economics Foundation, 1989).

Elgin, D. *Voluntary Simplicity* (New York, NY: William Morrow, 1981).

Elkin, T. and McLaren, D. *Reviving the City* (London: Friends of the Earth, 1991).

Elkington, J. *The Green Capitalists* (London: Victor Gollancz, 1987).

Elkington, J., Burke, T. and Hailes, J. *Green Pages: The Business of Saving the World* (London: Routledge, 1988).

Elkington, J. and Hailes, J. *The Green Consumer Guide* (London: Victor Gollancz, 1988).

Elliot, R. and Gare, A. (eds), *Environmental Philosophy* (St. Lucia, Australia: University of Queensland Press, 1983).

Environmental Resources Ltd, *Jobs and Energy Conservation* (London: Association for the Conservation of Energy, 1983).

—— *Charging Systems for Pollution Control in Some Member States* (London: ERL, 1985).

Enzensberger, H. 'A Critique of Political Ecology', *New Left Review*, 84, 1974.

Etzioni, A. *The Moral Dimension: Toward a New Economics* (New York, NY: Free Press, 1988).

Farer, D. 'Superfund Law Cleans Up the States', *The Law Society's Gazette*, 3 October 1990.

Fearnside, M. *Human Carrying Capacity of the Brazilian Rainforest* (New York, NY: Columbia University Press, 1986).

Feinberg, J. 'The Rights of Animals and Unborn Generations' in W. Blackstone, *Philosophy and the Environmental Crisis* (Athens, GA: University of Georgia Press, 1974).

Findlay, A.M., Rogerson, R.J. and Morris, A.S. 'Quality of Life in British Cities in 1988', *Cities*, 10, 1988.

Fisher, A.C. and Haneman, W.M. 'Endangered Species: The Economics of Irreversible Damage', in D. Hall, N. Myers, and N.S. Margolis (eds), *Economics of Ecosystem Management* (Dordrecht, The Netherlands: Dr. W. Junk Publishers, 1985).

—— 'Quasi-Option Value: Some Misconceptions Dispelled', *Journal of Environmental Economics and Management*, 14 (2), 1987.

Frankel, C. 'The Rights of Nature', in L.H. Tribe, C.S. Shelling and J. Voss (eds) *When Values Conflict* (New York, NY: John Wiley, 1976).

Freeman, A.M. 'The Sign and Size of Option Values', *Land Economics*, 60 (1), 1984.

—— 'Supply Uncertainty, Option Price and Option Value', *Land Economics*, 61 (2), 1985.

Freeman, R. 'Environmental Costs and International Competitiveness', in T. Barker (ed), *Green Futures for Economic Growth* (Cambridge: Cambridge Econometrics, 1991).

Friends of the Earth, *Efficiency of Electricity Use: Memorandum to the House of Lords European Communities Committee* (London: FoE, 1989).

—— *How Green is Britain?* (London: Hutchinson Radius, 1990).

Fromm, E. *To Have or To Be?* (London: Jonathan Cape, 1978).

Galbraith, J.K. *The New Industrial State* (Harmondsworth: Penguin, 1969).

Galtung, J., O'Brien, P. and Preiswerk, R. (eds), *Self Reliance* (London: Bogle L'Ouverture, 1980).

George, S. *Ill Fares the Land: Essays on Food, Hunger and Power* (London: Writers and Readers Publishing, 1985).

—— *A Fate Worse Than Debt* (Harmondsworth: Penguin Books, 1988).

Georgescu-Roegen, N. 'The Entropy Law and the Economic Problem', reprinted in H.E. Daly (ed), *Toward a Steady-State Economy* (San Francisco, CA: W.H. Freeman, 1973).

—— *The Entropy Law and the Economic Process* (Cambridge, MA: Harvard University Press, 1971).

Glomsrod, S. Vennemo, H. and Johnsen, T. *Stabilisation of Emissions of CO_2,* Discussion Paper No. 48, Central Bureau of Statistics, Oslo, 1990.

Glover, J. *Causing Death and Saving Lives* (Harmondsworth: Penguin, 1977).

Goldsmith, E. *The Great U-Turn: Deindustrialising Society* (Bideford: Green Books, 1988).

Goldsmith, E. and Hildyard, N. (eds), *Green Britain or Industrial Wasteland?* (Cambridge: Polity Press, 1986).

Goodin, R. 'Discounting Discounting', *Journal of Public Policy*, 2, 1982.

Goodland, R. and Ledoc, G. 'Neoclassical Economics and Principles of Sustainable Development', *Ecological Modelling*, 38, 1987.

Goodwin, P.B. 'Problems of Women's Mobility and Employment in the One Person Operation of Buses', in M. Grieco, L. Pickup and R. Whipp (eds), *Gender, Transport and Employment* (Aldershot: Gower, 1987).

—— *Evidence on Car and Public Transport Demand Elasticities, 1980–88*, Transport Studies Unit, Oxford University, June 1988.

Gorz, A. *Ecology as Politics* (London: Pluto Press, 1980).

Goudie, A. *The Human Impact on the Natural Environment* , 3rd edn (Oxford: Basil Blackwell, 1990).

Grainger, A. *The Threatening Desert: Controlling Desertification* (London: Earthscan, 1990).

Green Party, *Manifesto for a Sustainable Society* (London: Green Party, 1988).

Gregory, R. 'Interpreting Measures of Economic Loss: Evidence of Contingent Valuation and Experimental Studies', *Journal of Environmental Economics and Management*, 13 (4), 1986.

Gribbin, J. *The Hole in the Sky: Man's Threat to the Ozone Layer* (London: Corgi, 1988).

Grubb, M. *The Greenhouse Effect: Negotiating Targets* (London: Royal Institute of International Affairs, 1989).

—— *Energy Policies and the Greenhouse Effect* (Aldershot: Gower, 1990).

Gupta, A. *Ecology and Development in the Third World* (London: Routledge, 1988).

Hahn, R. and Hester, G. 'The Market for Bads', *Regulation*, 3/4, 1987.

Haigh, N. *EEC Environmental Policy and Britain*, 2nd edn (Harlow: Longman, 1989).

Haigh, N. and Baldock, D. *Environmental Policy and 1992* (London: Institute for European Environmental Policy, 1989).

Haigh, N. and Irwin, F. (eds) *Integrated Pollution Control in Europe and North America* (Washington, DC: The Conservation Foundation/London: Institute for European Environmental Policy, 1990).

Hall, D.C. and Hall, J.V. 'Concepts and Measures of Natural Resource Scarcity, with a Summary of Recent Trends', *Journal of Environmental Economics and Management*, 11 (3), 1984.

Hall, D., Myers, N. and Margolis, N.S. (eds), *Economics of Ecosystem Management* (Dordrecht, The Netherlands: Dr. W. Junk Publishers, 1985).

Hamer, M. *Wheels Within Wheels: A Study of the Road Lobby* (London: Routledge and Kegan Paul, 1987).

Hanley, N.D. 'Using Contingent Valuation to Value Environmental Improvements', *Applied Economics*, 20 (4), 1988.

—— 'Valuing Non-Market Goods Using Contingent Valuation', *Journal of Economic Surveys*, 3 (3), 1989.

Hanley, N., Hallett, S. and Moffatt, I. 'Why is More Notice Not Taken of Economists' Prescriptions for the Control of Pollution?', *Environment and Planning A*, 22, 1990.

Hardin, G. 'The Tragedy of the Commons', *Science*, 162, December 1968, reprinted in H.E. Daly (ed), *Toward a Steady-State Economy* (San Francisco: W.H. Freeman, 1973).

Harris, N. *Of Bread and Guns: The World Economic Crisis* (Harmondsworth: Penguin, 1983).

Harrison, P. *Inside the Third World* (Brighton: Harvester, 1980).

—— *The Greening of Africa* (London: Earthscan/Paladin, 1987).

Hartwick, J. and Olewiler, N. *The Economics of Natural Resource Use* (London: Harper and Row, 1986).

Hawkins, K. *Environment and Enforcement* (Oxford: Clarendon Press, 1984).

Hayek, F. *The Road to Serfdom* (London: Routledge and Kegan Paul, 1962).

Hayter, T. *The Creation of World Poverty* (London: Pluto Press, 1983).

Hayter, T. and Watson, C. *Aid: Rhetoric and Reality* (London: Pluto Press, 1985).

Hazarika, S. *Bhopal: The Lessons of a Tragedy* (New Delhi: Penguin, 1987).

Hecht, S. and Cockburn, A. *The Fate of the Forest* (London: Verso, 1989).

Held, D. *Models of Democracy* (Cambridge: Polity Press, 1987).

Helm. D. and Pearce D., 'The Assessment: Economic Policy Towards the Environment, *Oxford Review of Economic Policy*, 6 (1), 1990.

Henderson, H. *Creating Alternative Futures: The End of Economics* (New York, NY: Putman, 1978).

—— *The Politics of the Solar Age: Alternatives to Economics* (New York, NY: Doubleday, 1981).

Hewitt, P. *A Cleaner, Faster London: Road Pricing, Transport Policy and the Environment* (London: Institute for Public Policy Research, 1989).

Hick, J. *Value and Capital*, 2nd edn (Oxford: Oxford University Press, 1946).

Hirsch, F. *Social Limits to Growth* (London: Routledge and Kegan Paul, 1977).

Hirschhorn, J.S. and Oldenburg, K.V. *Prosperity Without Pollution* (New York, NY: Van Nostrand Reinhold, 1991).

Hodge, I.D. 'Approaches to the Value of the Rural Environment', paper given to the Annual Conference of the Rural Economy and Society Group of the British Sociological Association, University of Loughborough, 1986.

—— 'Uncertainty, Irreversibility and the Loss of Agricultural Land', *Journal of Agricultural Economics*, 35 (2), 1984.

Hodgson, G. *The Democratic Economy* (Harmondsworth: Penguin, 1984).

—— *Economics and Institutions* (Cambridge: Polity Press, 1988).

Holling, C.S. 'The Resilience of Terrestrial Ecosystems: Local Surprise and Global Change' in W.C. Clark and R.E. Munn (eds), *Sustainable Development of the Biosphere* (Cambridge: Cambridge University Press, 1986).

Hood, N. and Young, S. *The Economics of Multinational Enterprise* (Harlow: Longman, 1979).

Hope, C. and Parker, J. *Environmental Information for All: The Need for a Monthly Index*, Management Studies Group, University of Cambridge, 1990.

Hopkinson, P.G., Nash, C.A. and Sheehy, N. *How Much Do People Value the Environment? The Development of a Method to Identify How People Conceptualise and Value the Costs and Benefits of New Road Schemes*, Institute of Transport Studies and Department of Psychology, University of Leeds, 1990.

Hueting, R. *New Scarcity and Economic Growth: More Welfare Through Less Production?* (Amsterdam: North Holland, 1980).

—— 'Results of an Economic Scenario That Gives Top Priority to Saving the Environment Instead of Encouraging Production Growth', paper to The Other Economic Summit, London 1984, reprinted in P. Ekins (ed), *The Living Economy* (London: Routledge and Kegan Paul, 1986).

Illich, I. *Energy and Equity* (London: Calder and Boyars, 1974).

Ingham, A. and Ulph, A. *Carbon Taxes and the UK Manufacturing Sector*, Department of Economics, University of Southampton, 1990.

International Energy Agency, *Energy Conservation in IEA Countries* (Paris: International Energy Agency and OECD, 1987).

International Labour Organisation, *Employment and Training Implications of Environmental Policies in Europe* (Geneva: ILO, 1989).

International Union for the Conservation of Nature and Natural Resources, *World Conservation Strategy* (Gland, Switzerland: IUCN, 1980).

Irvine, S. *Beyond Green Consumerism* (London: Friends of the Earth, 1989).

—— 'No Growth in a Finite World', *New Statesman and Society*, 23 November 1991.

Jackson, B. *Poverty and the Planet: A Question of Survival* (Harmondsworth: Penguin, 1990).

Jackson, T. *Energy Policy in a Warming World* (London: Friends of the Earth, forthcoming).

Jackson, T. and Jacobs, M. 'Carbon Taxes and the Assumptions of Environmental Economics' in T. Barker (ed), *Green Futures for Economic Growth* (Cambridge: Cambridge Econometrics, 1991).

Jackson, T. and Roberts, S. *Getting Out of the Greenhouse* (London: Friends of the Earth, 1989).

Jochem, E. and Gruber, E. 'Obstacles to Rational Electricity Use and Measures to Alleviate Them', *Energy Policy*, 18 (4), 1990.

Johansson, P-O. *The Economic Theory and Measurement of Environmental Benefits* (Cambridge: Cambridge University Press, 1987).

—— 'Valuing Environmental Damage', *Oxford Review of Economic Policy*, 6 (1), 1990.

Johnson, P., McKay, S. and Smith, S. *The Distributional Consequences of Environmental Taxes* (London: Institute for Fiscal Studies, 1990).

Jones, R.R. and Wigley, T. (eds), *Ozone Depletion: Health and Environmental Consequences* (New York, NY: John Wiley, 1989).

Joseph, S. 'Green as a Class Issue', *New Ground*, 10, Summer 1986.

Kapp, K.W. 'Environmental Disruption and Social Costs: A Challenge to Economics', *Kyklos*, 23 (4), 1970.

Kelly, P. *Fighting for Hope* (London: Chatto and Windus, 1984).

Kemp, P. and Wall, D. *A Green Manifesto for the 1990s* (Harmondsworth: Penguin, 1990).

King, J., *Beyond Economic Choice: Population and Sustainable Development* (Centre for Human Ecology, University of Edinburgh/UNESCO, 1987).

Kneese, A., Ayres, R.U. and d'Arge, R. *Economics and the Environment* (Baltimore, MD: Johns Hopkins University Press, 1970).

Knetsch, J. and Sinden, J. 'Willingness to Pay and Compensation Demanded: Experimental Evidence of an Unexpected Disparity in Measures of Value', *Quarterly Journal of Economics*, August 1984.

Kohr, L. *The Breakdown of Nations* (London: Routledge and Kegan Paul, 1986).

Komarov, B. *The Destruction of Nature in the Soviet Union* (London: Pluto Press, 1978).

Krupnick, A. 'Costs of Alternative Policies for the Control of Nitrogen Dioxide in Baltimore', *Journal of Environmental Economics and Management*, 13, 1986.

Krutilla, J. and Fisher, A. *The Economics of Natural Environments* (Washington, DC: Resources for the Future, 1975).

Labour Party, *An Earthly Chance* (London: Labour Party, 1990).

Leipert, C. *Die Heimlichen Kosten des Fortschritts: Wie Umweltzerstörung das Wirtschaftswachstum Fördert* (Frankfurt: S. Fischer, 1989).

Leitch, G. *Report of the Advisory Committee on Trunk Road Assessment* (London: HMSO, 1977).

Leonard, H.J. *Pollution and the Struggle for the World Product* (Cambridge: Cambridge University Press, 1988).

Leontief, W. 'Environmental Repercussions and the Economic Structure: An Input-Output Approach', *Review of Economics and Statistics*, 11, August 1970.

Leopold, A. *A Sand County Almanac* (Oxford: Oxford University Press, 1949).

Liberal Democrats, *What Price Our Planet?* (Hebden Bridge: Association of Social and Liberal Democrat Councillors, 1990).

Liroff, R. *Reforming Air Pollution Regulation: The Toil and Trouble of EPA's Bubble* (Washington, DC: Conservation Foundation, 1986).

Lloyd, A. et al, 'Air Quality Management in Los Angeles: Perspectives on Past and Future Emission Control Strategies', *Journal of the Air and Waste Management Association*, 39 (5), 1989.

London Economics, *The Effects of Taxes on Fertiliser*, London, 1990.

Loomis, J.B. 'Expanding Contingent Value Sample Estimates to Aggregate Benefit Estimates: Current Practices and Proposed Solutions', *Land Economics*, 63 (4), 1987.

Lovelock, J. *Gaia: A New Look at Life on Earth* (Oxford: Oxford University Press, 1979).

Lovins, A. *Soft Energy Paths: Towards A Durable Peace* (London: Harper and Row, 1979).

Lutz, M.A. and Lux, K. *Humanistic Economics: The New Challenge* (New York, NY: Bootstrap Press, 1988).

McBurney, S. *Economics into Ecology Won't Go* (Bideford: Green Books, 1990).

McCormick, J. *Acid Earth* (London: Earthscan, 1985).

—— *The Global Environmental Movement* (London: Belhaven Press, 1989).

McIntyre, R. and Thornton, J. 'On the Environmental Efficiency of Economic Systems', *Soviet Studies*, April 1978.

McKay, S., Pearson, M. and Smith, S. 'Fiscal Instruments in Environmental Policy', *Fiscal Studies*, 11 (4), 1990.

McKibben, B. *The End of Nature* (Harmondsworth: Penguin, 1990).

McNeely, J.A. *Economics and Biological Diversity* (Gland, Switzerland: International Union for Conservation of Nature and Natural Resources, 1988).

McNeely, J. and Pitt, D. (eds), *Culture and Conservation: The Human Dimension in Environmental Planning* (London: Croom Helm, 1985).

Maler, K-G. 'International Environmental Problems', *Oxford Review of Economic Policy*, 6 (1), 1990.

Maltezou, S., Metry, A.A. and Irwin, W.A., *Industrial Risk Management and Clean Technology* (Vienna: Verlag Orac, 1990).

Manne, A.S. and Richels, R.G. 'Global CO_2 Emission Limits: An Economic Cost Analysis for the USA', *Energy Journal*, 11, Spring, 1990.

Mantegazzini, M. *The Environmental Risks of Biotechnology* (London: Frances Pinter, 1986).

Marcuse, H. *One Dimensional Man* (London: Sphere Books, 1968).

Marks, R.E. et al, 'The Cost of Australian Carbon Dioxide Abatement', *Energy Journal*, 11, Spring 1990.

Martinez-Alier, J. *Ecological Economics: Energy, Environment and Society* (Oxford: Basil Blackwell, 1987).

Marwell, G. and Ames, R. 'Economists Free Ride, Does Anyone Else?', *Journal of Public Economics*, 15, 1981.

Maslow, A.H. *Motivation and Personality* (New York, NY: Harper and Row, 1954).

Meadows, D.H. et al, *The Limits to Growth* (London: Pan, 1972).

Minay, C. and Weston, J. (eds), *The Future of Work: Jobs in the Environment*, Oxford Polytechnic School of Planning Working Paper No. 102, 1987.

Mishan, E.J. *The Costs of Economic Growth* (Harmondsworth: Penguin, 1969).

—— *Cost Benefit Analysis*, 4th edn (London: Allen and Unwin, 1988).

Mitchell, R.C. and Carson, R.T. *Using Surveys to Value Public Goods: The Contingent Valuation Method* (Washington, DC: Resources for the Future, 1989).

Mogridge, M.J.H. *Travel in Towns* (London: Macmillan, 1990).

Mortimer, N. 'Energy Analysis and Renewable Energy Sources', *Energy Policy*, 19, May 1991.

Mulberg, J., 'Environment, Growth and Value', *Journal of Interdisciplinary Economics*, 2 (2), 1987.

MVA Consultancy, Institute for Transport Studies (University of Leeds) and Transport Studies Unit (University of Oxford), *The Value of Travel Time Savings* (Newbury: Policy Journals, 1987).

Myers, N. *The Sinking Ark* (Oxford: Pergamon Press, 1979).

—— *A Wealth of Wild Species* (Boulder, CO: Westview Press, 1983).

—— *The Primary Source: Tropical Forests and Our Future* (New York, NY: W.W. Norton, 1984).

—— (ed), *The Gaia Atlas of Planet Management* (London: Pan, 1985).

Naess, A. 'The Shallow and the Deep, Long-Range Ecology Movement', *Inquiry*, 16, 1973.

Nash, C.A. 'The Treatment of Environmental Effects in Cost-Benefit Analysis: A Case Study of the Transport Sector', paper presented to the International Conference on Evaluation in Urban and Regional Planning, Capri, Italy, September 1989.

Nash, C.A. and Bowers, J.K. 'Alternative Approaches to the Valuation of Environmental Resources', in R.K. Turner (ed), *Sustainable Environmental Management: Principles and Practice* (London: Belhaven Press/Boulder, CO: Westview Press, 1988).

Nitze, W.A. *The Greenhouse Effect: Formulating a Convention* (London: Royal Institute of International Affairs, 1990).

Nordhaus, W.D. *To Slow Or Not To Slow: The Economics of the Greenhouse Effect*, Yale University, February 1990.

Norgaard, R. 'Coevolutionary Development Potential', *Land Economics*, 60 (2), 1984.

—— 'Environmental Economics: an Evolutionary Critique and a Plea for Pluralism', *Journal of Environmental Economics and Management*, 12 (4), 1985.

—— 'The Scarcity of Resource Economics', paper presented to the American Economics Association, New York, 1985.

—— 'Thermodynamic and Economic Concepts as Related to Resource-Use Policies: Synthesis', *Land Economics*, 62 (3), 1986.

—— 'Sustainable Development: A Co-Evolutionary View', *Futures*, 20 (6), 1988.

—— 'The Case for Methodological Pluralism', *Ecological Economics*, 1 (1), 1989.

Norton, B.G. 'Environmental Economics and Weak Anthropocentrism', *Environmental Ethics*, 6 (2), 1984.

—— *Why Preserve Natural Variety?* (Princeton: NJ: Princeton University Press, 1987).

Nove, A. *The Economics of Feasible Socialism* (London: Allen and Unwin, 1983).

—— *The Soviet Economic System*, 3rd edn (Boston, MA: Allen and Unwin, 1986).

Ophuls, W. *Ecology and the Politics of Scarcity* (San Francisco, CA: W.H. Freeman, 1977).

Opschoor, J.B. and Vos, H.B. *Economic Instruments for Environmental Protection* (Paris: Organisation for Economic Cooperation and Development, 1989).

Organisation for Economic Cooperation and Development, *The Polluter Pays Principle: Definition, Analysis and Implementation* (Paris: OECD, 1975).

—— 'The Impact of Environmental Policy on Employment', Background Paper, Conference on Environment and Economics, Paris, 1984.

—— *The State of the Environment* (Paris: OECD, 1985).

—— *OECD Environmental Data Compendium* (Paris: OECD, 1989).

O'Riordan, T. *Environmentalism* (London: Pion Press, 1981).

—— 'The Politics of Sustainability', in R.K. Turner (ed), *Sustainable Environmental Management: Principles and Practice* (London: Belhaven Press/Boulder, CO: Westview Press, 1988).

O'Riordan, T. et al, 'On Weighing Gains and Investments at the Margin of Risk Regulation', Working Paper, School of Environmental Sciences, University of East Anglia, 1985.

O'Riordan, T. and Turner, R.K. *An Annotated Reader in Environmental Planning and Management* (Oxford: Pergamon Press, 1983).

Owens, S. *Energy, Urban Form and Planning* (London: Pion Press, 1986).

Owens, S., Anderson, V. and Brunskill, I. *Green Taxes* (London: Institute for Public Policy Research,1990).

Oxfam, *Submission to the Treasury and Civil Service Select Committee on Management of Third World Debt*, December 1989.

Oyejide, T.A. 'Primary Commodities in the International Trading System' in J. Whalley (ed), *Developing Countries and the Global Trading System* (London: Macmillan, 1989).

Page, T. *Conservation and Economic Efficiency* (Baltimore, MD: Johns Hopkins University Press, 1977).

—— 'Intergenerational Justice as Opportunity', in P. Brown and D. Maclean (eds), *Energy and the Future* (Totowa, NJ: Rowman and Littlefield, 1983).

Palmer, J. *1992 and Beyond* (Luxembourg: Commission of the European Communities, 1989).

Parfit, D. 'Energy Policy and the Further Future: The Social Discount Rate', in D. Maclean and P. Brown (eds), *Energy and the Future* (Totowa, NJ: Rowman and Littlefield, 1983).

—— *Reasons and Persons* (Oxford: Oxford University Press, 1984).

Paterson, T. *The Green Conservative* (London: Bow Publications, 1989).

Patinkin, D. *Anticipations of the General Theory?* (Oxford: Basil Blackwell, 1982).

Pearce, D.W. *Cost-Benefit Analysis* (London: Macmillan, 1971).

—— *Environmental Economics* (London: Longman, 1976).

—— 'The Social Incidence of Environmental Costs and Benefits', in T. O'Riordan and R.K. Turner (eds), *Progress in Resource Management and Environmental Planning*, 2, 1980.

—— 'Sustainable Futures: Economics and the Environment', Inaugural Lecture, University College, London, 1985.

—— 'Foundations of an Ecological Economics', *Ecological Modeling* 38, 1986.

—— 'Optimal Prices for Sustainable Development', in D. Collard, D. Pearce and D. Ulph (eds), *Economics, Growth and Sustainable Environments* (London: Macmillan, 1988).

—— *An Economic Approach to Saving the Rainforest*, London Environmental Economics Centre, 1990.

Pearce, D.W., Barbier, E.B. and Markandya, A. *Sustainable Development and Cost Benefit Analysis*, London Environmental Economics Centre, 1988.

—— *Sustainable Development: Economics and Environment in the Third World* (London: Edward Elgar, 1989).

Pearce, D.W., Markandya, A. and Barbier, E.B. *Blueprint for a Green Economy* (London: Earthscan, 1989).

Pearce, D.W. and Nash, C.A. *The Social Appraisal of Projects* (London: Macmillan, 1981).

Pearce, D.W. and Turner, R.K. 'The Economic Evaluation of Low and Non-Waste Technology', *Resources and Conservation*, 11 (1), 1984.

—— *Economics of Natural Resources and the Environment* (Hemel Hempstead: Harvester Wheatsheaf, 1990).

Pearce, D. and Walter, I. *Resource Conservation: The Social and Economic Dimensions of Recycling* (London: Longman/New York, NY: New York University Press, 1977).

Pearce, F. *Turning Up the Heat* (London: Bodley Head, 1989).

Pearson, M. and Smith, S. *Taxation and Environmental Policy: Some Initial Evidence* (London: Institute for Fiscal Studies, 1990).

Pepper, D. *The Roots of Modern Environmentalism* (London: Croom Helm, 1984).

Perrings C. *Economy and Environment* (Cambridge: Cambridge University Press, 1987).

Peskin, H.M. 'Environmental Policy and the Distribution of Benefits and Costs', in P.R. Portney (ed), *Current Issues in US Environmental Policy* (Baltimore, MD: Johns Hopkins University Press, 1977).

Peters, C.M., Gentry, A.H. and Mendelsohn, R.O. 'Valuation of an Amazonian Rainforest', *Nature*, 339, 29 June 1989.

Pettit, P. *Rawls: A Theory of Justice and Its Critics* (Cambridge: Polity Press, 1990).

Pezzey, J. 'Market Mechanisms of Pollution Control: "Polluter Pays", Economic and Practical Aspects' in R.K. Turner (ed), *Sustainable Environmental Management: Principles and Practice* (London: Belhaven Press/Boulder CO: Westview Press, 1988).

—— *Economic Analysis of Sustainable Growth and Sustainable Development*, World Bank Environment Department, Working Paper No. 15, Washington, DC: May 1989.

Pigou, A. *The Economics of Welfare* (London: Macmillan, 1920).

Plant, G. 'Institutional and Legal Responses to Global Climate Change', *Millenium*, 19 (3), 1990.

Poore, D. *No Timber Without Trees: Sustainability in the Tropical Forest* (London: Earthscan 1989).

Porritt, J. *Seeing Green* (Oxford: Basil Blackwell, 1984).

Porritt, J. and Winner, D. *The Coming of the Greens* (London: Fontana, 1988).

Porter, A., Spence, M. and Thompson, R. *The Energy Fix* (London: Pluto Press, 1986).

Porter, R. 'The New Approach to Wilderness Preservation Through Benefit Cost Analysis', *Journal of Environmental Economics and Management*, 9, 1982.

Princeton Protocol on Factors that Contribute to Global Warming, Woodrow Wilson School of Public and International Affairs, Princeton University, 1988.

Proops, J.L.R. 'Ecological Economics: Rationale and Problem Areas', *Ecological Economics*, 1 (1), 1989.

Pye-Smith, C. and Rose, C. *Crisis and Conservation: Conflict in the British Countryside* (Harmondsworth: Penguin, 1984).

Ramakrishna, K. 'North–South Issues, Common Heritage of Mankind and Global Climate Change', *Millenium*, 19 (3), 1990.

Rawls, J. *A Theory of Justice* (Cambridge, MA: Harvard University Press, 1971).

Redclift, M. *Development and the Environmental Crisis: Red or Green Alternatives* (London: Methuen, 1984).

—— *Sustainable Development: Exploring the Contradictions* (London: Methuen, 1987).

—— 'Economic Models and Environmental Values: A Discourse on Theory', in R.K. Turner (ed), *Sustainable Environmental Management: Principles and Practice* (London: Belhaven Press/Boulder, CO: Westview Press, 1988).

—— 'Sustainable Development and the Market: A Framework for Analysis', *Futures*, December 1988.

Rees, J. *Natural Resources: Allocation, Efficiency and Policy*, 2nd edn (London: Routledge, 1990).

—— 'Pollution Control Objectives and the Regulatory Framework', in R.K. Turner (ed), *Sustainable Environmental Management: Principles and Practice* (London: Belhaven Press/Boulder, CO: Westview Press, 1988).

Regan, T. 'On the Nature and Possibility of an Environmental Ethic', *Environmental Ethics*, 3 (1), 1981.

Reid, W.V. and Miller, K.R. *Keeping Options Alive* (Washington, DC: World Resources Institute, 1989).

Repetto, R. (ed), *The Global Possible* (New Haven, CT: Yale University Press, 1985).

—— *World Enough and Time* (New Haven, CT: Yale University Press, 1986).

Riddell, R. *Ecodevelopment* (Farnborough: Gower, 1981).

Rifkin, J. *Declaration of a Heretic* (London: Routledge and Kegan Paul, 1985).

Roberts, J. *User Friendly Cities* (London: TEST, 1989).

Roberts, T. and Porter, R. (eds), *Energy Saving from Waste Recycling* (London: Elsevier Applied Science Publishers, 1985).

Robertson, J. *The Sane Alternative*, 2nd edn (Ironbridge: James Robertson, 1983).

—— *Future Wealth* (London: Cassell, 1990).

Robison, H.D. 'Who Pays for Industrial Pollution Abatement?', *Review of Economics and Statistics*, 67 (4), 1985.

Rogerson, R. et al, *Quality of Life in Britain's Intermediate Cities* (Glasgow: Quality of Life Group, Glasgow University, 1989).

Rosen, S. 'Hedonic Prices and Implicit Markets', *Journal of Political Economy*, 82, 1974.

Roszak, T. *Where the Wasteland Ends* (London: Faber and Faber, 1973).

—— *Person/Planet: The Creative Disintegration of Industrial Society* (London: Victor Gollancz, 1979).

Routley, R. and Routley, V. 'Against the Inevitability of Human Chauvinism' in K.E. Goodpaster and K.M. Sayer (eds), *Ethics and Problems of the 21st Century* (Notre Dame, IN: University of Notre Dame Press, 1979).

Rowe, R., d'Arge, R. and Brookshire, D. 'An Experiment on the Economic Value of Visibility', *Journal of Environmental Economics and Management*, 7 (1), 1980.

Rowe, R.D. and Chestnut, L.G. 'Valuing Environmental Commodities: Revisited', *Land Economics*, 59 (4), 1983.

Royal Commission on Environmental Pollution, *Tackling Pollution: Experience and Prospects*, 10th Report (London: HMSO, 1984).

—— *Best Practicable Environmental Option*, 12th Report (London: HMSO, 1988).

Russell, P. *The Awakening Earth: Our Next Evolutionary Leap* (London: RKP, 1982).

Ryle, M. *Ecology and Socialism* (London: Hutchinson, 1989).

Sagoff, M. 'Some Problems with Environment Economics', *Environmental Ethics*, Spring 1981.

—— *The Economy of the Earth* (Cambridge: Cambridge University Press, 1988).

Sale, K. *Human Scale* (London: Secker and Warburg, 1980).

Samuelson, S. and Nordhaus, W. *Economics*, 13th edn (New York, NY: McGraw-Hill 1989).

Sandbach F. *Environment, Ideology and Policy* (Oxford: Basil Blackwell, 1980).

—— *Principles of Pollution Control* (Harlow: Longman, 1982).

Schatan, J. *World Debt: Who Is To Pay?* (London: Zed Books, 1987).

Schmidt, A. *The Concept of Nature in Marx* (London: New Left Books, 1971).

Schneider, S. *Global Warming: Are We Entering the Greenhouse Century?* (San Francisco, CA: Sierra Club Books, 1989).

Schulze, W. et al, 'The Economic Benefits of Preserving Visibility in the National Parklands of the South West', *Natural Resources Journal*, 23, July 1983.

Schulze, W.D., d'Arge, R.C. and Brookshire, D.S. 'Valuing Environmental Commodities: Some Recent Experiments', *Land Economics*, 57 (2), 1981.

Schumacher, E.F. *Small Is Beautiful* (London: Blond and Briggs, 1973).

Schwarz, W. and Schwarz, D. *Breaking Through* (Bideford: Green Books, 1987).

Seabrook, J. *The Myth of the Market* (Bideford: Green Books, 1990).

—— *The Race to Riches* (Basingstoke: Green Print, 1988).

Secrett, C. *Rainforest* (London: Friends of the Earth, 1986).

Self, P. 'Nonsense on Stilts: The Futility of Roskill', *Political Quarterly*, July 1970.

Seller, C., Stoll, J. and Chevas, J-P. 'Validation of Empirical Measures of Welfare Change: A Comparison of Non-Market Techniques', *Land Economics*, 61 (2), 1985.

Sen, A. *Poverty and Famines: An Essay On Entitlement and Deprivation* (Oxford: Clarendon Press, 1981).

Simon, J.L. *The Ultimate Resource* (Oxford; Martin Robertson, 1981).

Simon, J.L. and Kahn, H. *The Resourceful Earth: A Response to Global 2000* (Oxford: Basil Blackwell, 1984).

Singer, P. 'Not for Humans Only: The Place of Nonhumans in Environmental Issues' in K.E. Goodpaster and K.M. Sayers (eds), *Ethics and Problems of the 21st Century* (Notre Dame, IN: University of Notre Dame Press, 1979).

Singh, N. *Economics and the Crisis of Ecology*, 3rd edn (London: Bellew 1989).

Slesser, M. *Enhancement of Carrying Capacity Options*, Part II: Introductory Guide (Pitlochry: Resource Use Institute, 1990).

Smith, K. *The British Economic Crisis* (Harmondsworth: Penguin, 1984).

Smith, K. *Global Warming and the Natural Debt* (Hawaii: Environment and Policy Institute, East West Centre, 1989).

Smith, V.K. 'Supply Uncertainty, Option Price and Indirect Benefit Estimation', *Land Economics*, 61 (3), 1985.

Smith, V.K. and Desvouges, W. *Measuring Water Quality Benefits* (Boston, MA: Kluwer Nijhoff, 1986).

Söderbaum, 'Economics, Ethics and Environmental Problems', *Journal of Interdisciplinary Economics*, 2 (2), 1987.

Solow, R. 'On the Integenerational Allocation of Natural Resources', *Scandinavian Journal of Economics*, 88 (1), 1986.

Sondheimer, J. 'The Macroeconomic Effects of a Carbon Tax', in T. Barker (ed), *Green Futures for Economic Growth* (Cambridge: Cambridge Econometrics, 1991).

Spulber, D.F. 'Effluent Regulation and Long-Run Optimality', *Journal of Environmental Economics and Management*, 12 (2), 1985.

State of the Environment in the European Community 1986 (Brussels: Commission of the European Communities, 1987).

Steer Davies and Gleave Ltd, 'Turning Trucks Into Trains', report prepared for Transport 2000, 1987.

Stretton, H. *Capitalism, Socialism and the Environment* (Cambridge: Cambridge University Press, 1976).

Sweet, C. *The Price of Nuclear Power* (London: Heinemann, 1983).

Sylvan, R. 'Deep Ecology', *Radical Philosophy*, 40 and 41, 1985.

Task Force on the Environment and the Internal Market, *'1992': The Environmental Dimension* (Brussels: Commission of the European Communities, 1990).

Taylor, M. *Anarchy and Cooperation* (Chichester: John Wiley, 1976).

Taylor, P.W. *Respect for Nature* (Princeton, NJ: Princeton University Press, 1986).

Terkla, S. 'The Efficiency Value of Effluent Tax Revenues', *Journal of Environmental Economics and Management*, 11 (2), 1984.

Thayer, M. 'Contingent Valuation Techniques for Assessing Environmental Impacts: Further Evidence', *Journal of Environmental Economics and Management*, 8 (1), 1981.

Thomas, K. *Man and the Natural World* (London: Allen Lane, 1983).

Tietenberg, T.H. *Emissions Trading: An Exercise in Reforming Pollution Policy* (Washington, DC: Resources for the Future, 1985).

—— 'Economic Instruments for Environmental Regulation', *Oxford Review of Economic Policy*, 6 (1), 1990.

Timberlake, L. *Africa in Crisis* (London: Earthscan, 1985).

To Choose or to Lose: National Environmental Policy Plan (The Hague: Ministry of Housing, Physical Planning and Environment, 1989).

Tobias, M. (ed), *Deep Ecology* (San Diego, CA: Avant Books, 1984).

Toke, D. *Green Energy* (London: Green Print, 1990).

Tolba, M. *Sustainable Development: Constraints and Opportunities* (London: Butterworths, 1987).

Trainer, F.E. *Abandon Affluence!* (London: Zed Books, 1985).

Turner, R.K. 'Wetlands Conservation: Economics and Ethics', in D. Collard, D. Pearce and D. Ulph (eds), *Economics, Growth and Sustainable Environments* (London: Macmillan, 1988).

—— 'Sustainability, Resource Conservation and Pollution Control: An Overview', in R.K. Turner (ed), *Sustainable Environmental Management: Principles and Practice* (London: Belhaven Press/Boulder CO: Westview Press, 1988).

—— (ed), *Sustainable Environmental Management: Principles and Practice* (London: Belhaven Press/Boulder CO: Westview Press, 1988).

UK Government, *This Common Inheritance: Britain's Environmental Strategy* (London: HMSO, 1990).

Victor, P. *Pollution: Economy and Environment* (London: Allen and Unwin, 1972).

Von Moltke, K. 'Debt for Nature: An Overview', World Wildlife Fund, undated.

Von Weizsäcker, E.U. 'Global Warming and Environmental Taxes', paper given to International Conference on 'Atmosphere, Climate and Man', Torino, Italy, January 1989.

Walsh, R., Loomis, J. and Gillman, R. 'Valuing Option, Existence and Bequest Demands for Wilderness', *Land Economics*, 60 (1), 1984.

Ward, B. and Dubos, R. *Only One Earth* (Harmondsworth: Penguin, 1972).

Waring, M. *If Women Counted* (London: Macmillan, 1989).

Weston, J. (ed), *Red and Green* (London: Pluto Press, 1986).

Whalley, J. (ed), *Developing Countries and the Global Trading System* (London: Macmillan, 1989).

Wheale, P. and McNally, R. *Genetic Engineering: Catastrophe or Utopia?* (Hemel Hempstead: Harvester Wheatsheaf, 1988).

White, P.R. 'Man and His Transport Behaviour: User Response to Price Changes: The Application of the the Threshold Concept', *Transport Reviews*, 4 (4), 1984.

Williams, R. *Towards 2000* (Harmondsworth: Penguin, 1984).

—— *Socialism and Ecology* (London: Socialist Environment and Resources Association pamphlet, undated).

Williams, R. 'Innovative Approaches to Marketing Electric Efficiency', in T. Johansson, B. Bodlund and R. Williams (eds), *Electricity: Efficient End-Use and New Generation Technologies and Their Planning Implications* (Lund, Sweden: Lund University Press, 1989)

Wilson, D. *The Lead Scandal* (London: Heinemann, 1983).

Wilson, E.O. 'Threats to Biodiversity', *Scientific American*, 261 (3), 1989.

World Commission on Environment and Development, *Our Common Future* (Oxford: Oxford University Press, 1987).

World Meteorological Organisation/United Nations Environment Programme/ J.T. Houghton, G.J. Jenkins and J.J. Ephraums (eds), *Climate Change: The IPCC Scientific Assessment* (Cambridge: Cambridge University Press, 1990).

World Resources Institute, *World Resources 1988–9* (New York, NY: Basic Books, 1988).

—— *Natural Endowments: Financing Resource Conservation for Development* (Washington, DC: WRI, 1989).

—— *World Resources 1990–91* (New York, NY/Oxford: Oxford University Press, 1990).

'World Status: Environmental Taxation?', *Energy Economist*, February 1990.

Young, J. *Post-Environmentalism* (London: Belhaven Press, 1990).

Ziegler, C. 'Soviet Environmental Policy and Soviet Central Planning: A Reply to McIntyre and Thornton', *Soviet Studies*, January 1980.

—— *Environmental Policy in the USSR* (London: Frances Pinter, 1987).

Index